ZATCH BELL!™

ZATCH BELL!
Vol. 8

STORY AND ART BY
MAKOTO RAIKU

English Adaptation/Fred Burke
Translation/David Ury
Touch-up Art & Lettering/Gabe Crate
Design/Izumi Hirayama
Special Thanks/Jessica Villat, Miki Macaluso,
Mitsuko Kitajima, and Akane Matsuo
Editor/Kit Fox

Managing Editor/Annette Roman
Editorial Director/Elizabeth Kawasaki
Editor in Chief/Alvin Lu
Sr. Director of Acquisitions/Rika Inouye
Senior VP of Marketing/Liza Coppola
Exec. VP of Sales & Marketing/John Easum
Publisher/Hyoe Narita

Printed in the U.S.A.

Published by VIZ Media, LLC
P.O. Box 77010
San Francisco, CA 94107

10 9 8 7 6 5 4 3 2 1
First printing, August 2006

RATED T FOR TEEN

PARENTAL ADVISORY
ZATCH BELL! is rated T for Teen and is recommended for ages 13 and up. This volume contains realistic and fantasy violence.

www.viz.com
store.viz.com

ZATCH BELL!

™

STORY AND ART BY
MAKOTO RAIKU

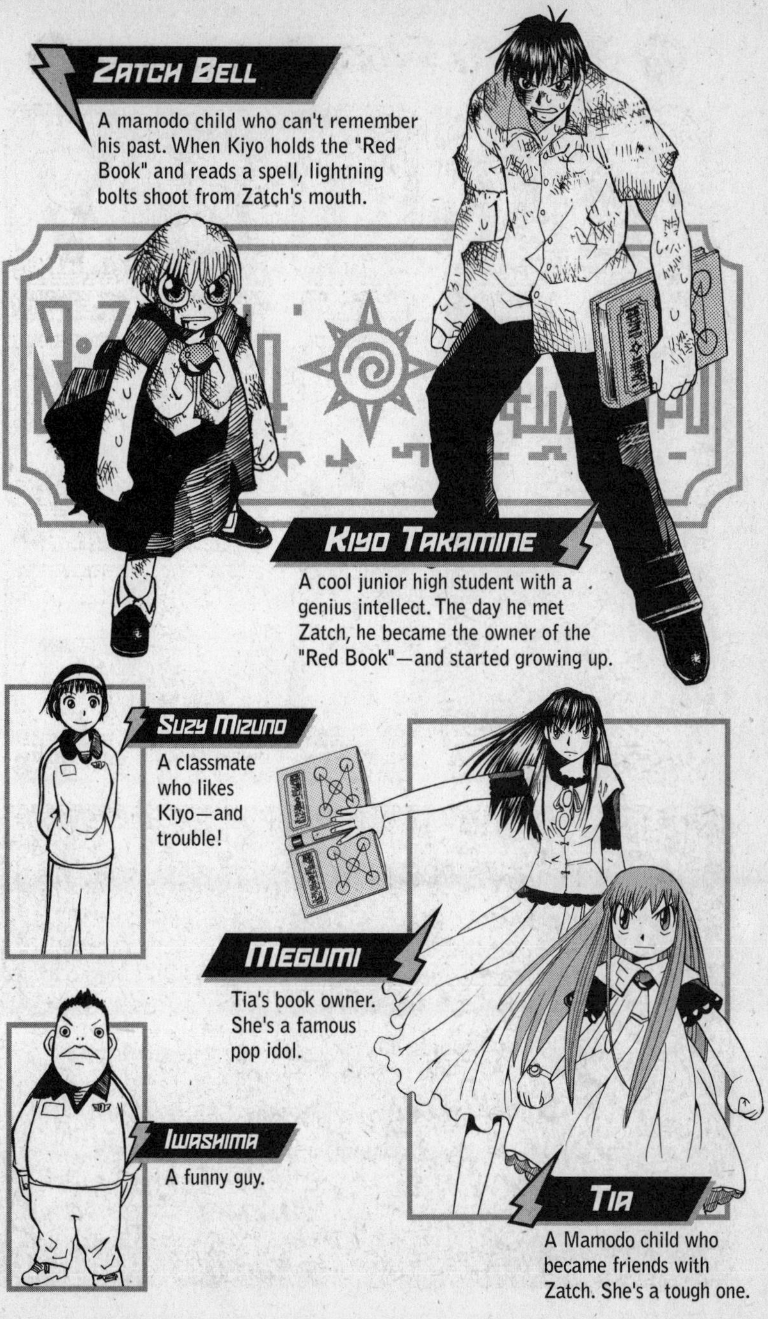
ZATCH BELL
A mamodo child who can't remember his past. When Kiyo holds the "Red Book" and reads a spell, lightning bolts shoot from Zatch's mouth.
KIYO TAKAMINE
A cool junior high student with a genius intellect. The day he met Zatch, he became the owner of the "Red Book"—and started growing up.
SUZY MIZUNO
A classmate who likes Kiyo—and trouble!
MEGUMI
Tia's book owner. She's a famous pop idol.
IWASHIMA
A funny guy.
TIA
A Mamodo child who became friends with Zatch. She's a tough one.

ZATCH'S PAST OPPONENTS

KOLULU

SUGINO

GOFURE

BRAGO

REYCOM

MARUSS

ROBNOS

KANCHOMÉ

ESHROS

FEIN

DANNY

ROPS

KIKUROPU

BALTRO

THE STORY THUS FAR

Kiyo is a junior high student who's so intelligent that he's bored by life and doesn't even go to school. Kiyo's father sends him an amazing child named Zatch as a birthday present. When Kiyo holds the "Red Book" (which only Kiyo can read) and reads a spell, Zatch displays various powers. Zatch is one of 100 mamodo children chosen to fight in a battle which will determine who is king of the mamodo world for the next 1,000 years. The bond between Zatch and Kiyo deepens as they're forced to fight for their own survival.

Zatch and Kiyo visit England, where Zatch's look-alike has been spotted. After surviving another difficult match with the mamodo, they reunite with Kiyo's father, who had been kidnapped. Many mamodo have already disappeared from the human world—and now only the strong remain!

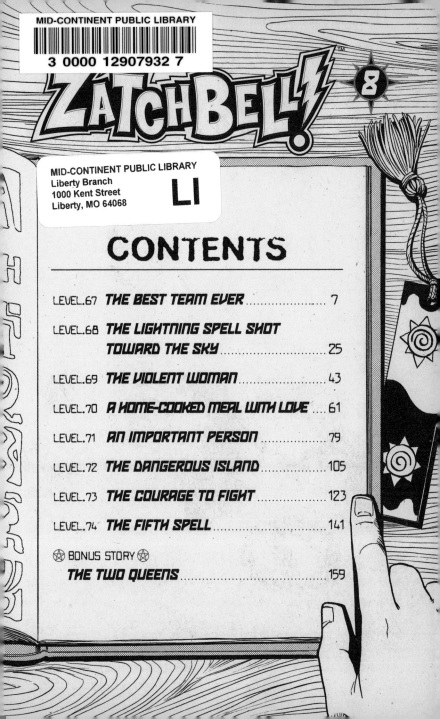

ZATCHBELL!

8

CONTENTS

LEVEL 67:
The Best Team Ever

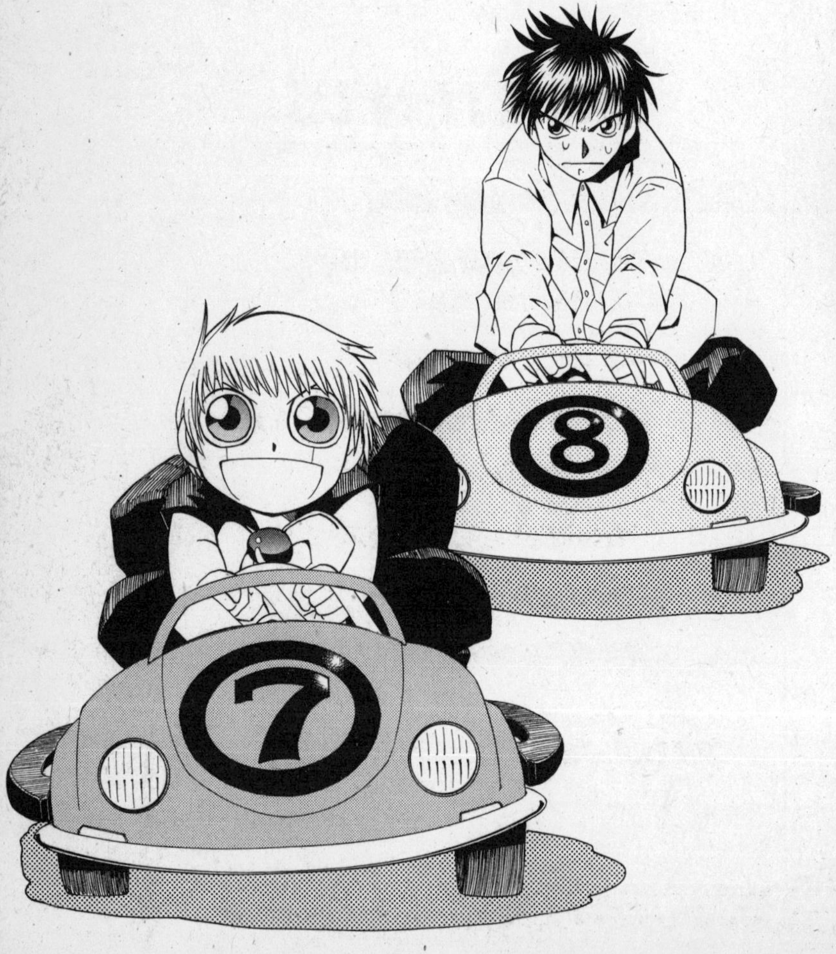

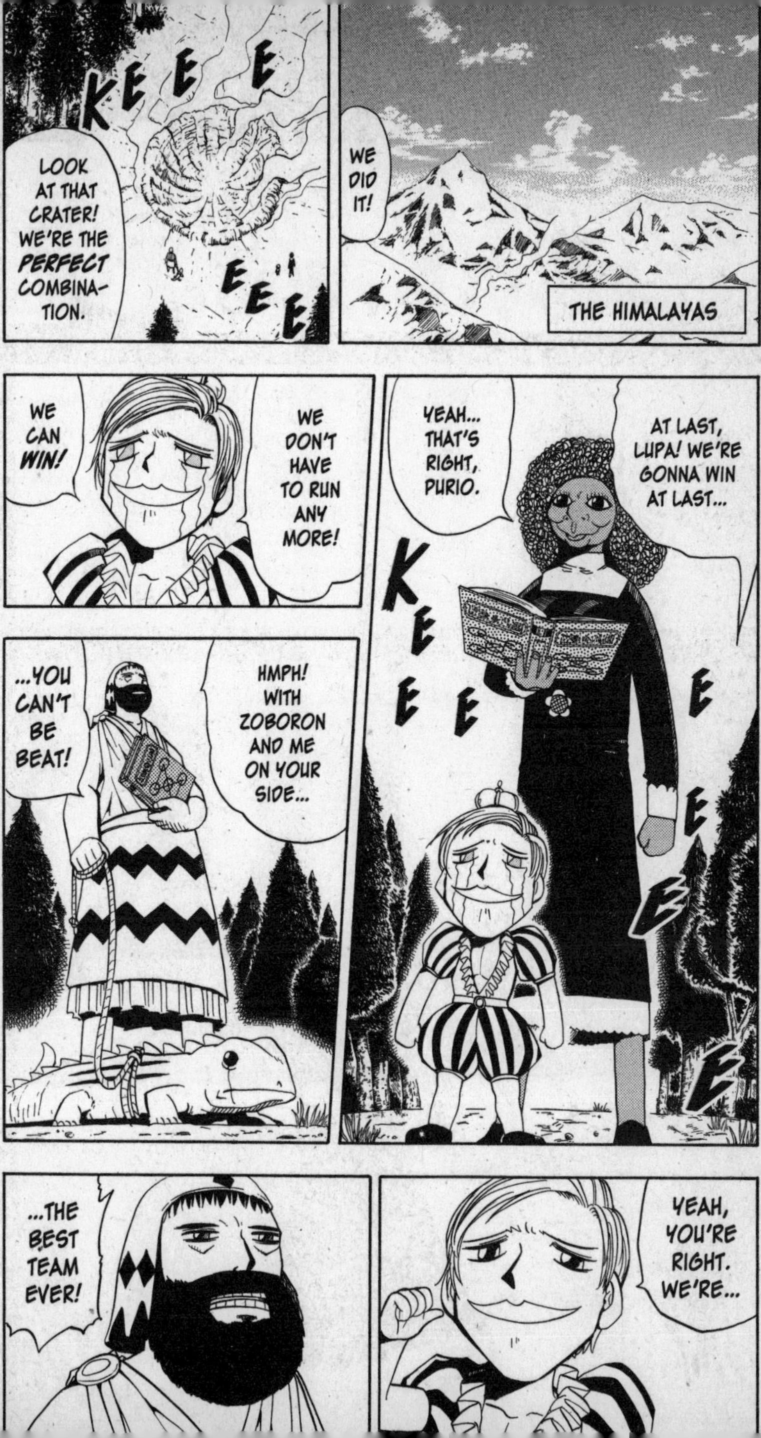

KEEEE
LOOK AT THAT CRATER! WE'RE THE PERFECT COMBINATION.
EEEE
WE DID IT!
THE HIMALAYAS
WE CAN WIN!
WE DON'T HAVE TO RUN ANY MORE!
YEAH... THAT'S RIGHT, PURIO.
AT LAST, LUPA! WE'RE GONNA WIN AT LAST...
KEEEEEEEE
...YOU CAN'T BE BEAT!
HMPH! WITH ZOBORON AND ME ON YOUR SIDE...
...THE BEST TEAM EVER!
YEAH, YOU'RE RIGHT. WE'RE...

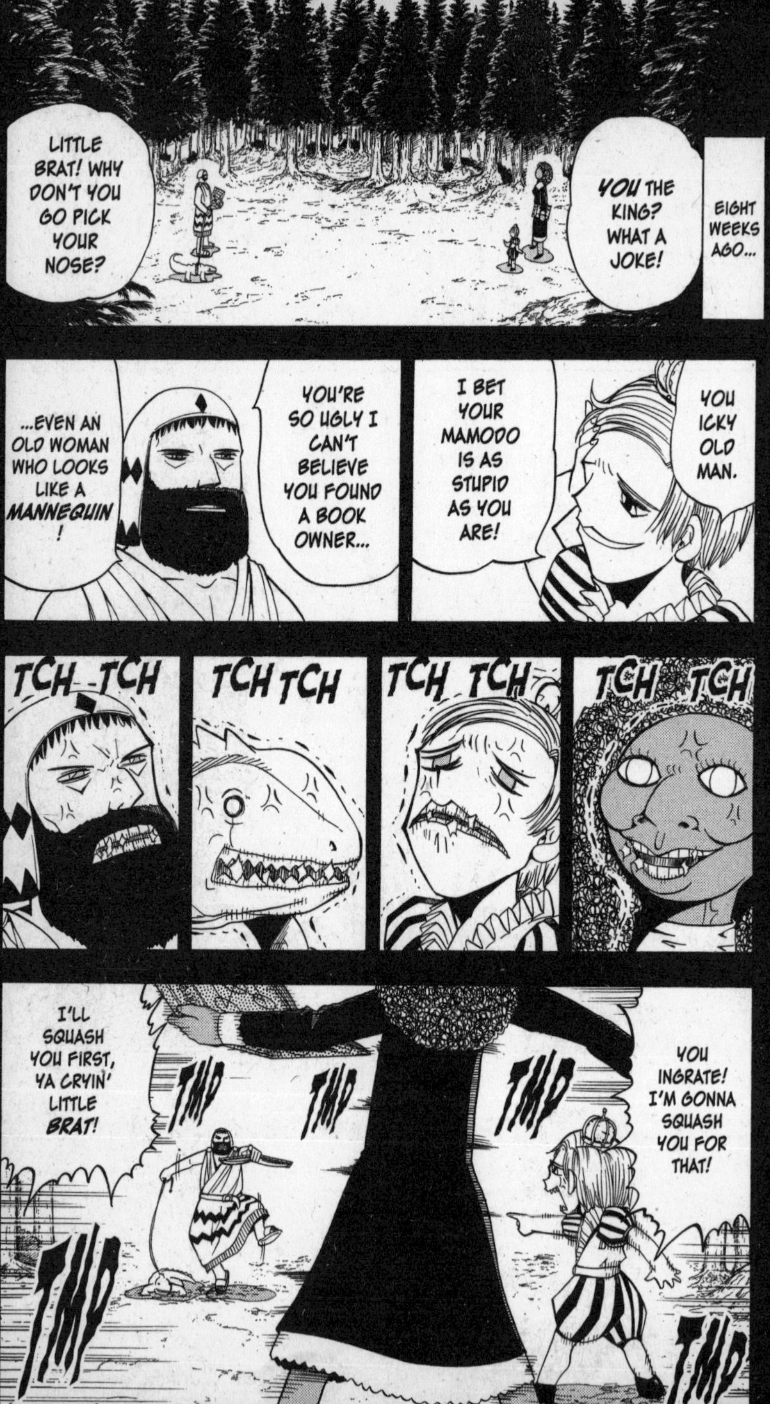
EIGHT WEEKS AGO...
YOU THE KING? WHAT A JOKE!
LITTLE BRAT! WHY DON'T YOU GO PICK YOUR NOSE?
YOU ICKY OLD MAN.
I BET YOUR MAMODO IS AS STUPID AS YOU ARE!
YOU'RE SO UGLY I CAN'T BELIEVE YOU FOUND A BOOK OWNER...
...EVEN AN OLD WOMAN WHO LOOKS LIKE A MANNEQUIN!
TCH TCH
TCH TCH
TCH TCH
TCH TCH
YOU INGRATE! I'M GONNA SQUASH YOU FOR THAT!
I'LL SQUASH YOU FIRST, YA CRYIN' LITTLE BRAT!
TMP TMP TMP TMP TMP

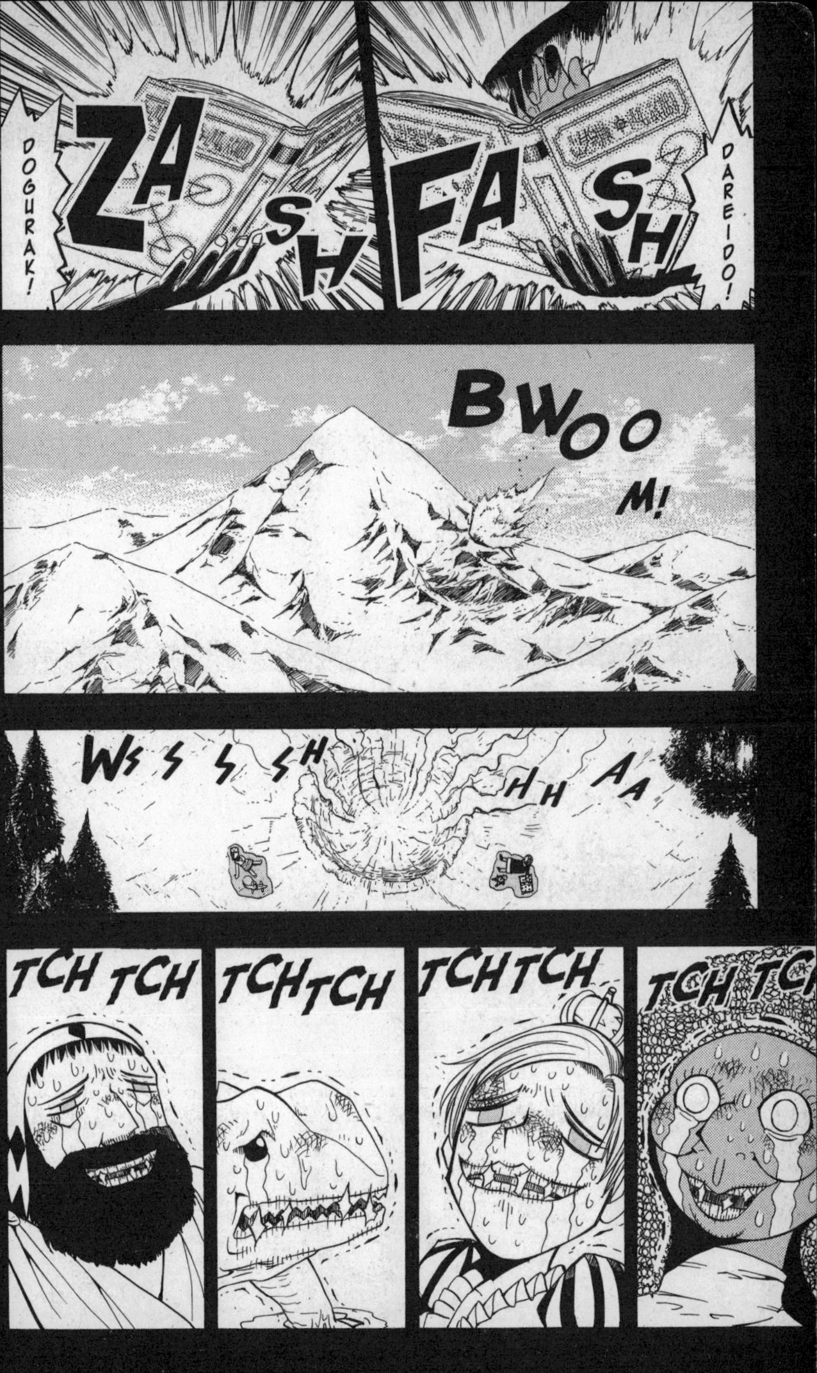

DAREIDO!
FASH
DOGURAK!
ZASH
BWOOOM!
WSSSSHHHAA
TCH TCH
TCHTCH
TCHTCH
TCH TCH

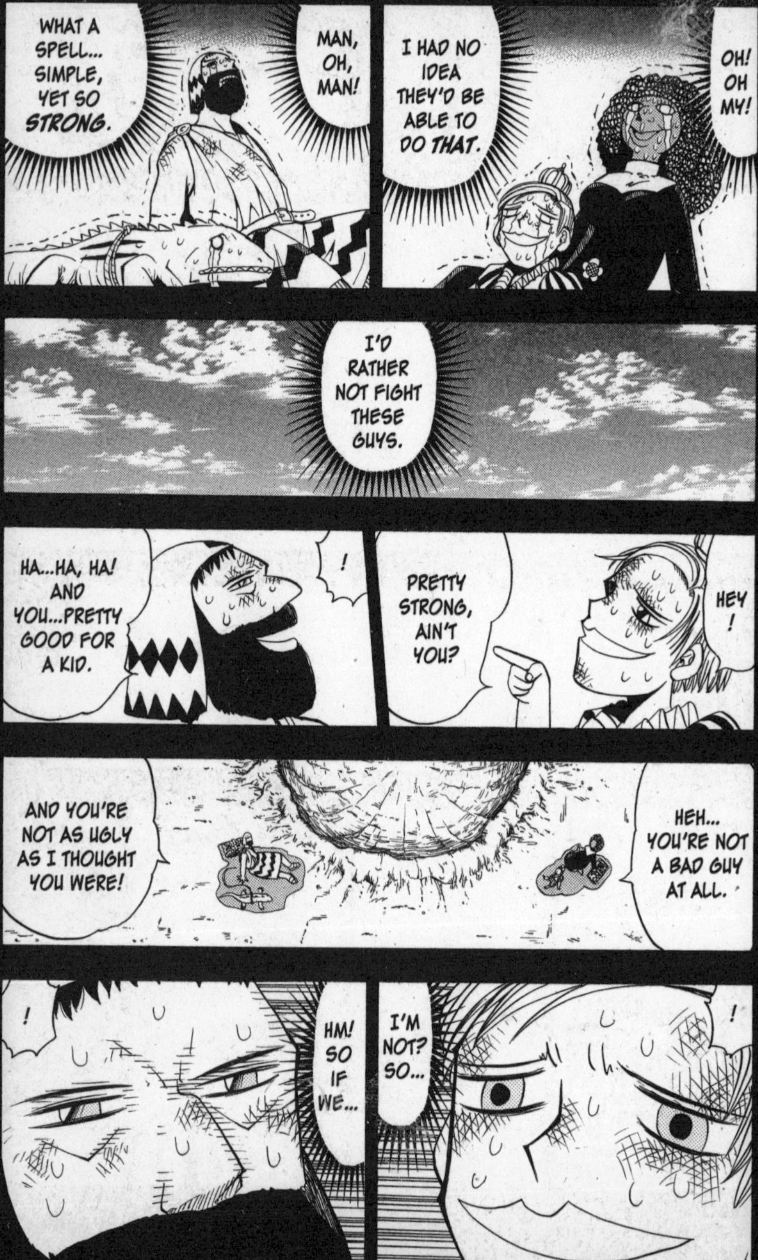
OH! OH MY!
I HAD NO IDEA THEY'D BE ABLE TO DO *THAT*.
MAN, OH, MAN!
WHAT A SPELL... SIMPLE, YET SO *STRONG*.
I'D RATHER NOT FIGHT THESE GUYS.
HEY!
PRETTY STRONG, AIN'T YOU?
!
HA...HA, HA! AND YOU...PRETTY GOOD FOR A KID.
HEH... YOU'RE NOT A BAD GUY AT ALL.
AND YOU'RE NOT AS UGLY AS I THOUGHT YOU WERE!
!
I'M NOT? SO...
HM! SO IF WE...
!

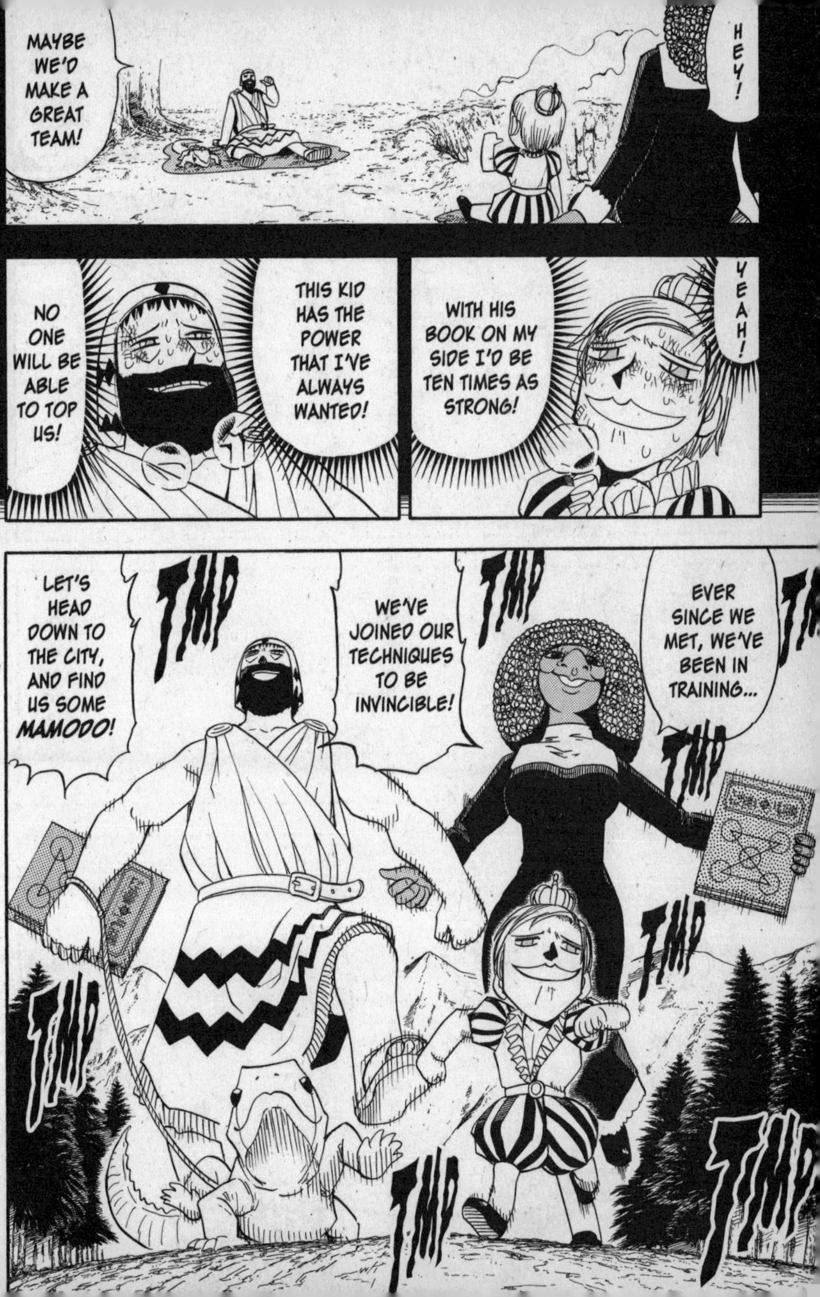
HEY!
MAYBE WE'D MAKE A GREAT TEAM!
YEAH!
WITH HIS BOOK ON MY SIDE I'D BE TEN TIMES AS STRONG!
THIS KID HAS THE POWER THAT I'VE ALWAYS WANTED!
NO ONE WILL BE ABLE TO TOP US!
EVER SINCE WE MET, WE'VE BEEN IN TRAINING...
WE'VE JOINED OUR TECHNIQUES TO BE INVINCIBLE!
LET'S HEAD DOWN TO THE CITY, AND FIND US SOME MAMODO!
TMP TMP TMP TMP TMP TMP TMP TMP TMP

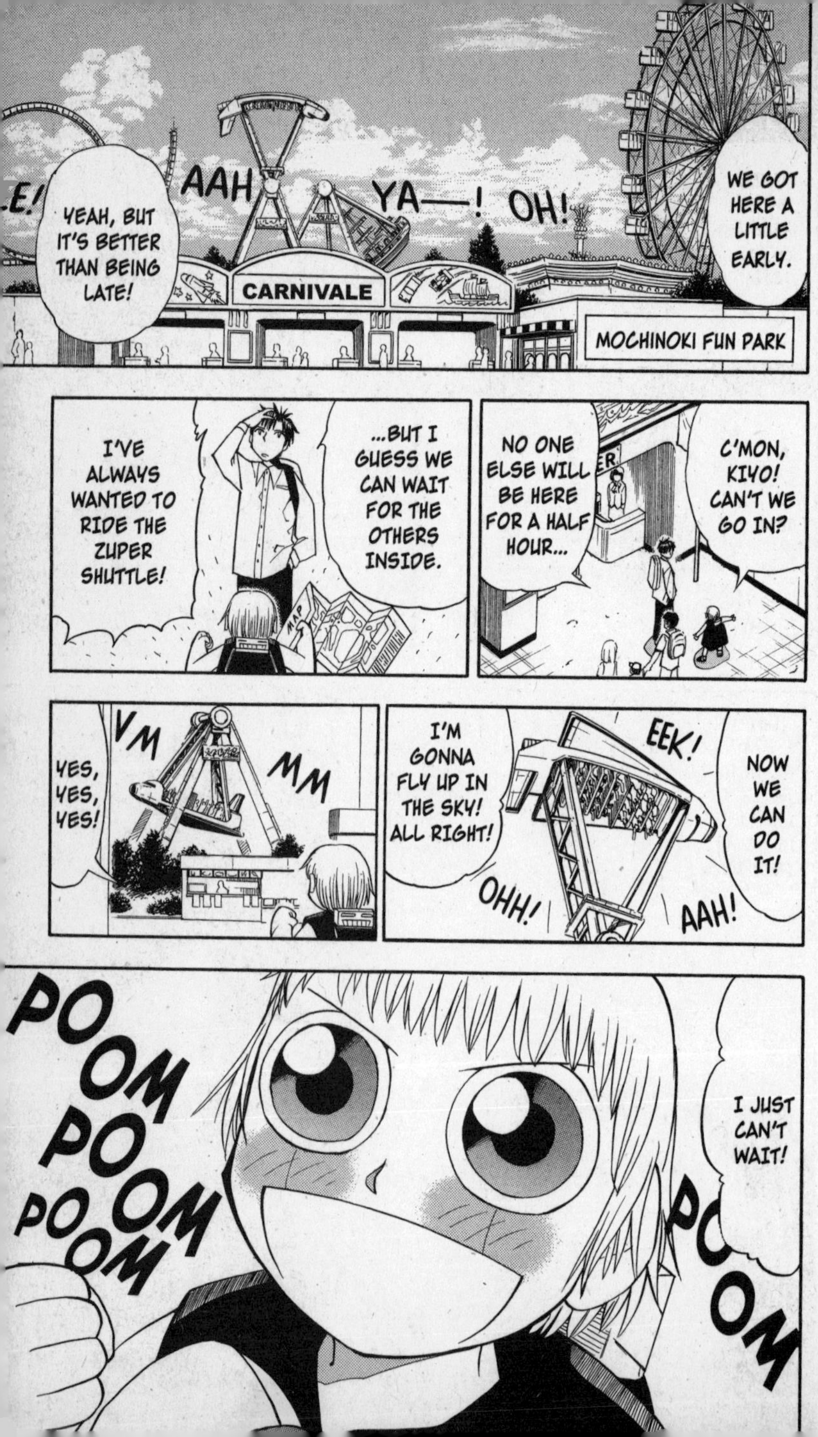
AAH
YA—!
OH!
E!
MOCHINOKI FUN PARK
CARNIVALE
WE GOT HERE A LITTLE EARLY.
YEAH, BUT IT'S BETTER THAN BEING LATE!
C'MON, KIYO! CAN'T WE GO IN?
NO ONE ELSE WILL BE HERE FOR A HALF HOUR...
...BUT I GUESS WE CAN WAIT FOR THE OTHERS INSIDE.
I'VE ALWAYS WANTED TO RIDE THE ZUPER SHUTTLE!
MAP
NOW WE CAN DO IT!
EEK!
I'M GONNA FLY UP IN THE SKY! ALL RIGHT!
OHH!
AAH!
VM
MM
YES, YES, YES!
I JUST CAN'T WAIT!
POOM
POOM
POOM
POOM
POOM

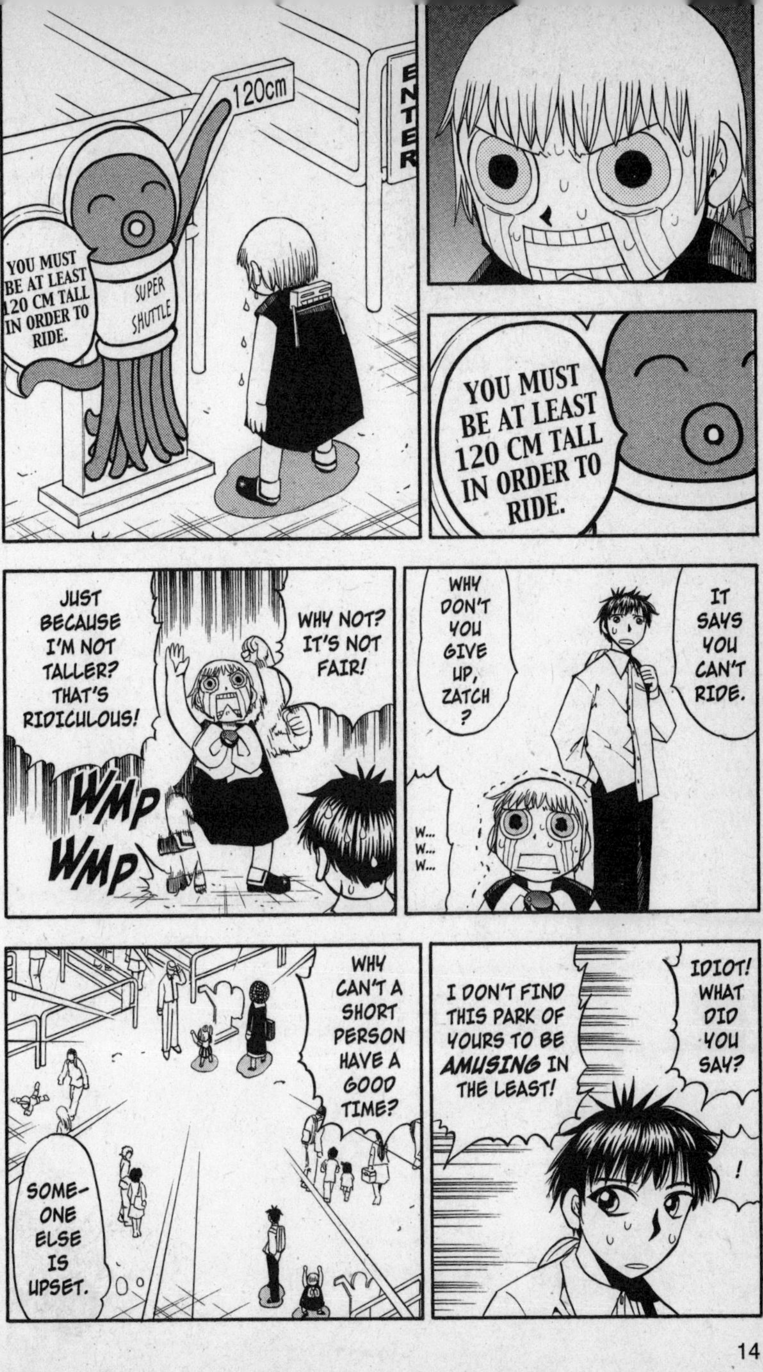
ENTER
120cm
YOU MUST BE AT LEAST 120 CM TALL IN ORDER TO RIDE.
YOU MUST BE AT LEAST 120 CM TALL IN ORDER TO RIDE.
SUPER SHUTTLE
IT SAYS YOU CAN'T RIDE.
WHY DON'T YOU GIVE UP, ZATCH?
W... W... W...
WHY NOT? IT'S NOT FAIR!
JUST BECAUSE I'M NOT TALLER? THAT'S RIDICULOUS!
WMP WMP
IDIOT! WHAT DID YOU SAY?
I DON'T FIND THIS PARK OF YOURS TO BE AMUSING IN THE LEAST!
!
WHY CAN'T A SHORT PERSON HAVE A GOOD TIME?
SOME-ONE ELSE IS UPSET.

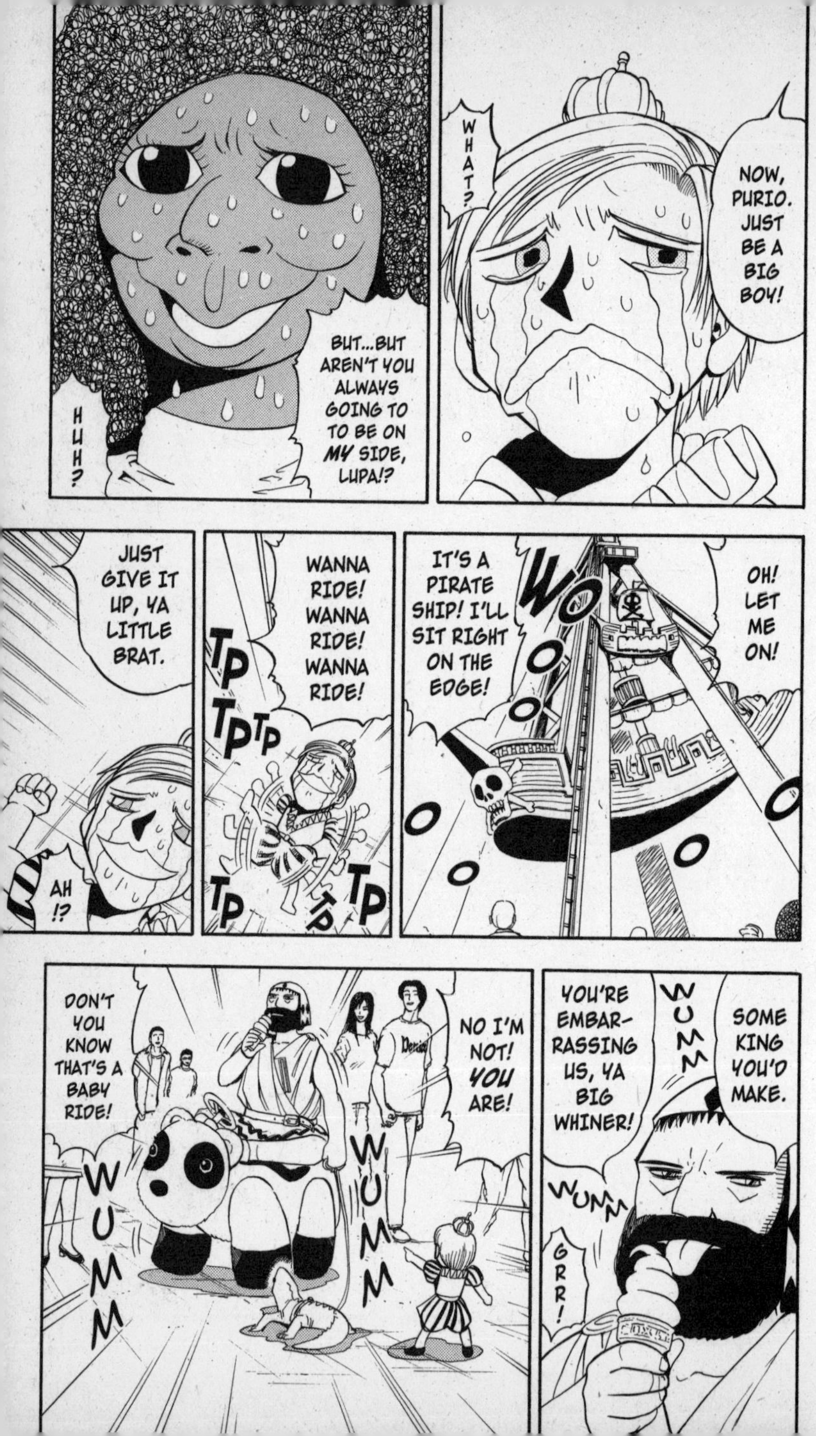
NOW, PURIO. JUST BE A BIG BOY!
WHAT?
BUT...BUT AREN'T YOU ALWAYS GOING TO TO BE ON MY SIDE, LUPA!?
HUH?
OH! LET ME ON!
WOOOOOOOO
IT'S A PIRATE SHIP! I'LL SIT RIGHT ON THE EDGE!
WANNA RIDE! WANNA RIDE! WANNA RIDE!
TP TP TP TP TP TP TP
JUST GIVE IT UP, YA LITTLE BRAT.
AH!?
SOME KING YOU'D MAKE.
WUMM
YOU'RE EMBARRASSING US, YA BIG WHINER!
WUMM
GRR!
NO I'M NOT! YOU ARE!
WUMM
DON'T YOU KNOW THAT'S A BABY RIDE!
WUMM

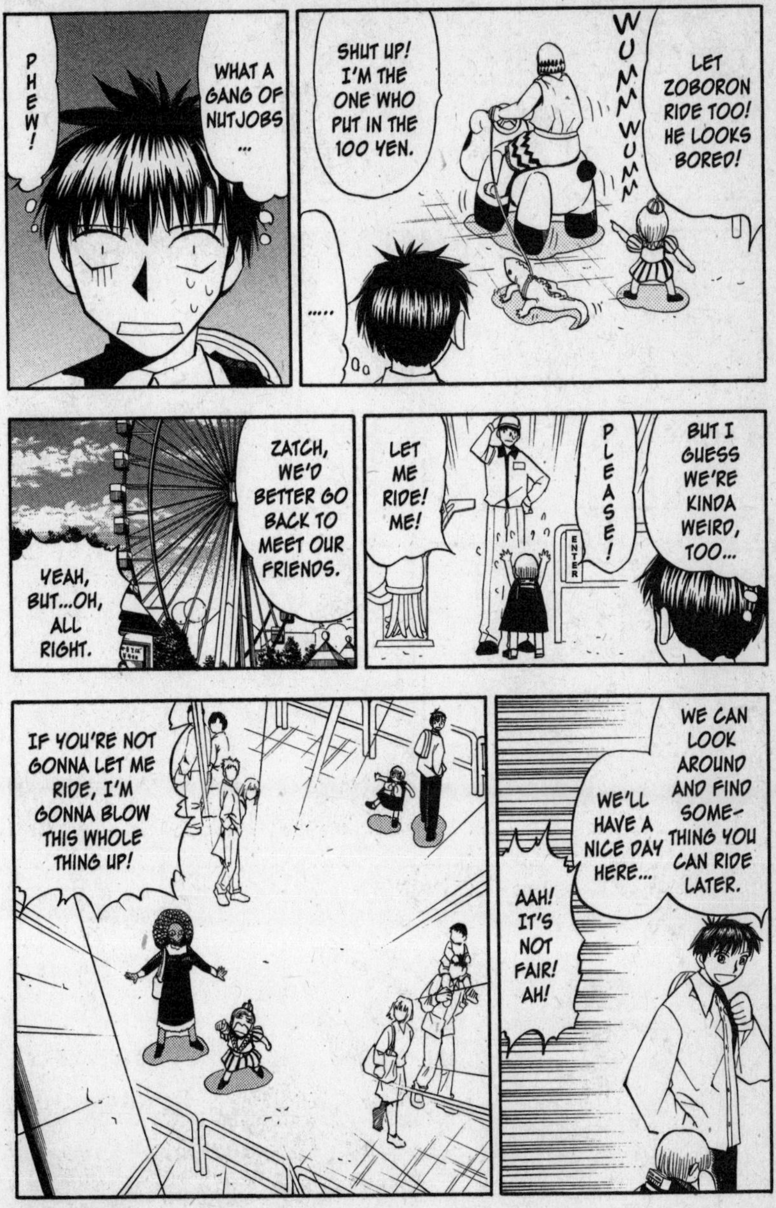

LET ZOBORON RIDE TOO! HE LOOKS BORED!
WUMM WUMM
SHUT UP! I'M THE ONE WHO PUT IN THE 100 YEN.
.....
WHAT A GANG OF NUTJOBS ...
PHEW!
BUT I GUESS WE'RE KINDA WEIRD, TOO...
PLEASE!
ENTER
LET ME RIDE! ME!
ZATCH, WE'D BETTER GO BACK TO MEET OUR FRIENDS.
YEAH, BUT...OH, ALL RIGHT.
WE CAN LOOK AROUND AND FIND SOME-THING YOU CAN RIDE LATER.
WE'LL HAVE A NICE DAY HERE...
AAH! IT'S NOT FAIR! AH!
IF YOU'RE NOT GONNA LET ME RIDE, I'M GONNA BLOW THIS WHOLE THING UP!

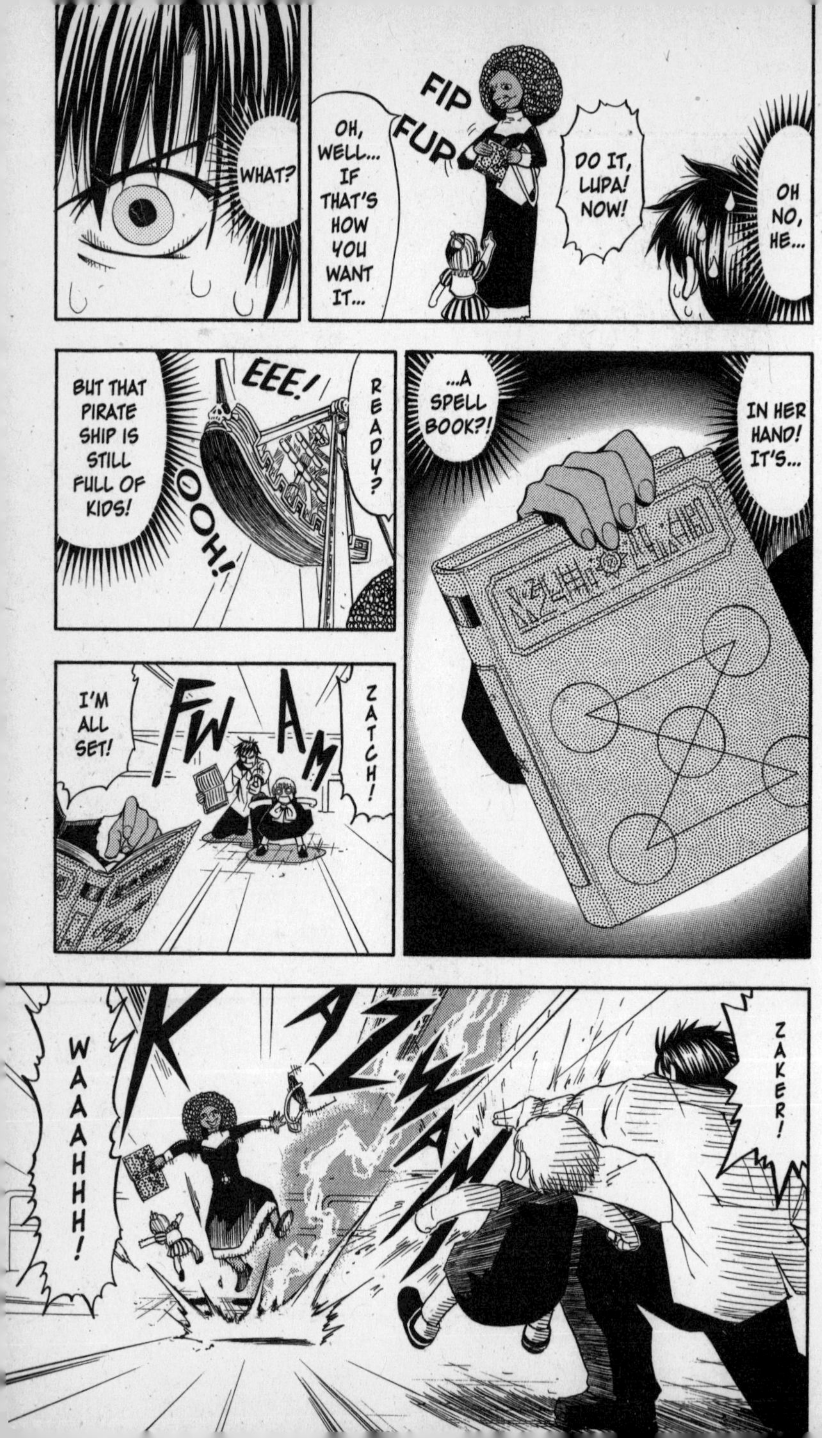
OH NO, HE...
DO IT, LUPA! NOW!
FIP FUP
OH, WELL... IF THAT'S HOW YOU WANT IT...
WHAT?
IN HER HAND! IT'S...
...A SPELL BOOK?!
READY?
EEE!
OOOH!
BUT THAT PIRATE SHIP IS STILL FULL OF KIDS!
ZATCH!
FWAM
I'M ALL SET!
ZAKER!
KAZWAM
WAAAAHHH!

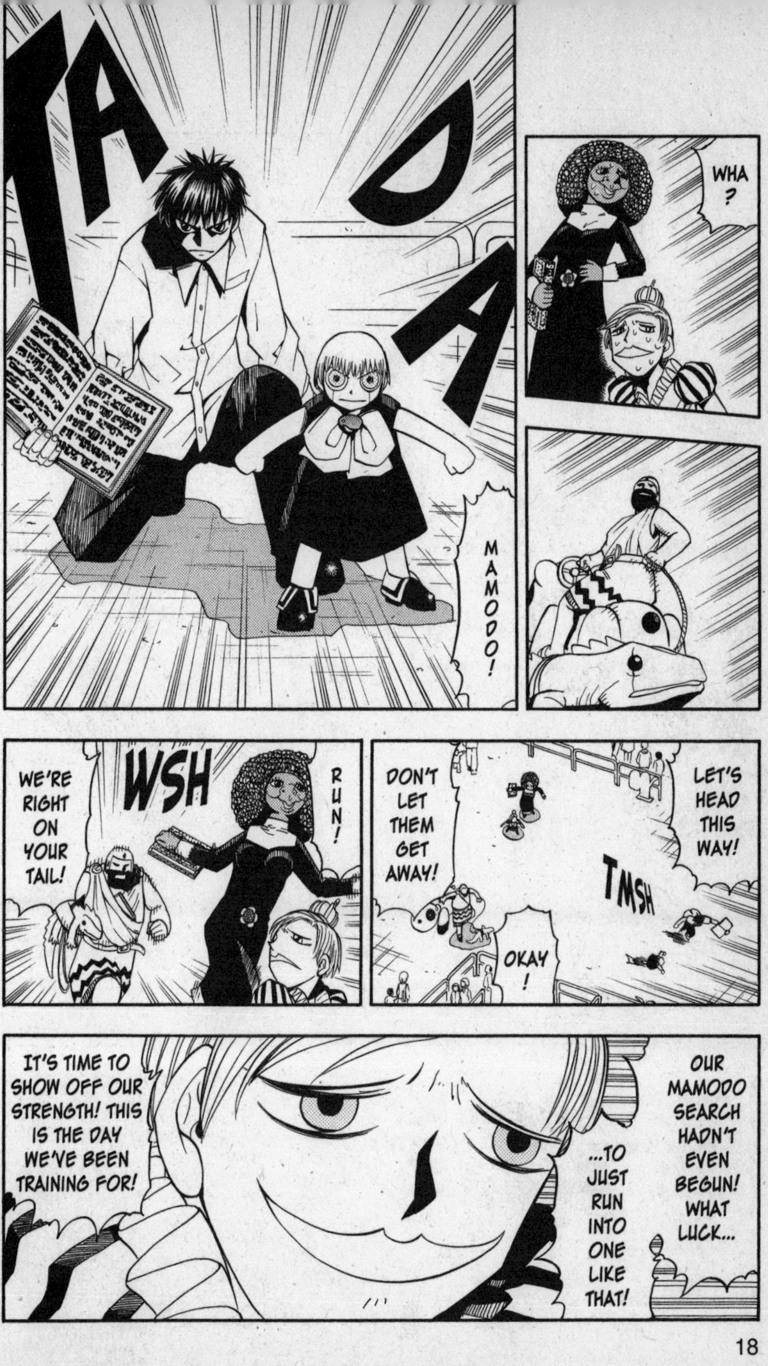
TA
DA
MAMODO!
WHA?
RUN!
WSH
WE'RE RIGHT ON YOUR TAIL!
LET'S HEAD THIS WAY!
TMSH
OKAY!
DON'T LET THEM GET AWAY!
OUR MAMODO SEARCH HADN'T EVEN BEGUN! WHAT LUCK...
...TO JUST RUN INTO ONE LIKE THAT!
IT'S TIME TO SHOW OFF OUR STRENGTH! THIS IS THE DAY WE'VE BEEN TRAINING FOR!

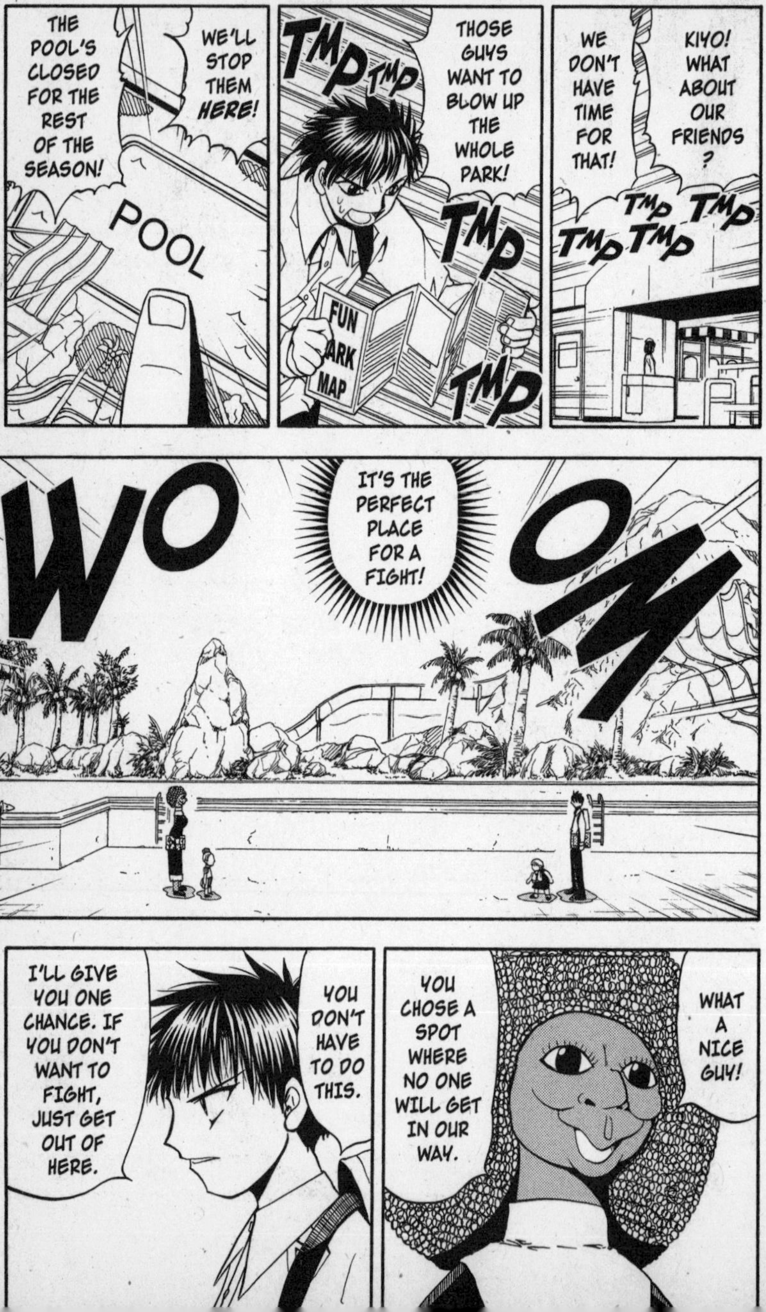
TMP TMP TMP TMP
KIYO! WHAT ABOUT OUR FRIENDS?
WE DON'T HAVE TIME FOR THAT!
TMP TMP TMP TMP
THOSE GUYS WANT TO BLOW UP THE WHOLE PARK!
FUN PARK MAP
WE'LL STOP THEM HERE!
THE POOL'S CLOSED FOR THE REST OF THE SEASON!
POOL
WOOM
IT'S THE PERFECT PLACE FOR A FIGHT!
WHAT A NICE GUY!
YOU CHOSE A SPOT WHERE NO ONE WILL GET IN OUR WAY.
YOU DON'T HAVE TO DO THIS.
I'LL GIVE YOU ONE CHANCE. IF YOU DON'T WANT TO FIGHT, JUST GET OUT OF HERE.

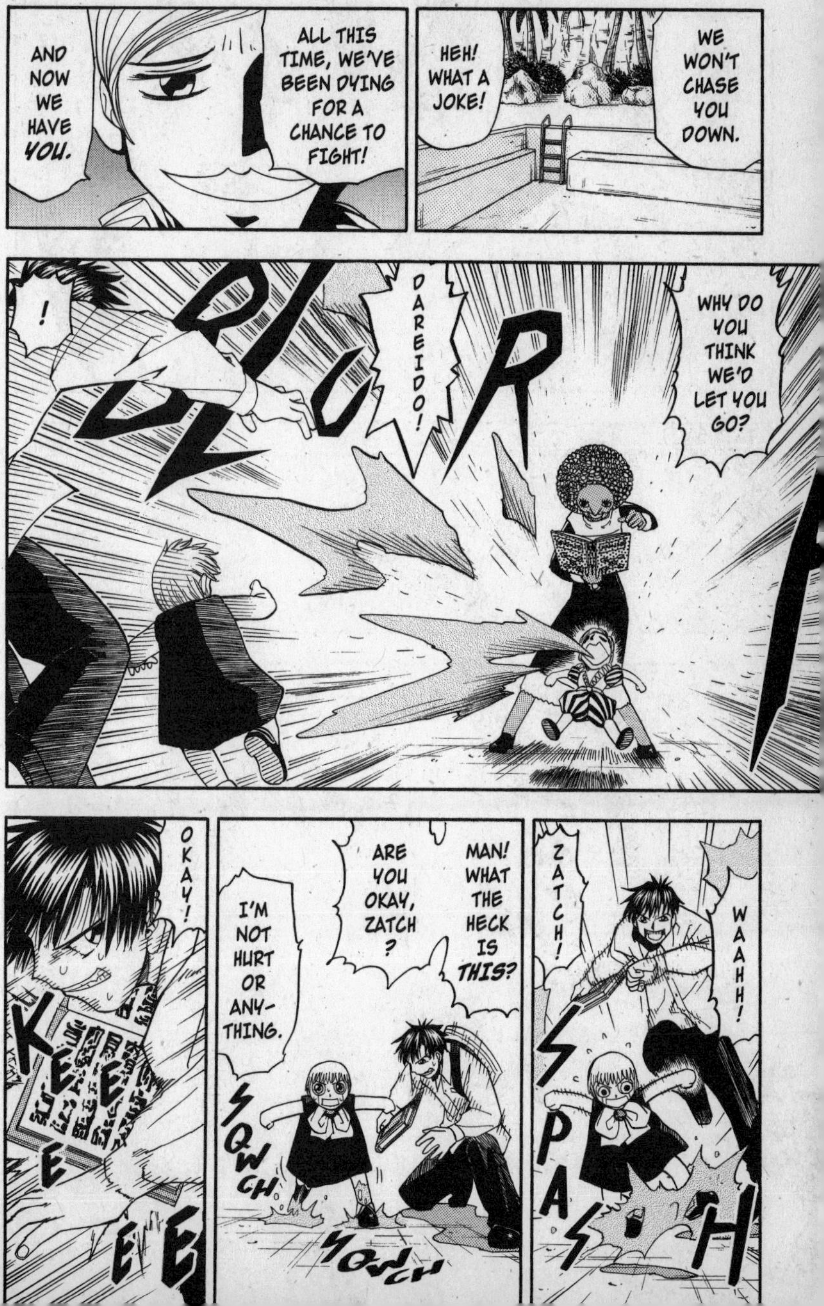
WE WON'T CHASE YOU DOWN.
HEH! WHAT A JOKE!
ALL THIS TIME, WE'VE BEEN DYING FOR A CHANCE TO FIGHT!
AND NOW WE HAVE YOU.
WHY DO YOU THINK WE'D LET YOU GO?
DAREIDO!
!
WAAHH!
ZATCH!
MAN! WHAT THE HECK IS THIS?
ARE YOU OKAY, ZATCH?
I'M NOT HURT OR ANYTHING.
SQWCH
SQWCH
OKAY!

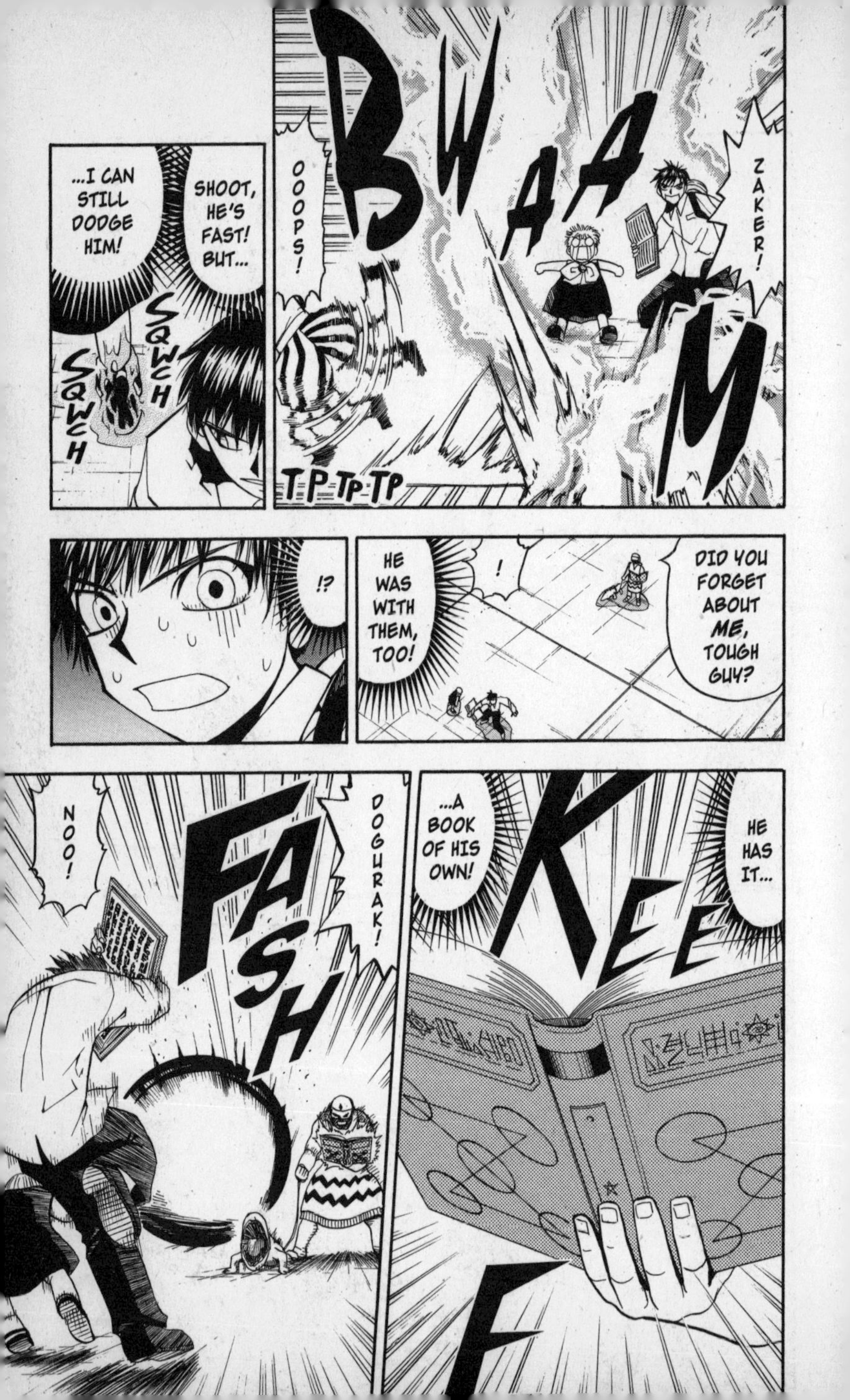
ZAKER!
BWAAM
OOOPS!
TP TP TP TP
SHOOT, HE'S FAST! BUT...
...I CAN STILL DODGE HIM!
SQWCH
SQWCH
DID YOU FORGET ABOUT ME, TOUGH GUY?
!
HE WAS WITH THEM, TOO!
!?
HE HAS IT...
...A BOOK OF HIS OWN!
KEE
F
DOGURAK!
FASH
NOO!

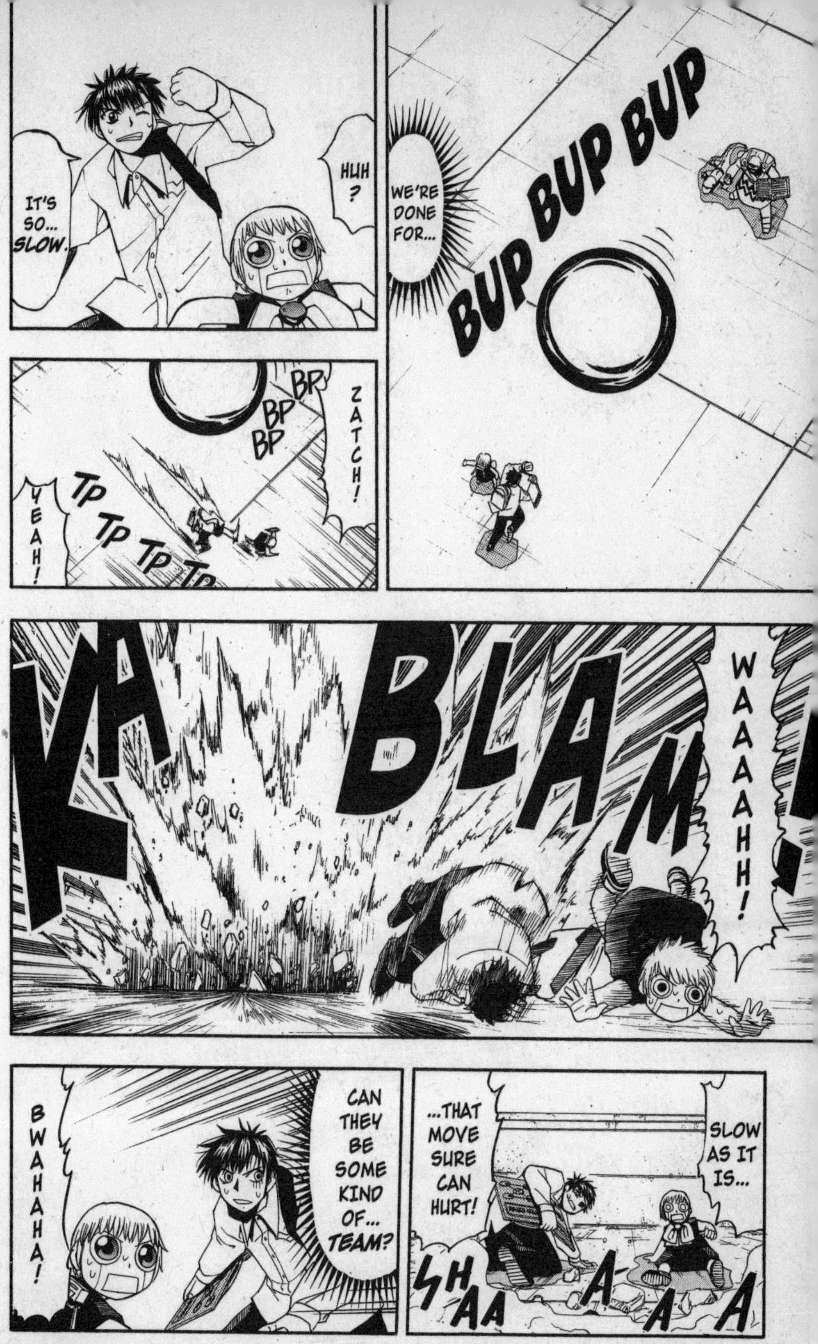

BUP BUP BUP
WE'RE DONE FOR...
HUH?
IT'S SO... SLOW.
ZATCH!
BP BP BP
YEAH!
TP TP TP TP
KA BLAM!
WAAAAAHH!
SLOW AS IT IS...
...THAT MOVE SURE CAN HURT!
SHAAAAA
CAN THEY BE SOME KIND OF... TEAM?
BWAHAHA!

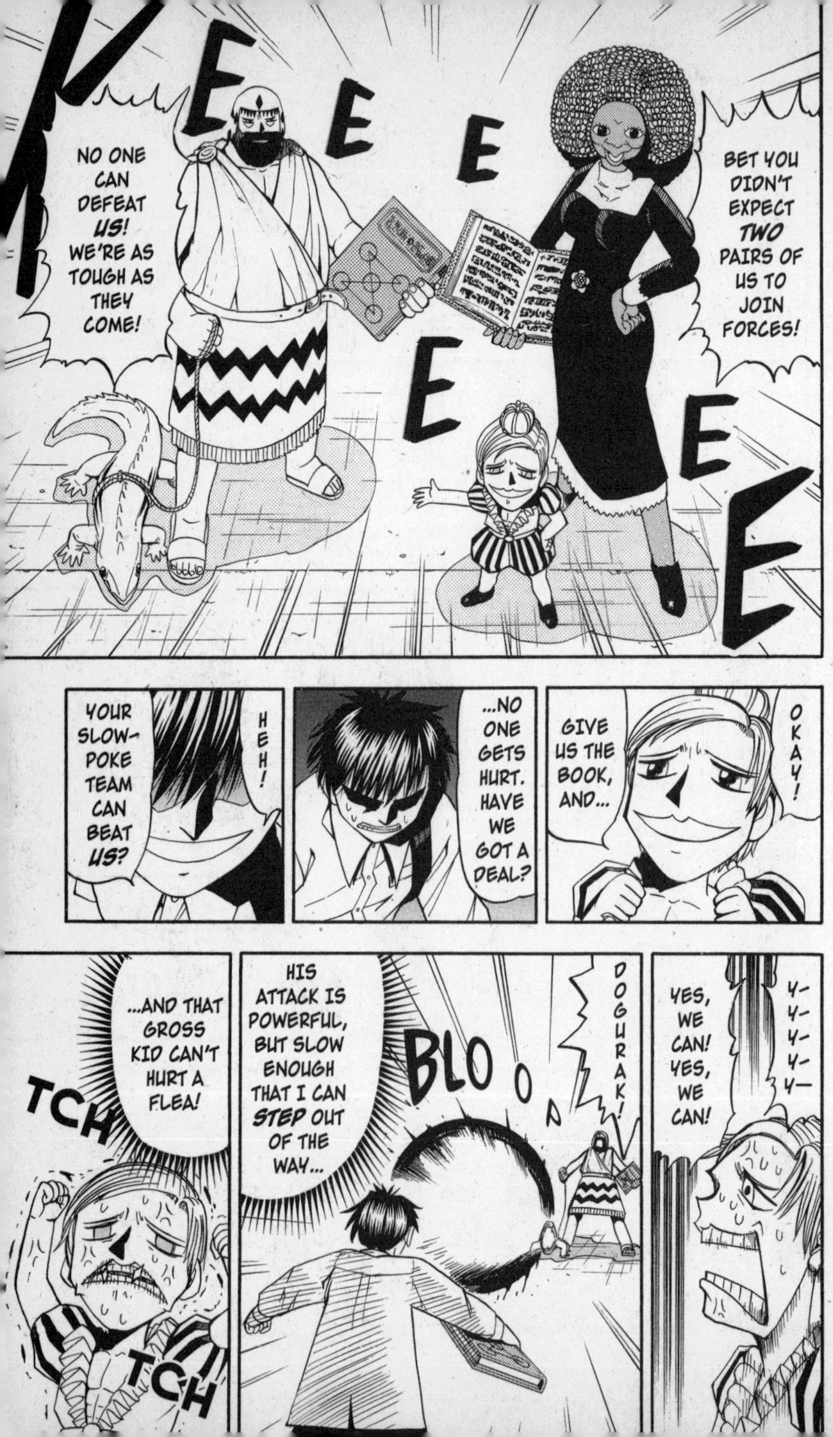
BET YOU DIDN'T EXPECT TWO PAIRS OF US TO JOIN FORCES!
NO ONE CAN DEFEAT US! WE'RE AS TOUGH AS THEY COME!
KEEEEEEE
OKAY!
GIVE US THE BOOK, AND...
...NO ONE GETS HURT. HAVE WE GOT A DEAL?
HEH!
YOUR SLOW-POKE TEAM CAN BEAT US?
Y-Y-Y-Y-Y—
YES, WE CAN! YES, WE CAN!
DOGURAK!
BLO
HIS ATTACK IS POWERFUL, BUT SLOW ENOUGH THAT I CAN STEP OUT OF THE WAY...
...AND THAT GROSS KID CAN'T HURT A FLEA!
TCH
TCH

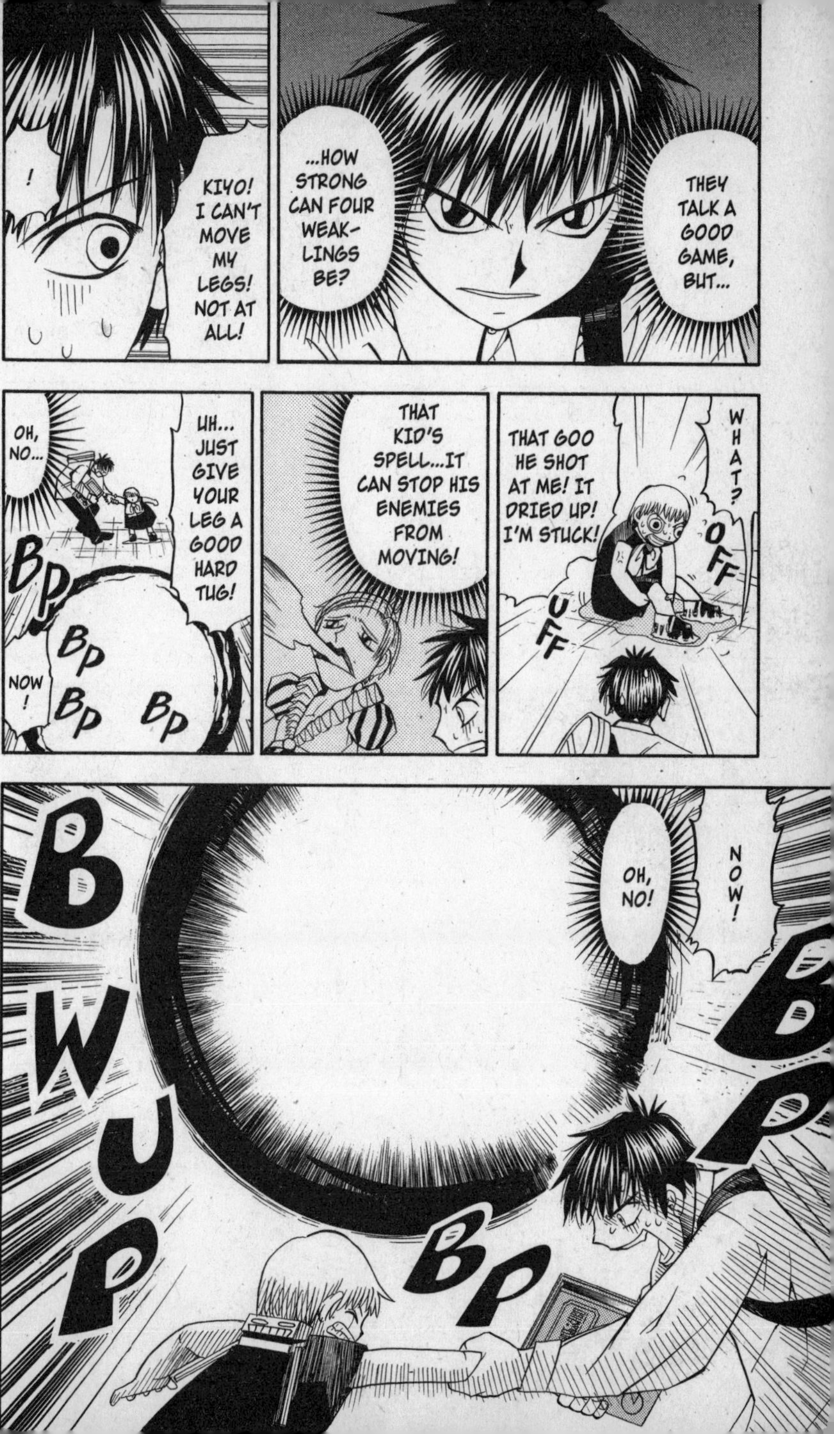
THEY TALK A GOOD GAME, BUT...
...HOW STRONG CAN FOUR WEAK-LINGS BE?
!
KIYO! I CAN'T MOVE MY LEGS! NOT AT ALL!
WHAT?
THAT GOO HE SHOT AT ME! IT DRIED UP! I'M STUCK!
OFF
UFF
THAT KID'S SPELL...IT CAN STOP HIS ENEMIES FROM MOVING!
UH... JUST GIVE YOUR LEG A GOOD HARD TUG!
OH, NO...
BP
BP BP BP
NOW!
NOW!
OH, NO!
BP
BP
BWUP

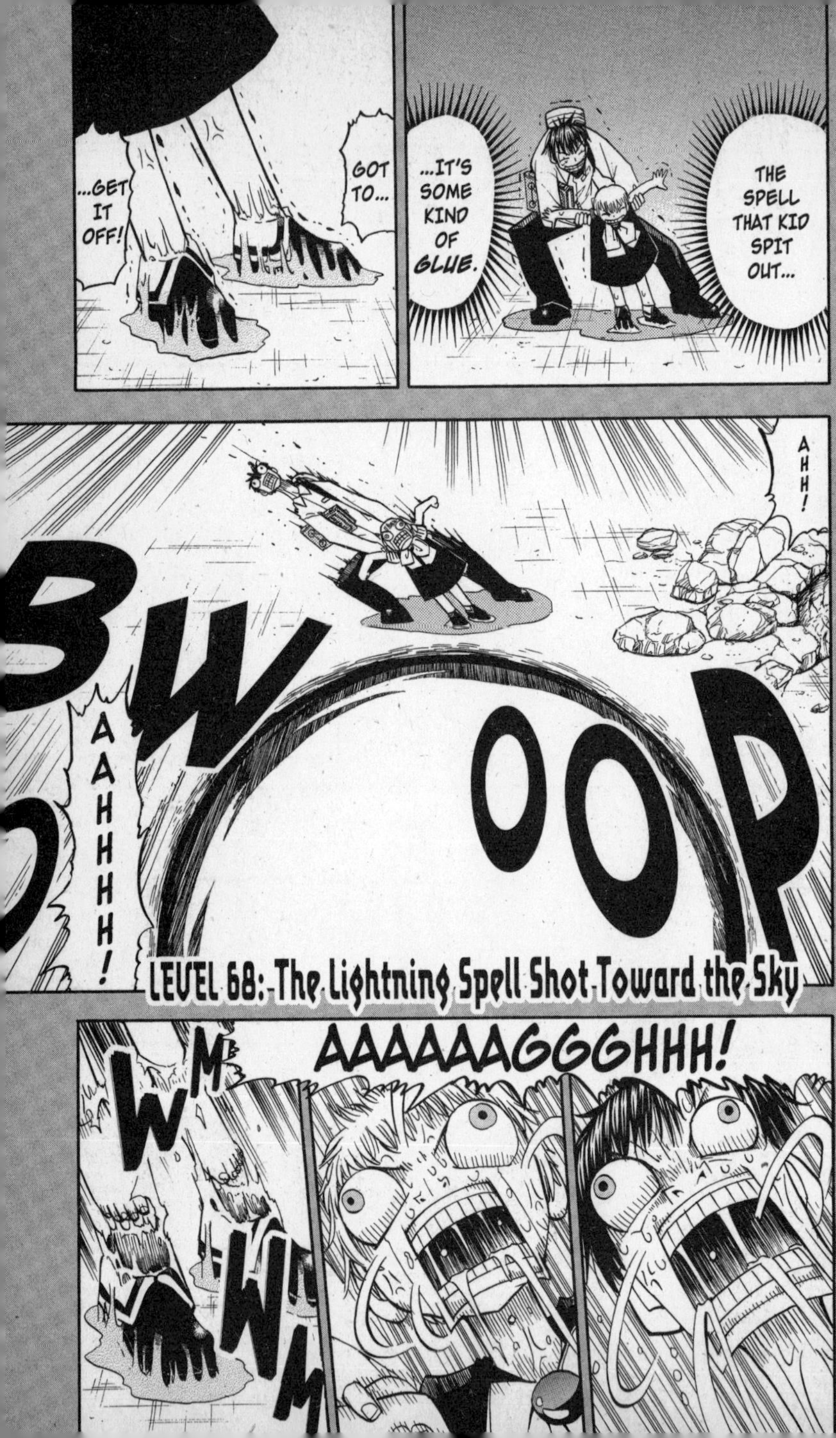
THE SPELL THAT KID SPIT OUT...
...IT'S SOME KIND OF GLUE.
GOT TO...
...GET IT OFF!
AHH!
BWOOP
AAHHHHH!
AAAAAAGGGHHH!

LEVEL 68: The Lightning Spell Shot Toward the Sky

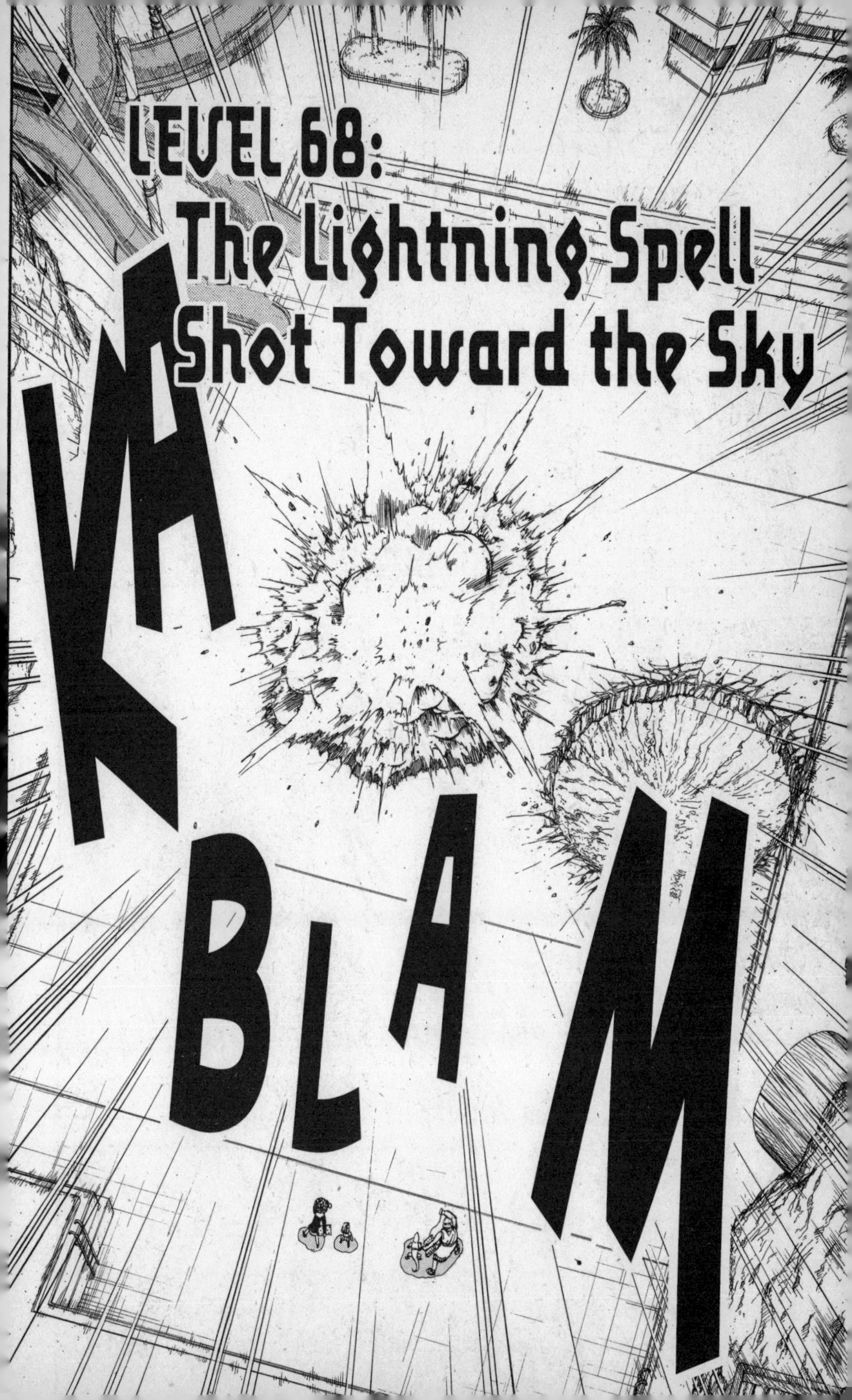
LEVEL 68:
The Lightning Spell Shot Toward the Sky
KA
BLAM

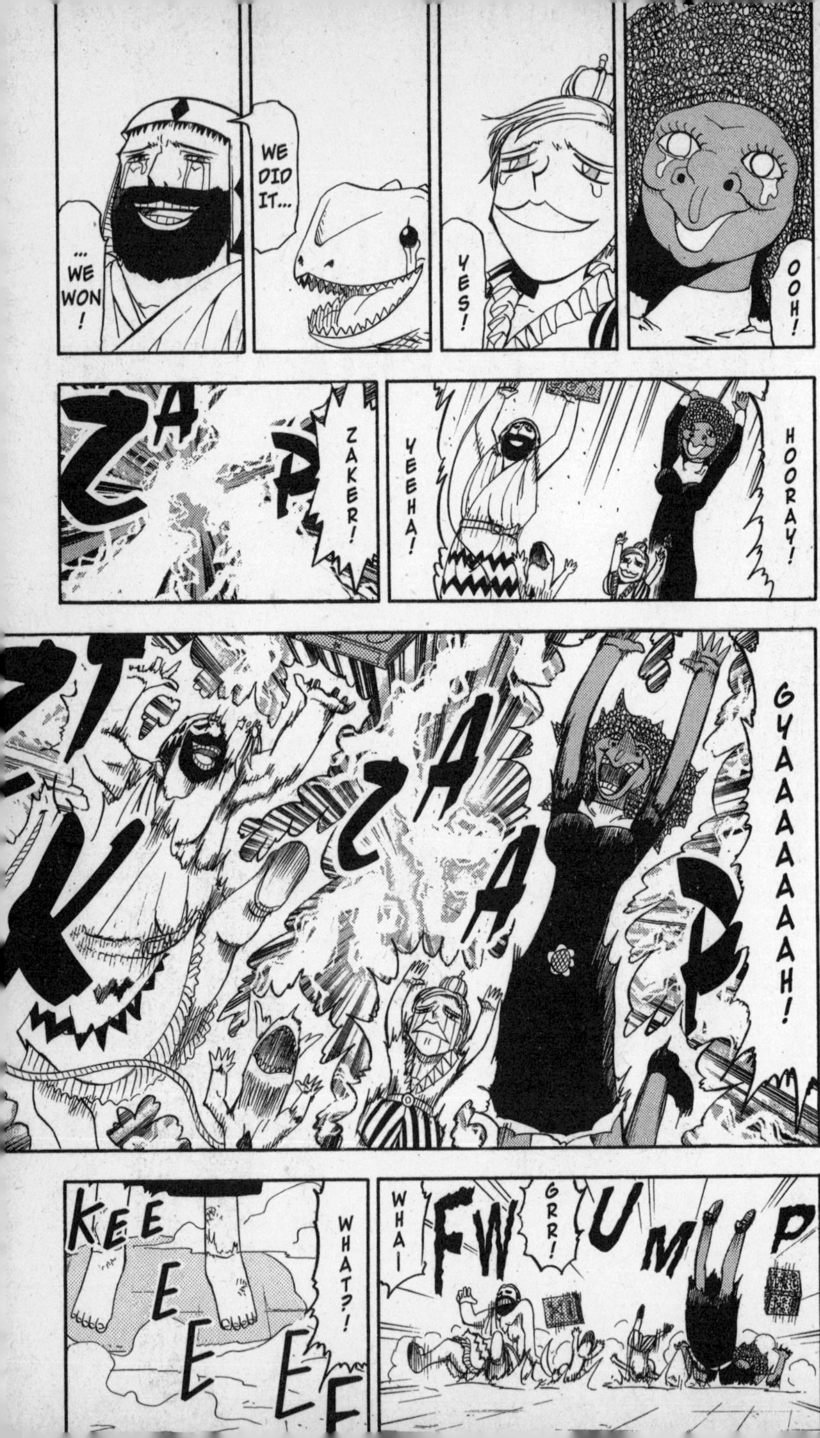
OOH!
YES!
WE DID IT...
...WE WON!
HOORAY!
YEEHA!
ZAKER!
ZAP
GYAAAAAAAAH!
FWUMP
GRR!
WHA!
WHAT?!

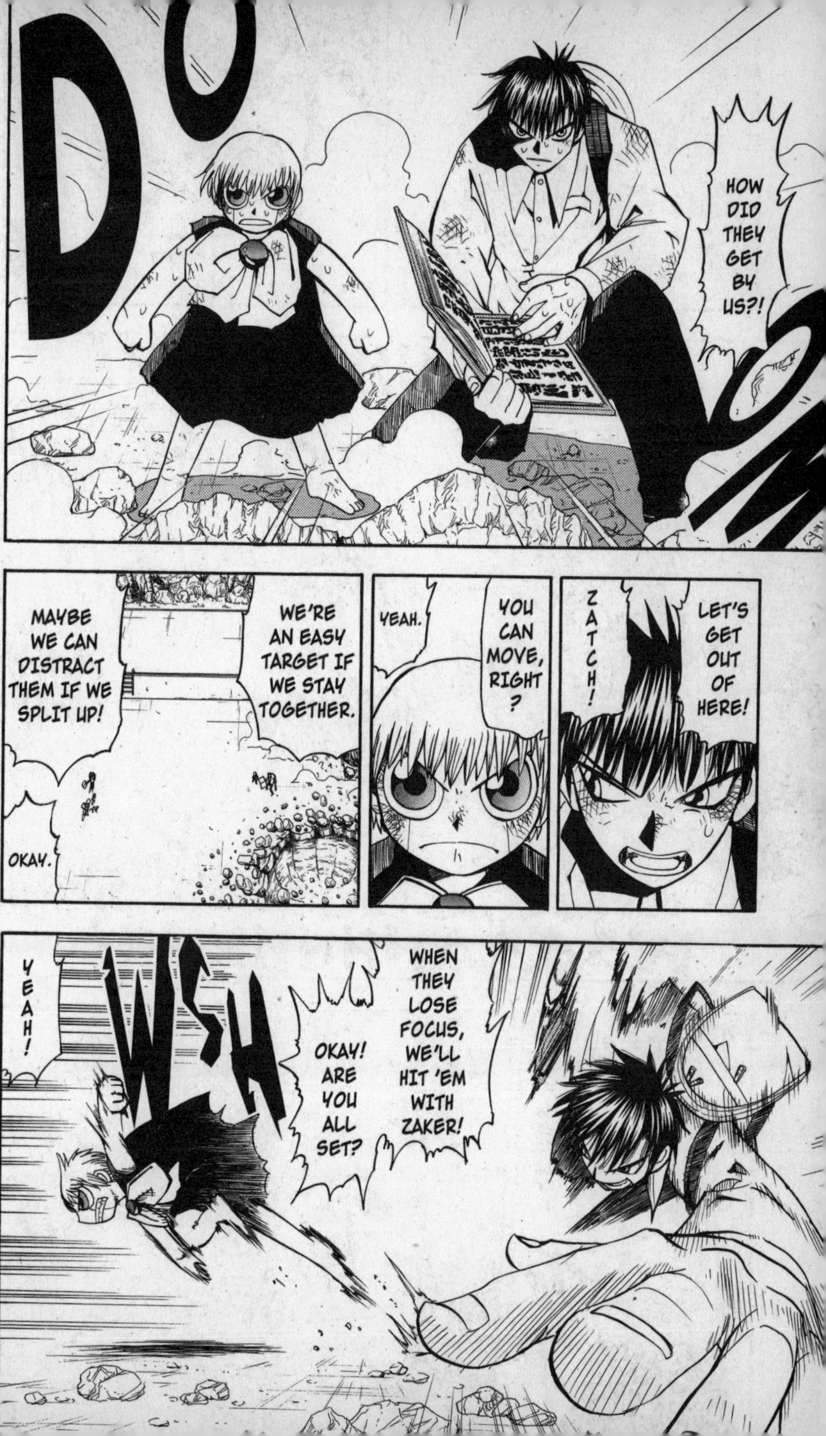
DOOM
HOW DID THEY GET BY US?!
LET'S GET OUT OF HERE!
ZATCH!
YOU CAN MOVE, RIGHT?
YEAH.
WE'RE AN EASY TARGET IF WE STAY TOGETHER.
MAYBE WE CAN DISTRACT THEM IF WE SPLIT UP!
OKAY.
WHEN THEY LOSE FOCUS, WE'LL HIT 'EM WITH ZAKER!
OKAY! ARE YOU ALL SET?
WSH
YEAH!

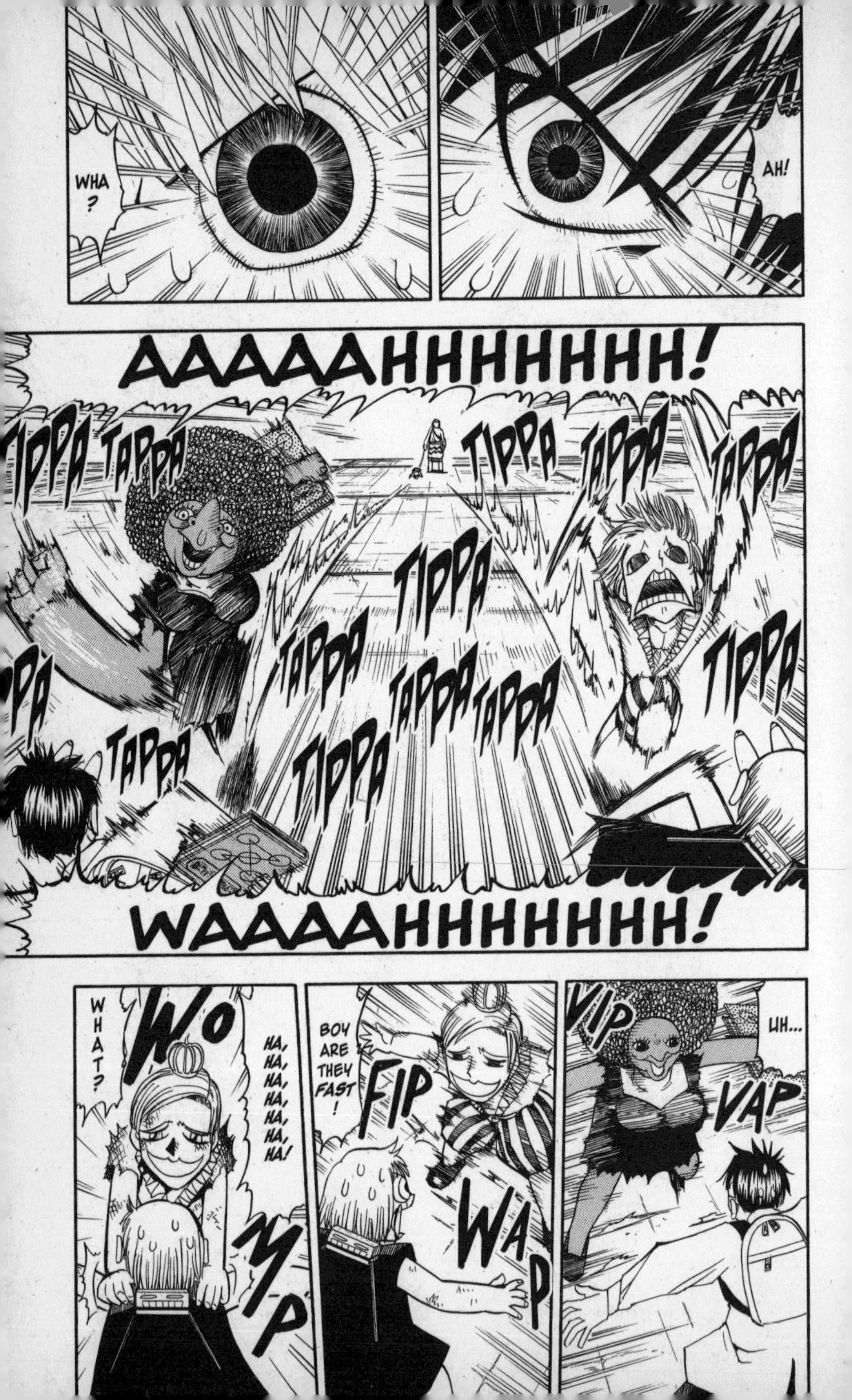
AH!
WHA?
AAAAAHHHHHHH!
TAPPA
TIPPA
TAPPA
TIPPA
TIPPA
TAPPA
TAPPA
TAPPA
TIPPA
TAPPA
TAPPA
TIPPA
TAPPA
WAAAAHHHHHHH!
UH...
VIP
VAP
BOY ARE THEY FAST!
FIP
WAP
WHAT?
WO
HA, HA, HA, HA, HA, HA, HA, HA!
MP

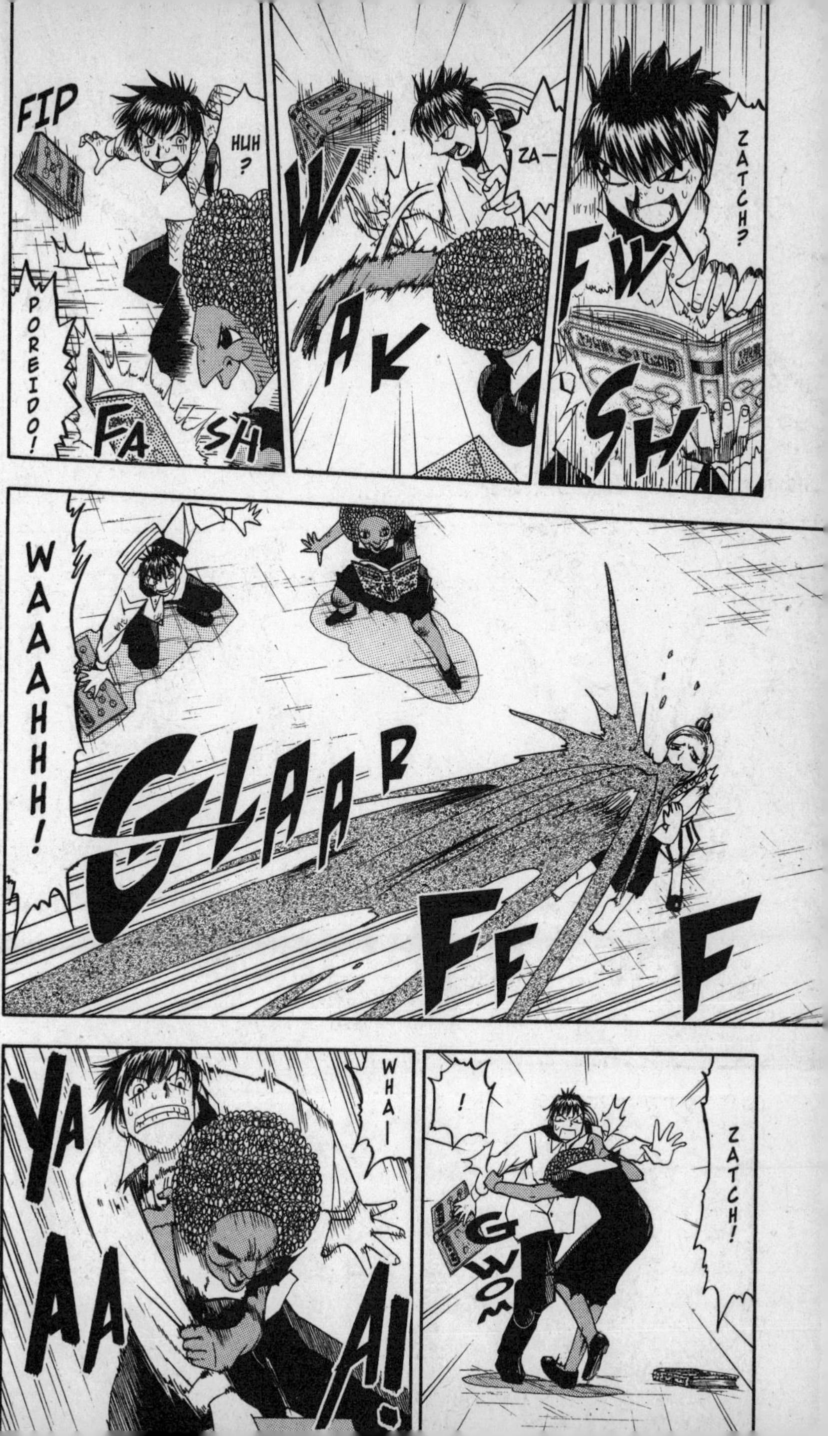
ZATCH?
FWSH
ZA—
WAK
HUH?
FIP
POREIDO!
FASH
WAAAAHHHH!
GLAAR
FFF
ZATCH!
!
GWOM
WHAI
YAAAAI!

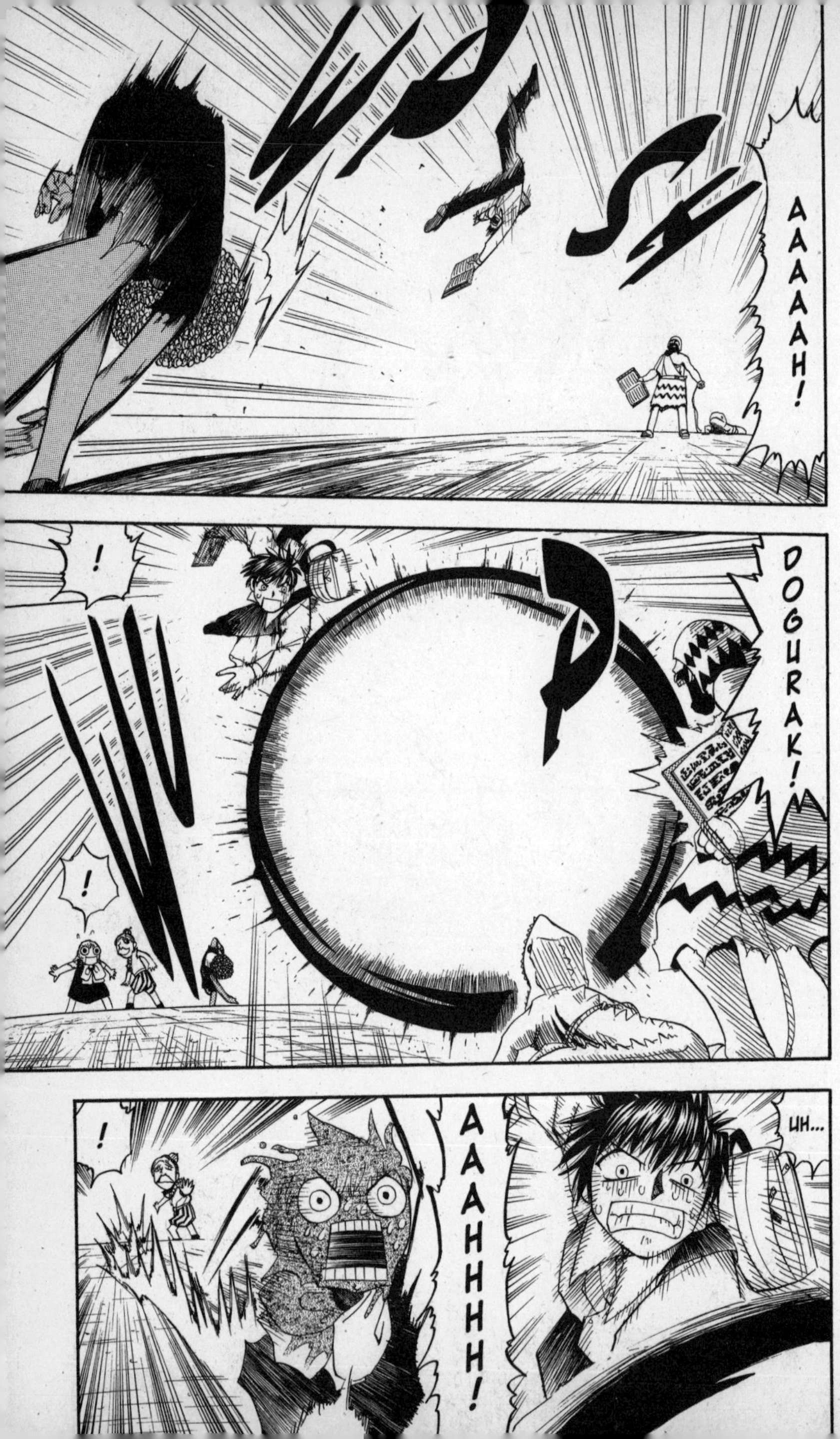
AAAAAAH!
!
DOGURAK!
!
UH...
AAAHHHHH!
!

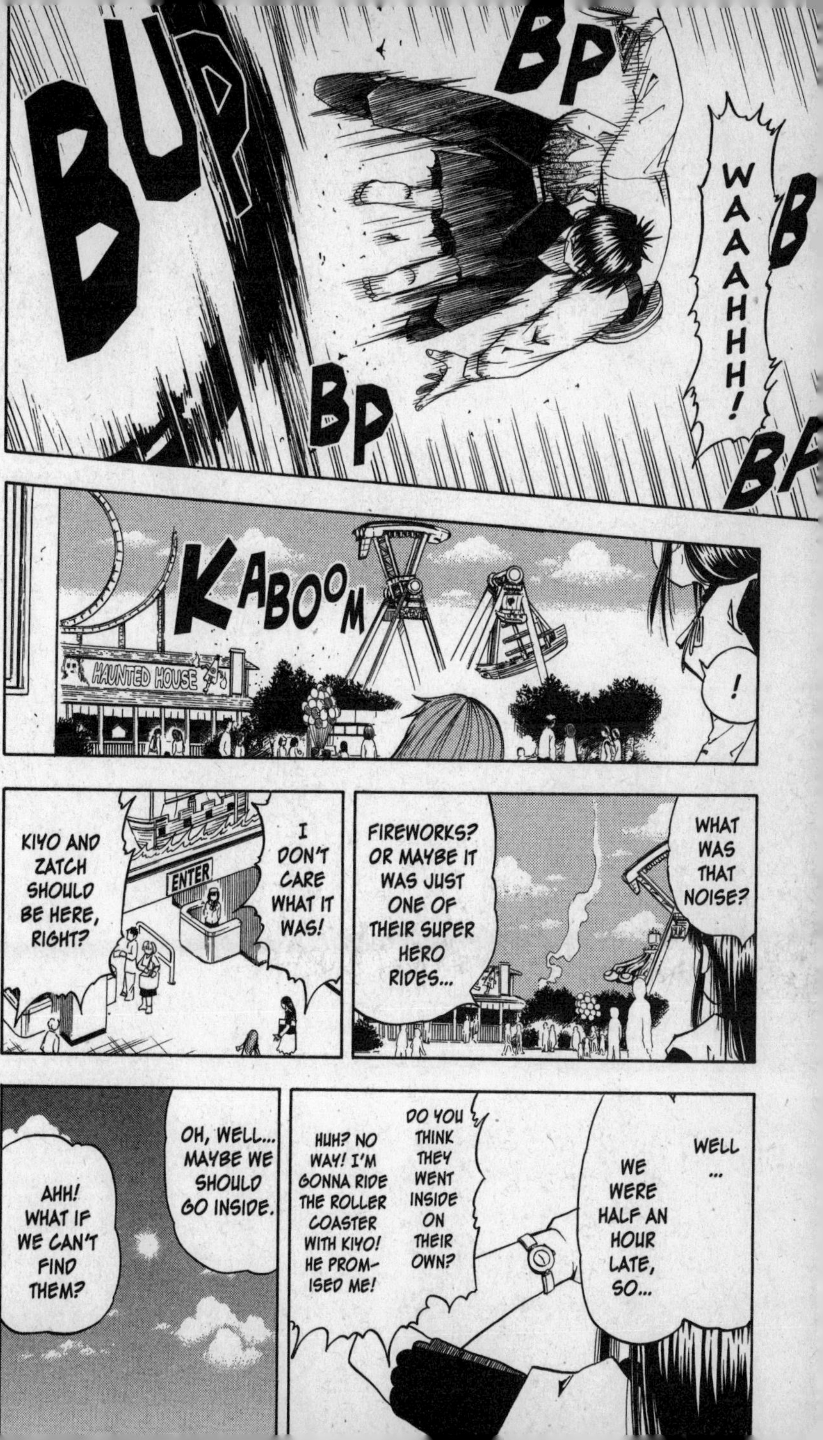
BP
WAAAAHHH!
B
BUP
BP
BP
KABOOM
HAUNTED HOUSE
!
WHAT WAS THAT NOISE?
FIREWORKS? OR MAYBE IT WAS JUST ONE OF THEIR SUPER HERO RIDES...
I DON'T CARE WHAT IT WAS!
ENTER
KIYO AND ZATCH SHOULD BE HERE, RIGHT?
WELL...
WE WERE HALF AN HOUR LATE, SO...
DO YOU THINK THEY WENT INSIDE ON THEIR OWN?
HUH? NO WAY! I'M GONNA RIDE THE ROLLER COASTER WITH KIYO! HE PROM-ISED ME!
OH, WELL... MAYBE WE SHOULD GO INSIDE.
AHH! WHAT IF WE CAN'T FIND THEM?

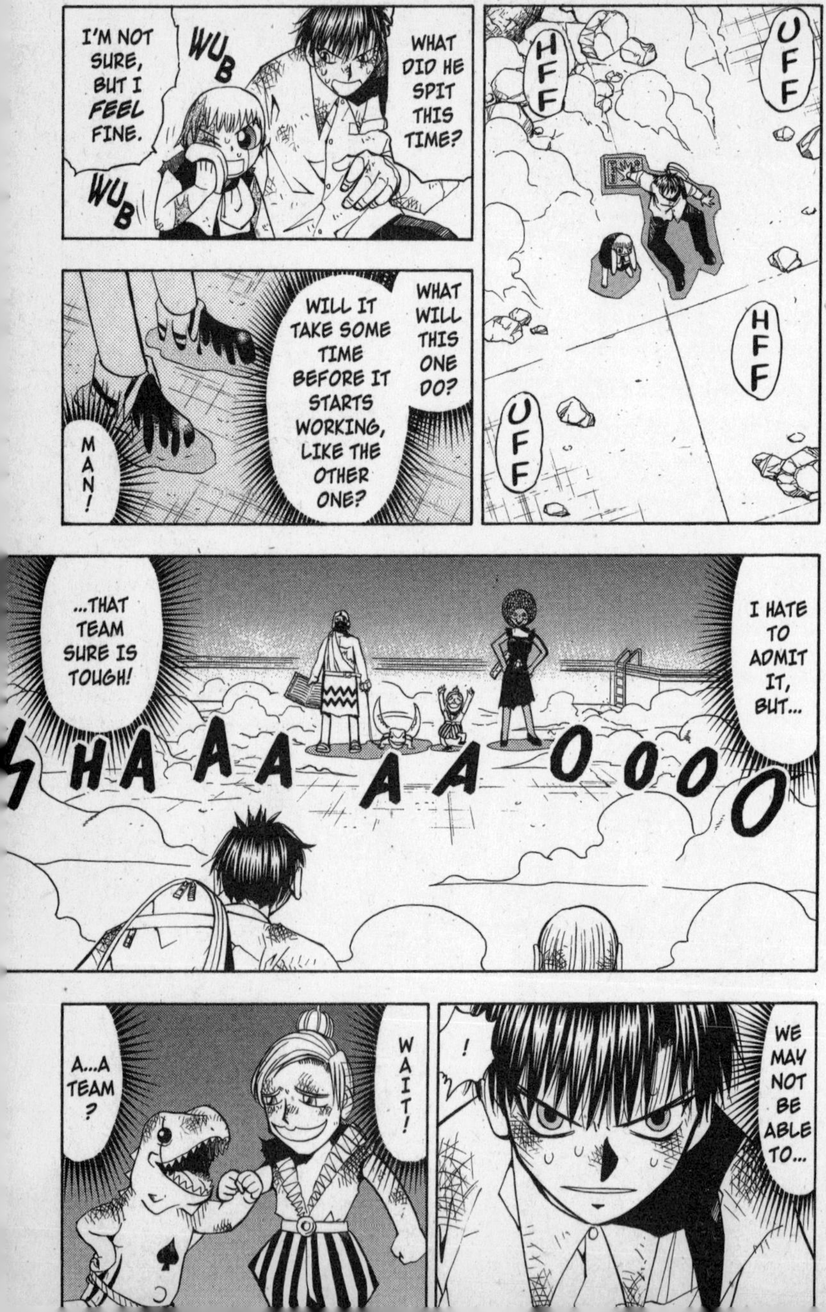
UFF
HFF
HFF
UFF
WHAT DID HE SPIT THIS TIME?
WUB
I'M NOT SURE, BUT I FEEL FINE.
WUB
WHAT WILL THIS ONE DO?
WILL IT TAKE SOME TIME BEFORE IT STARTS WORKING, LIKE THE OTHER ONE?
MAN!
I HATE TO ADMIT IT, BUT...
...THAT TEAM SURE IS TOUGH!
SHAAAAAOOOO
WE MAY NOT BE ABLE TO...
!
WAIT!
A...A TEAM?

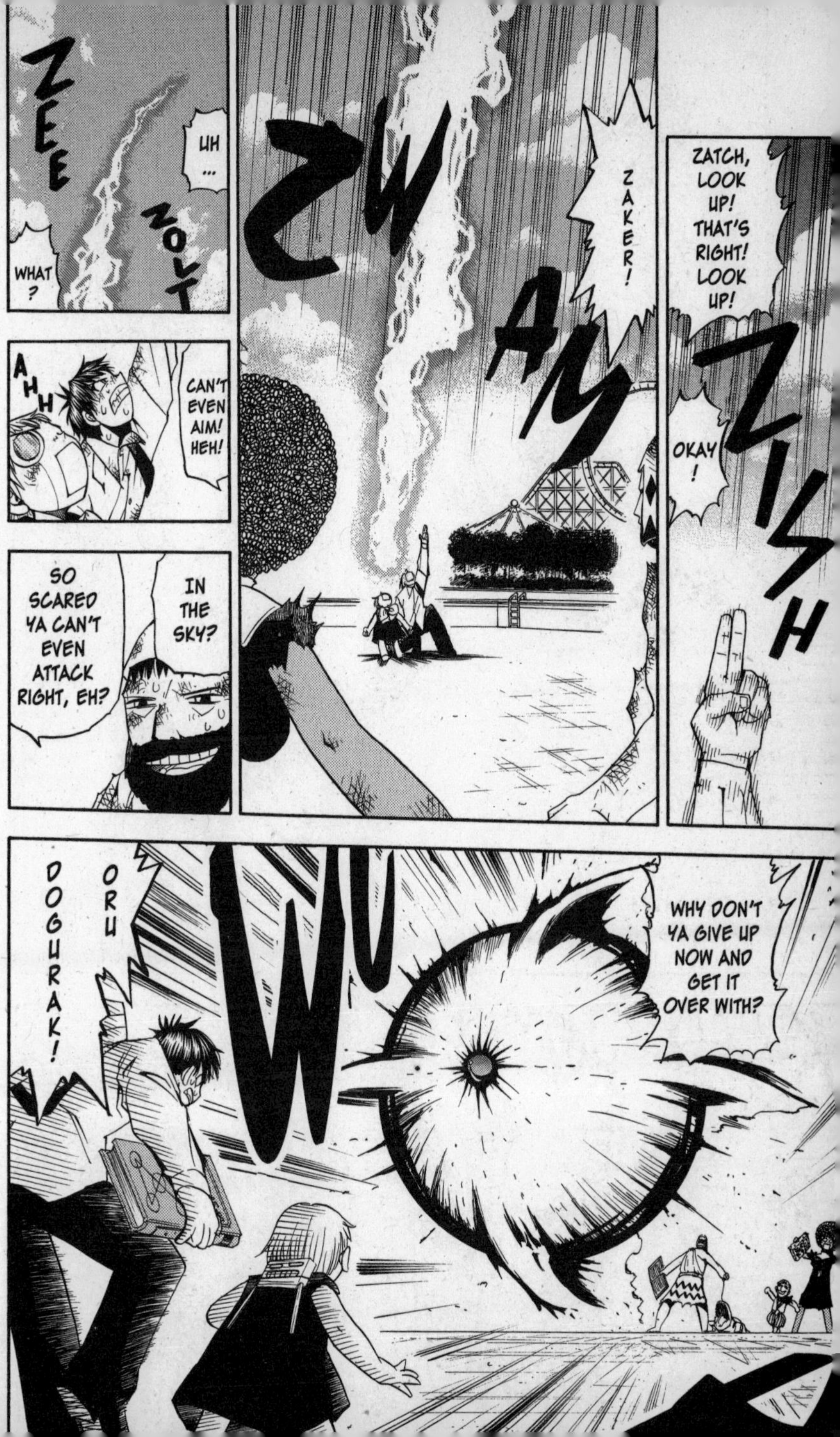
ZATCH, LOOK UP! THAT'S RIGHT! LOOK UP!
OKAY!
ZWISH
ZAKER!
ZWAM
UH ...
WHAT?
ZEE
ZOLT
CAN'T EVEN AIM! HEH!
AHH
IN THE SKY?
SO SCARED YA CAN'T EVEN ATTACK RIGHT, EH?
WHY DON'T YA GIVE UP NOW AND GET IT OVER WITH?
ORU DOGURAK!
WUW

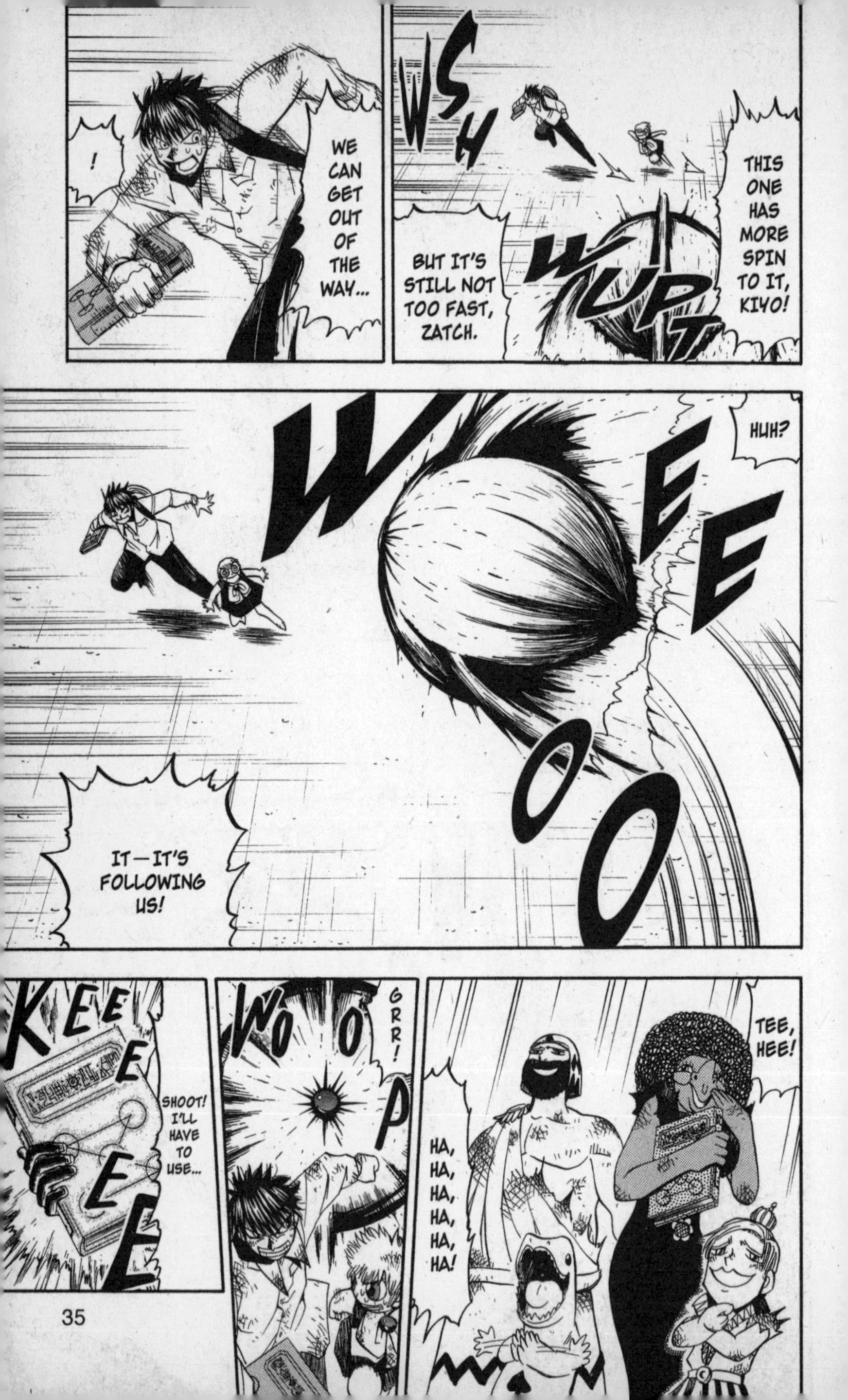
THIS ONE HAS MORE SPIN TO IT, KIYO!
WUPT
BUT IT'S STILL NOT TOO FAST, ZATCH.
WSH
WE CAN GET OUT OF THE WAY...
!
HUH?
WEEOO
IT—IT'S FOLLOWING US!
TEE, HEE!
HA, HA, HA, HA, HA, HA!
GRR!
WOOP
SHOOT! I'LL HAVE TO USE...
KEEEEE

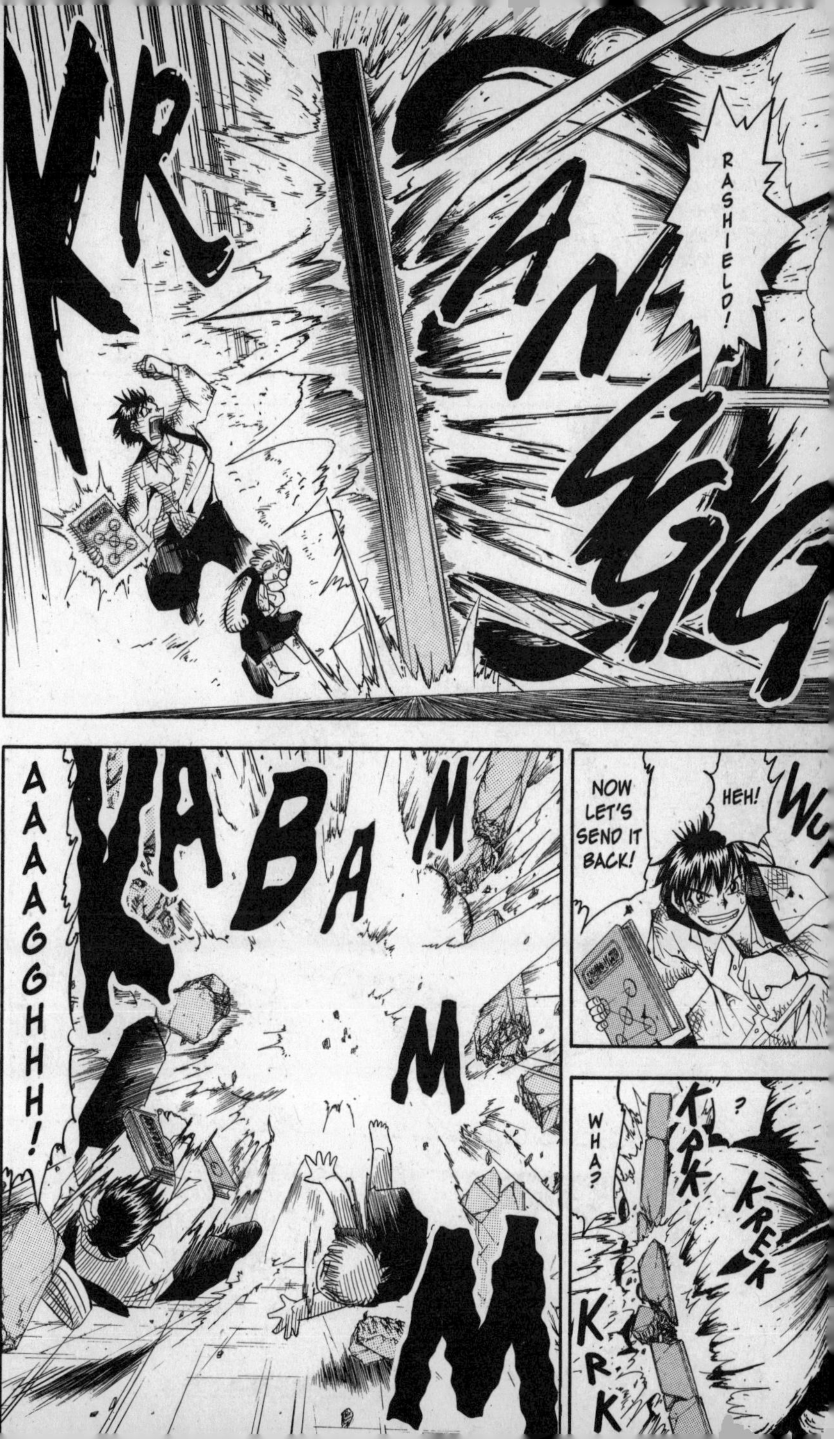
RASHIELD!
KRANGGG
HEH!
NOW LET'S SEND IT BACK!
?
WHA?
KRK
KREK
KRK
KABAMMM
AAAAGGHHH!

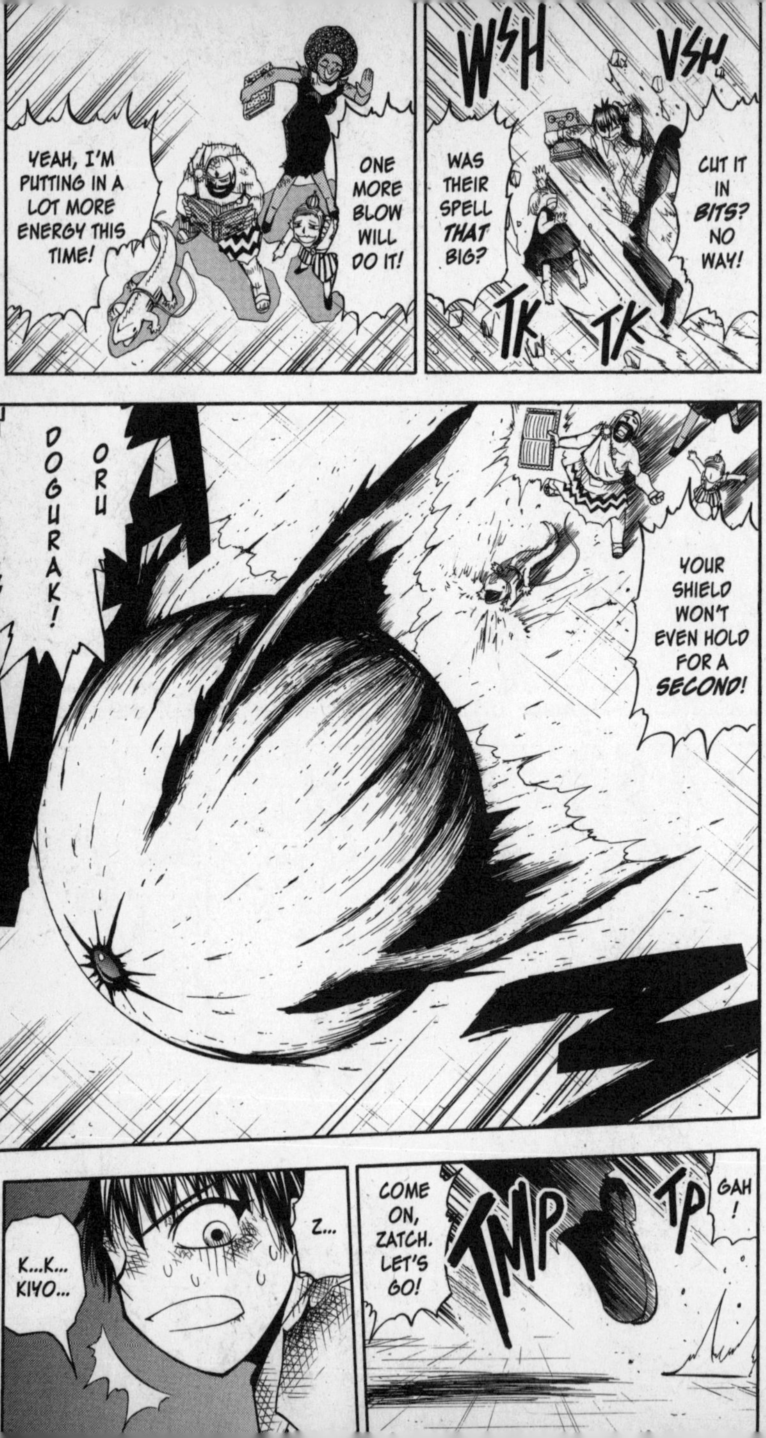

VSH
WSH
CUT IT IN BITS? NO WAY!
WAS THEIR SPELL THAT BIG?
TK
TK
ONE MORE BLOW WILL DO IT!
YEAH, I'M PUTTING IN A LOT MORE ENERGY THIS TIME!
YOUR SHIELD WON'T EVEN HOLD FOR A SECOND!
ORU DOGURAK!
GAH!
TP
TMP
COME ON, ZATCH. LET'S GO!
Z...
K...K... KIYO...

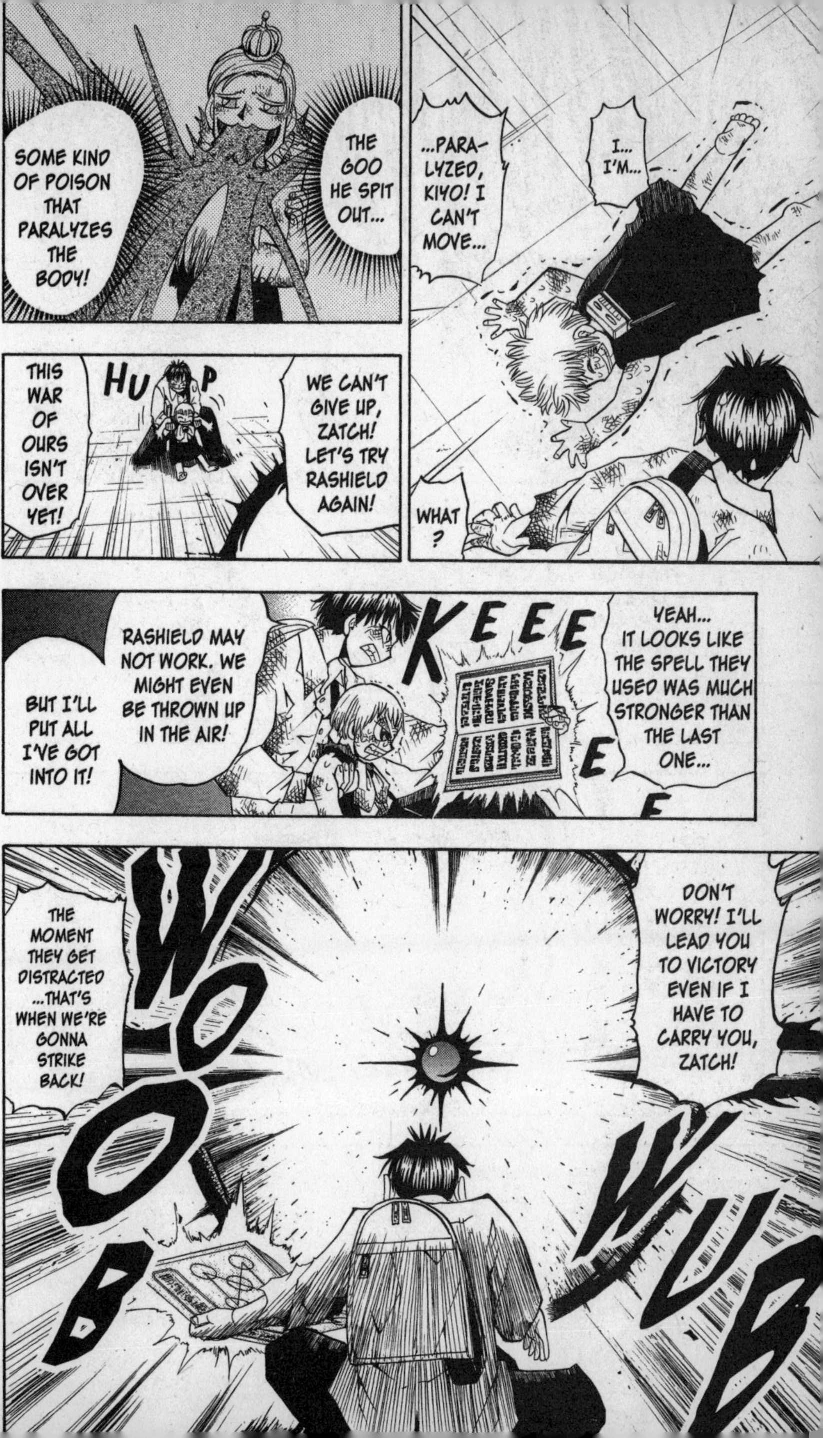
I... I'M...
...PARALYZED, KIYO! I CAN'T MOVE...
WHAT?
THE GOO HE SPIT OUT...
SOME KIND OF POISON THAT PARALYZES THE BODY!
WE CAN'T GIVE UP, ZATCH! LET'S TRY RASHIELD AGAIN!
HUP
THIS WAR OF OURS ISN'T OVER YET!
YEAH... IT LOOKS LIKE THE SPELL THEY USED WAS MUCH STRONGER THAN THE LAST ONE...
KEEEEE
RASHIELD MAY NOT WORK. WE MIGHT EVEN BE THROWN UP IN THE AIR!
BUT I'LL PUT ALL I'VE GOT INTO IT!
DON'T WORRY! I'LL LEAD YOU TO VICTORY EVEN IF I HAVE TO CARRY YOU, ZATCH!
WUB
WOOB
THE MOMENT THEY GET DISTRACTED ...THAT'S WHEN WE'RE GONNA STRIKE BACK!

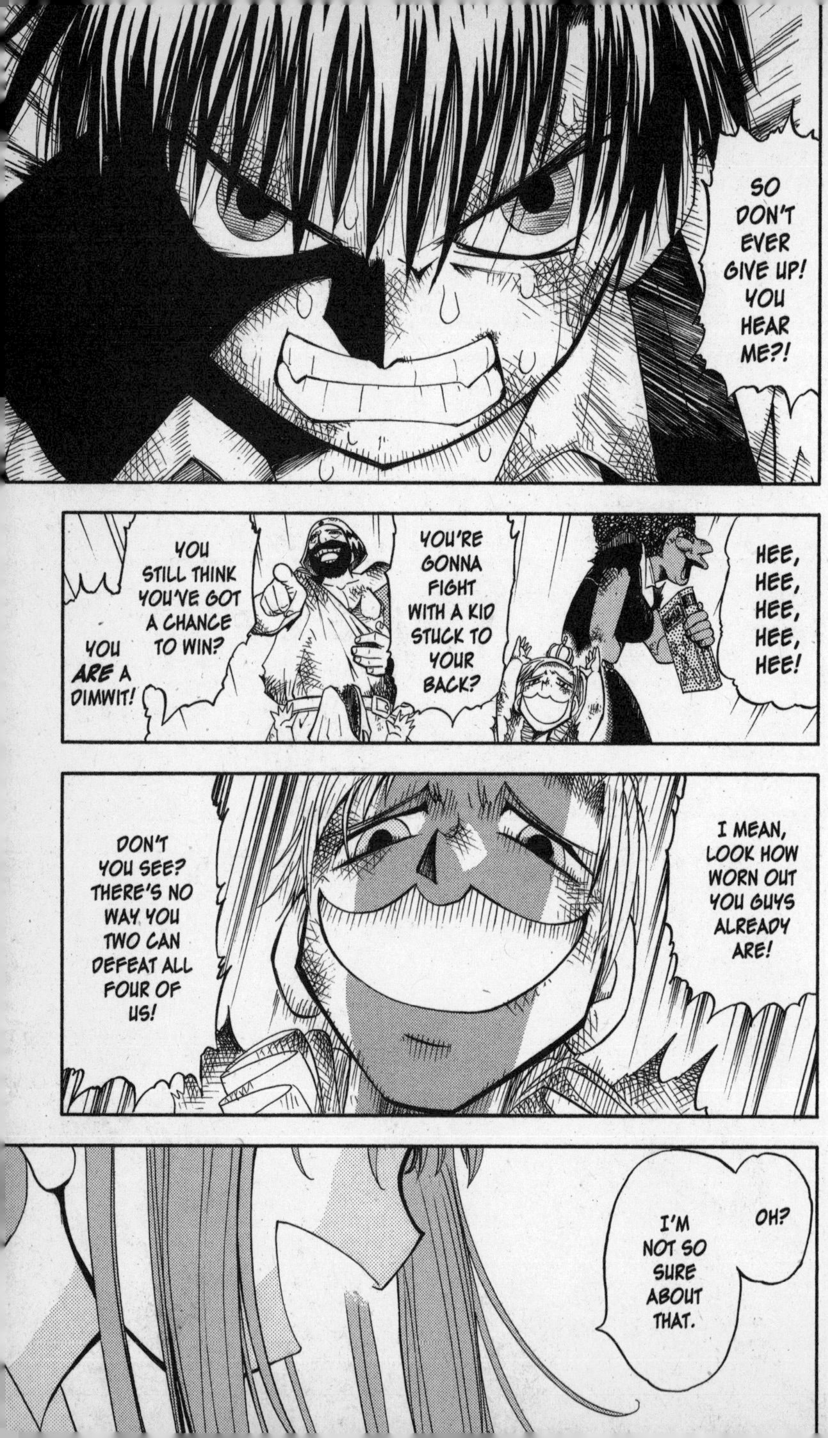
SO DON'T EVER GIVE UP! YOU HEAR ME?!
HEE, HEE, HEE, HEE, HEE!
YOU'RE GONNA FIGHT WITH A KID STUCK TO YOUR BACK?
YOU STILL THINK YOU'VE GOT A CHANCE TO WIN?
YOU ARE A DIMWIT!
I MEAN, LOOK HOW WORN OUT YOU GUYS ALREADY ARE!
DON'T YOU SEE? THERE'S NO WAY YOU TWO CAN DEFEAT ALL FOUR OF US!
OH?
I'M NOT SO SURE ABOUT THAT.

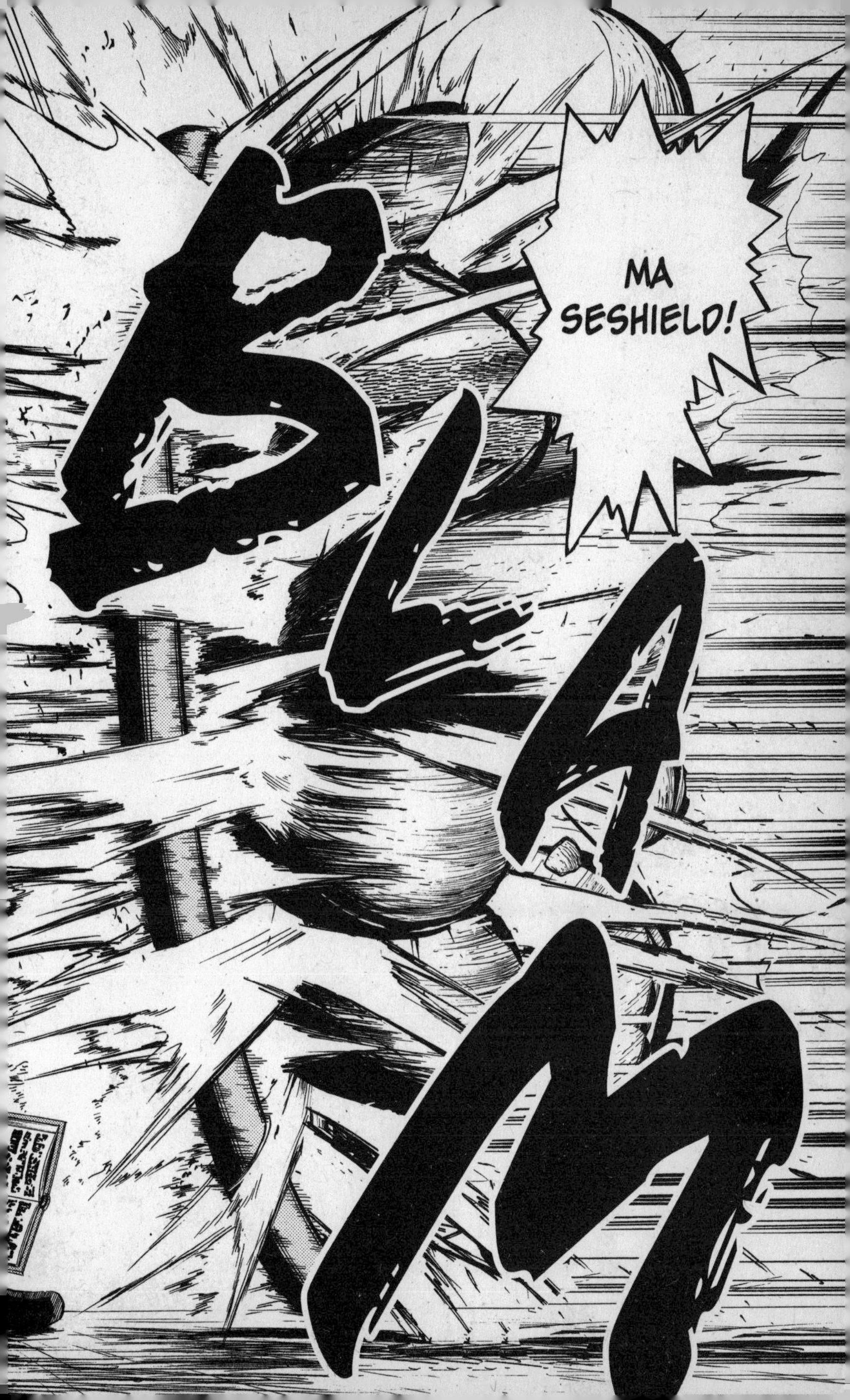
MA SESHIELD!

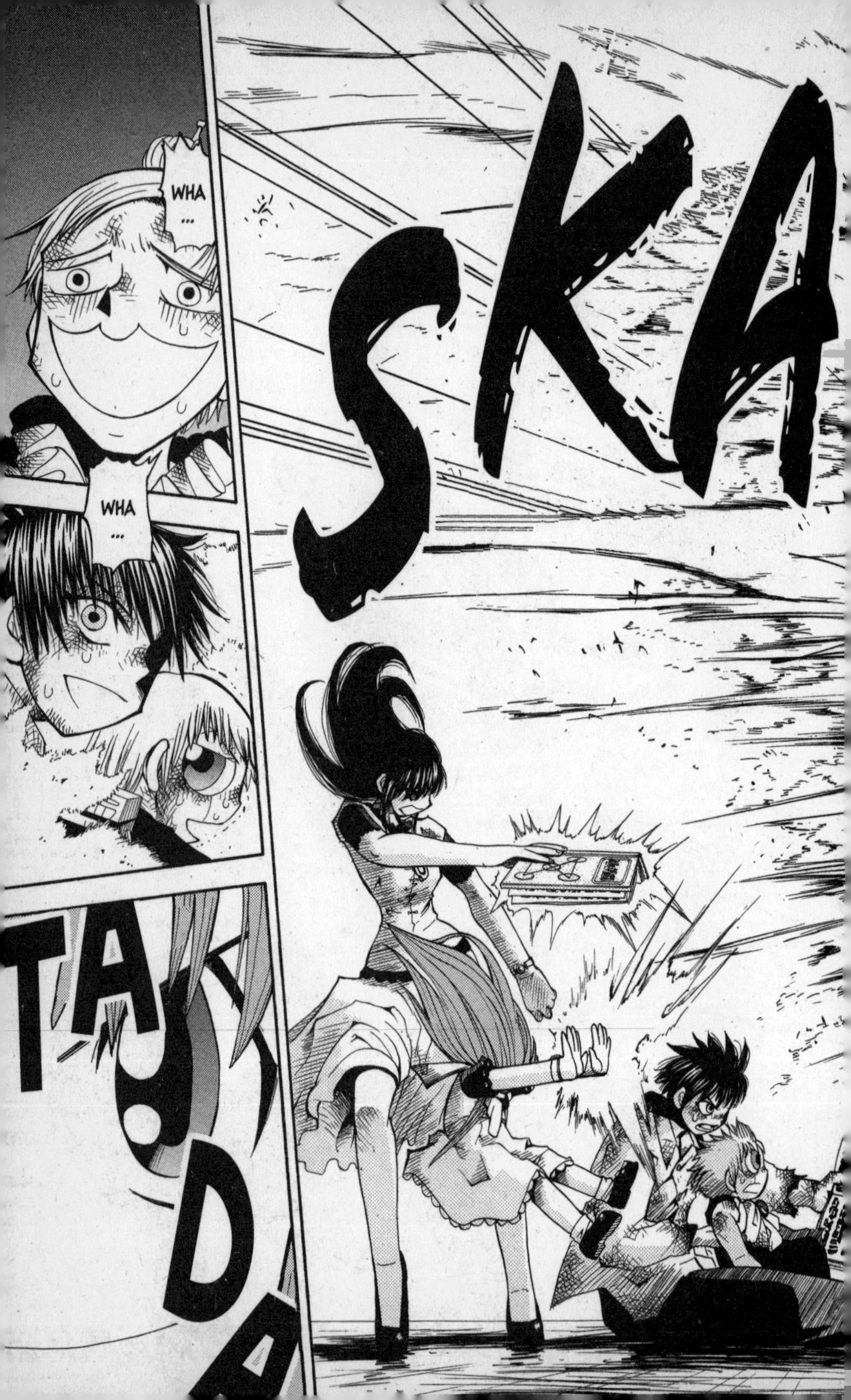
SKA
WHA ...
WHA ...
TA
D
A

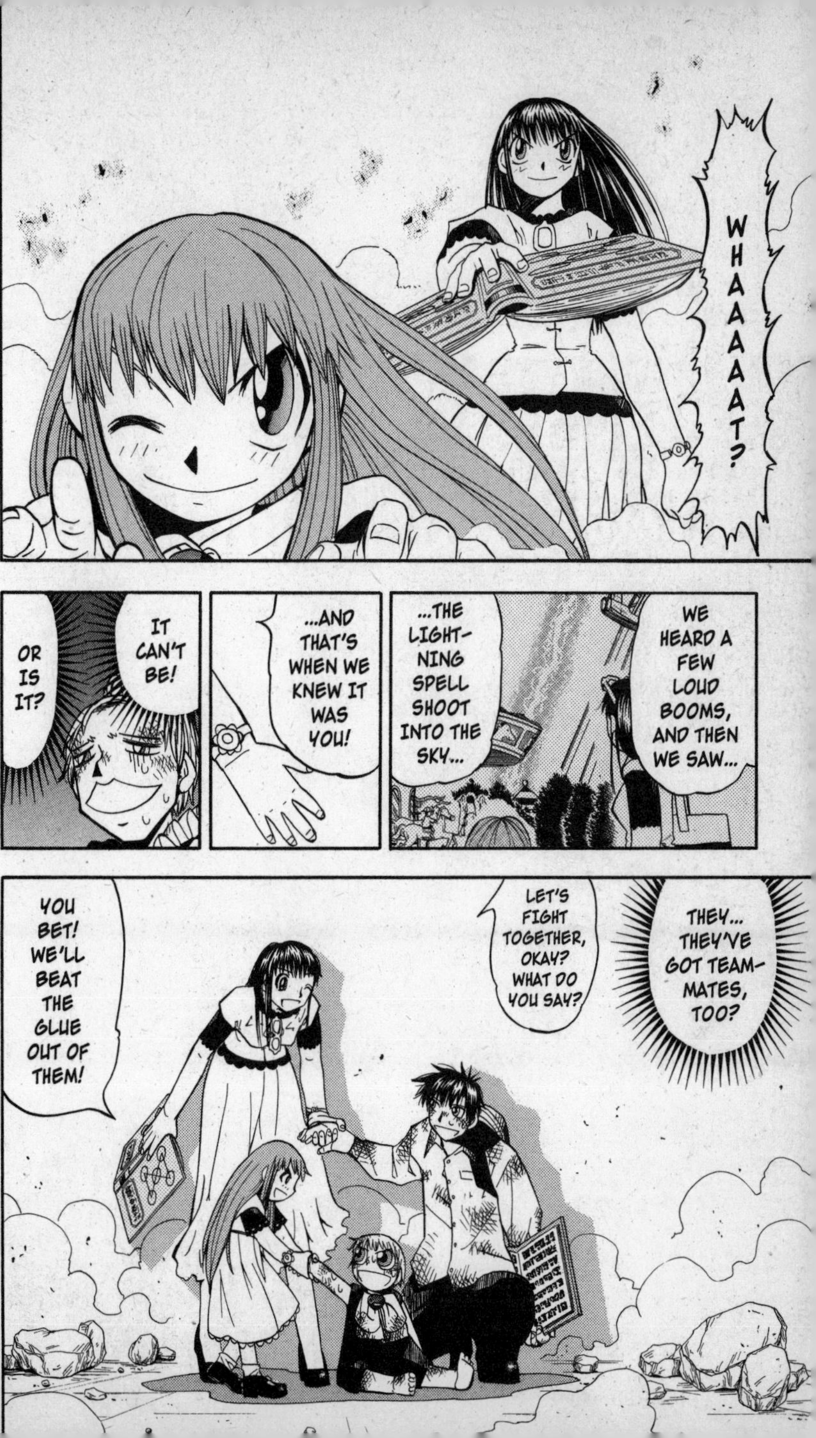
WHAAAAAT?
WE HEARD A FEW LOUD BOOMS, AND THEN WE SAW...
...THE LIGHTNING SPELL SHOOT INTO THE SKY...
...AND THAT'S WHEN WE KNEW IT WAS YOU!
IT CAN'T BE!
OR IS IT?
THEY... THEY'VE GOT TEAMMATES, TOO?
LET'S FIGHT TOGETHER, OKAY? WHAT DO YOU SAY?
YOU BET! WE'LL BEAT THE GLUE OUT OF THEM!

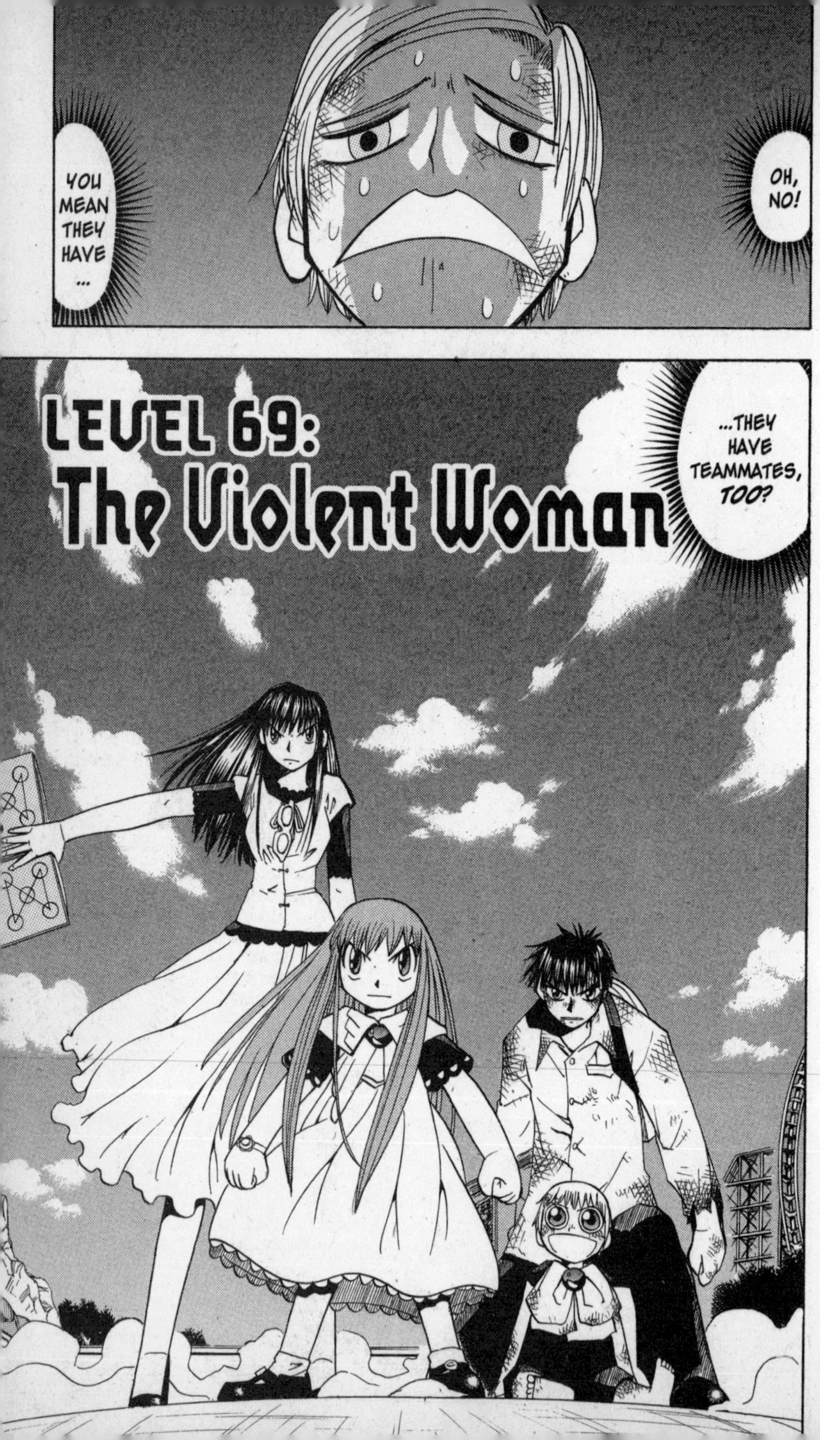
OH, NO!
YOU MEAN THEY HAVE ...
...THEY HAVE TEAMMATES, TOO?
LEVEL 69:
The Violent Woman

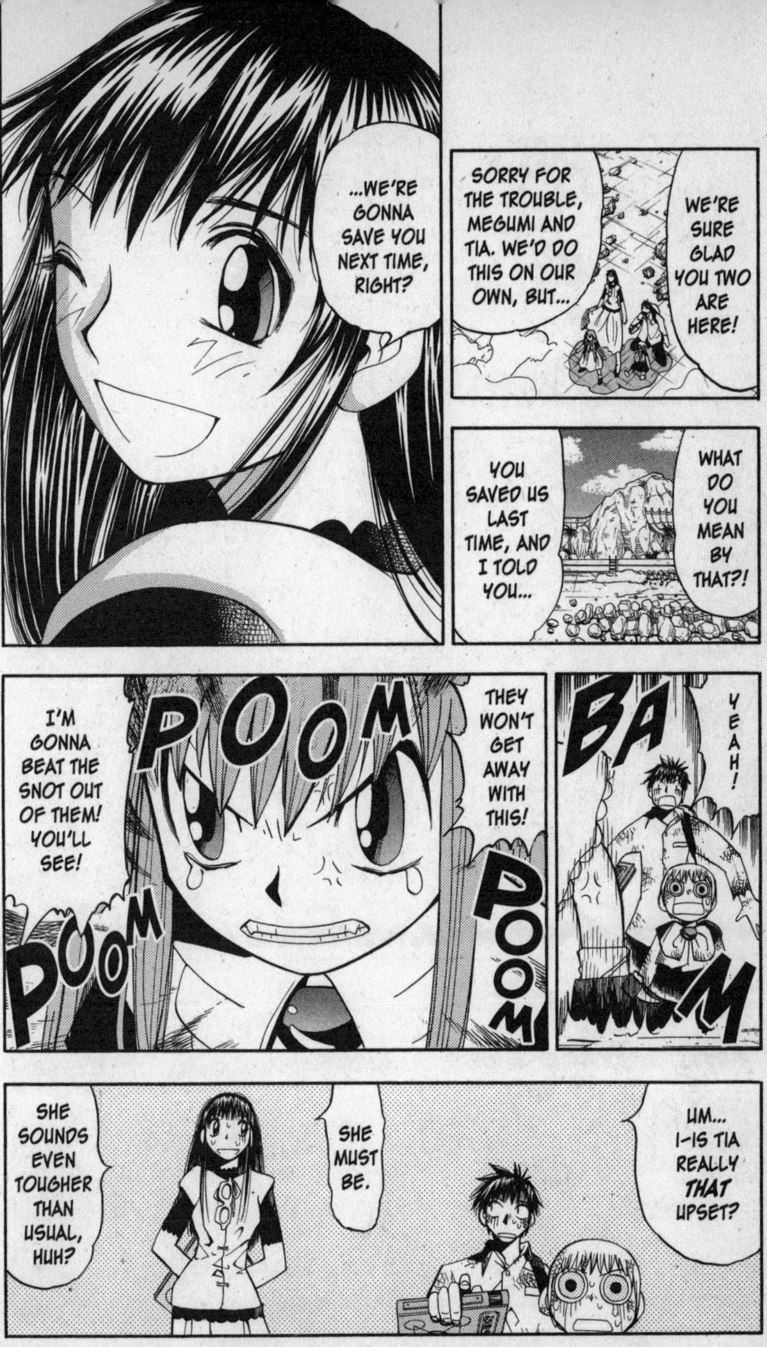
WE'RE SURE GLAD YOU TWO ARE HERE!
SORRY FOR THE TROUBLE, MEGUMI AND TIA. WE'D DO THIS ON OUR OWN, BUT...
WHAT DO YOU MEAN BY THAT?!
YOU SAVED US LAST TIME, AND I TOLD YOU...
...WE'RE GONNA SAVE YOU NEXT TIME, RIGHT?
BAM
YEAH!
THEY WON'T GET AWAY WITH THIS!
I'M GONNA BEAT THE SNOT OUT OF THEM! YOU'LL SEE!
POOM
POOM
POOM
UM... I-IS TIA REALLY *THAT* UPSET?
SHE MUST BE.
SHE SOUNDS EVEN TOUGHER THAN USUAL, HUH?

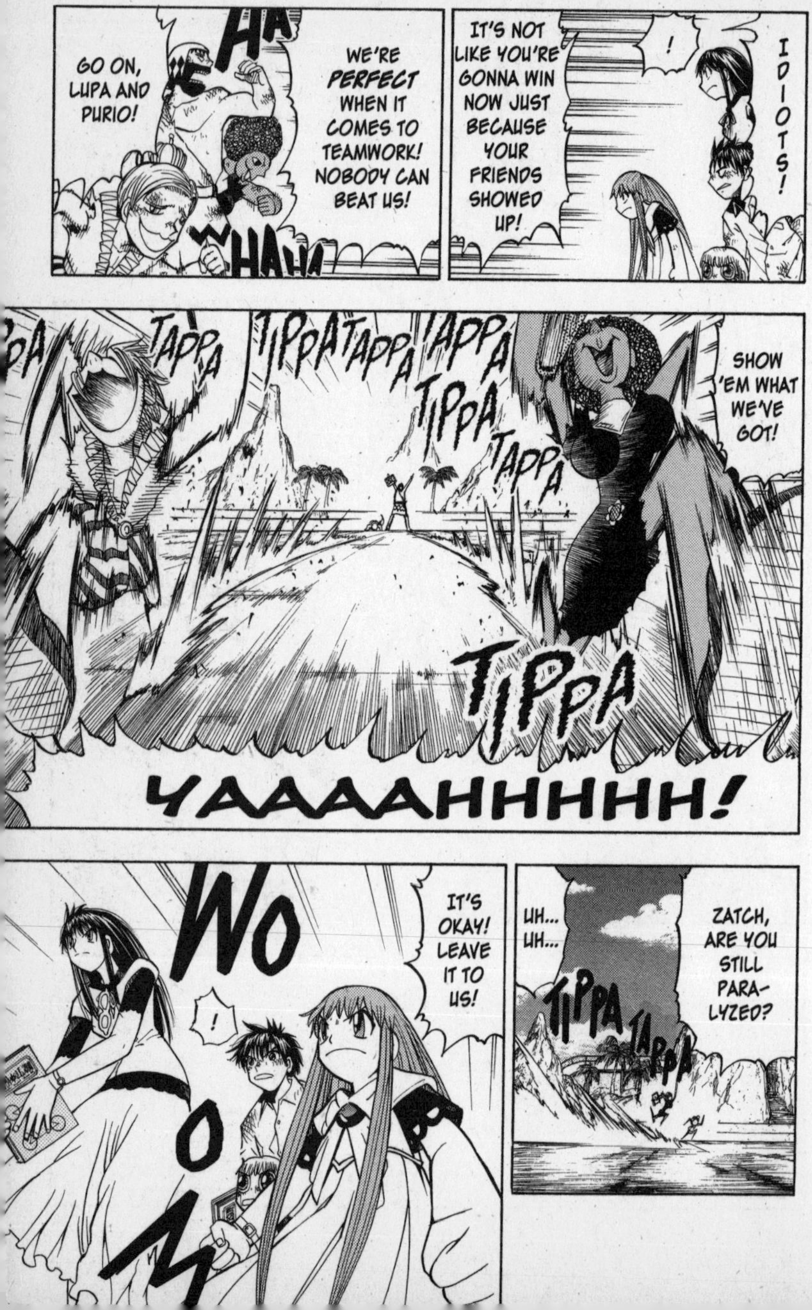
GO ON, LUPA AND PURIO!
HA
WHAHA
WE'RE *PERFECT* WHEN IT COMES TO TEAMWORK! NOBODY CAN BEAT US!
IT'S NOT LIKE YOU'RE GONNA WIN NOW JUST BECAUSE YOUR FRIENDS SHOWED UP!
!
IDIOTS!
TAPPA
TIPPA TAPPA TAPPA
TIPPA
TAPPA
SHOW 'EM WHAT WE'VE GOT!
TIPPA
YAAAAHHHHH!
WOOM
!
IT'S OKAY! LEAVE IT TO US!
UH... UH...
ZATCH, ARE YOU STILL PARA-LYZED?
TIPPA TAPPA

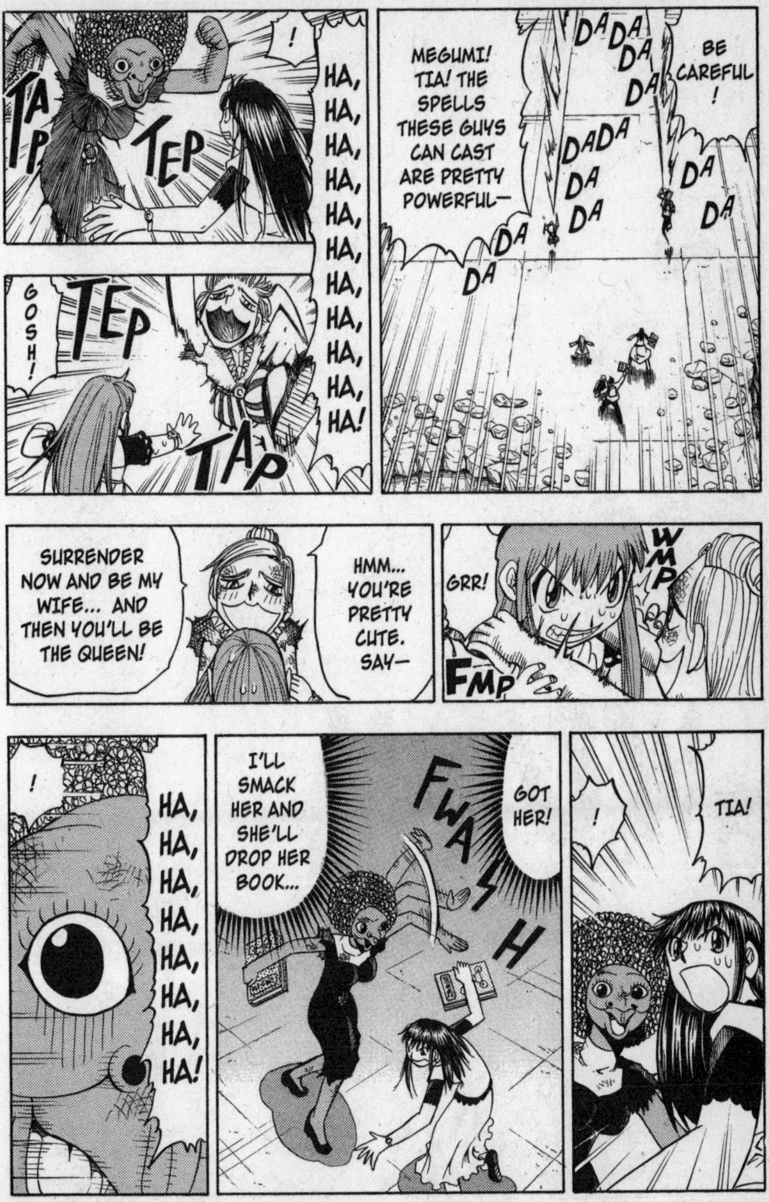
MEGUMI! TIA! THE SPELLS THESE GUYS CAN CAST ARE PRETTY POWERFUL—
BE CAREFUL!
DADADADA DADADADA DADADA DADA
!
TAP TEP
HA, HA, HA, HA, HA, HA, HA, HA, HA, HA, HA!
GOSH!
TEP
TAP
WMP
GRR!
FMP
HMM... YOU'RE PRETTY CUTE. SAY—
SURRENDER NOW AND BE MY WIFE... AND THEN YOU'LL BE THE QUEEN!
!
TIA!
GOT HER!
FWASH
I'LL SMACK HER AND SHE'LL DROP HER BOOK...
!
HA, HA, HA, HA, HA, HA, HA, HA!

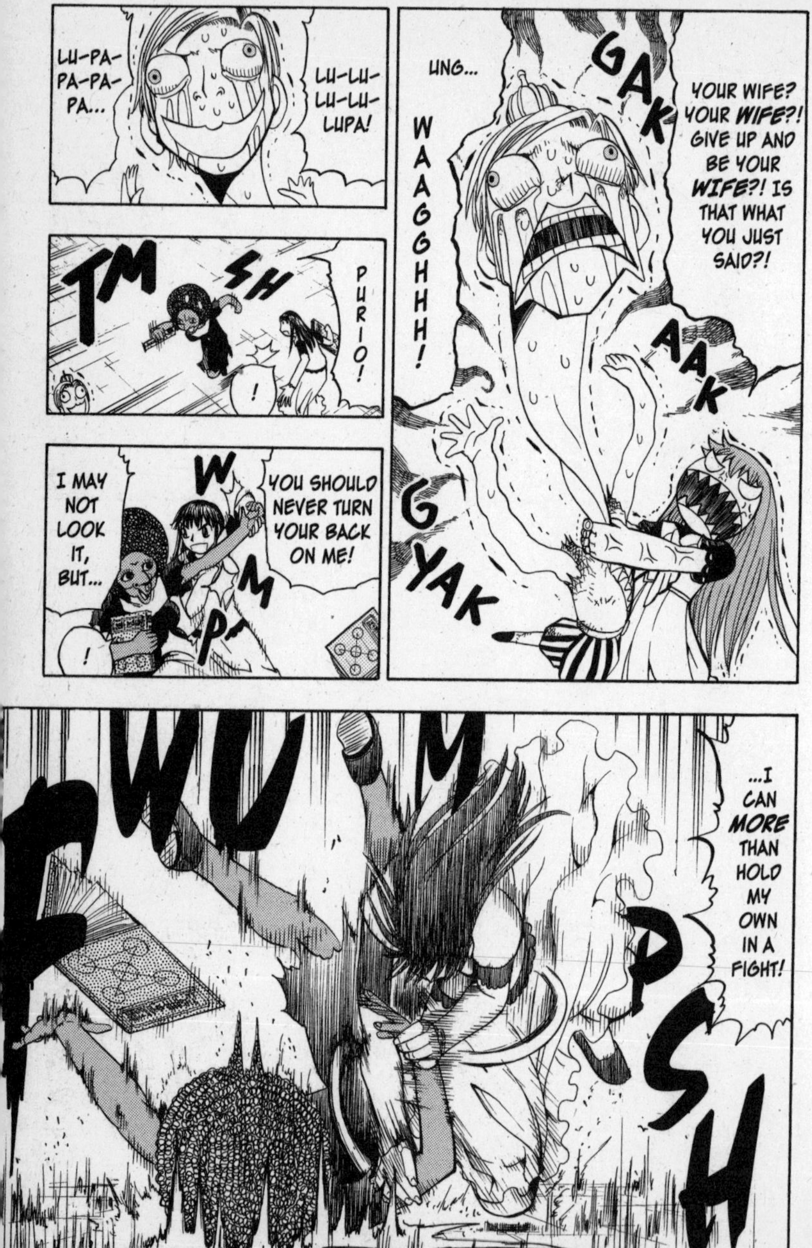

LU-PA-PA-PA-PA...
LU-LU-LU-LU-LUPA!
UNG...
WAAGGHHH!
GAK
YOUR WIFE? YOUR WIFE?! GIVE UP AND BE YOUR WIFE?! IS THAT WHAT YOU JUST SAID?!
AAK
GYAK
TMSH
PURIO!
!
I MAY NOT LOOK IT, BUT...
WMP
YOU SHOULD NEVER TURN YOUR BACK ON ME!
!
FWOOM
...I CAN MORE THAN HOLD MY OWN IN A FIGHT!
PSH

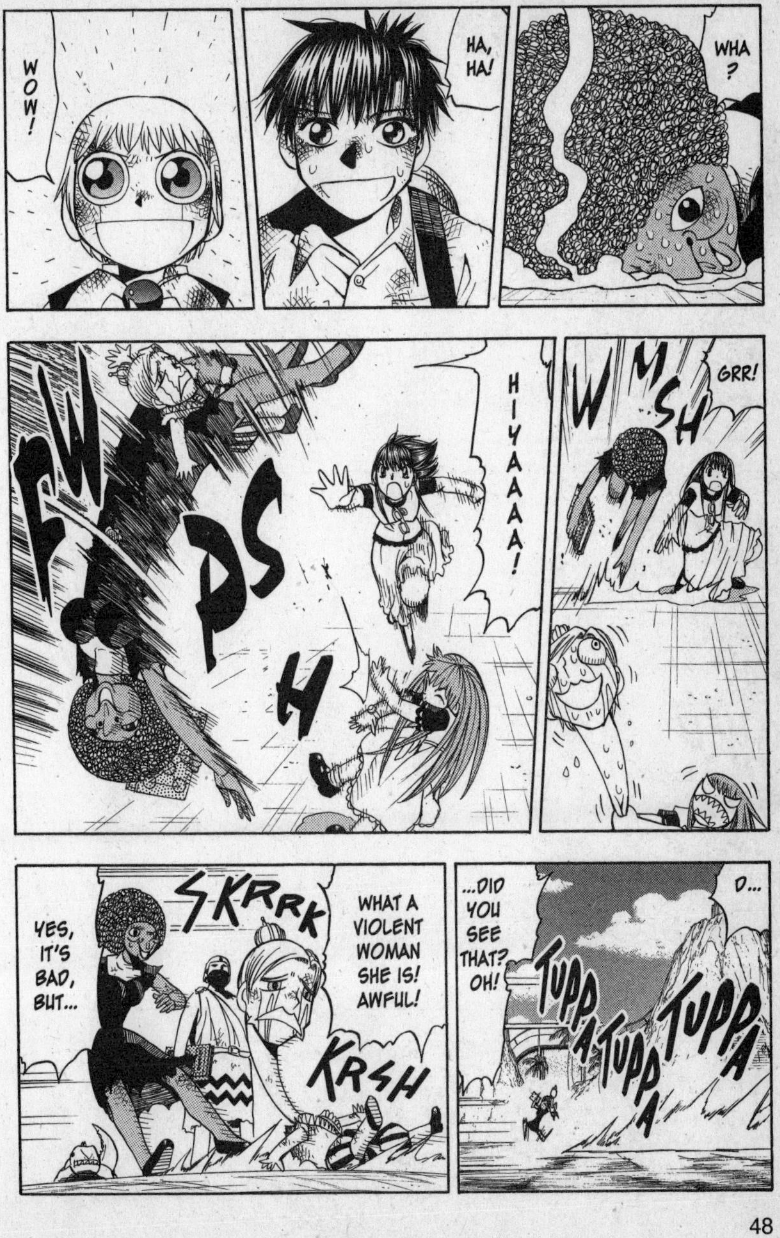
WHA?
HA, HA!
WOW!
WMSH
GRR!
HIYAAAAA!
FWPSH
D...
...DID YOU SEE THAT? OH!
TUPPA TUPPA TUPPA
WHAT A VIOLENT WOMAN SHE IS! AWFUL!
SKRRK
YES, IT'S BAD, BUT...
KRSH

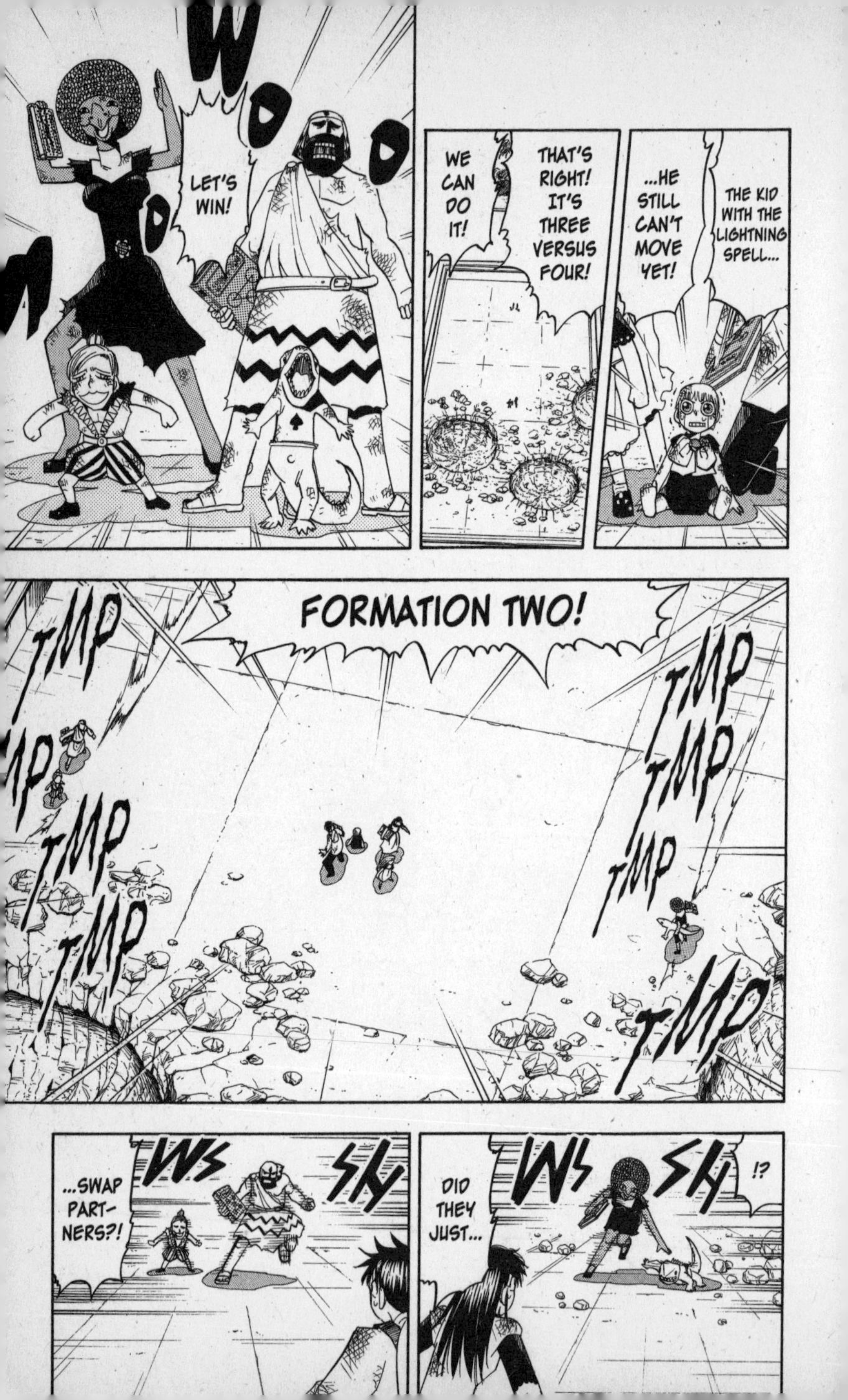
THE KID WITH THE LIGHTNING SPELL...
...HE STILL CAN'T MOVE YET!
THAT'S RIGHT! IT'S THREE VERSUS FOUR!
WE CAN DO IT!
LET'S WIN!
FORMATION TWO!
TMP
TMP
TMP
TMP
TMP
TMP
TMP
!?
DID THEY JUST...
...SWAP PARTNERS?!

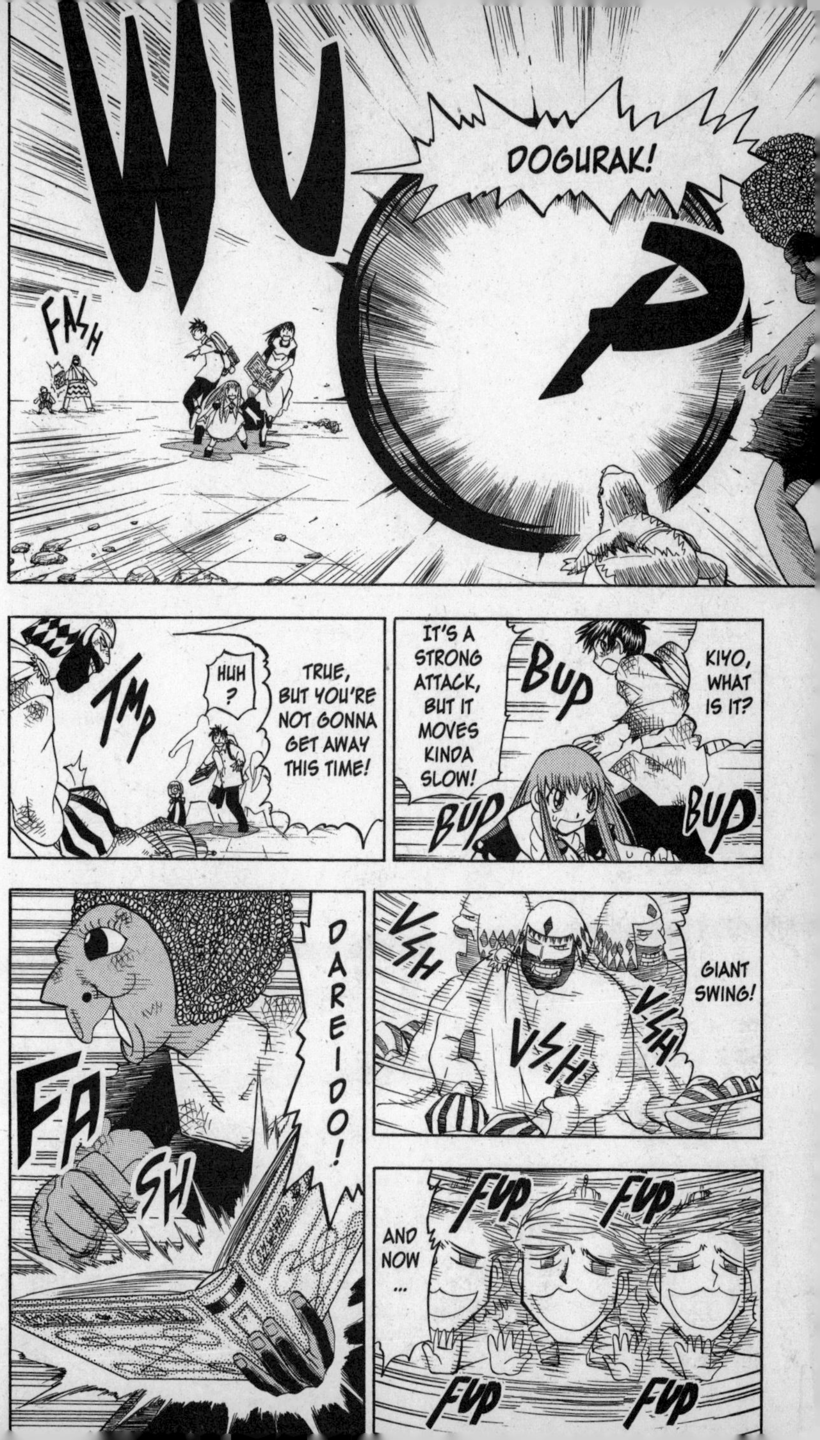
DOGURAK!
WU
FASH
KIYO, WHAT IS IT?
IT'S A STRONG ATTACK, BUT IT MOVES KINDA SLOW!
BUP
BUP
BUP
TRUE, BUT YOU'RE NOT GONNA GET AWAY THIS TIME!
HUH?
TMP
GIANT SWING!
VSH
VSH
VSH
DAREIDO!
FASH
AND NOW ...
FUP
FUP
FUP
FUP

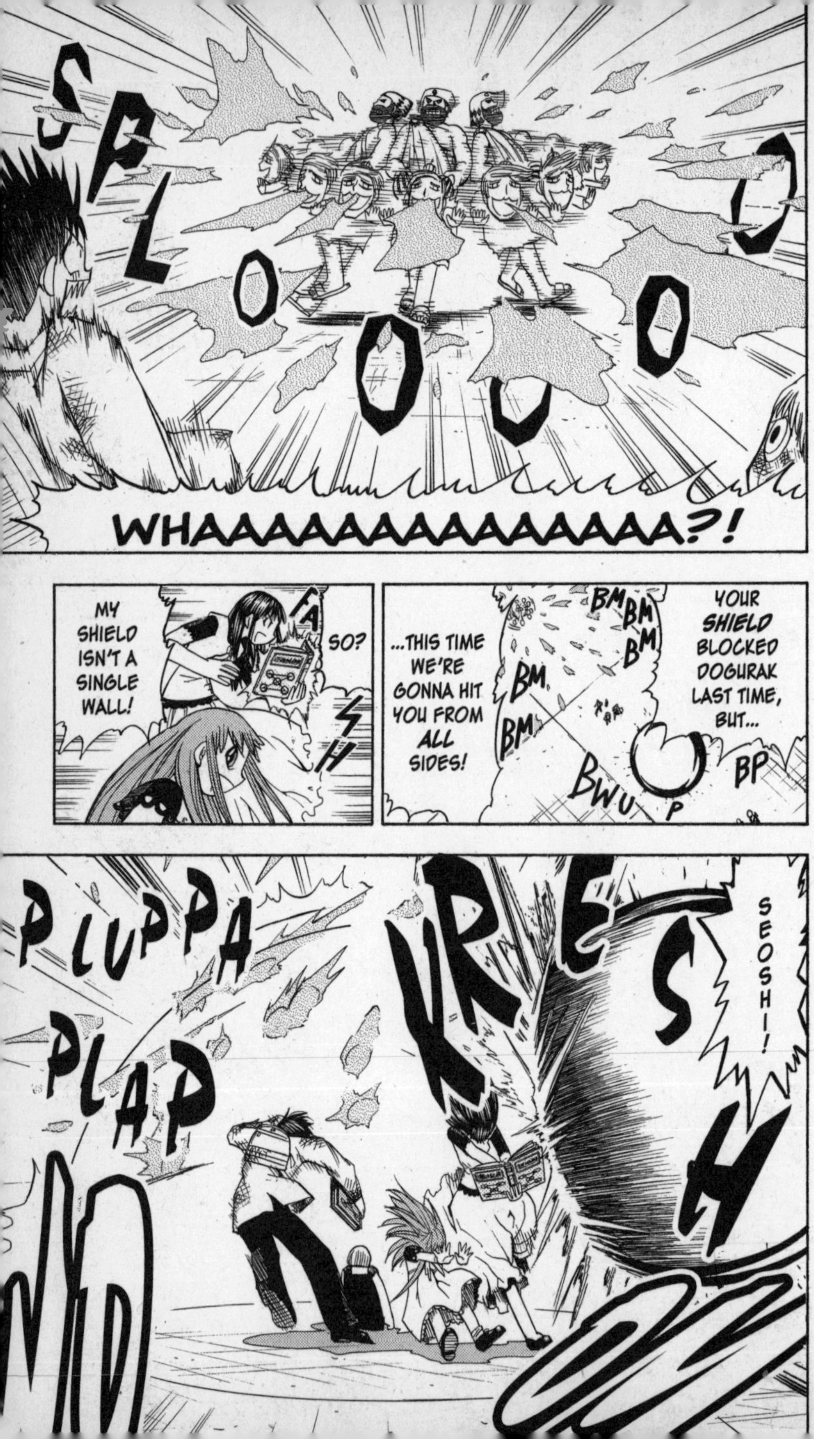
SPLOOOOOO
WHAAAAAAAAAAAAAA?!
YOUR SHIELD BLOCKED DOGURAK LAST TIME, BUT...
BM BM BM BM BM
BWUP
BP
...THIS TIME WE'RE GONNA HIT YOU FROM ALL SIDES!
SO?
FA
SHH
MY SHIELD ISN'T A SINGLE WALL!
SEOSHI!
KRESH
PLUPPA
PLAP

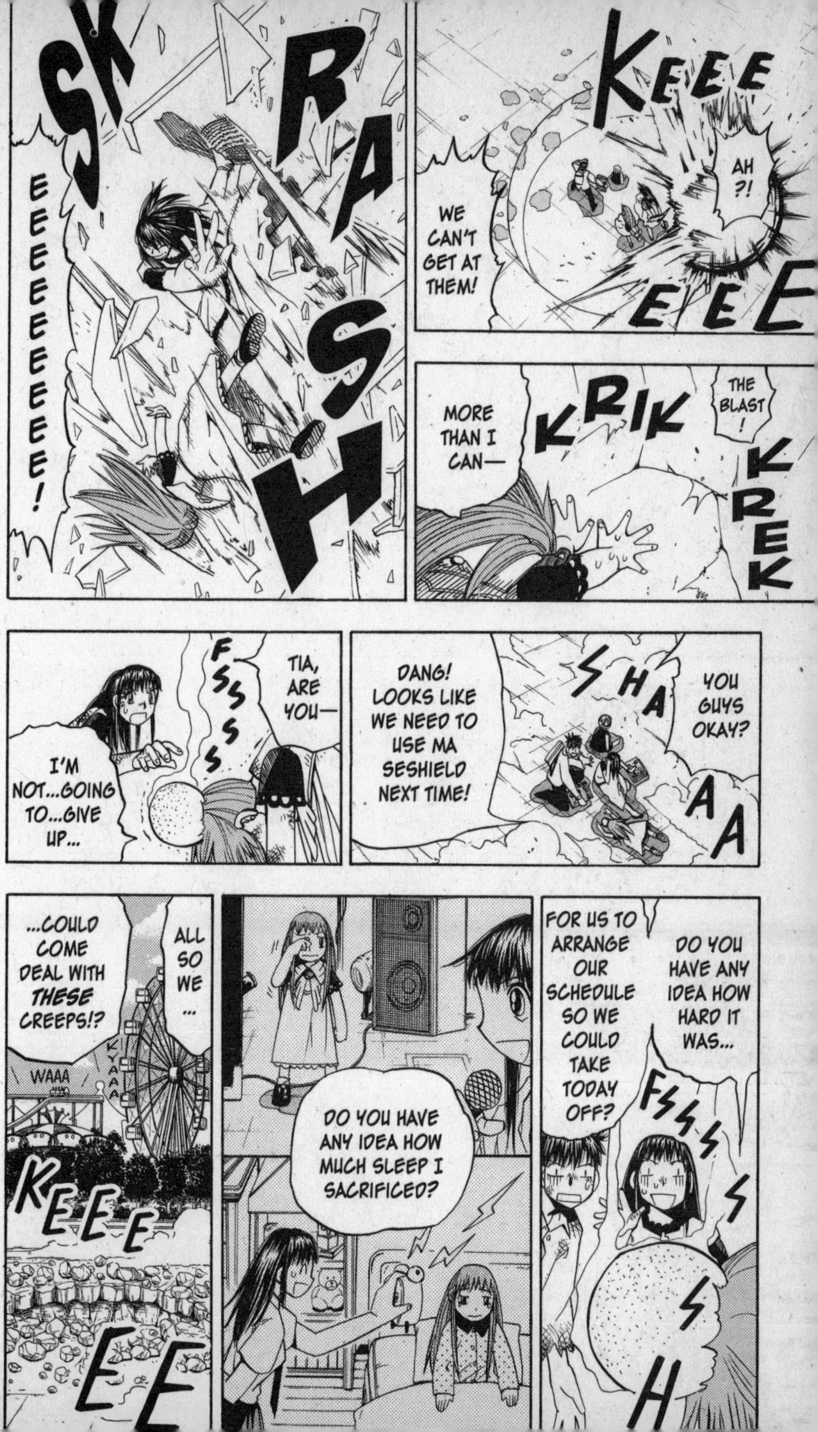

KEEEEEE
AH ?!
WE CAN'T GET AT THEM!
THE BLAST!
KRIK
KREK
MORE THAN I CAN—
SKRASH
EEEEEEEEEEEEE!
YOU GUYS OKAY?
SHAAA
DANG! LOOKS LIKE WE NEED TO USE MA SESHIELD NEXT TIME!
TIA, ARE YOU—
FSSSS
I'M NOT...GOING TO...GIVE UP...
DO YOU HAVE ANY IDEA HOW HARD IT WAS...
FOR US TO ARRANGE OUR SCHEDULE SO WE COULD TAKE TODAY OFF?
FSSSSH
DO YOU HAVE ANY IDEA HOW MUCH SLEEP I SACRIFICED?
ALL SO WE ...
...COULD COME DEAL WITH THESE CREEPS!?
KYAAA
WAAA
KEEEEE

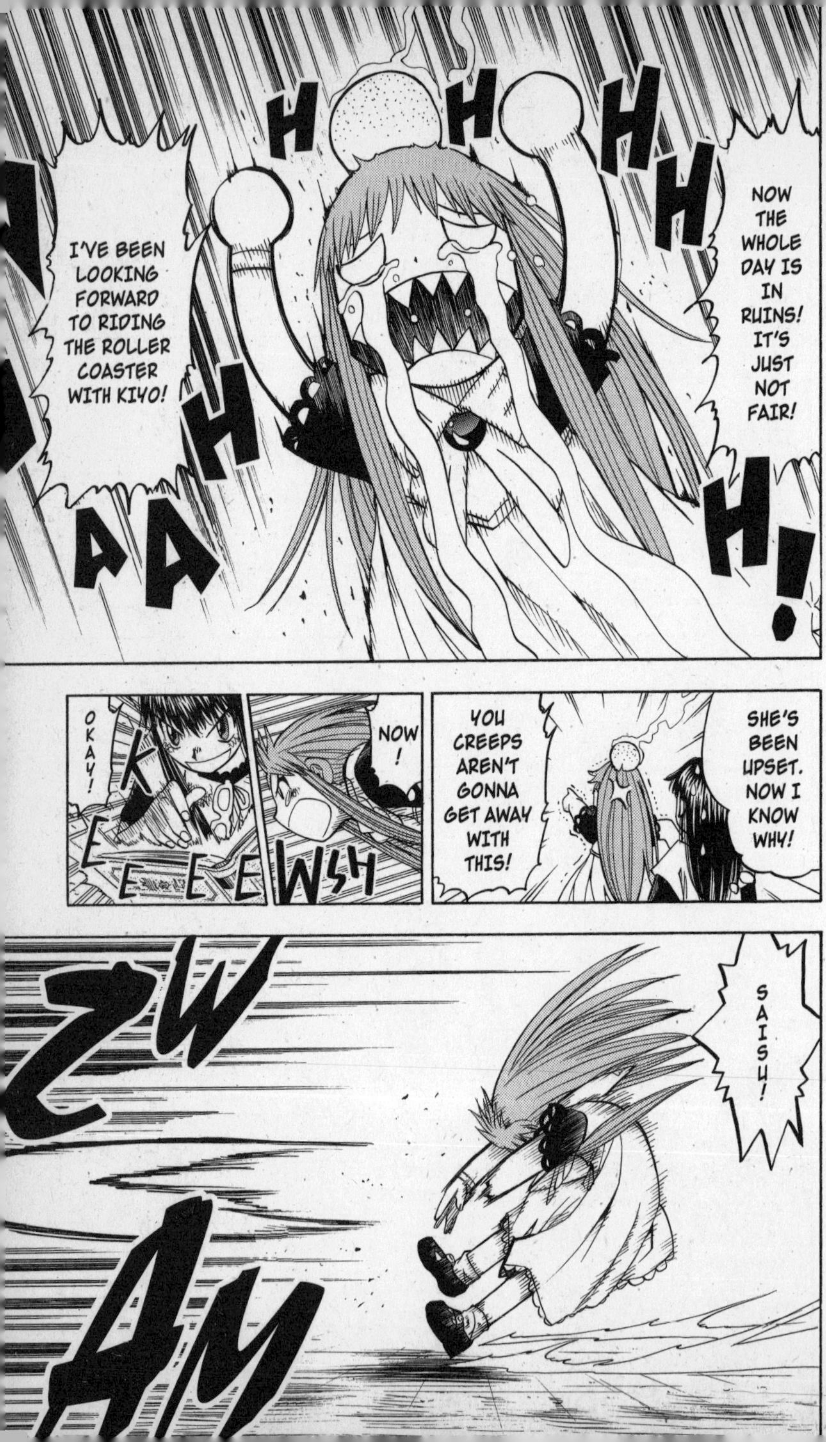

AAHHHHHHHH!
NOW THE WHOLE DAY IS IN RUINS! IT'S JUST NOT FAIR!
I'VE BEEN LOOKING FORWARD TO RIDING THE ROLLER COASTER WITH KIYO!
SHE'S BEEN UPSET. NOW I KNOW WHY!
YOU CREEPS AREN'T GONNA GET AWAY WITH THIS!
NOW!
OKAY!
KEEEEWSH
SAISU!
ZWAM

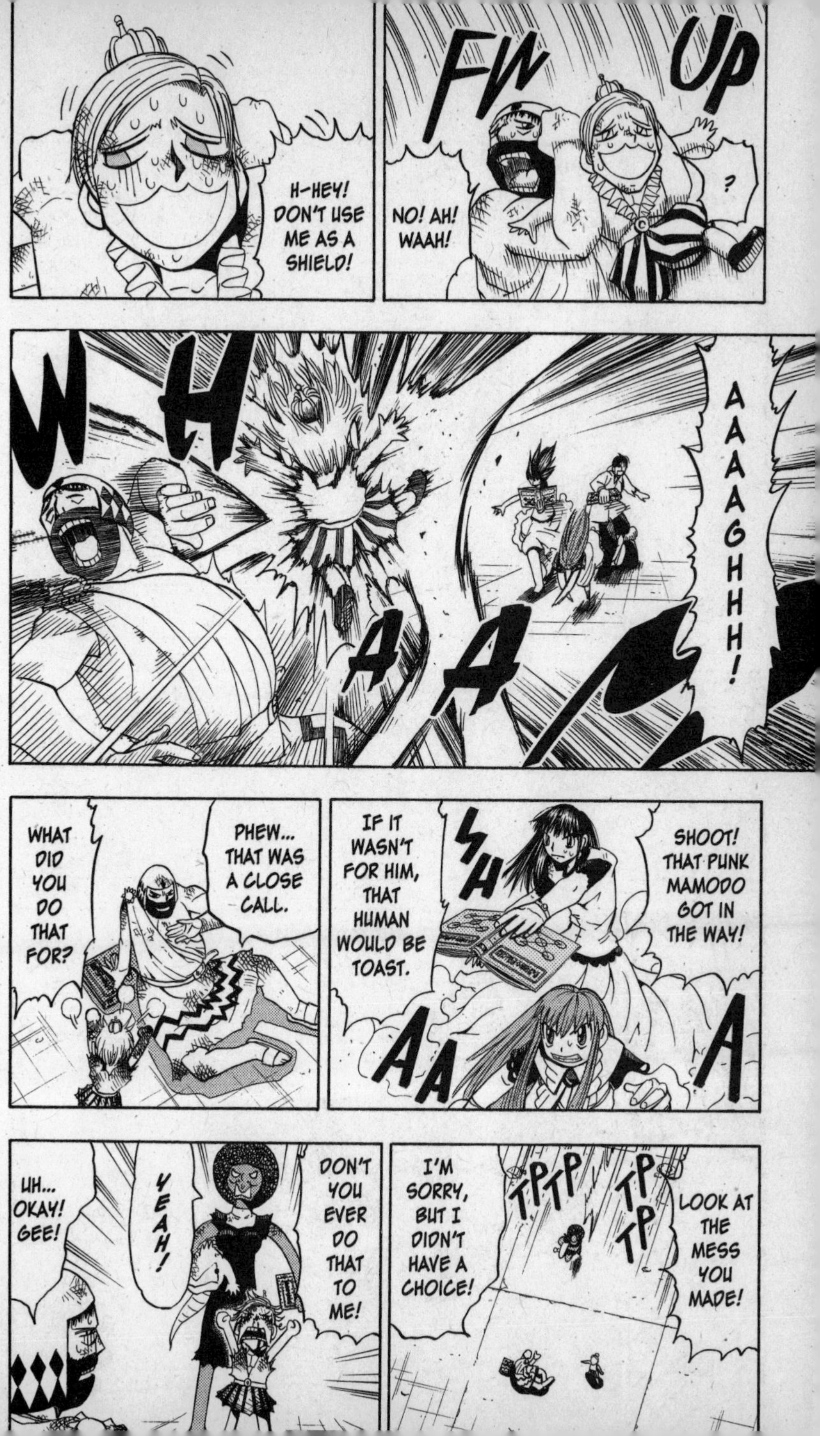
FW UP
?
NO! AH! WAAH!
H-HEY! DON'T USE ME AS A SHIELD!
AAAAAGHHHH!
WH
AAA
SHOOT! THAT PUNK MAMODO GOT IN THE WAY!
SH
IF IT WASN'T FOR HIM, THAT HUMAN WOULD BE TOAST.
AAA
PHEW... THAT WAS A CLOSE CALL.
WHAT DID YOU DO THAT FOR?
LOOK AT THE MESS YOU MADE!
TPTP TPTP
I'M SORRY, BUT I DIDN'T HAVE A CHOICE!
DON'T YOU EVER DO THAT TO ME!
YEAH!
UH... OKAY! GEE!

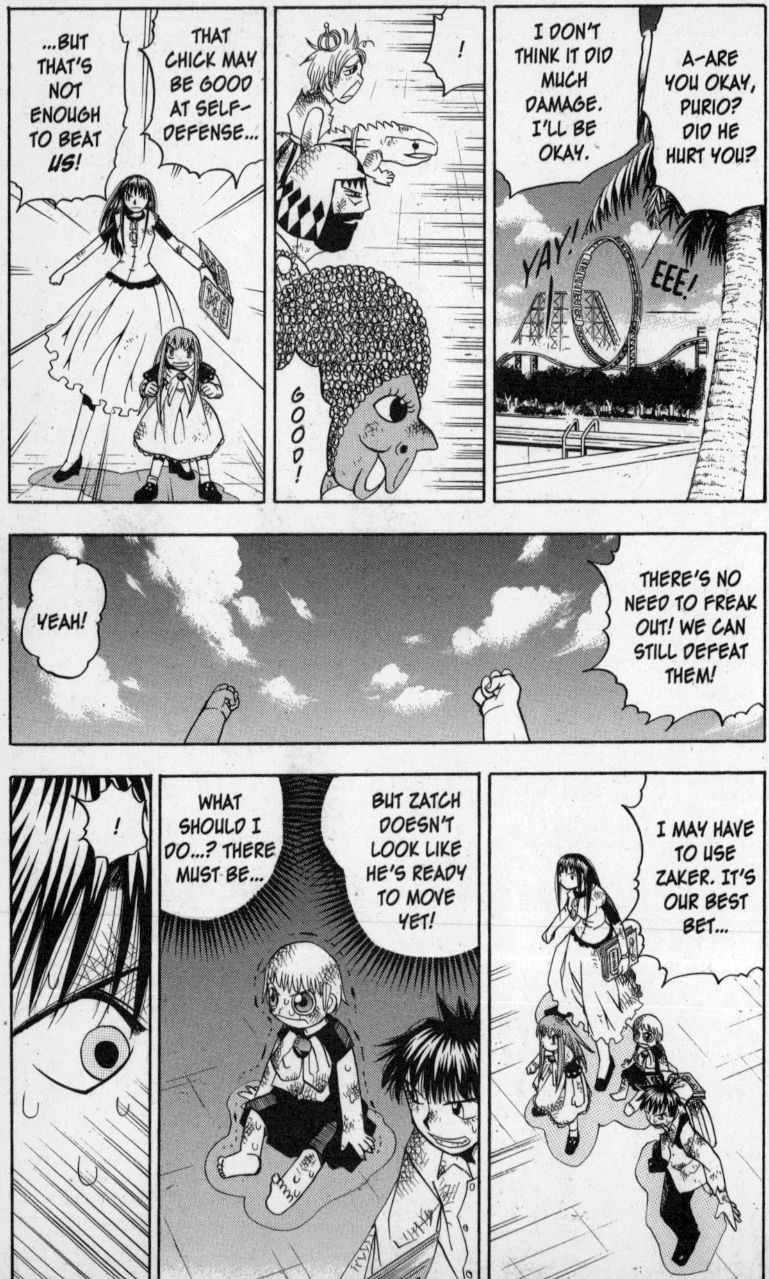
A-ARE YOU OKAY, PURIO? DID HE HURT YOU?
I DON'T THINK IT DID MUCH DAMAGE. I'LL BE OKAY.
YAY!
EEE!
!
GOOD!
THAT CHICK MAY BE GOOD AT SELF-DEFENSE...
...BUT THAT'S NOT ENOUGH TO BEAT US!
THERE'S NO NEED TO FREAK OUT! WE CAN STILL DEFEAT THEM!
YEAH!
I MAY HAVE TO USE ZAKER. IT'S OUR BEST BET...
BUT ZATCH DOESN'T LOOK LIKE HE'S READY TO MOVE YET!
WHAT SHOULD I DO...? THERE MUST BE...
!

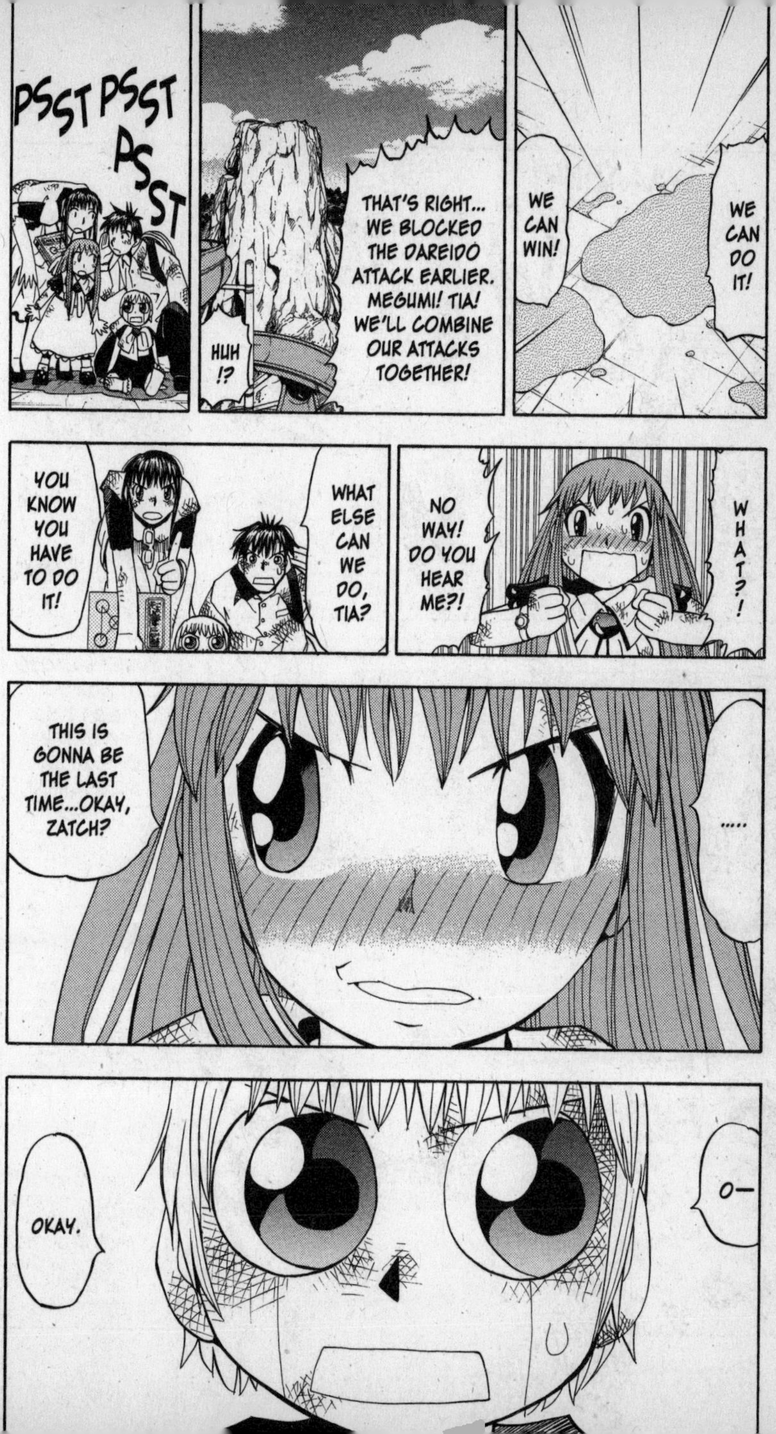

WE CAN DO IT!
WE CAN WIN!
THAT'S RIGHT... WE BLOCKED THE DAREIDO ATTACK EARLIER. MEGUMI! TIA! WE'LL COMBINE OUR ATTACKS TOGETHER!
HUH!?
PSST PSST PSST
WHAT?!
NO WAY! DO YOU HEAR ME?!
WHAT ELSE CAN WE DO, TIA?
YOU KNOW YOU HAVE TO DO IT!
.....
THIS IS GONNA BE THE LAST TIME...OKAY, ZATCH?
O—
OKAY.

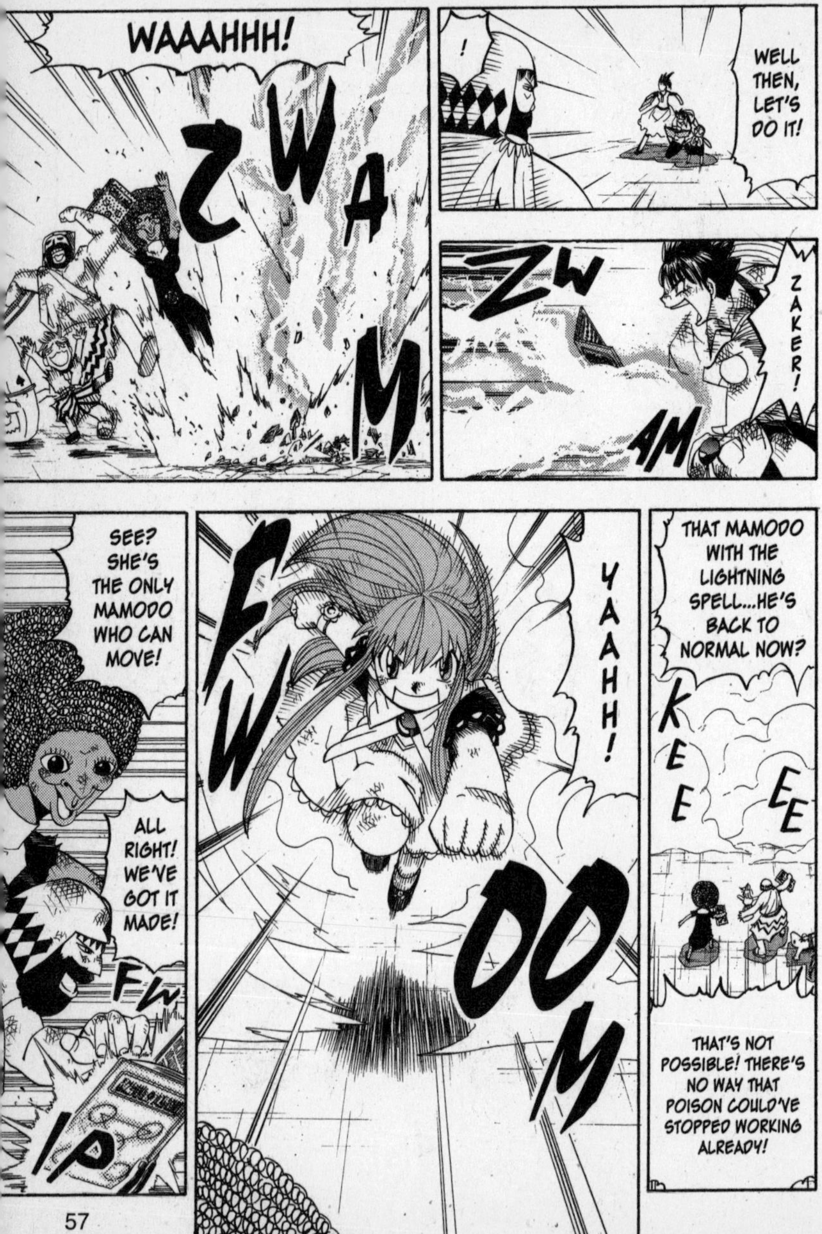
!
WELL THEN, LET'S DO IT!
ZW
AM
ZAKER!
WAAAHHH!
ZWAM
THAT MAMODO WITH THE LIGHTNING SPELL...HE'S BACK TO NORMAL NOW?
KEEEE
THAT'S NOT POSSIBLE! THERE'S NO WAY THAT POISON COULD'VE STOPPED WORKING ALREADY!
FWW
YAAAHH!
DOOM
SEE? SHE'S THE ONLY MAMODO WHO CAN MOVE!
ALL RIGHT! WE'VE GOT IT MADE!
FWIP

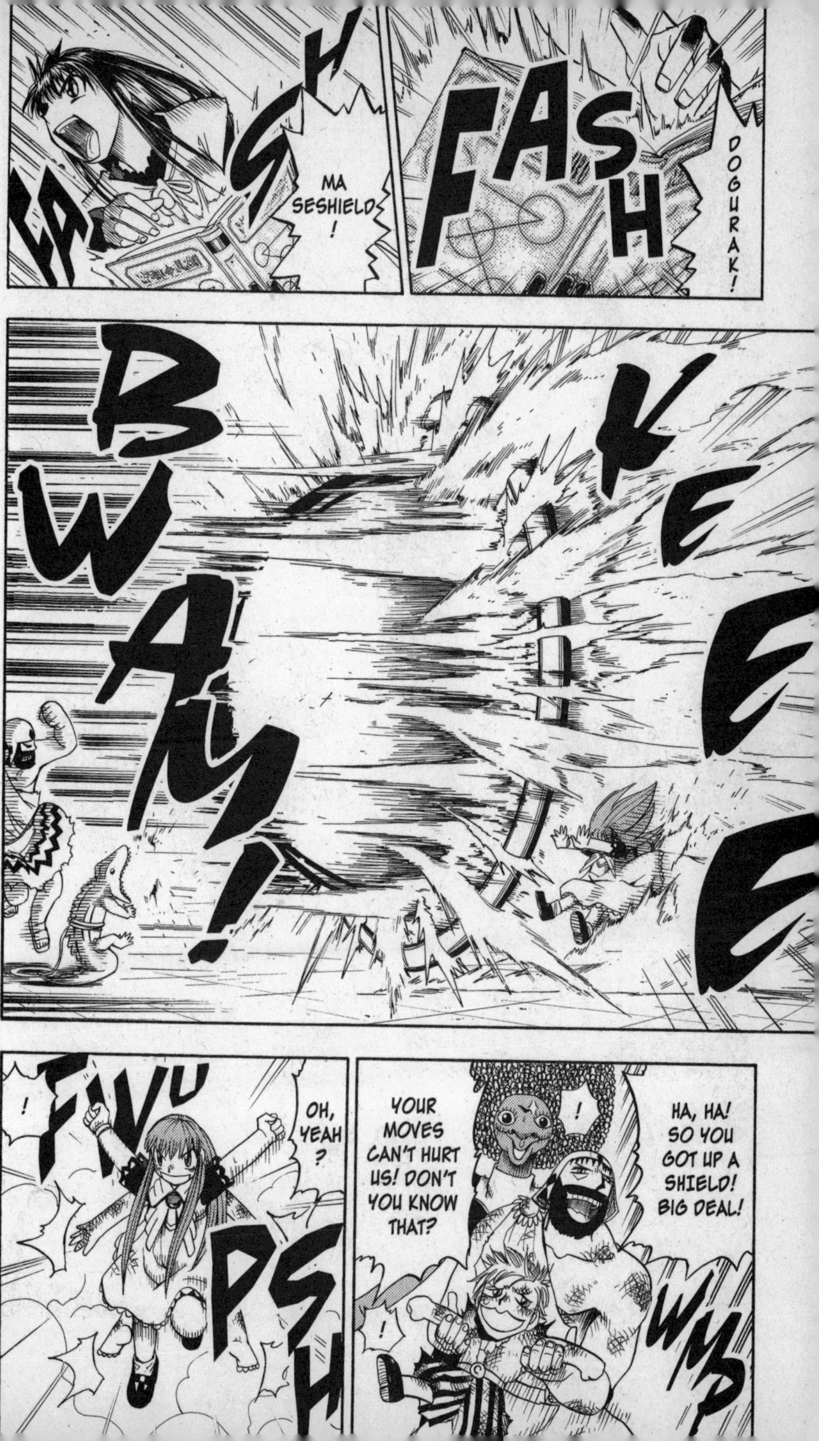
DOGURAK!
FASH
MA SESHIELD!
FASH
BWAM!
KEEEE
HA, HA! SO YOU GOT UP A SHIELD! BIG DEAL!
YOUR MOVES CAN'T HURT US! DON'T YOU KNOW THAT?
WMP
OH, YEAH?
PSH

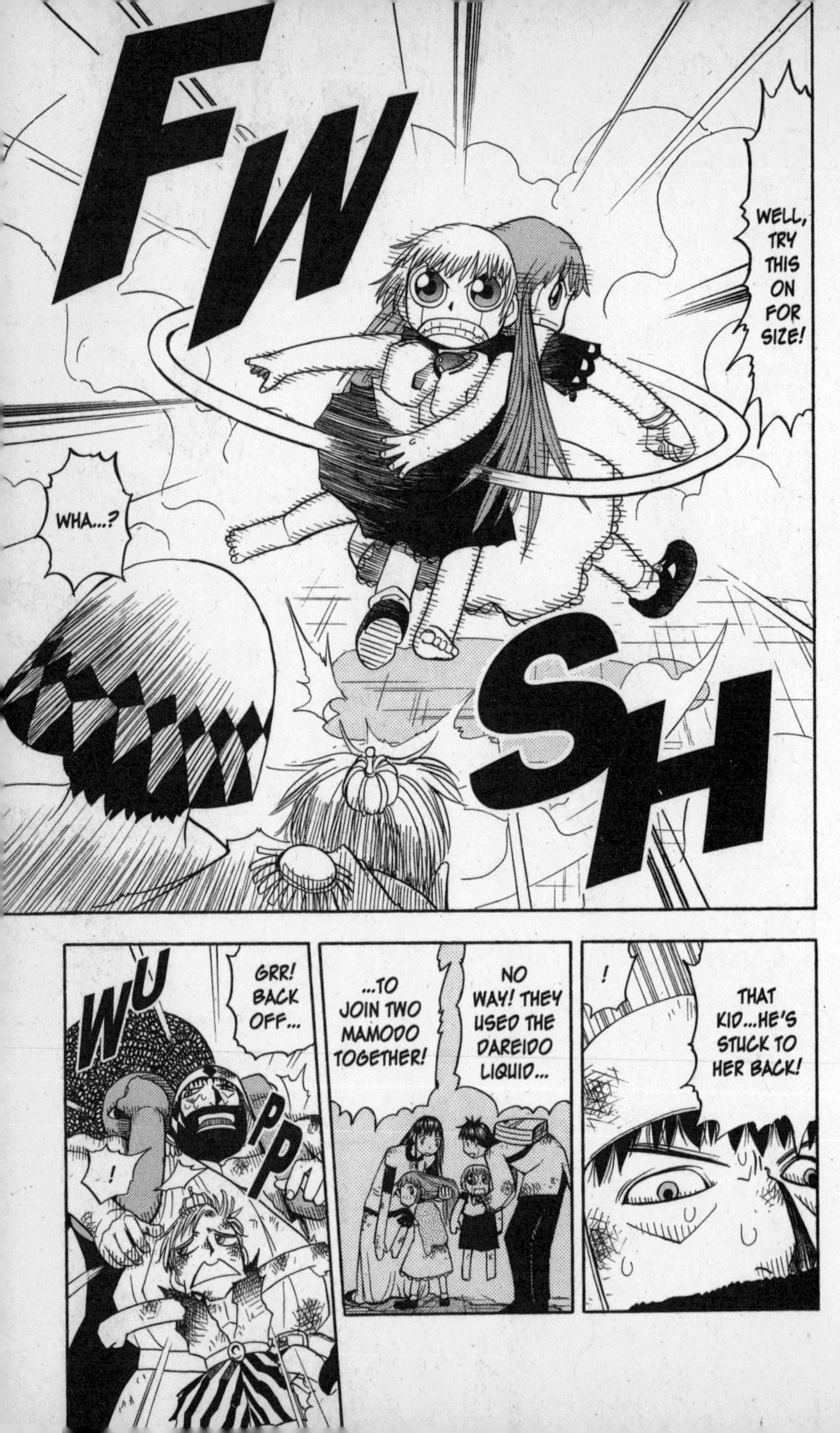
WELL, TRY THIS ON FOR SIZE!
FW
WHA...?
SH
!
THAT KID...HE'S STUCK TO HER BACK!
NO WAY! THEY USED THE DAREIDO LIQUID...
...TO JOIN TWO MAMODO TOGETHER!
GRR! BACK OFF...
WU
PP
!

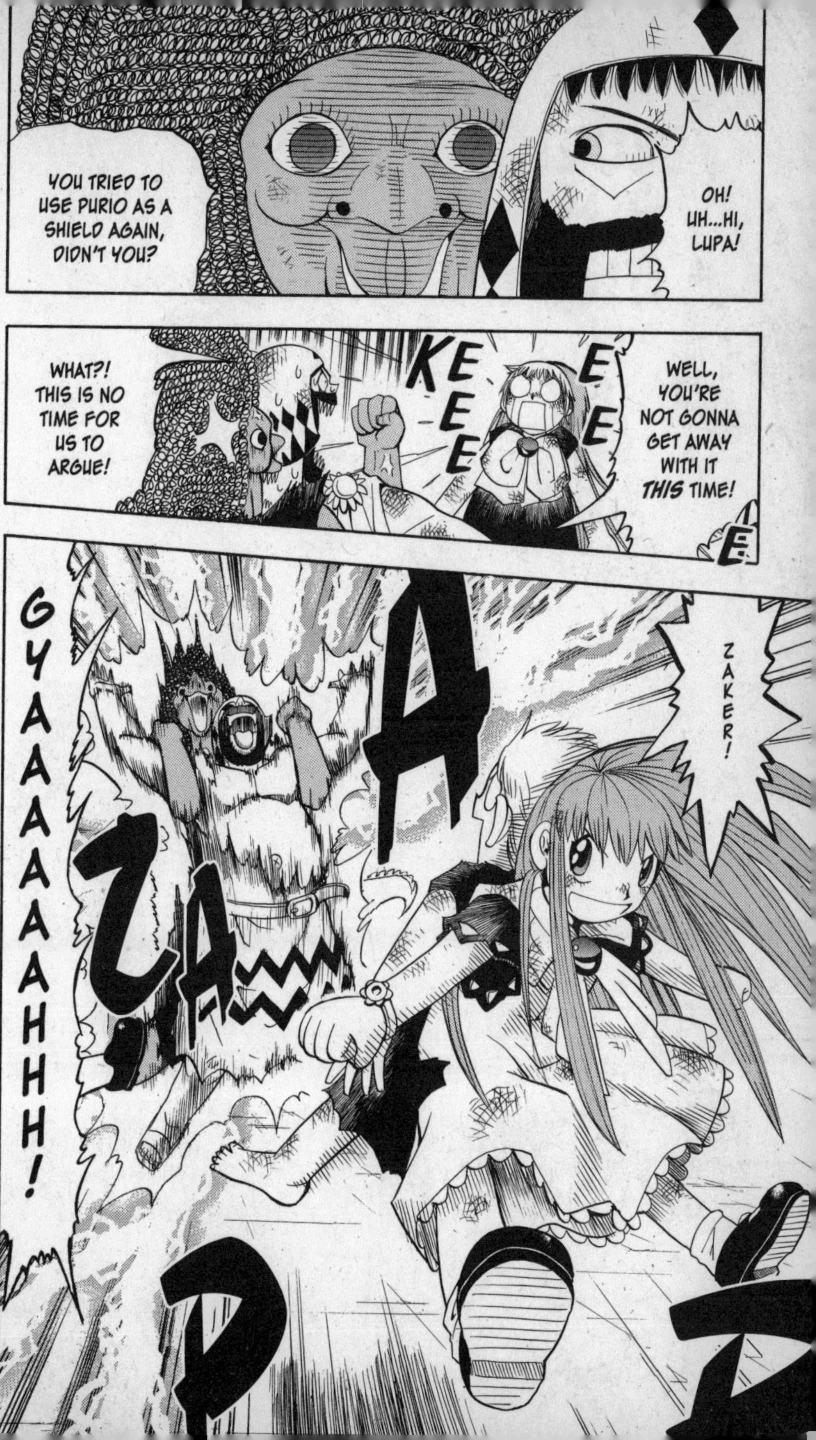
OH! UH...HI, LUPA!
YOU TRIED TO USE PURIO AS A SHIELD AGAIN, DIDN'T YOU?
WELL, YOU'RE NOT GONNA GET AWAY WITH IT THIS TIME!
WHAT?! THIS IS NO TIME FOR US TO ARGUE!
ZAKER!
GYAAAAAAHHH!
ZA

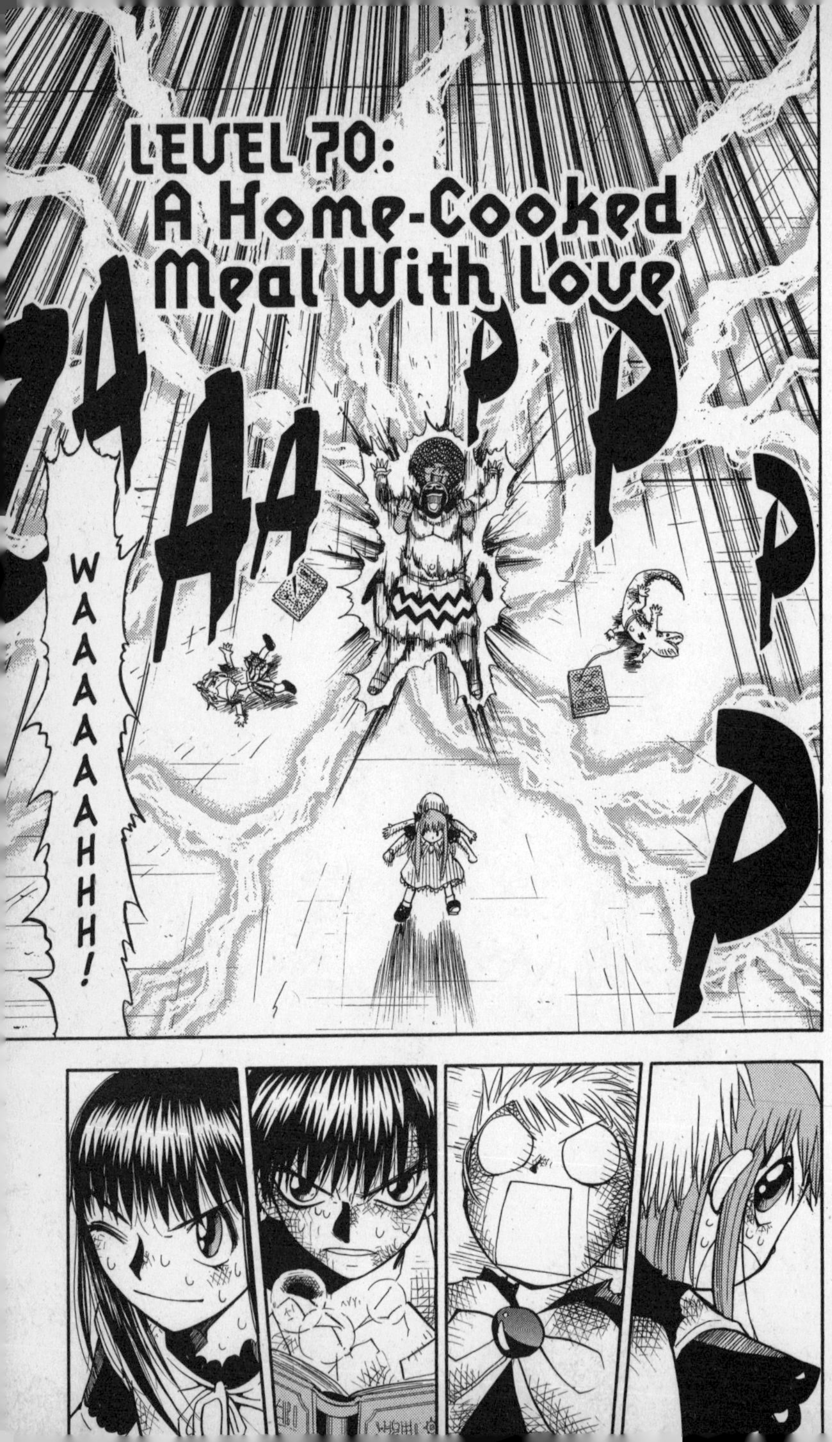

LEVEL 70:
A Home-Cooked Meal With Love
WAAAAAAHHH!

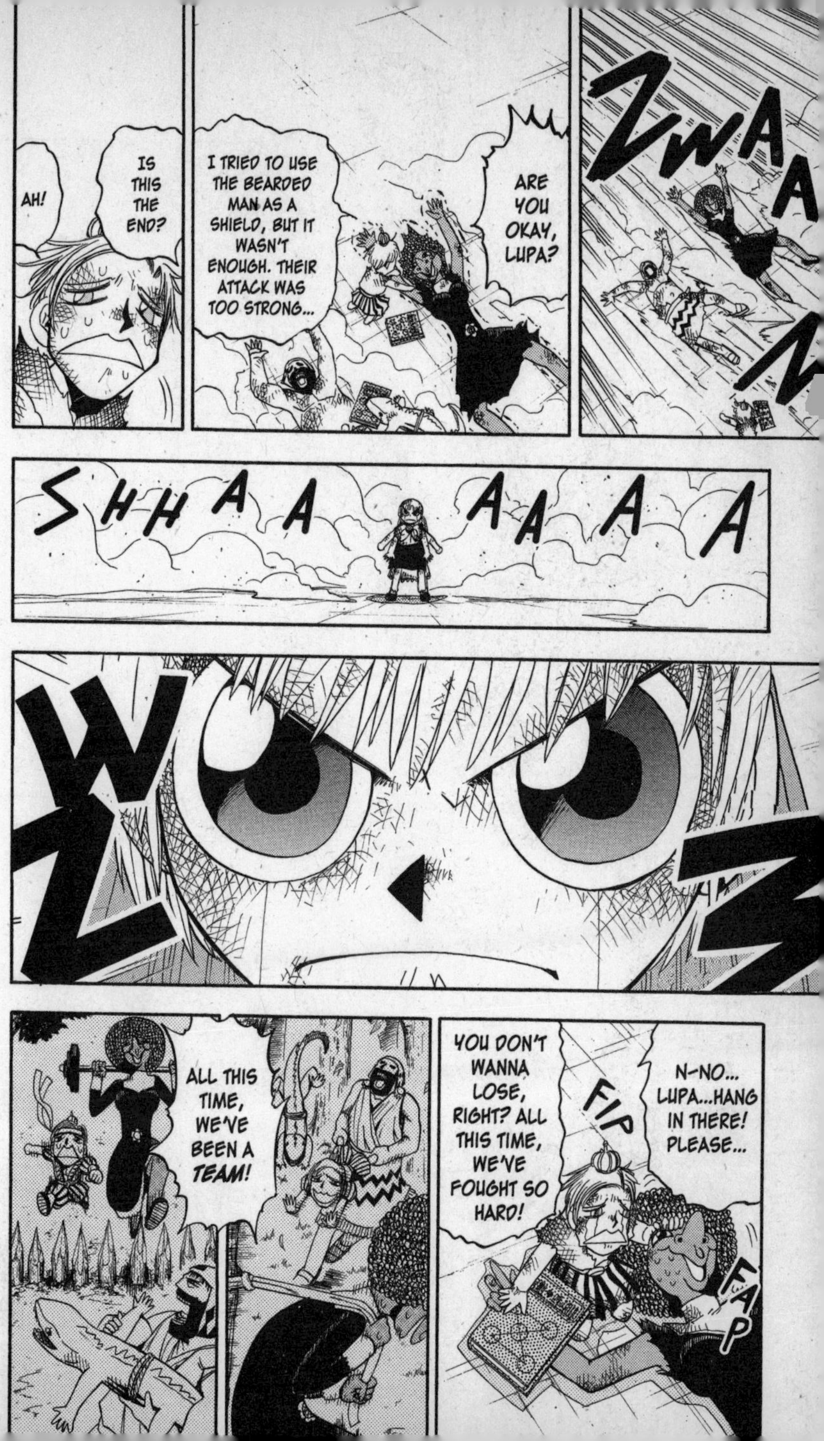
ZWAAAN
ARE YOU OKAY, LUPA?
I TRIED TO USE THE BEARDED MAN AS A SHIELD, BUT IT WASN'T ENOUGH. THEIR ATTACK WAS TOO STRONG...
IS THIS THE END?
AH!
SHHAAAAAA
ZWM
N-NO... LUPA...HANG IN THERE! PLEASE...
FIP
FAP
YOU DON'T WANNA LOSE, RIGHT? ALL THIS TIME, WE'VE FOUGHT SO HARD!
ALL THIS TIME, WE'VE BEEN A *TEAM*!

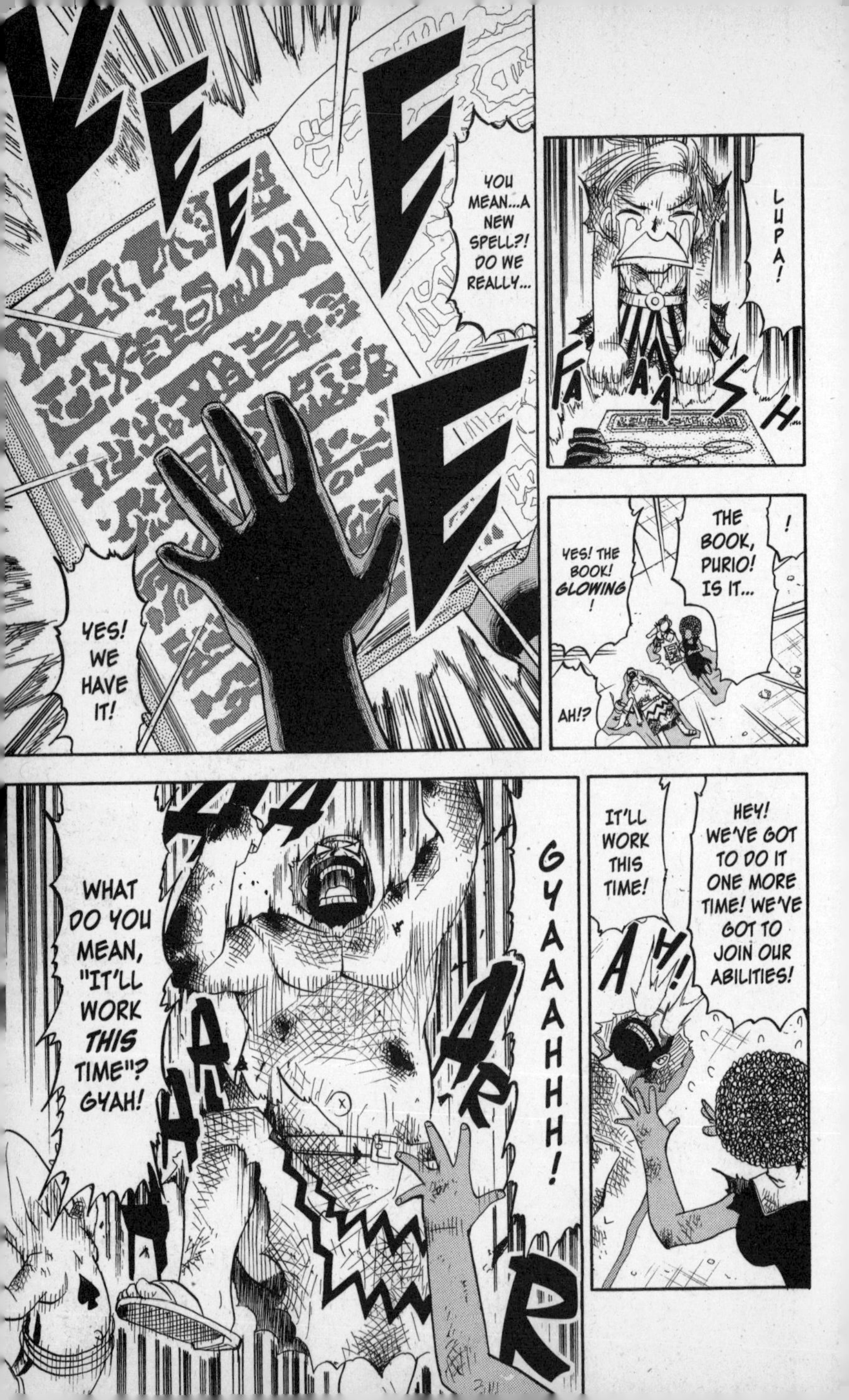
LUPA!
FAAASH
!
THE BOOK, PURIO! IS IT...
YES! THE BOOK! GLOWING!
AH!?
YOU MEAN...A NEW SPELL?! DO WE REALLY...
YES! WE HAVE IT!
HEY! WE'VE GOT TO DO IT ONE MORE TIME! WE'VE GOT TO JOIN OUR ABILITIES!
AH!
IT'LL WORK THIS TIME!
GYAAAAHHH!
WHAT DO YOU MEAN, "IT'LL WORK *THIS* TIME"? GYAH!

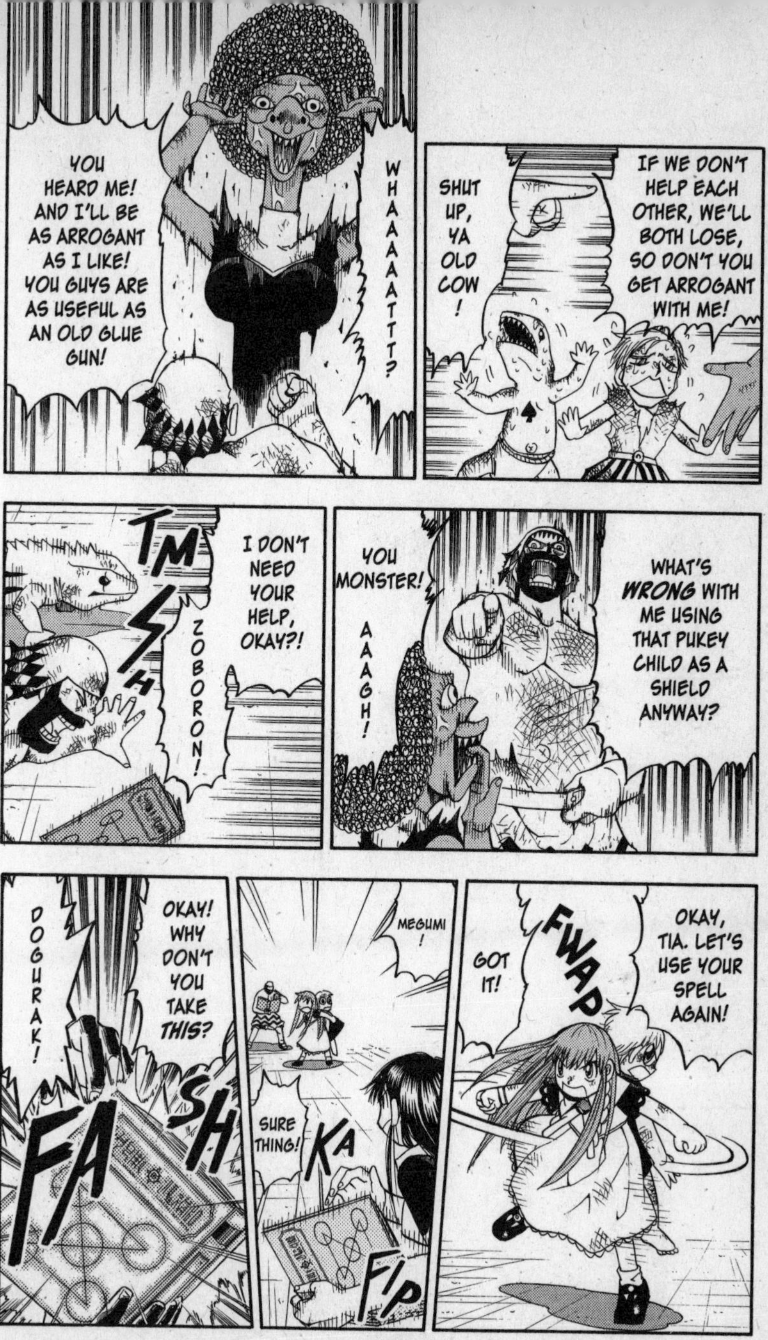
IF WE DON'T HELP EACH OTHER, WE'LL BOTH LOSE, SO DON'T YOU GET ARROGANT WITH ME!
SHUT UP, YA OLD COW!
WHAAAAAATTT?
YOU HEARD ME! AND I'LL BE AS ARROGANT AS I LIKE! YOU GUYS ARE AS USEFUL AS AN OLD GLUE GUN!
WHAT'S *WRONG* WITH ME USING THAT PUKEY CHILD AS A SHIELD ANYWAY?
YOU MONSTER!
AAAGH!
I DON'T NEED YOUR HELP, OKAY?!
ZOBORON!
TMSSH
OKAY, TIA. LET'S USE YOUR SPELL AGAIN!
GOT IT!
FWAP
MEGUMI!
SURE THING!
KA
FLIP
OKAY! WHY DON'T YOU TAKE *THIS*?
DOGURAK!
FASH

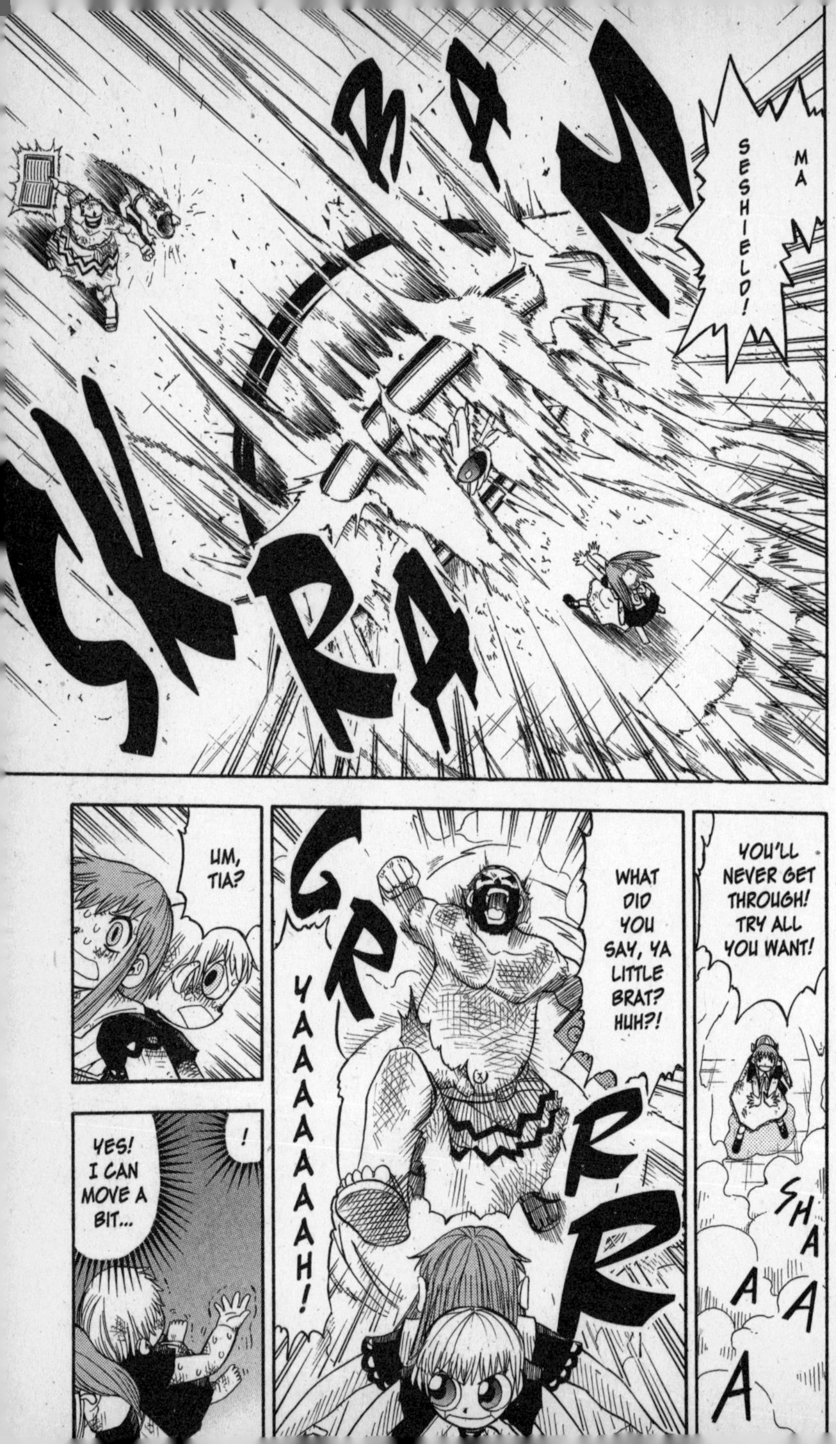
MA
SESHIELD!
BAM
SKRA
YOU'LL NEVER GET THROUGH! TRY ALL YOU WANT!
SHAAAAA
WHAT DID YOU SAY, YA LITTLE BRAT? HUH?!
GRRR
YAAAAAAAAAAH!
UM, TIA?
!
YES! I CAN MOVE A BIT...

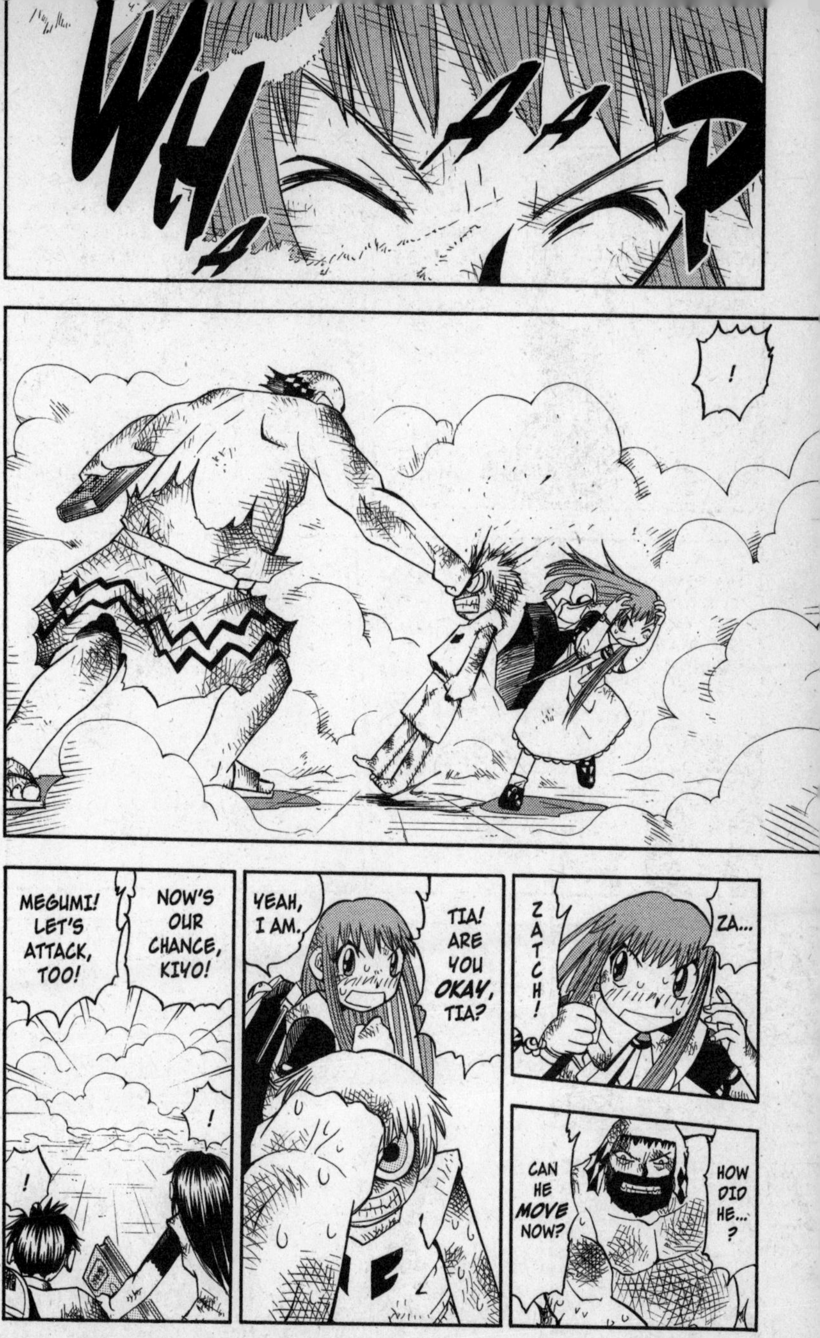
WHAAAA?
!
ZA...
ZATCH!
HOW DID HE...?
CAN HE MOVE NOW?
TIA! ARE YOU OKAY, TIA?
YEAH, I AM.
NOW'S OUR CHANCE, KIYO!
MEGUMI! LET'S ATTACK, TOO!
!
!

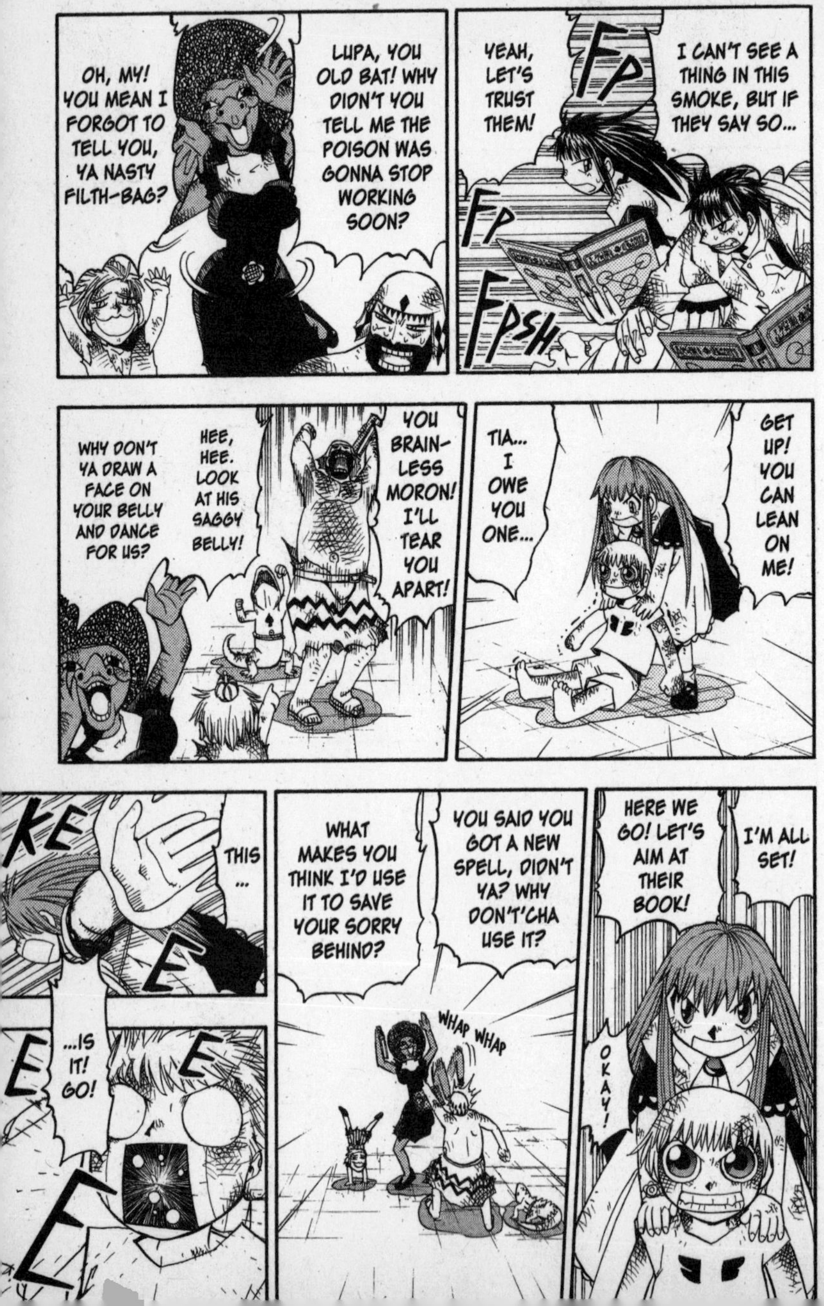
I CAN'T SEE A THING IN THIS SMOKE, BUT IF THEY SAY SO...
YEAH, LET'S TRUST THEM!
FP
FP
FPSH
LUPA, YOU OLD BAT! WHY DIDN'T YOU TELL ME THE POISON WAS GONNA STOP WORKING SOON?
OH, MY! YOU MEAN I FORGOT TO TELL YOU, YA NASTY FILTH-BAG?
GET UP! YOU CAN LEAN ON ME!
TIA... I OWE YOU ONE...
YOU BRAINLESS MORON! I'LL TEAR YOU APART!
HEE, HEE. LOOK AT HIS SAGGY BELLY!
WHY DON'T YA DRAW A FACE ON YOUR BELLY AND DANCE FOR US?
I'M ALL SET!
HERE WE GO! LET'S AIM AT THEIR BOOK!
OKAY!
YOU SAID YOU GOT A NEW SPELL, DIDN'T YA? WHY DON'T'CHA USE IT?
WHAT MAKES YOU THINK I'D USE IT TO SAVE YOUR SORRY BEHIND?
WHAP WHAP
THIS ...
...IS IT! GO!
KEEEEE

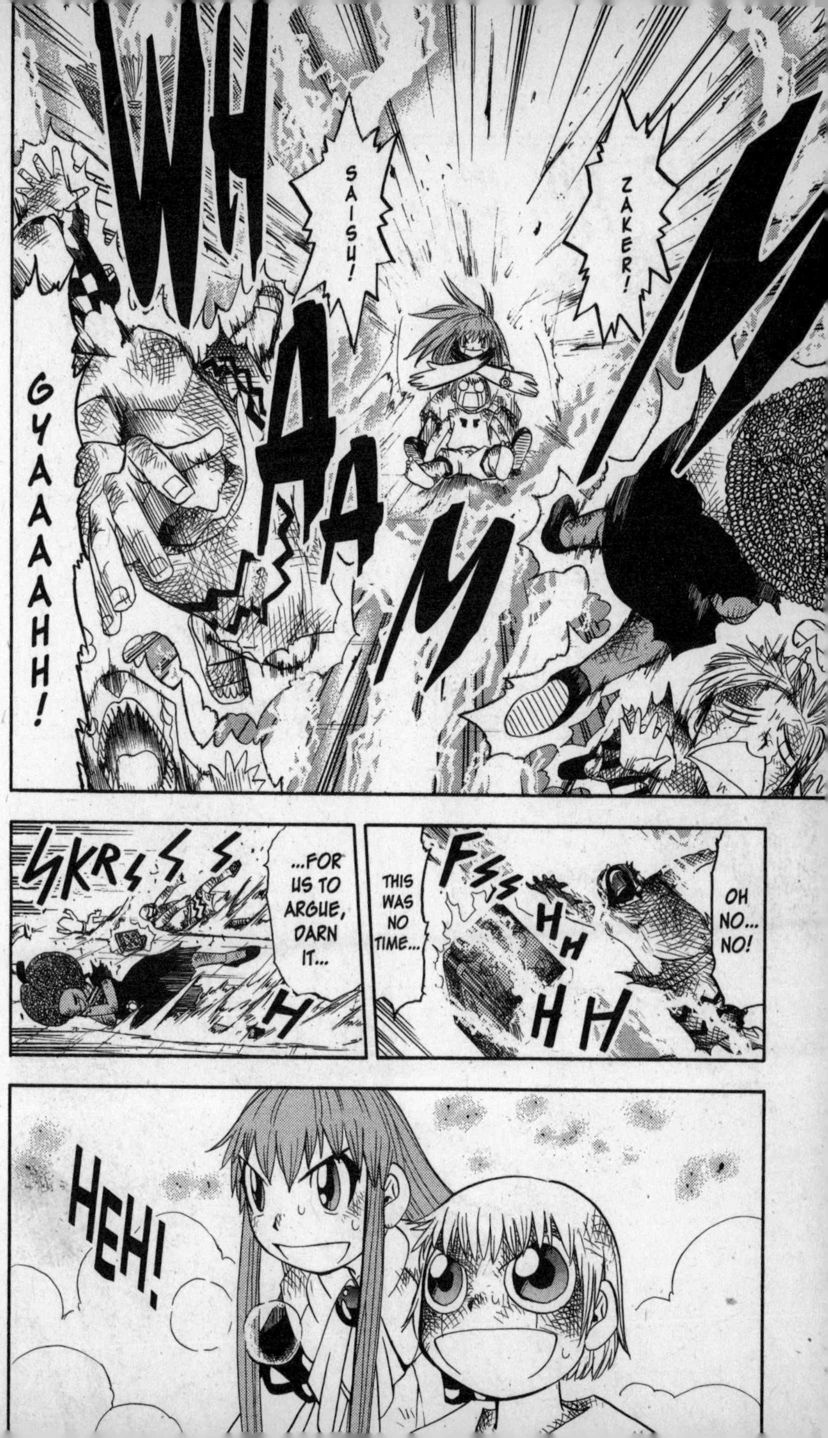

ZAKER!
SAISU!
WHAAMMM
GYAAAAAHH!
OH NO... NO!
FSSHHHH
THIS WAS NO TIME...
...FOR US TO ARGUE, DARN IT...
SKRSSSH
HEH!

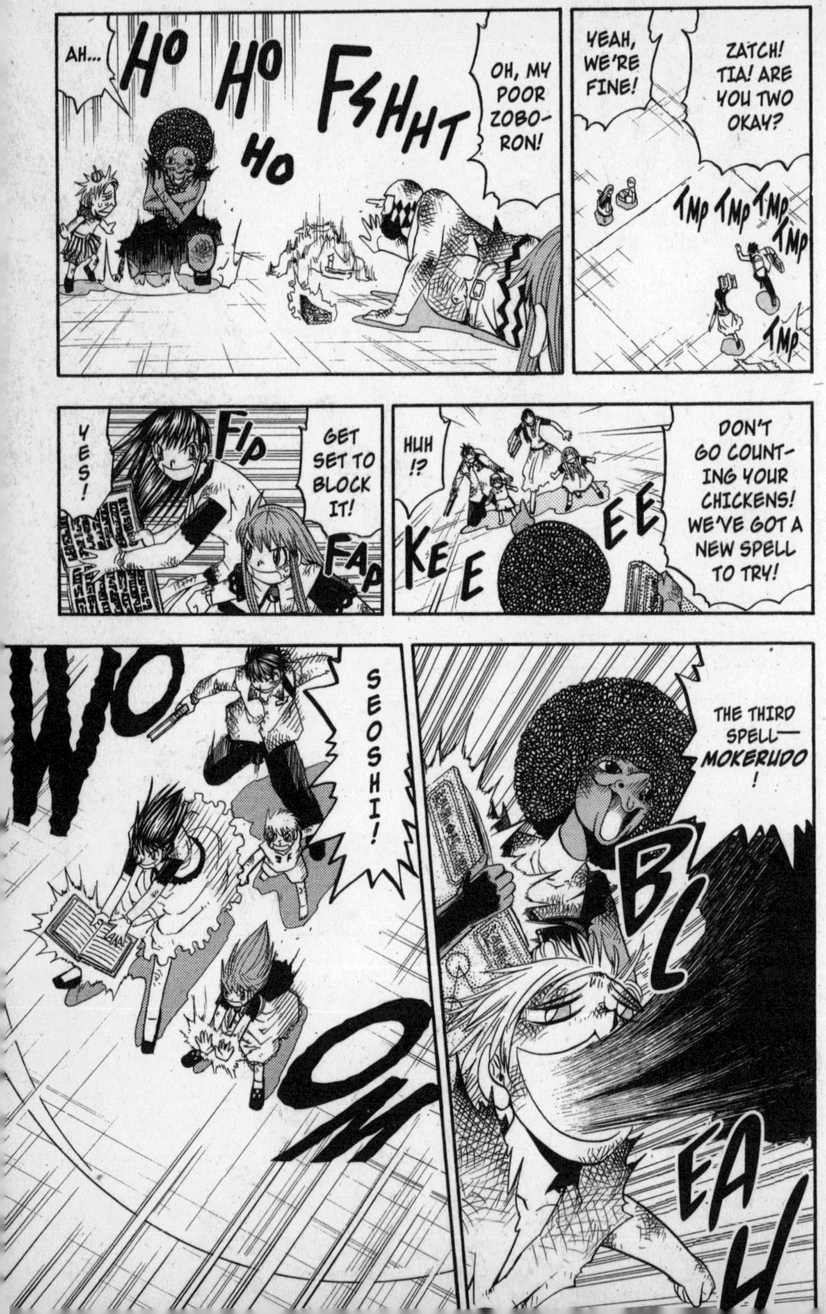
ZATCH! TIA! ARE YOU TWO OKAY?
YEAH, WE'RE FINE!
TMP TMP TMP TMP TMP
OH, MY POOR ZOBORON!
FSHHT
HO HO HO
AH...
DON'T GO COUNTING YOUR CHICKENS! WE'VE GOT A NEW SPELL TO TRY!
KEEEE
HUH !?
GET SET TO BLOCK IT!
FLIP
FAP
YES!
THE THIRD SPELL— MOKERUDO !
BLEAH
SEOSHI!
WOOM

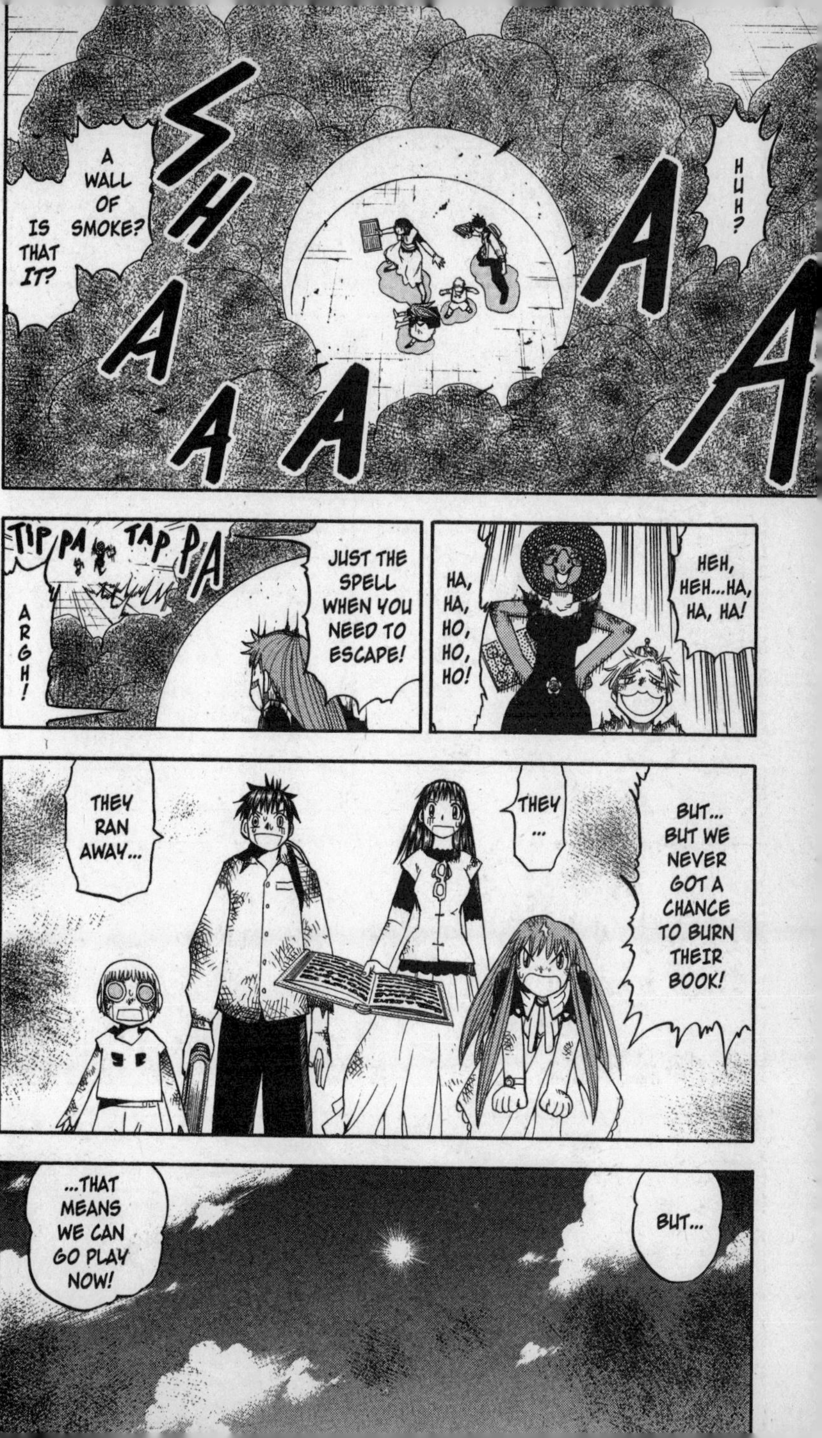
HUH?
A WALL OF SMOKE? IS THAT IT?
SHAAAAAA
HEH, HEH...HA, HA, HA!
HA, HA, HO, HO, HO!
JUST THE SPELL WHEN YOU NEED TO ESCAPE!
TIP PA TAP PA
ARGH!
BUT... BUT WE NEVER GOT A CHANCE TO BURN THEIR BOOK!
THEY ...
THEY RAN AWAY...
BUT...
...THAT MEANS WE CAN GO PLAY NOW!

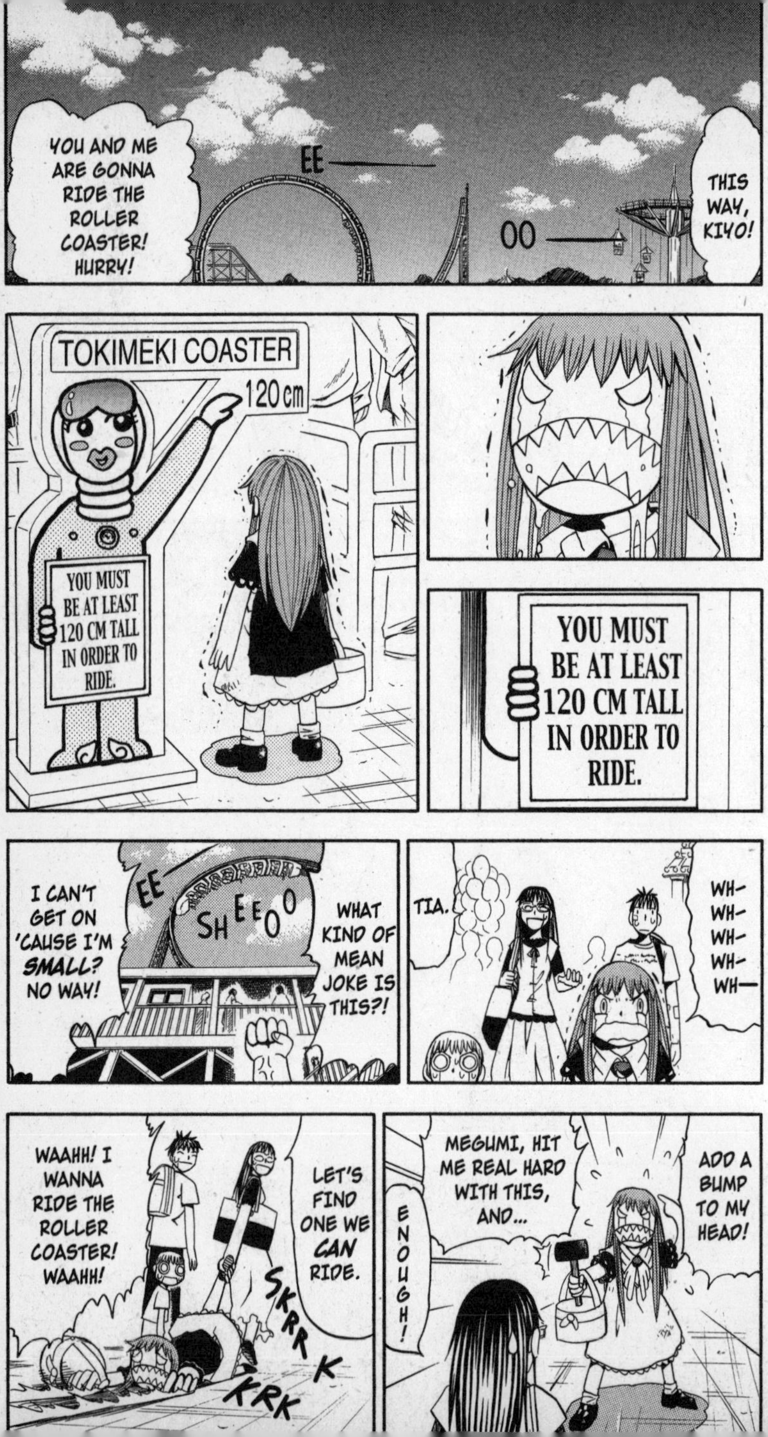

THIS WAY, KIYO!
EE——
OO——
YOU AND ME ARE GONNA RIDE THE ROLLER COASTER! HURRY!
TOKIMEKI COASTER
120 cm
YOU MUST BE AT LEAST 120 CM TALL IN ORDER TO RIDE.
YOU MUST BE AT LEAST 120 CM TALL IN ORDER TO RIDE.
WHAT KIND OF MEAN JOKE IS THIS?!
I CAN'T GET ON 'CAUSE I'M SMALL? NO WAY!
EE
SHEEOO
WH- WH- WH- WH- WH—
TIA.
ADD A BUMP TO MY HEAD!
MEGUMI, HIT ME REAL HARD WITH THIS, AND...
ENOUGH!
LET'S FIND ONE WE CAN RIDE.
WAAHH! I WANNA RIDE THE ROLLER COASTER! WAAHH!
SKRRK
KRK

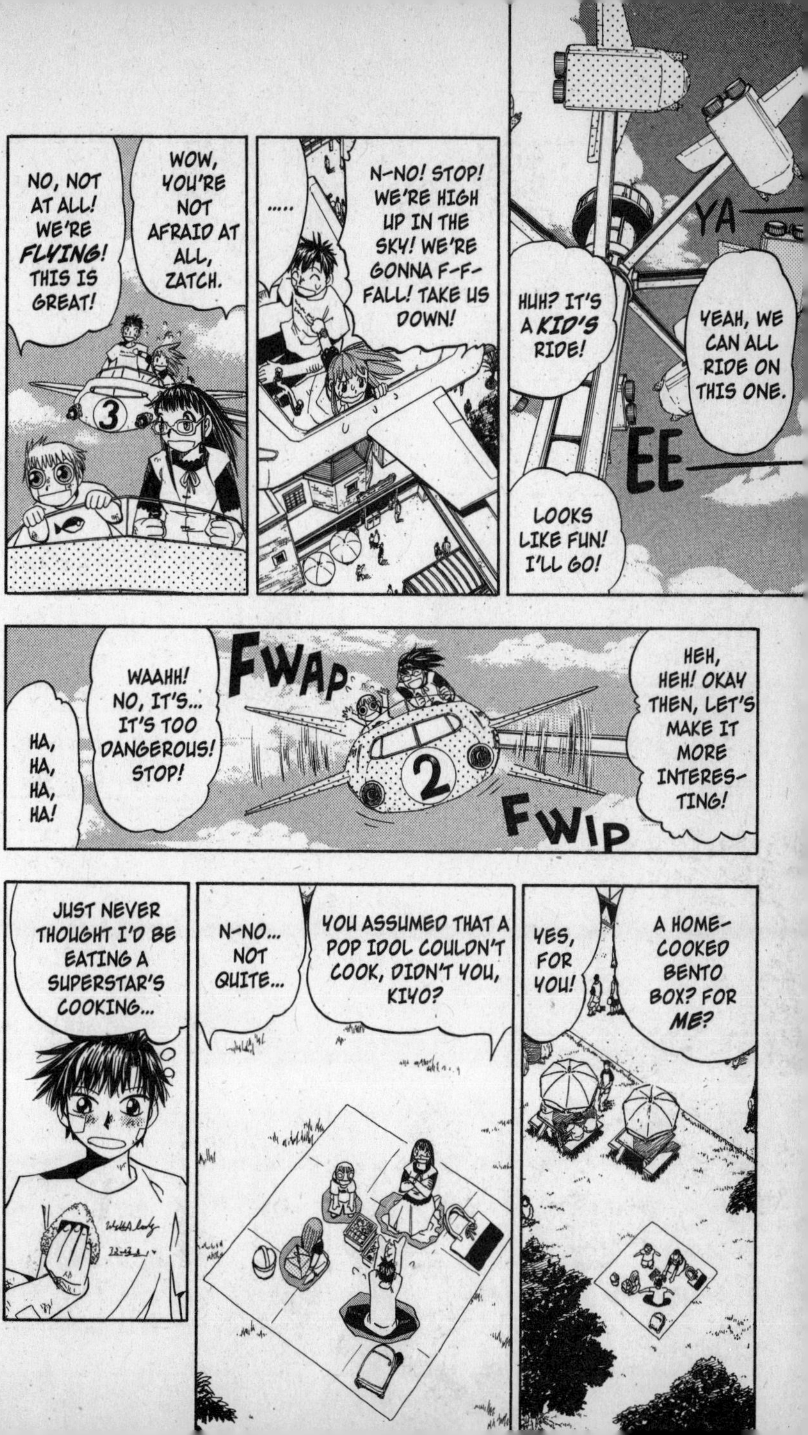
YEAH, WE CAN ALL RIDE ON THIS ONE.
HUH? IT'S A KID'S RIDE!
YA
EE
LOOKS LIKE FUN! I'LL GO!
N-NO! STOP! WE'RE HIGH UP IN THE SKY! WE'RE GONNA F-F-FALL! TAKE US DOWN!
.....
WOW, YOU'RE NOT AFRAID AT ALL, ZATCH.
NO, NOT AT ALL! WE'RE FLYING! THIS IS GREAT!
HEH, HEH! OKAY THEN, LET'S MAKE IT MORE INTERES-TING!
FWIP
FWAP
WAAHH! NO, IT'S... IT'S TOO DANGEROUS! STOP!
HA, HA, HA, HA!
A HOME-COOKED BENTO BOX? FOR ME?
YES, FOR YOU!
YOU ASSUMED THAT A POP IDOL COULDN'T COOK, DIDN'T YOU, KIYO?
N-NO... NOT QUITE...
JUST NEVER THOUGHT I'D BE EATING A SUPERSTAR'S COOKING...

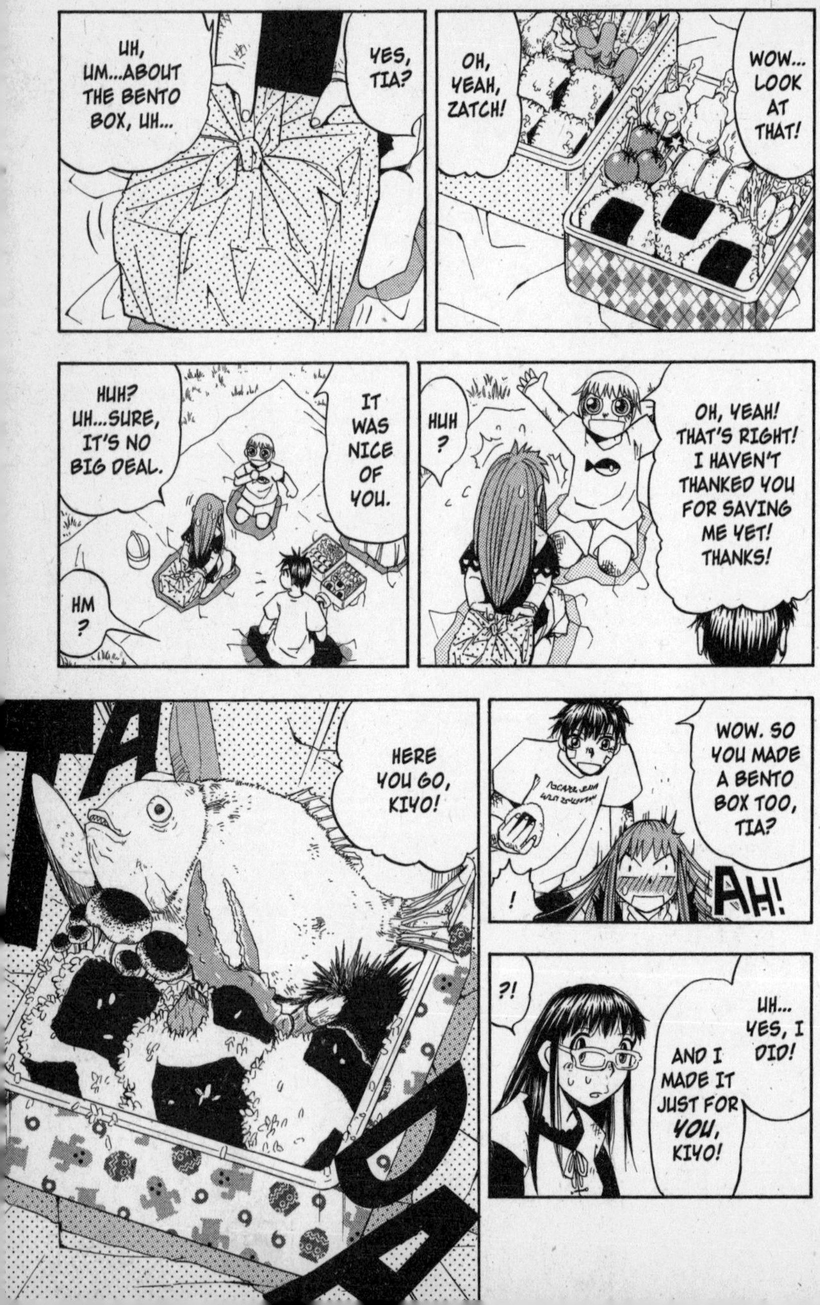
WOW... LOOK AT THAT!
OH, YEAH, ZATCH!
YES, TIA?
UH, UM...ABOUT THE BENTO BOX, UH...
OH, YEAH! THAT'S RIGHT! I HAVEN'T THANKED YOU FOR SAVING ME YET! THANKS!
HUH?
IT WAS NICE OF YOU.
HUH? UH...SURE, IT'S NO BIG DEAL.
HM?
WOW. SO YOU MADE A BENTO BOX TOO, TIA?
AH!
!
UH... YES, I DID!
AND I MADE IT JUST FOR YOU, KIYO!
?!
HERE YOU GO, KIYO!

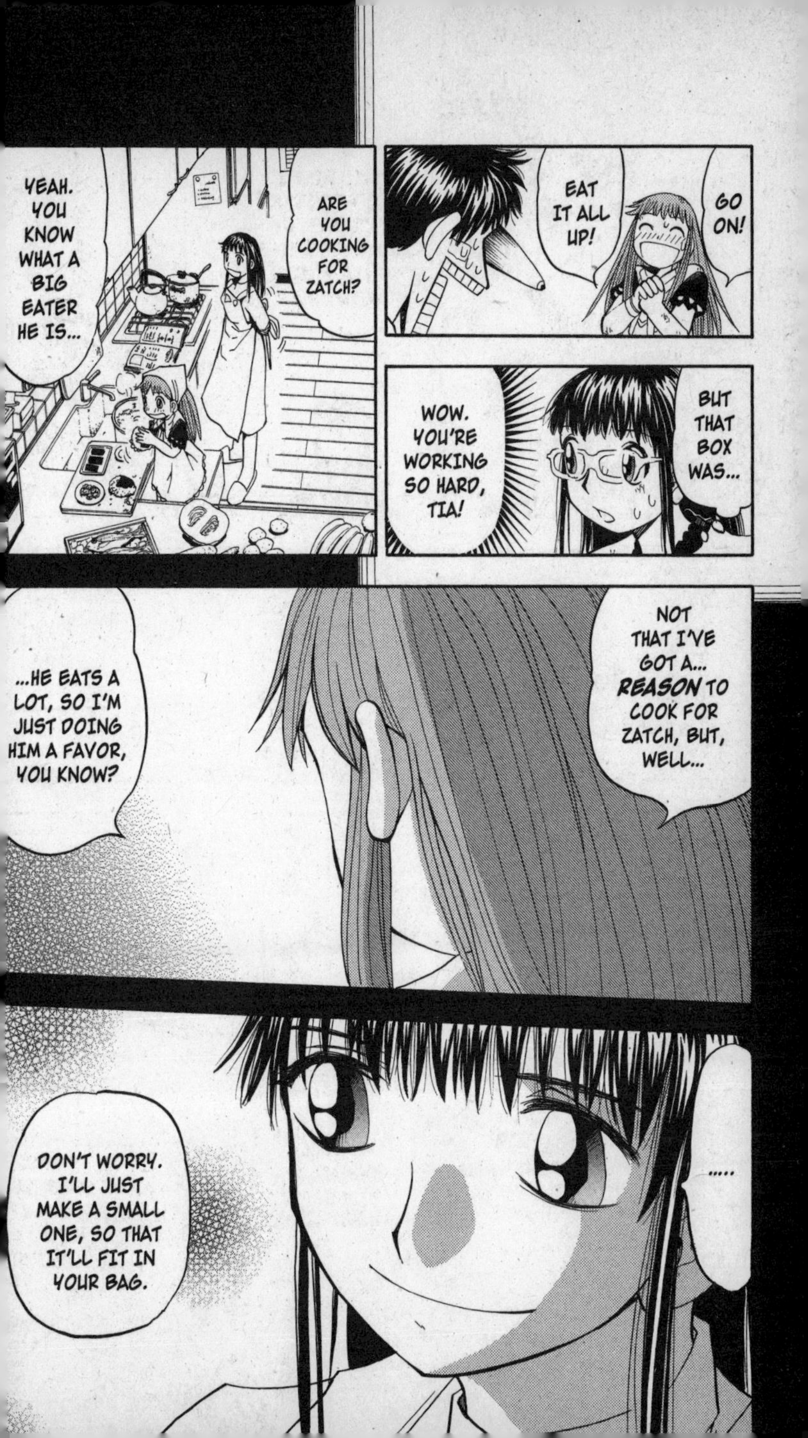

GO ON!
EAT IT ALL UP!
BUT THAT BOX WAS...
WOW. YOU'RE WORKING SO HARD, TIA!
ARE YOU COOKING FOR ZATCH?
YEAH. YOU KNOW WHAT A BIG EATER HE IS...
NOT THAT I'VE GOT A... **REASON** TO COOK FOR ZATCH, BUT, WELL...
...HE EATS A LOT, SO I'M JUST DOING HIM A FAVOR, YOU KNOW?
.....
DON'T WORRY. I'LL JUST MAKE A SMALL ONE, SO THAT IT'LL FIT IN YOUR BAG.

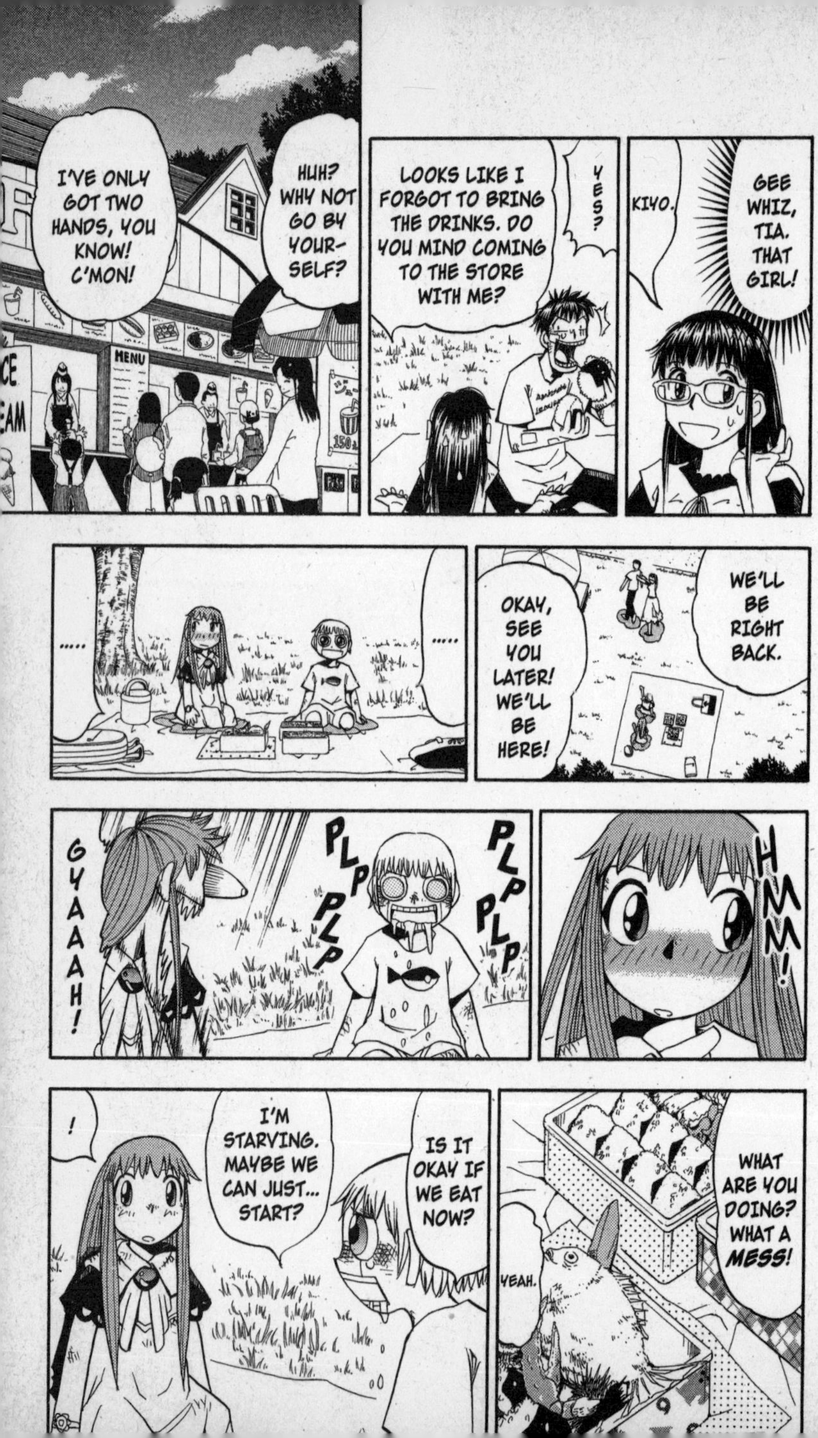
GEE WHIZ, TIA. THAT GIRL!
KIYO.
YES?
LOOKS LIKE I FORGOT TO BRING THE DRINKS. DO YOU MIND COMING TO THE STORE WITH ME?
HUH? WHY NOT GO BY YOURSELF?
I'VE ONLY GOT TWO HANDS, YOU KNOW! C'MON!
MENU
WE'LL BE RIGHT BACK.
OKAY, SEE YOU LATER! WE'LL BE HERE!
.....
.....
HMMM!
PLP PLP
PLP PLP
GYAAAAH!
WHAT ARE YOU DOING? WHAT A MESS!
YEAH.
IS IT OKAY IF WE EAT NOW?
I'M STARVING. MAYBE WE CAN JUST... START?
!

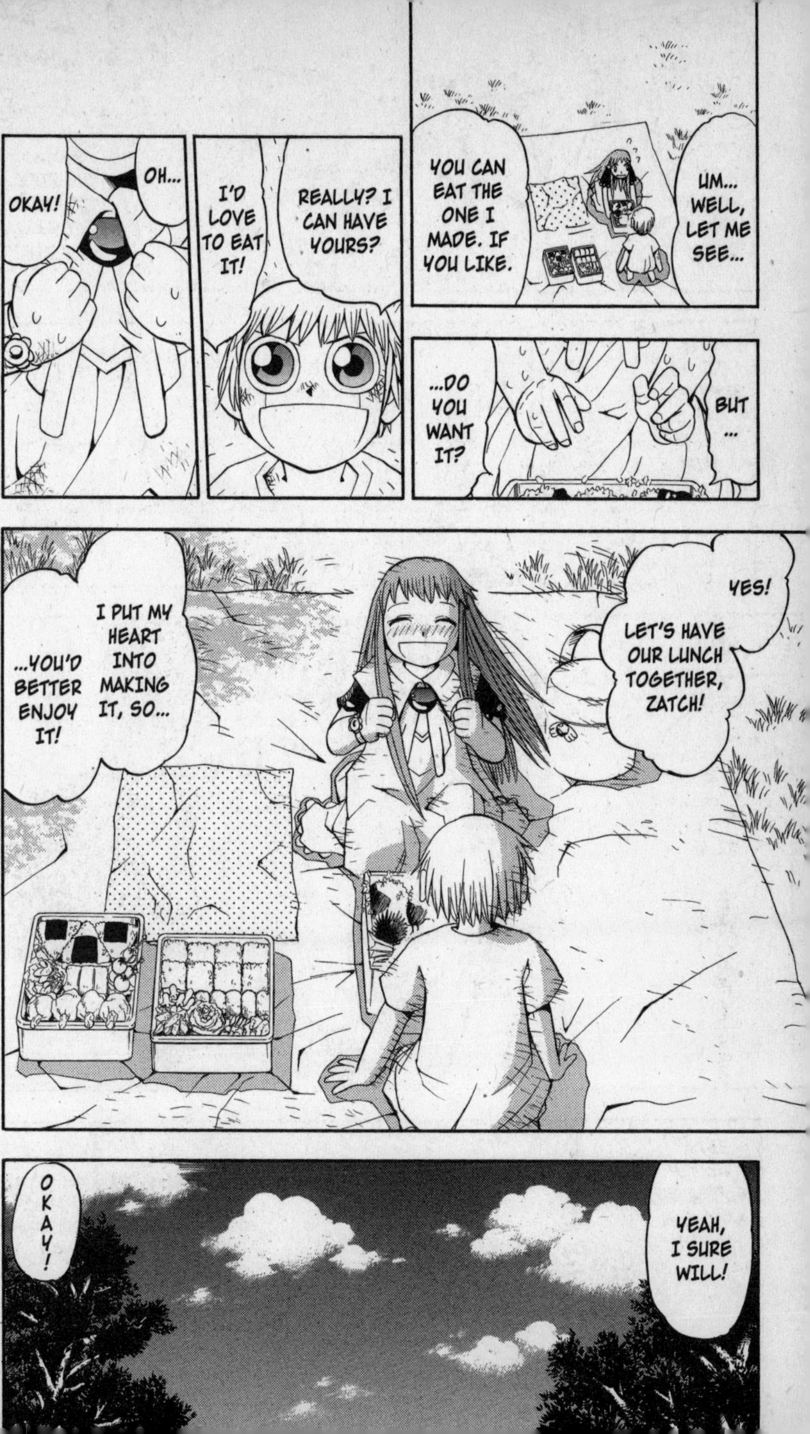
UM... WELL, LET ME SEE...
YOU CAN EAT THE ONE I MADE. IF YOU LIKE.
BUT ...
...DO YOU WANT IT?
REALLY? I CAN HAVE YOURS?
I'D LOVE TO EAT IT!
OH...
OKAY!
YES!
LET'S HAVE OUR LUNCH TOGETHER, ZATCH!
I PUT MY HEART INTO MAKING IT, SO...
...YOU'D BETTER ENJOY IT!
YEAH, I SURE WILL!
OKAY!

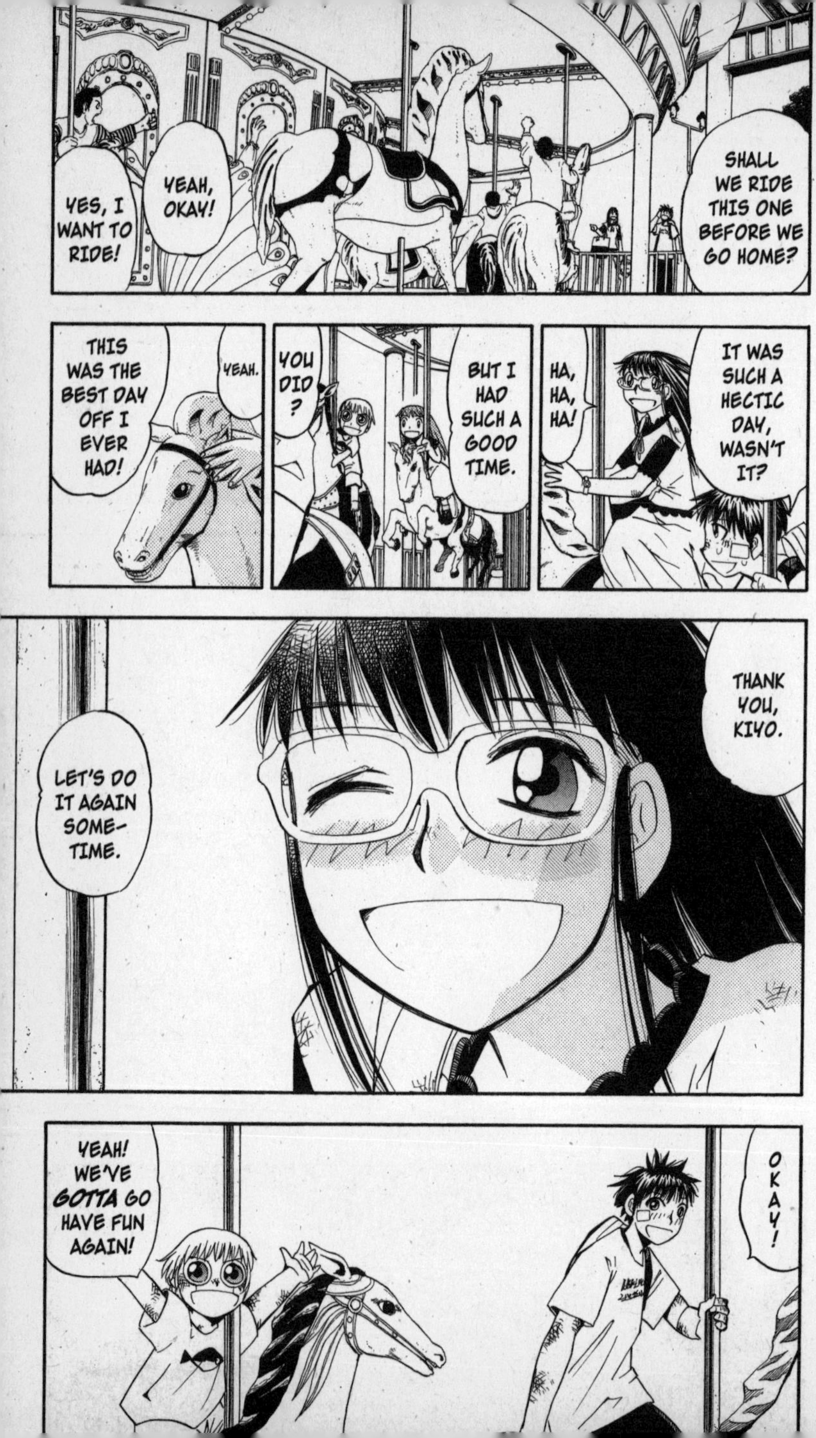
SHALL WE RIDE THIS ONE BEFORE WE GO HOME?
YEAH, OKAY!
YES, I WANT TO RIDE!
IT WAS SUCH A HECTIC DAY, WASN'T IT?
HA, HA, HA!
BUT I HAD SUCH A GOOD TIME.
YOU DID?
YEAH.
THIS WAS THE BEST DAY OFF I EVER HAD!
THANK YOU, KIYO.
LET'S DO IT AGAIN SOMETIME.
OKAY!
YEAH! WE'VE *GOTTA* GO HAVE FUN AGAIN!

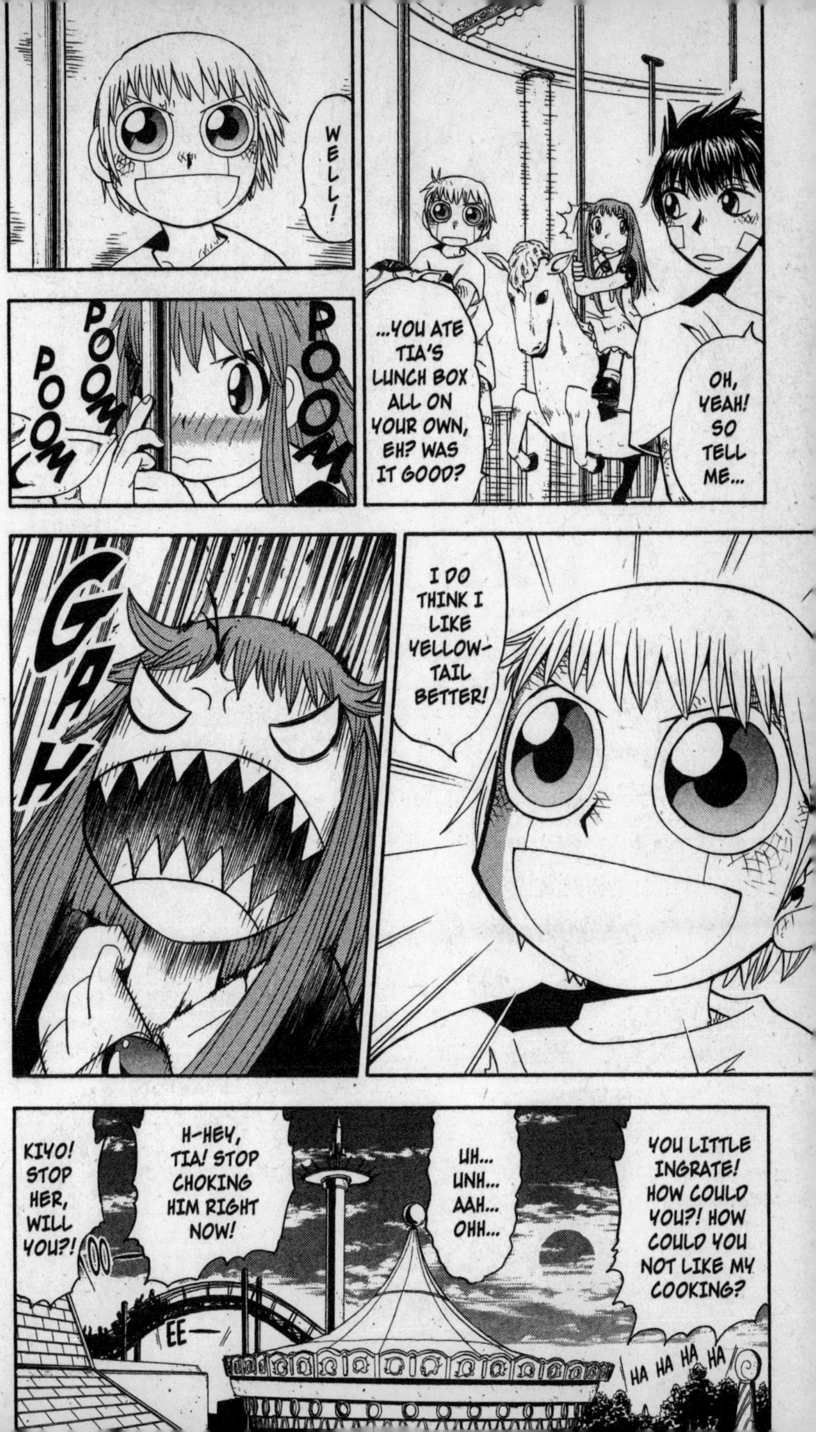
OH, YEAH! SO TELL ME...
...YOU ATE TIA'S LUNCH BOX ALL ON YOUR OWN, EH? WAS IT GOOD?
WELL!
POOM POOM POOM POOM
I DO THINK I LIKE YELLOW-TAIL BETTER!
GAAH
YOU LITTLE INGRATE! HOW COULD YOU?! HOW COULD YOU NOT LIKE MY COOKING?
HA HA HA HA
UH... UNH... AAH... OHH...
H-HEY, TIA! STOP CHOKING HIM RIGHT NOW!
KIYO! STOP HER, WILL YOU?!
EE—

LEVEL 71: An Important Person

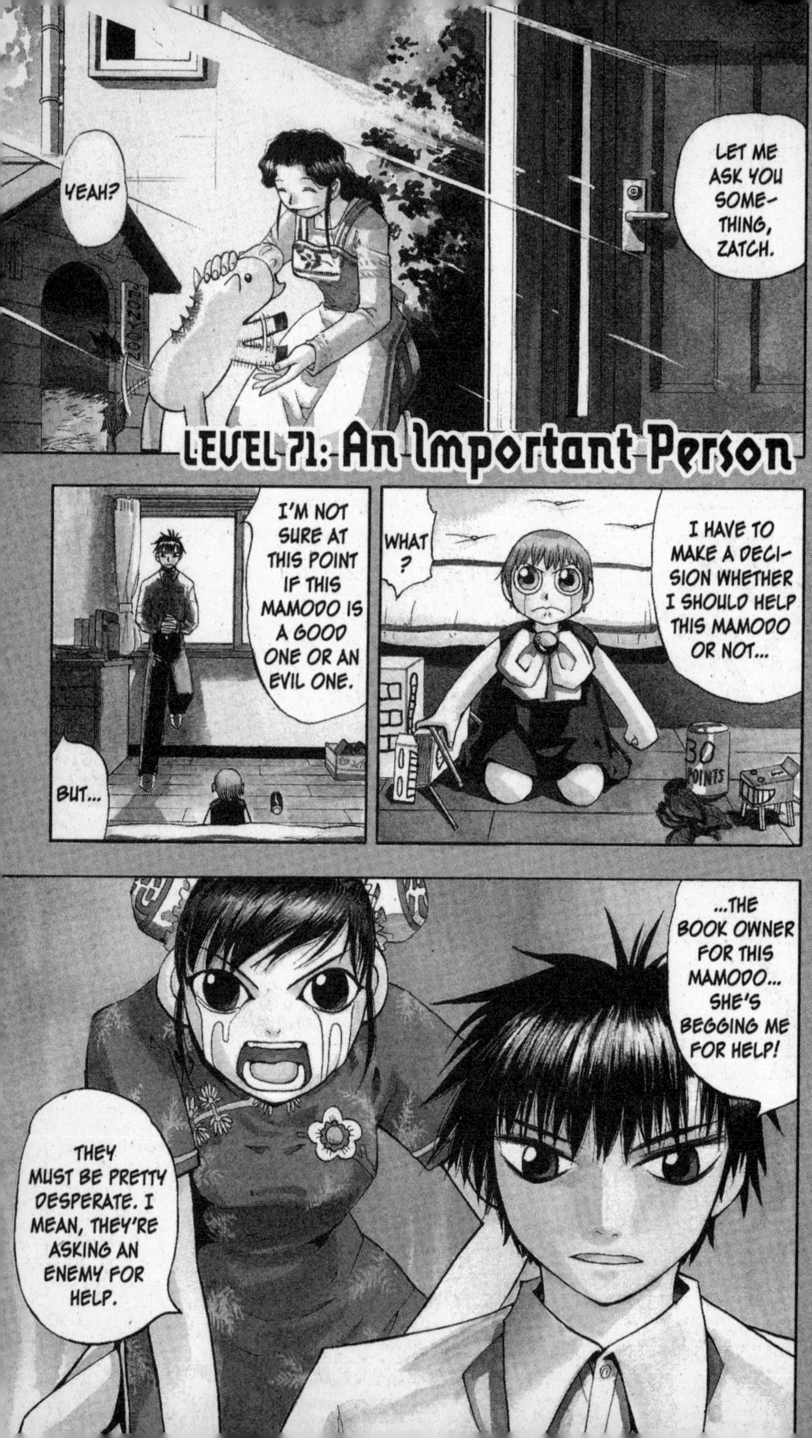
LET ME ASK YOU SOME-THING, ZATCH.
YEAH?
I HAVE TO MAKE A DECI-SION WHETHER I SHOULD HELP THIS MAMODO OR NOT...
WHAT?
I'M NOT SURE AT THIS POINT IF THIS MAMODO IS A GOOD ONE OR AN EVIL ONE.
BUT...
...THE BOOK OWNER FOR THIS MAMODO... SHE'S BEGGING ME FOR HELP!
THEY MUST BE PRETTY DESPERATE. I MEAN, THEY'RE ASKING AN ENEMY FOR HELP.
30 POINTS

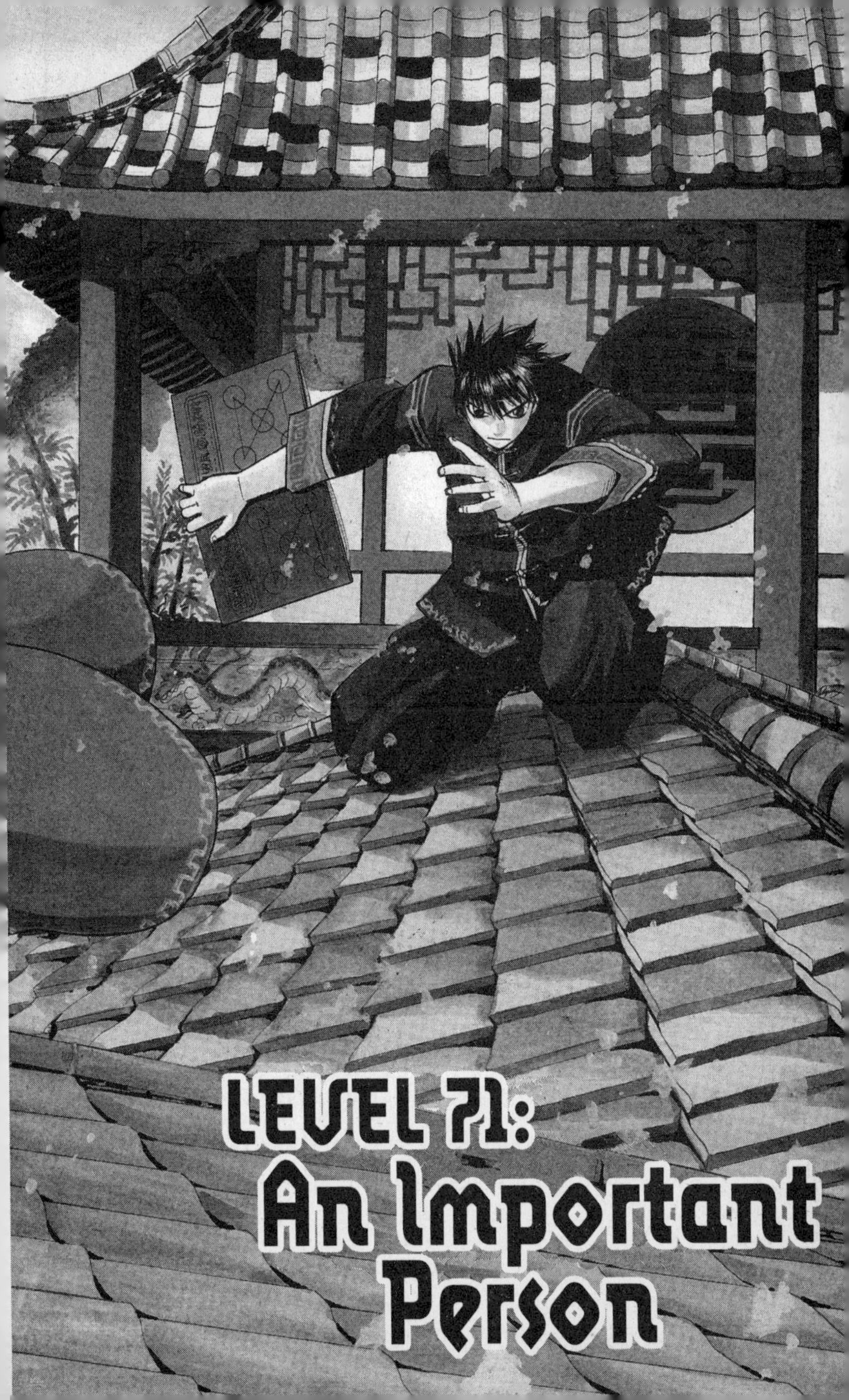
LEVEL 71:
An Important Person

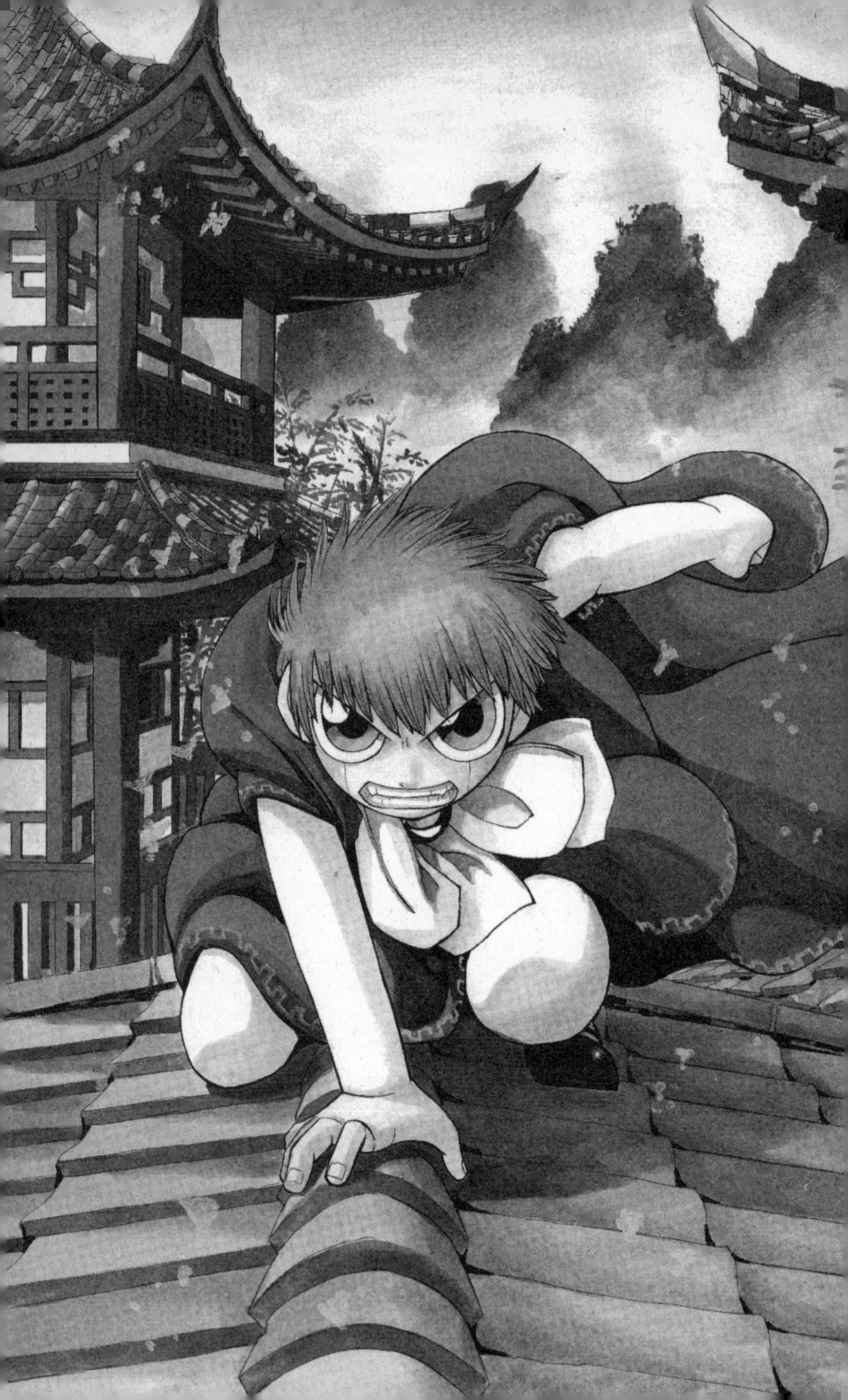

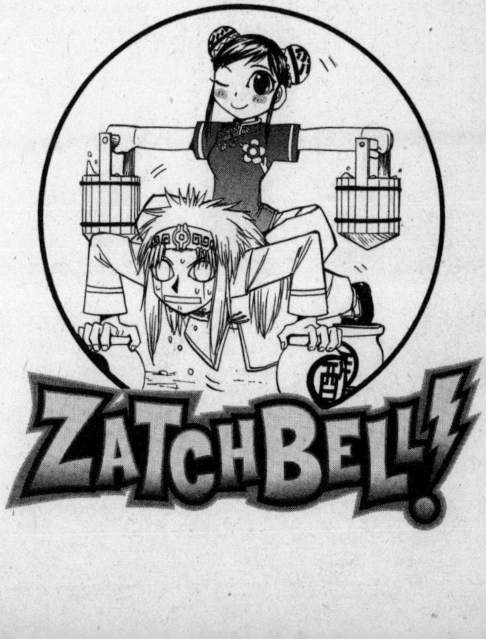

ZATCHBELL!

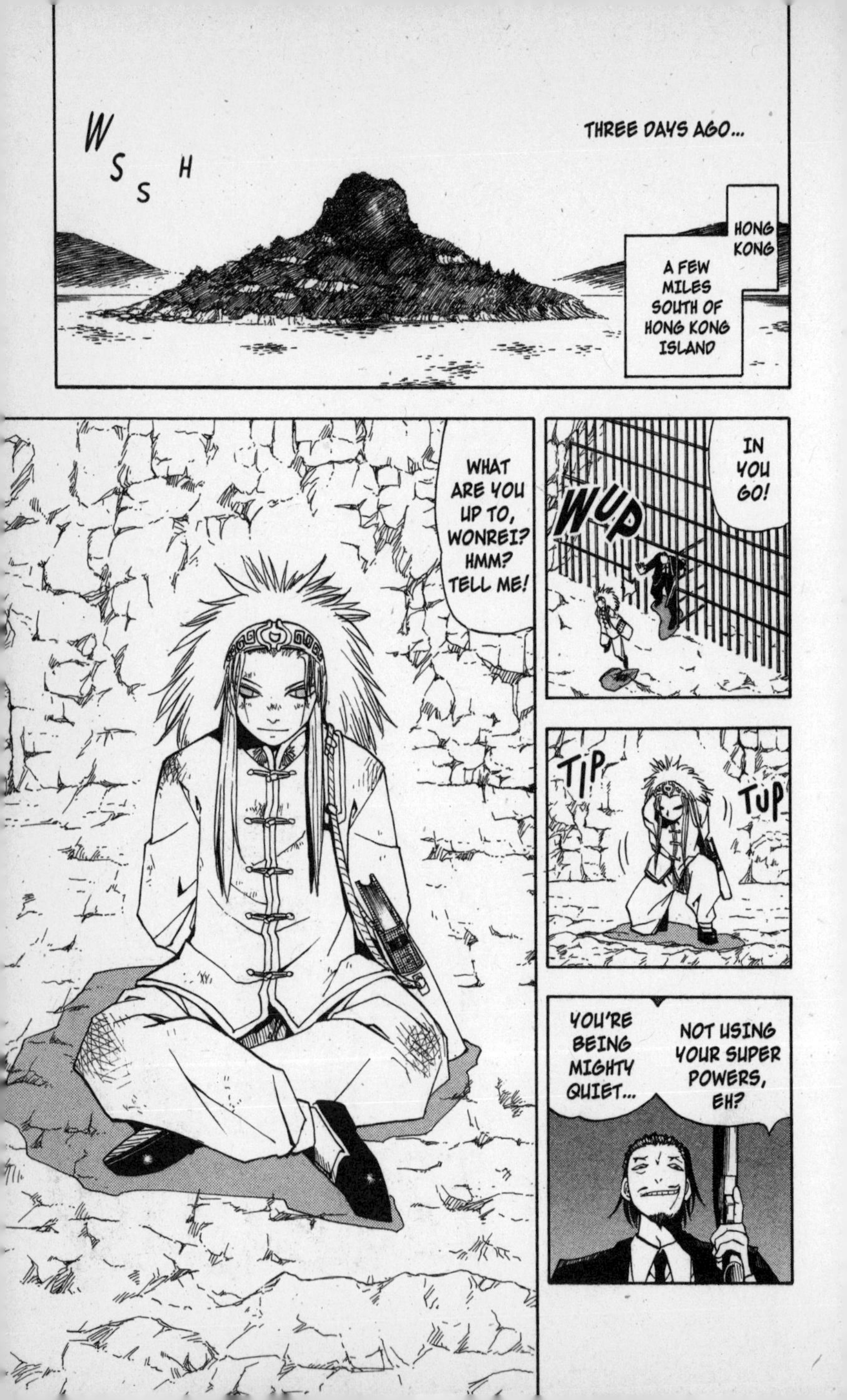
THREE DAYS AGO...
HONG KONG
A FEW MILES SOUTH OF HONG KONG ISLAND
WSSH
IN YOU GO!
WUP
TIP
TUP
YOU'RE BEING MIGHTY QUIET...
NOT USING YOUR SUPER POWERS, EH?
WHAT ARE YOU UP TO, WONREI? HMM? TELL ME!

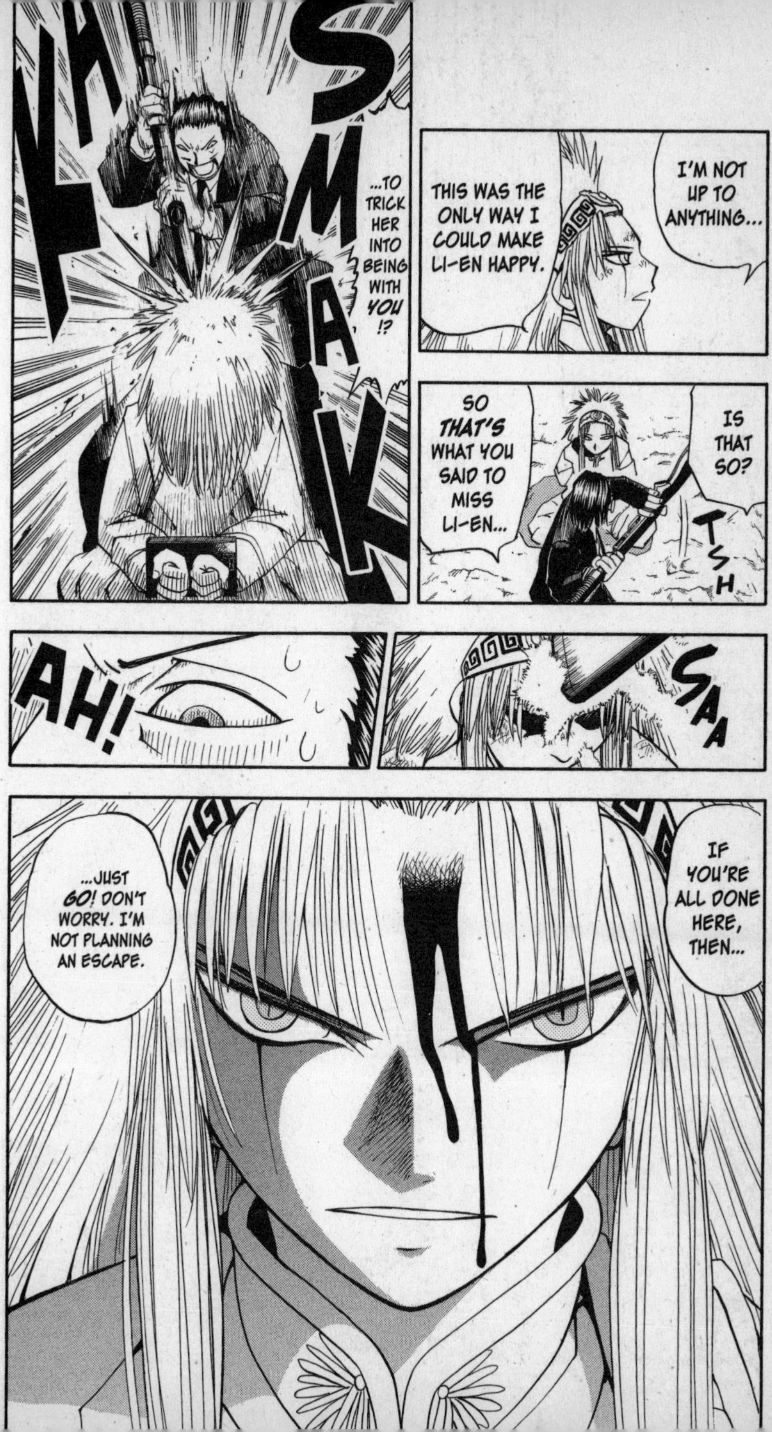
I'M NOT UP TO ANYTHING...
THIS WAS THE ONLY WAY I COULD MAKE LI-EN HAPPY.
IS THAT SO?
SO THAT'S WHAT YOU SAID TO MISS LI-EN...
TSH
...TO TRICK HER INTO BEING WITH YOU!?
SMAK
SAAA
AH!
IF YOU'RE ALL DONE HERE, THEN...
...JUST GO! DON'T WORRY. I'M NOT PLANNING AN ESCAPE.

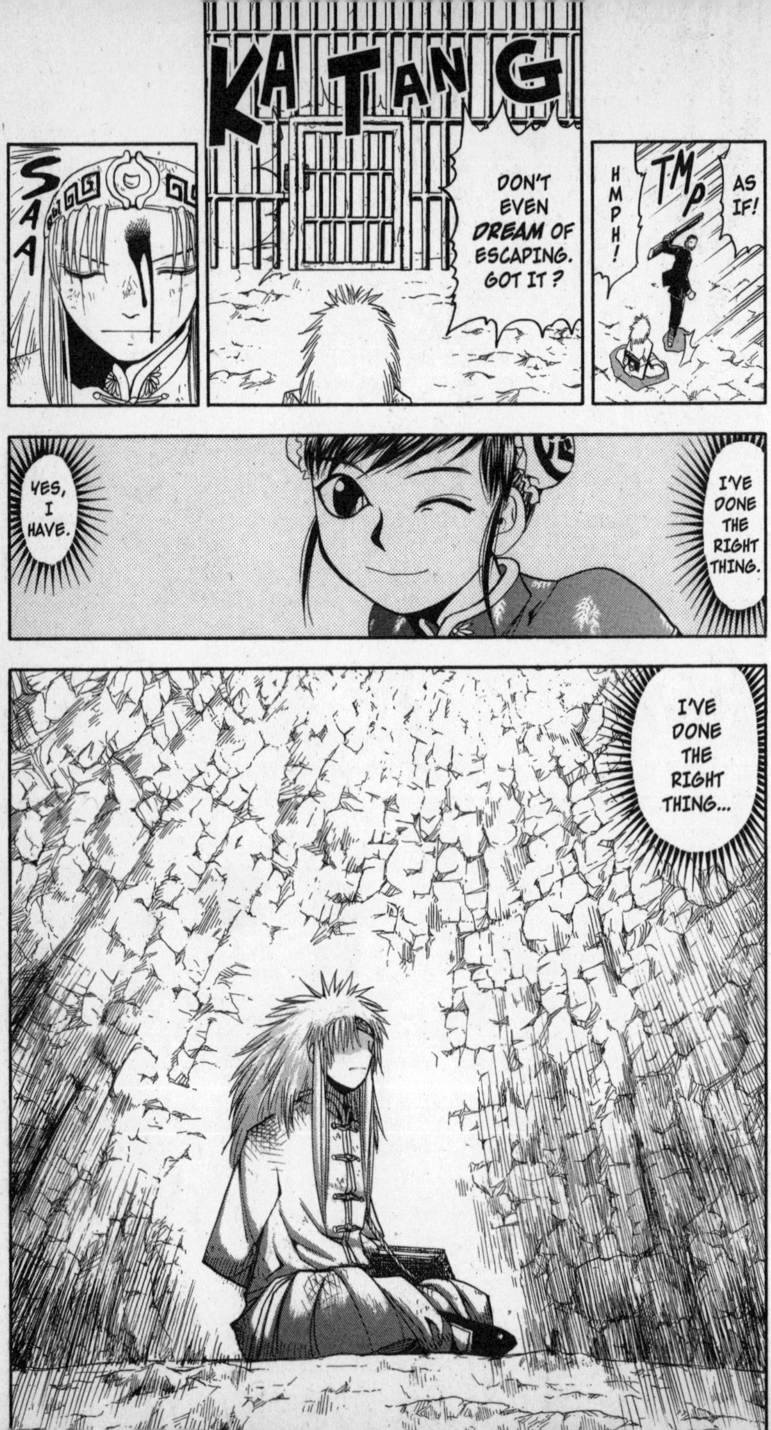
KATANG
DON'T EVEN DREAM OF ESCAPING. GOT IT?
HMPH!
TMP
AS IF!
SAA
I'VE DONE THE RIGHT THING.
YES, I HAVE.
I'VE DONE THE RIGHT THING...

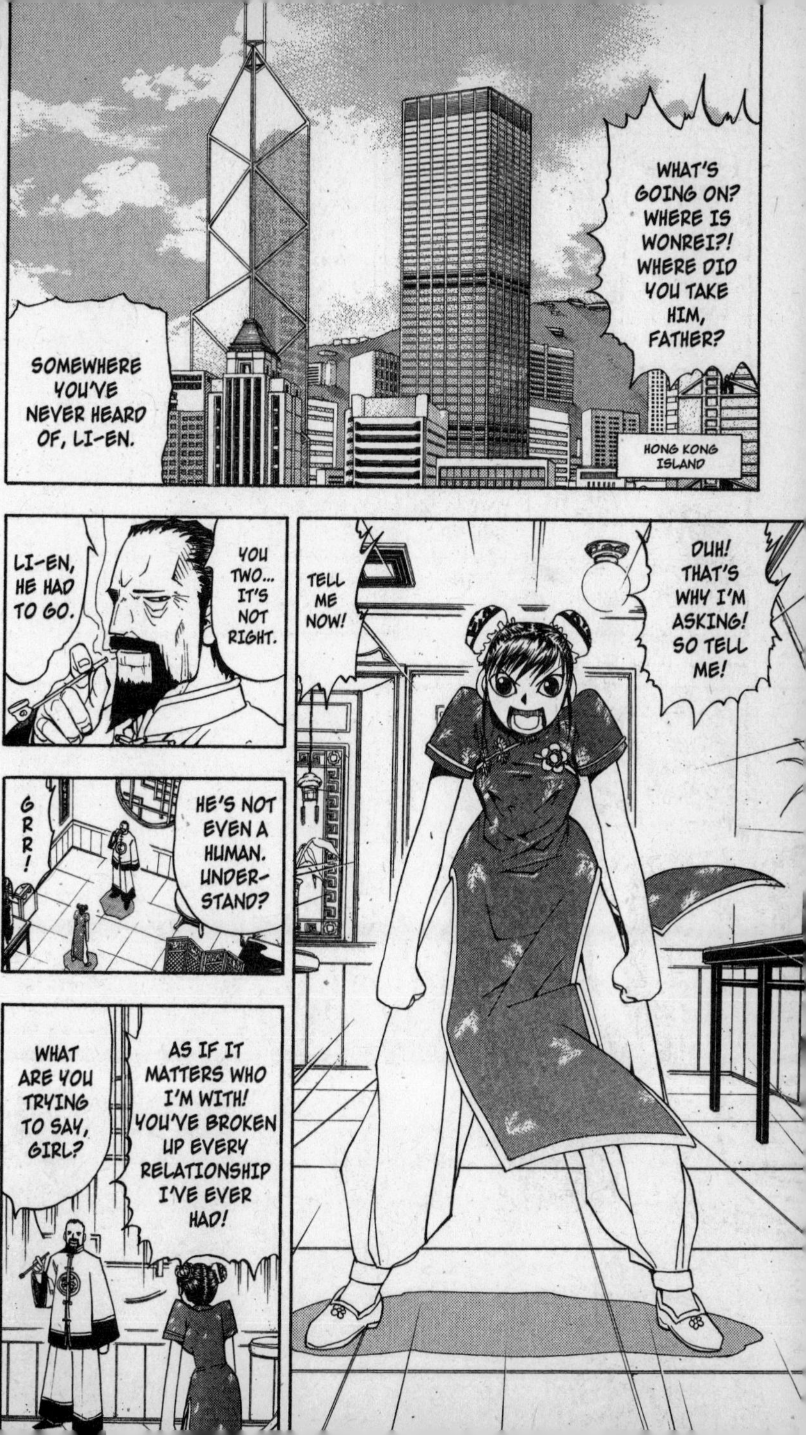
WHAT'S GOING ON? WHERE IS WONREI?! WHERE DID YOU TAKE HIM, FATHER?
SOMEWHERE YOU'VE NEVER HEARD OF, LI-EN.
HONG KONG ISLAND
TELL ME NOW!
LI-EN, HE HAD TO GO.
YOU TWO... IT'S NOT RIGHT.
HE'S NOT EVEN A HUMAN. UNDER-STAND?
GRR!
DUH! THAT'S WHY I'M ASKING! SO TELL ME!
AS IF IT MATTERS WHO I'M WITH! YOU'VE BROKEN UP EVERY RELATIONSHIP I'VE EVER HAD!
WHAT ARE YOU TRYING TO SAY, GIRL?

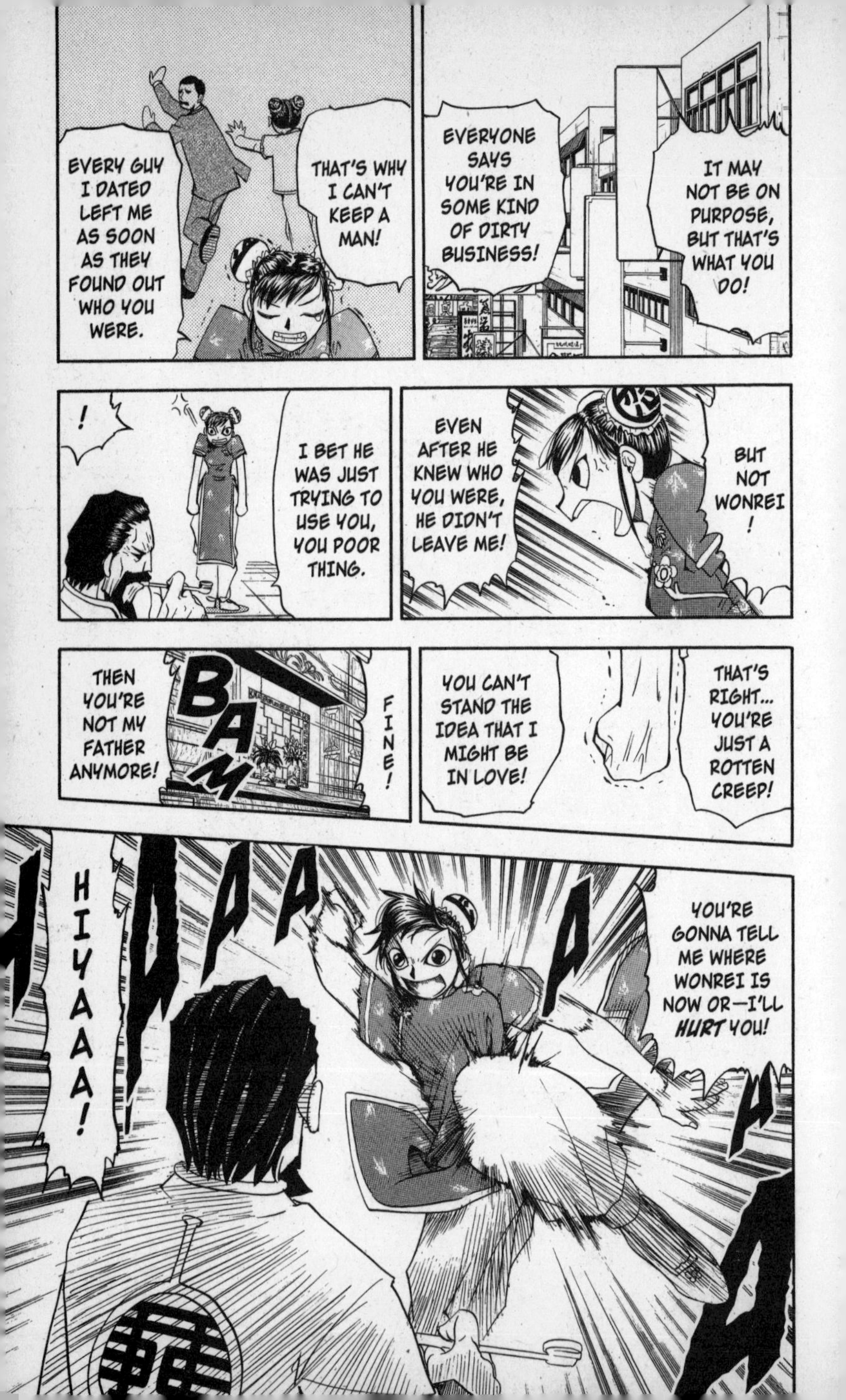
IT MAY NOT BE ON PURPOSE, BUT THAT'S WHAT YOU DO!
EVERYONE SAYS YOU'RE IN SOME KIND OF DIRTY BUSINESS!
THAT'S WHY I CAN'T KEEP A MAN!
EVERY GUY I DATED LEFT ME AS SOON AS THEY FOUND OUT WHO YOU WERE.
BUT NOT WONREI!
EVEN AFTER HE KNEW WHO YOU WERE, HE DIDN'T LEAVE ME!
I BET HE WAS JUST TRYING TO USE YOU, YOU POOR THING.
!
THAT'S RIGHT... YOU'RE JUST A ROTTEN CREEP!
YOU CAN'T STAND THE IDEA THAT I MIGHT BE IN LOVE!
FINE!
BAM
THEN YOU'RE NOT MY FATHER ANYMORE!
YOU'RE GONNA TELL ME WHERE WONREI IS NOW OR—I'LL *HURT* YOU!
HIYAAAA!

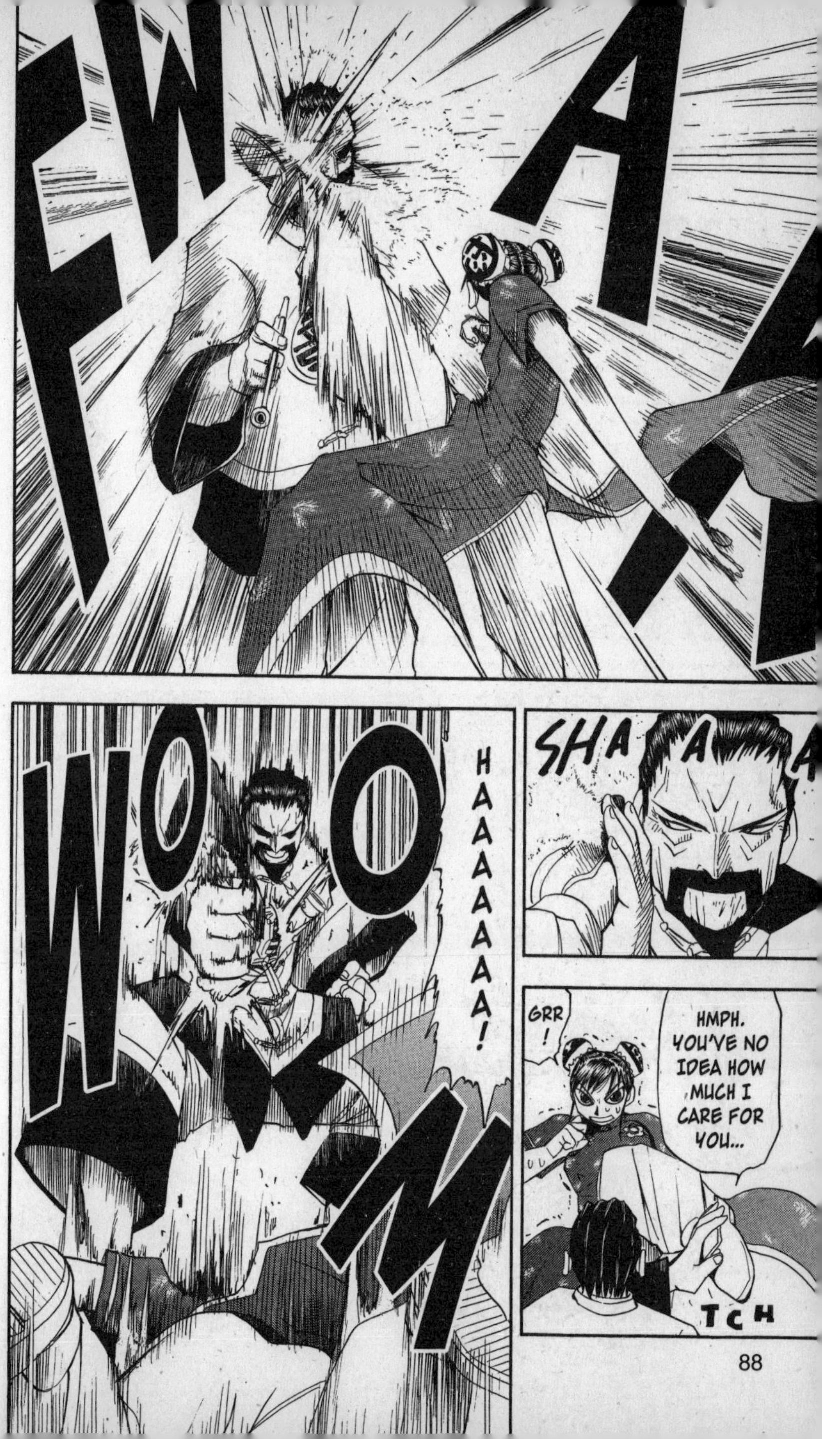
FW
A
SHAAA
GRR!
HMPH. YOU'VE NO IDEA HOW MUCH I CARE FOR YOU...
TCH
WOOM
HAAAAAAAAA!

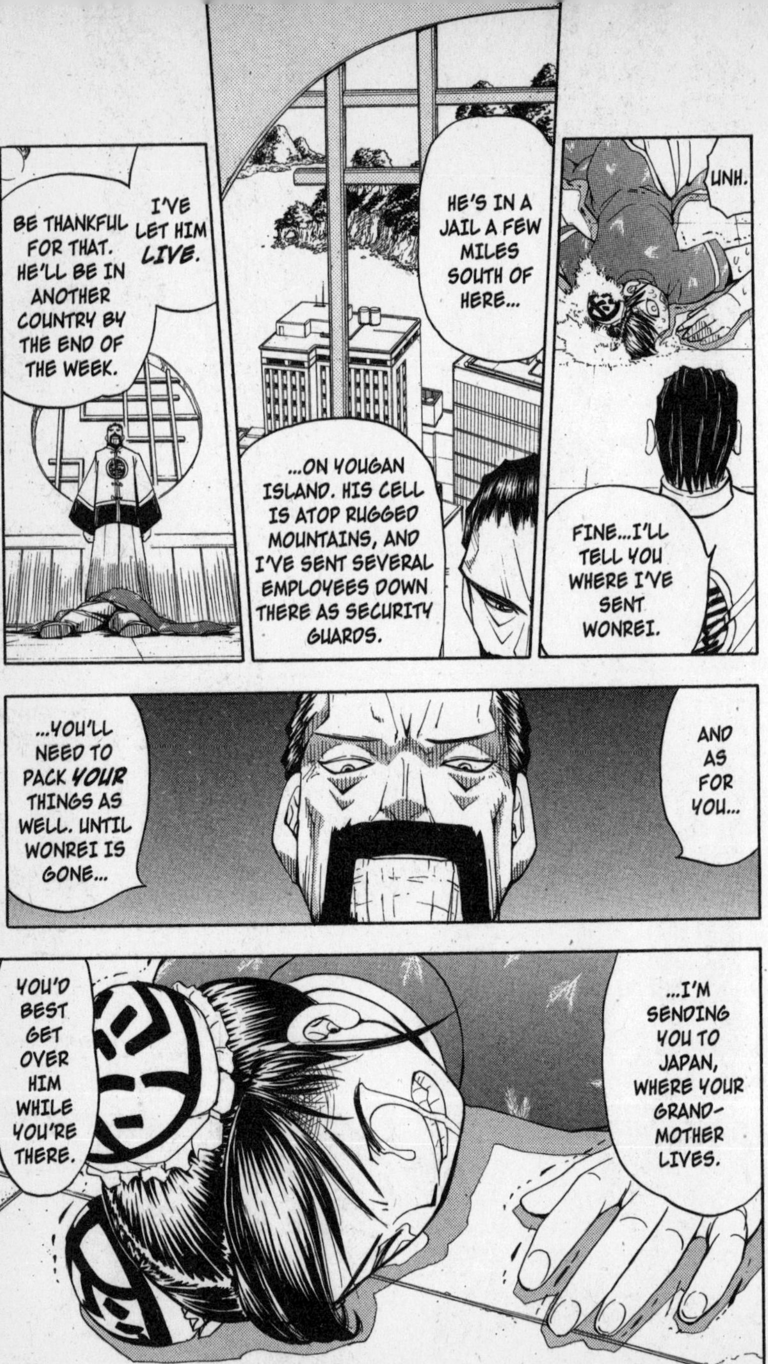
UNH.
FINE...I'LL TELL YOU WHERE I'VE SENT WONREI.
HE'S IN A JAIL A FEW MILES SOUTH OF HERE...
...ON YOUGAN ISLAND. HIS CELL IS ATOP RUGGED MOUNTAINS, AND I'VE SENT SEVERAL EMPLOYEES DOWN THERE AS SECURITY GUARDS.
I'VE LET HIM *LIVE*.
BE THANKFUL FOR THAT. HE'LL BE IN ANOTHER COUNTRY BY THE END OF THE WEEK.
AND AS FOR YOU...
...YOU'LL NEED TO PACK *YOUR* THINGS AS WELL. UNTIL WONREI IS GONE...
...I'M SENDING YOU TO JAPAN, WHERE YOUR GRAND-MOTHER LIVES.
YOU'D BEST GET OVER HIM WHILE YOU'RE THERE.

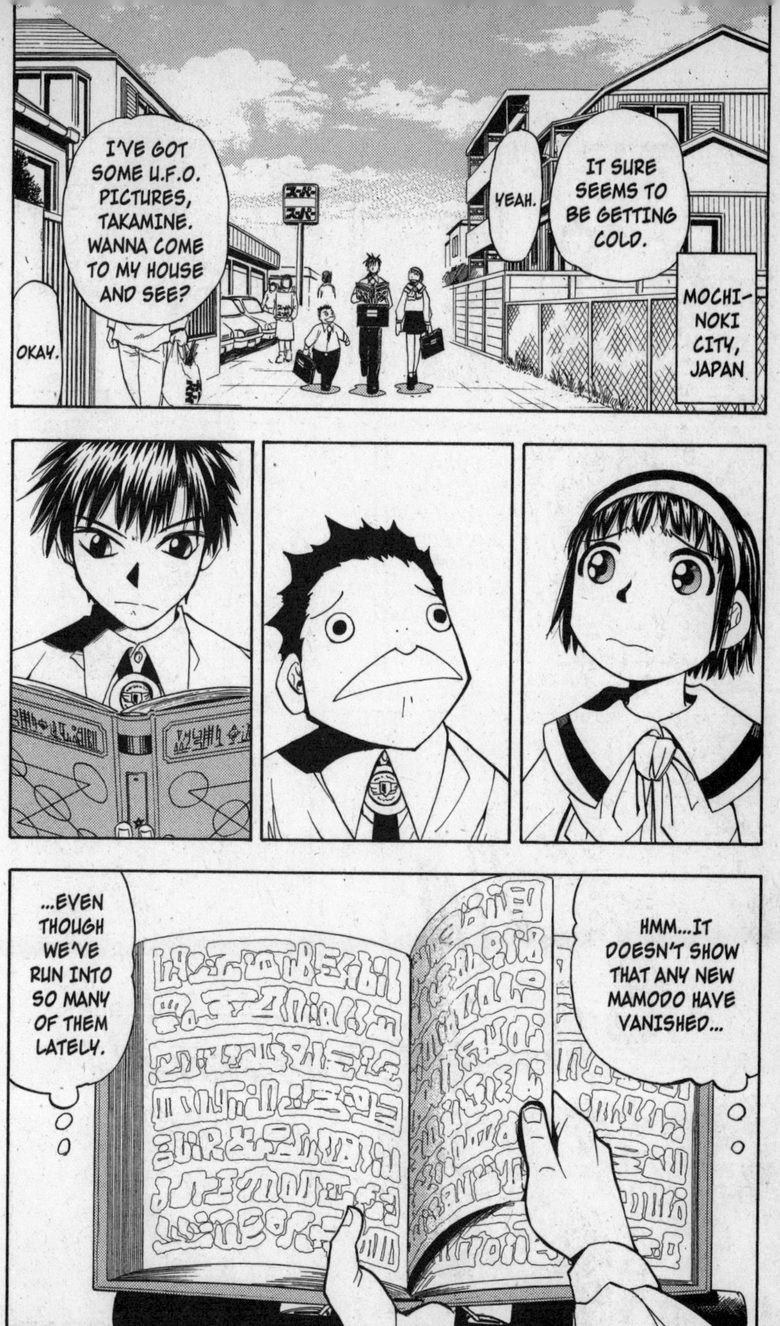
MOCHI-NOKI CITY, JAPAN
IT SURE SEEMS TO BE GETTING COLD.
YEAH.
I'VE GOT SOME U.F.O. PICTURES, TAKAMINE. WANNA COME TO MY HOUSE AND SEE?
OKAY.
HMM...IT DOESN'T SHOW THAT ANY NEW MAMODO HAVE VANISHED...
...EVEN THOUGH WE'VE RUN INTO SO MANY OF THEM LATELY.

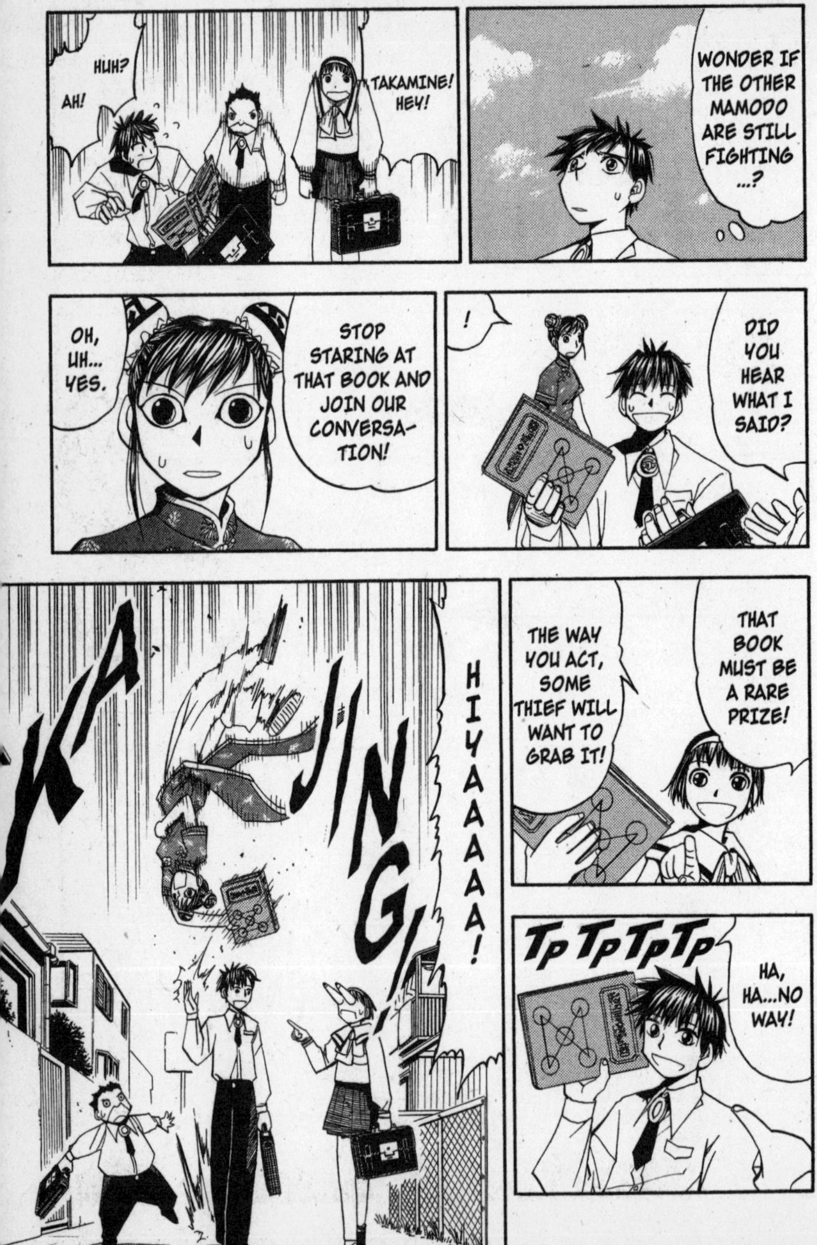
WONDER IF THE OTHER MAMODO ARE STILL FIGHTING ...?
TAKAMINE! HEY!
HUH?
AH!
DID YOU HEAR WHAT I SAID?
!
STOP STARING AT THAT BOOK AND JOIN OUR CONVERSA-TION!
OH, UH... YES.
THAT BOOK MUST BE A RARE PRIZE!
THE WAY YOU ACT, SOME THIEF WILL WANT TO GRAB IT!
TP TP TP TP
HA, HA...NO WAY!
HIYAAAAAA!
KA JING!

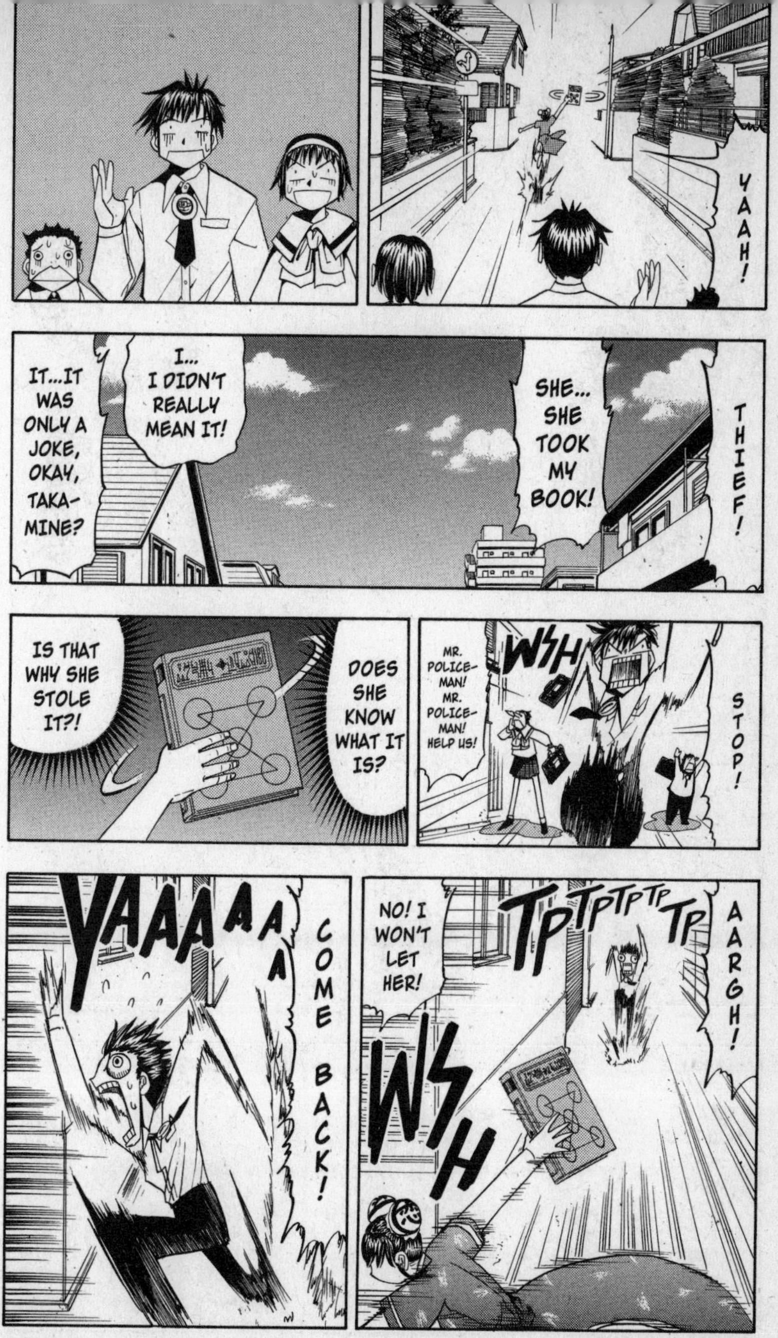
YAAAH!
THIEF!
SHE... SHE TOOK MY BOOK!
I... I DIDN'T REALLY MEAN IT!
IT...IT WAS ONLY A JOKE, OKAY, TAKAMINE?
STOP!
WSH
MR. POLICEMAN! MR. POLICEMAN! HELP US!
DOES SHE KNOW WHAT IT IS?
IS THAT WHY SHE STOLE IT?!
AARGH!
TPTPTPTPTP
NO! I WON'T LET HER!
WSH
COME BACK!
YAAAAAAA

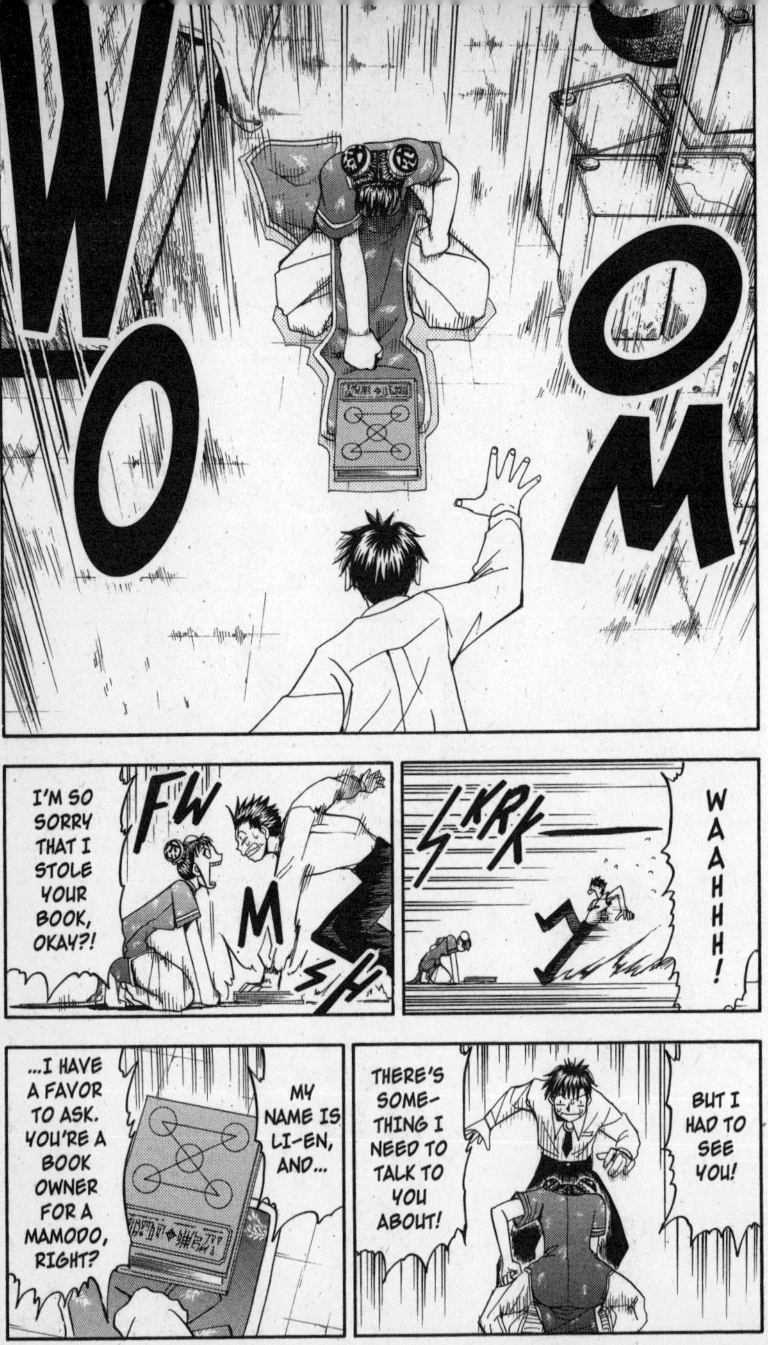
WOOM
SKRK
WAAHHH!
FWMSH
I'M SO SORRY THAT I STOLE YOUR BOOK, OKAY?!
BUT I HAD TO SEE YOU!
THERE'S SOME-THING I NEED TO TALK TO YOU ABOUT!
MY NAME IS LI-EN, AND...
...I HAVE A FAVOR TO ASK. YOU'RE A BOOK OWNER FOR A MAMODO, RIGHT?

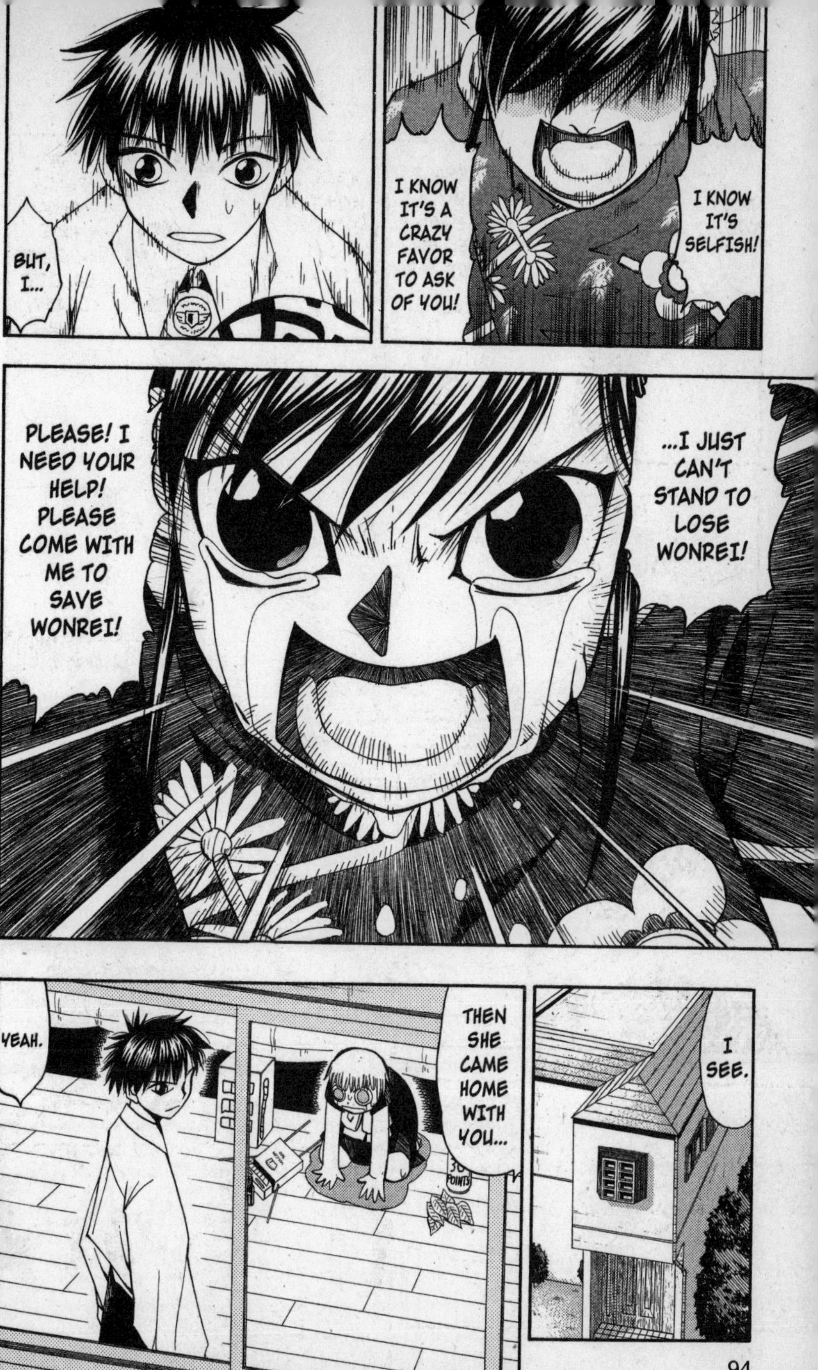
I KNOW IT'S SELFISH!
I KNOW IT'S A CRAZY FAVOR TO ASK OF YOU!
BUT, I...
...I JUST CAN'T STAND TO LOSE WONREI!
PLEASE! I NEED YOUR HELP! PLEASE COME WITH ME TO SAVE WONREI!
I SEE.
THEN SHE CAME HOME WITH YOU...
YEAH.
30 POINTS

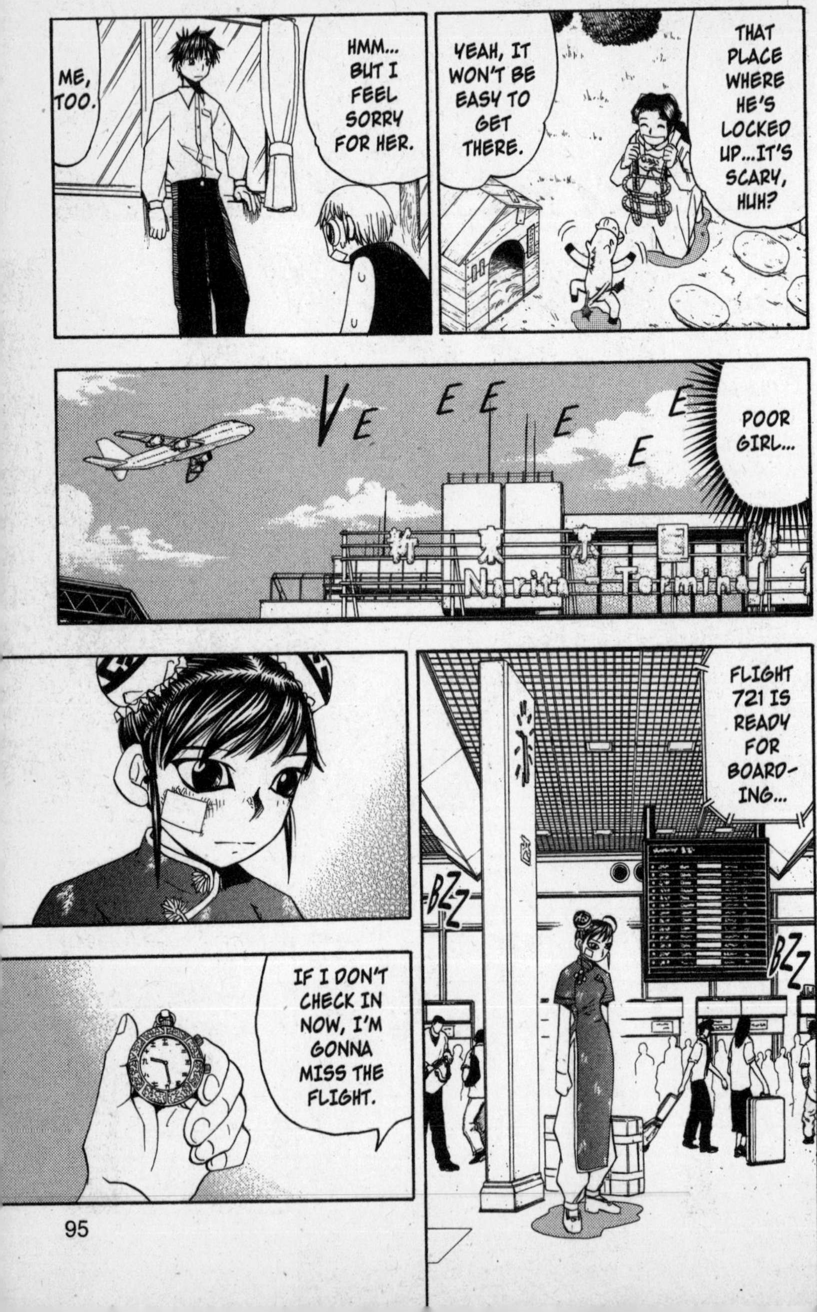
THAT PLACE WHERE HE'S LOCKED UP...IT'S SCARY, HUH?
YEAH, IT WON'T BE EASY TO GET THERE.
HMM... BUT I FEEL SORRY FOR HER.
ME, TOO.
POOR GIRL...
VEEEEEE
Narita Terminal 1
FLIGHT 721 IS READY FOR BOARDING...
BZZ
BZZ
IF I DON'T CHECK IN NOW, I'M GONNA MISS THE FLIGHT.

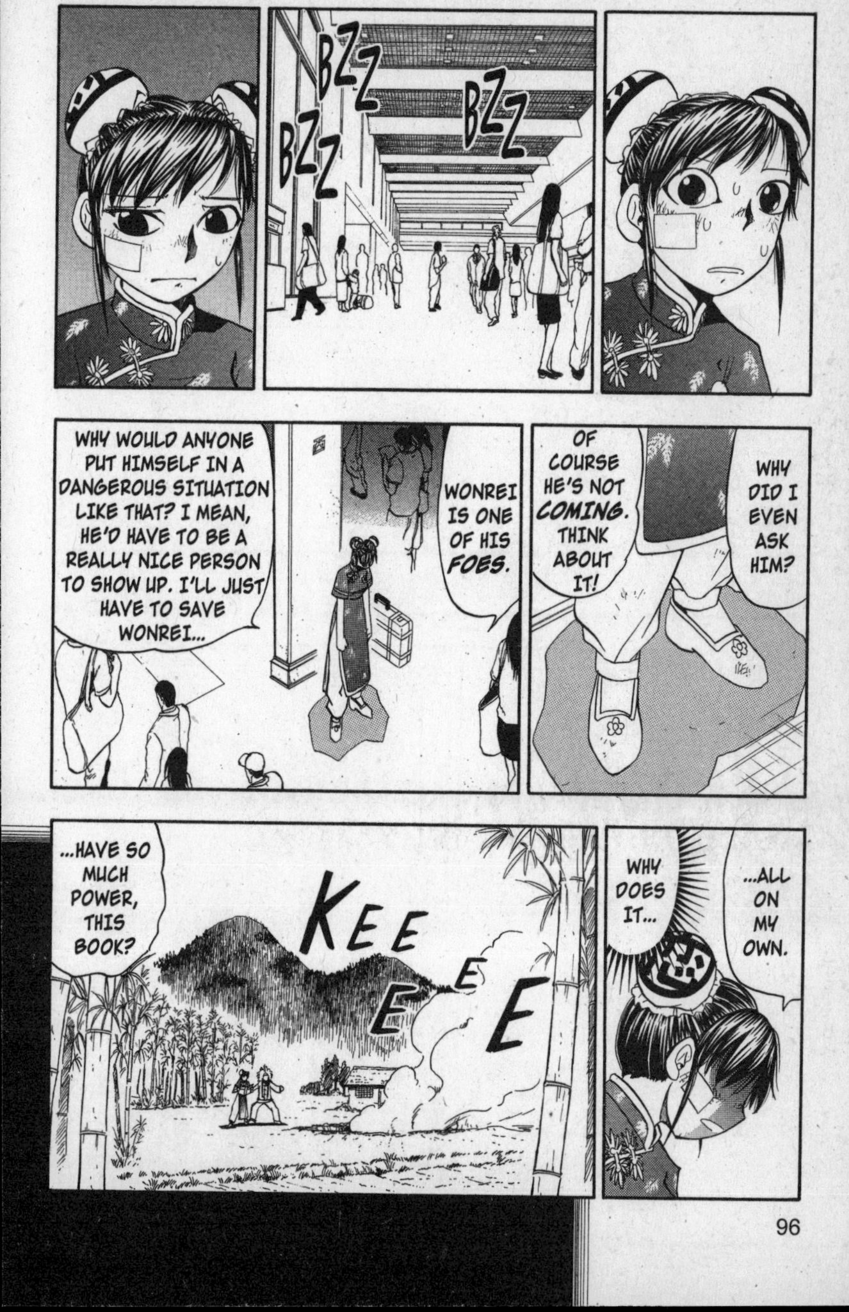
BZZ
BZZ
WHY DID I EVEN ASK HIM?
OF COURSE HE'S NOT COMING. THINK ABOUT IT!
WONREI IS ONE OF HIS FOES.
WHY WOULD ANYONE PUT HIMSELF IN A DANGEROUS SITUATION LIKE THAT? I MEAN, HE'D HAVE TO BE A REALLY NICE PERSON TO SHOW UP. I'LL JUST HAVE TO SAVE WONREI...
...ALL ON MY OWN.
WHY DOES IT...
...HAVE SO MUCH POWER, THIS BOOK?
KEEEEE

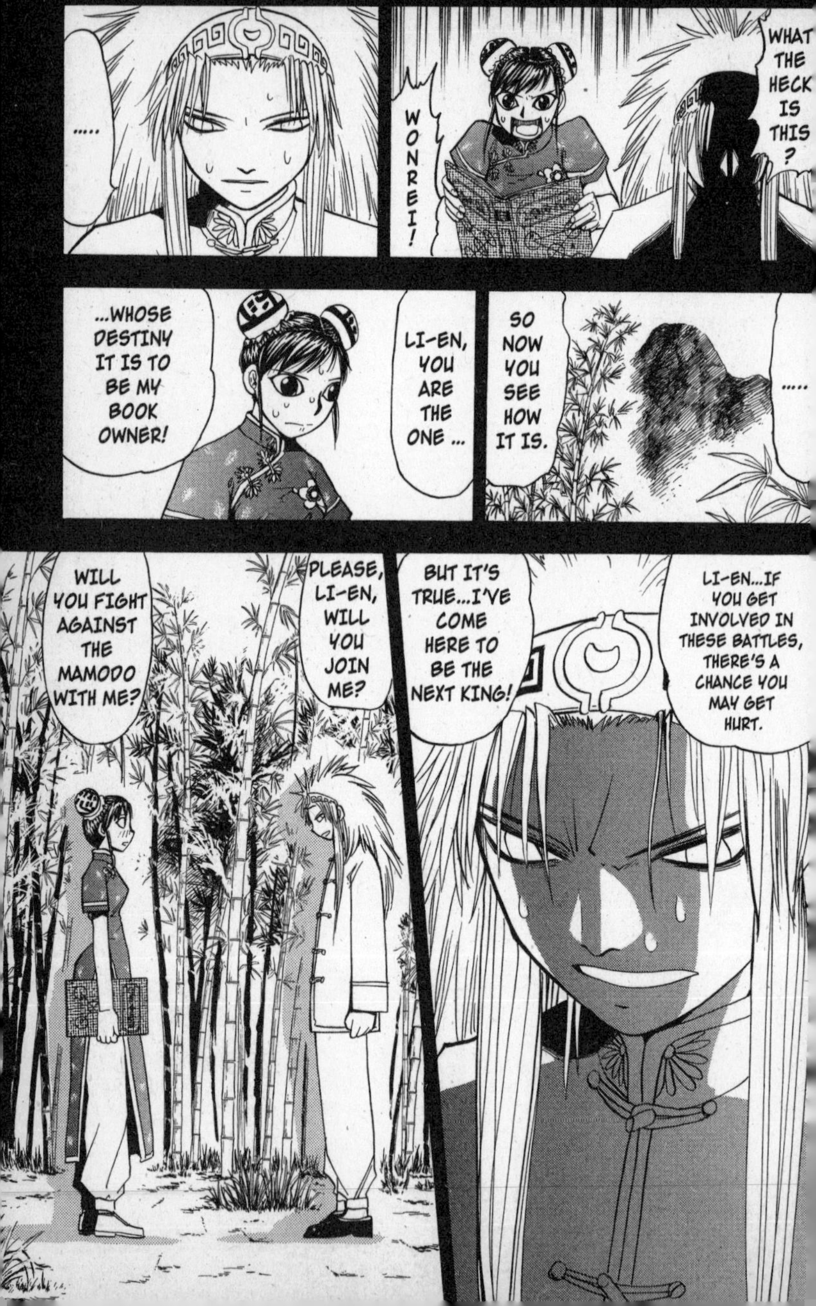
WHAT THE HECK IS THIS?
WONREI!
.....
.....
SO NOW YOU SEE HOW IT IS.
LI-EN, YOU ARE THE ONE ...
...WHOSE DESTINY IT IS TO BE MY BOOK OWNER!
LI-EN...IF YOU GET INVOLVED IN THESE BATTLES, THERE'S A CHANCE YOU MAY GET HURT.
BUT IT'S TRUE...I'VE COME HERE TO BE THE NEXT KING!
PLEASE, LI-EN, WILL YOU JOIN ME?
WILL YOU FIGHT AGAINST THE MAMODO WITH ME?

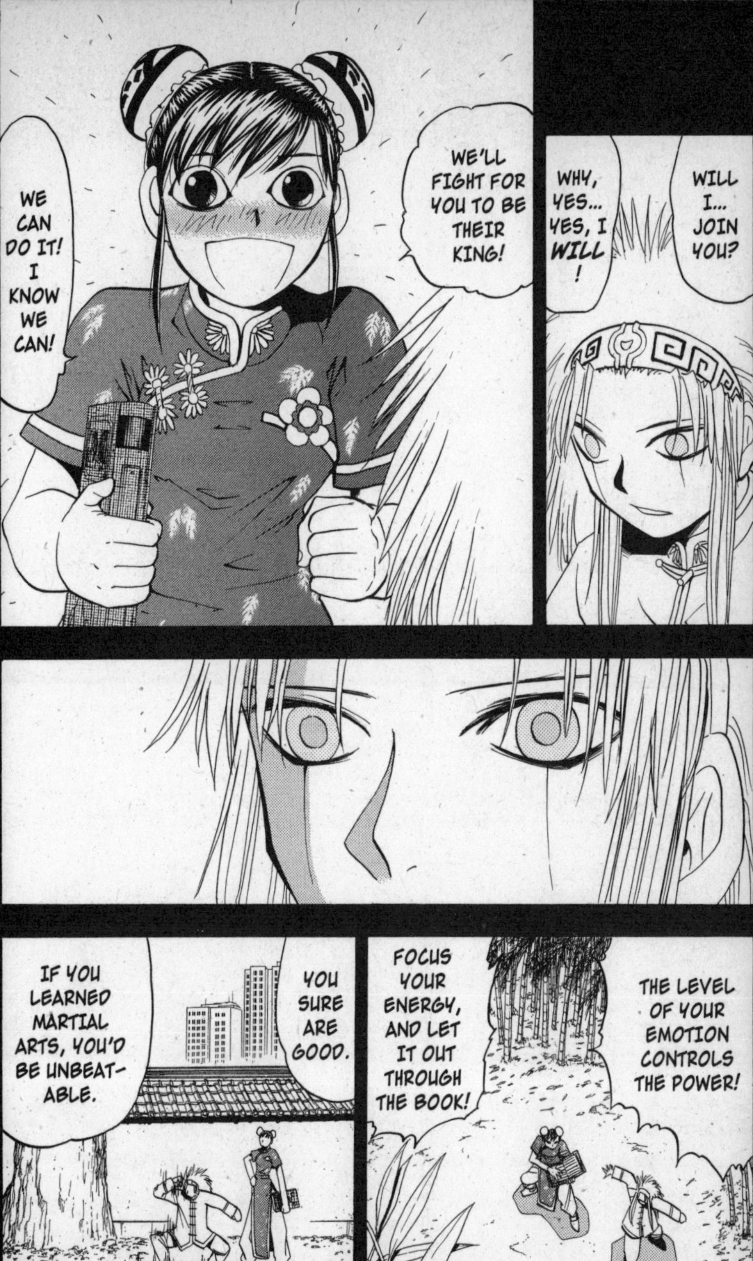
WILL I... JOIN YOU?
WHY, YES... YES, I WILL!
WE'LL FIGHT FOR YOU TO BE THEIR KING!
WE CAN DO IT! I KNOW WE CAN!
THE LEVEL OF YOUR EMOTION CONTROLS THE POWER!
FOCUS YOUR ENERGY, AND LET IT OUT THROUGH THE BOOK!
YOU SURE ARE GOOD.
IF YOU LEARNED MARTIAL ARTS, YOU'D BE UNBEAT-ABLE.

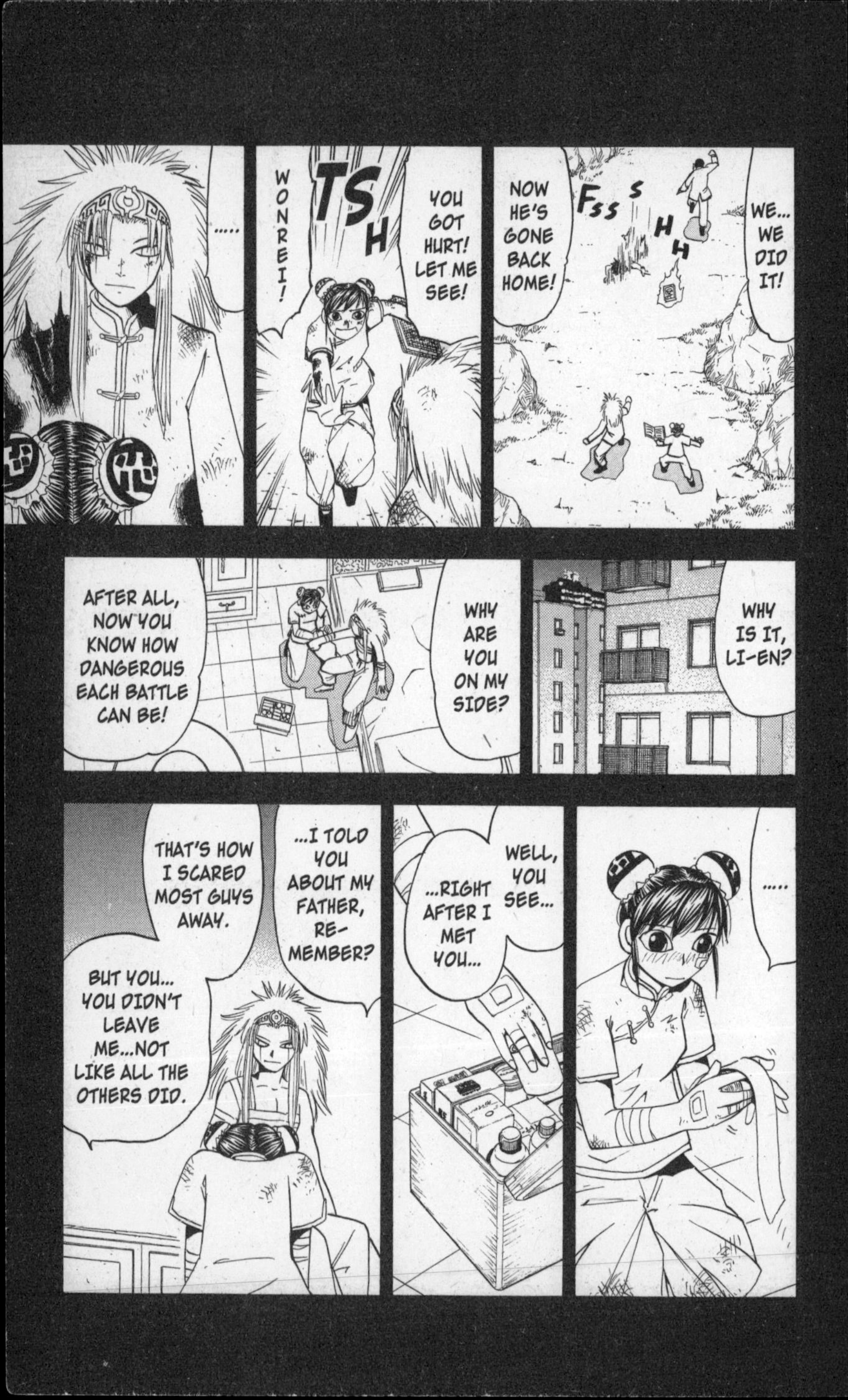
WE... WE DID IT!
FSSSHHH
NOW HE'S GONE BACK HOME!
YOU GOT HURT! LET ME SEE!
TSH
WONREI!
.....
WHY IS IT, LI-EN?
WHY ARE YOU ON MY SIDE?
AFTER ALL, NOW YOU KNOW HOW DANGEROUS EACH BATTLE CAN BE!
.....
WELL, YOU SEE...
...RIGHT AFTER I MET YOU...
...I TOLD YOU ABOUT MY FATHER, RE-MEMBER?
THAT'S HOW I SCARED MOST GUYS AWAY.
BUT YOU... YOU DIDN'T LEAVE ME...NOT LIKE ALL THE OTHERS DID.

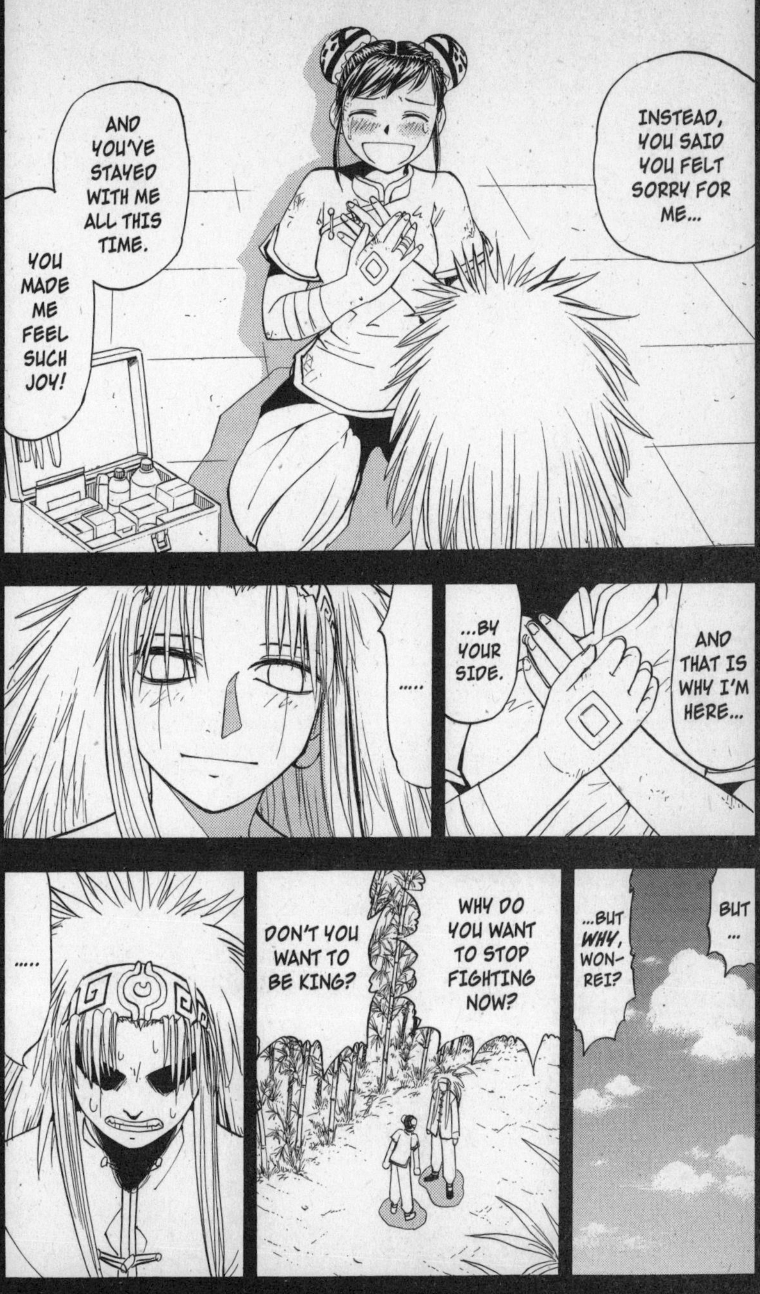
INSTEAD, YOU SAID YOU FELT SORRY FOR ME...
AND YOU'VE STAYED WITH ME ALL THIS TIME.
YOU MADE ME FEEL SUCH JOY!
AND THAT IS WHY I'M HERE...
...BY YOUR SIDE.
.....
BUT ...
...BUT WHY, WON-REI?
WHY DO YOU WANT TO STOP FIGHTING NOW?
DON'T YOU WANT TO BE KING?
.....

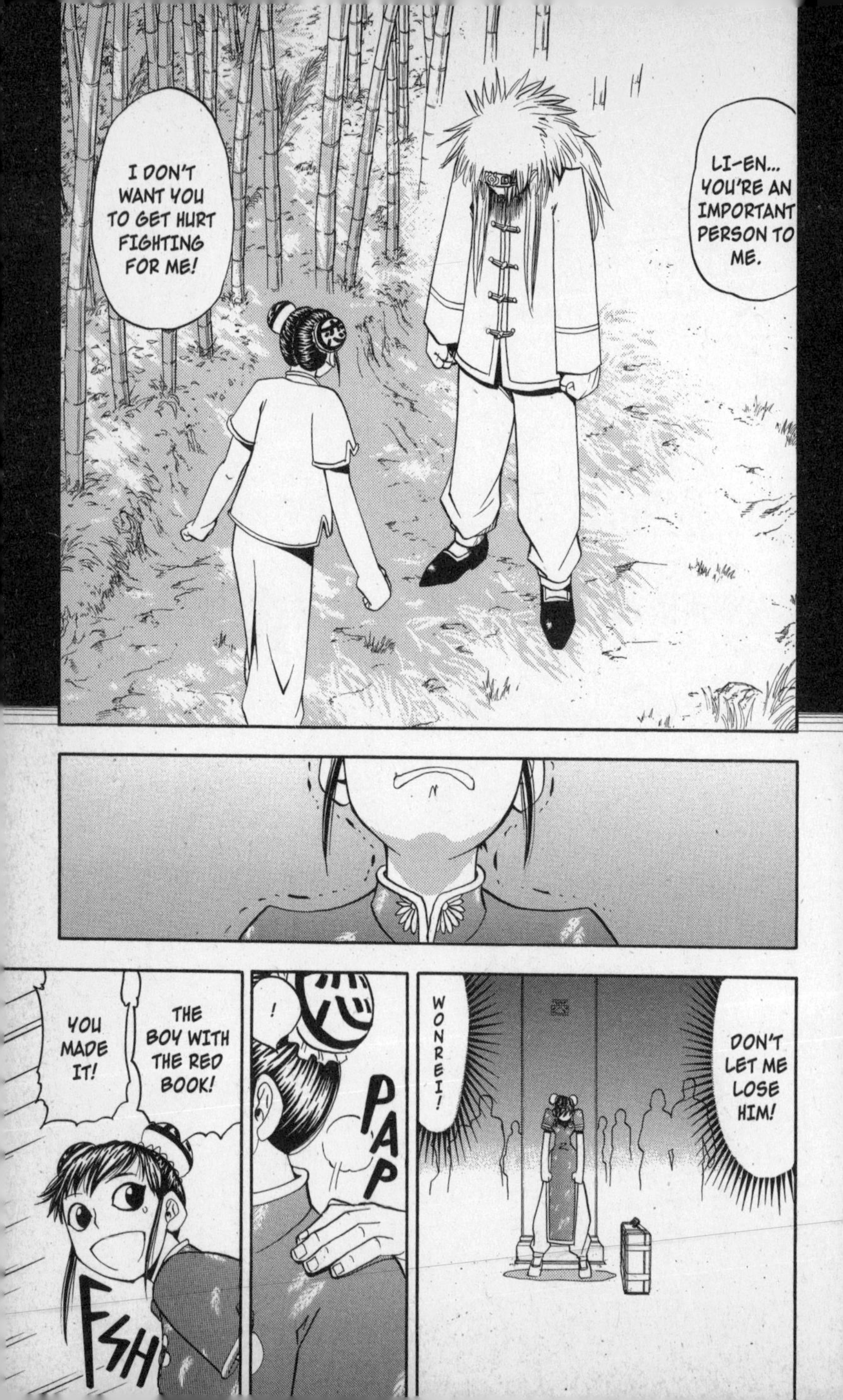
LI-EN... YOU'RE AN IMPORTANT PERSON TO ME.
I DON'T WANT YOU TO GET HURT FIGHTING FOR ME!
DON'T LET ME LOSE HIM!
WONREI!
!
PAP
THE BOY WITH THE RED BOOK!
YOU MADE IT!
FSH

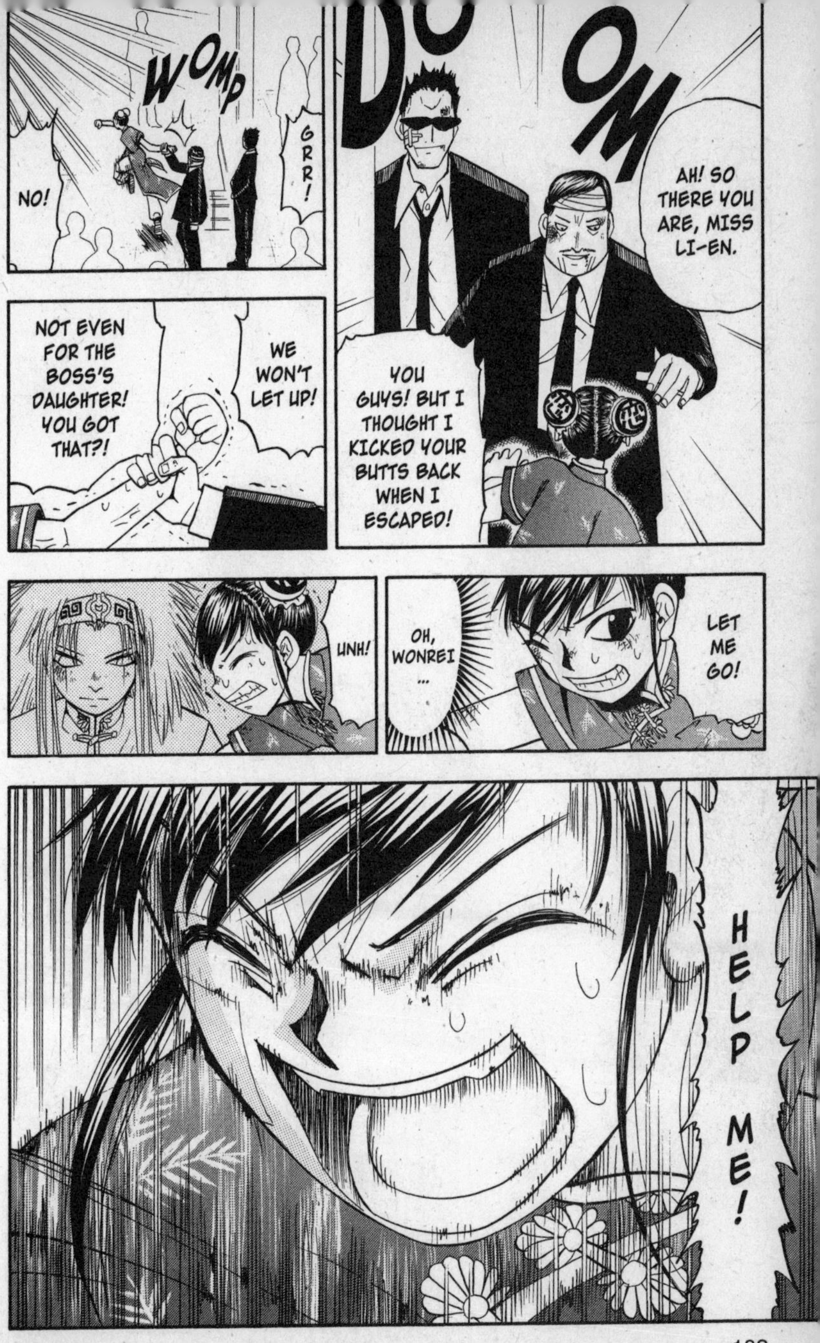
DOOM
AH! SO THERE YOU ARE, MISS LI-EN.
YOU GUYS! BUT I THOUGHT I KICKED YOUR BUTTS BACK WHEN I ESCAPED!
GRR!
WOMP
NO!
WE WON'T LET UP!
NOT EVEN FOR THE BOSS'S DAUGHTER! YOU GOT THAT?!
LET ME GO!
OH, WONREI ...
UNH!
HELP ME!

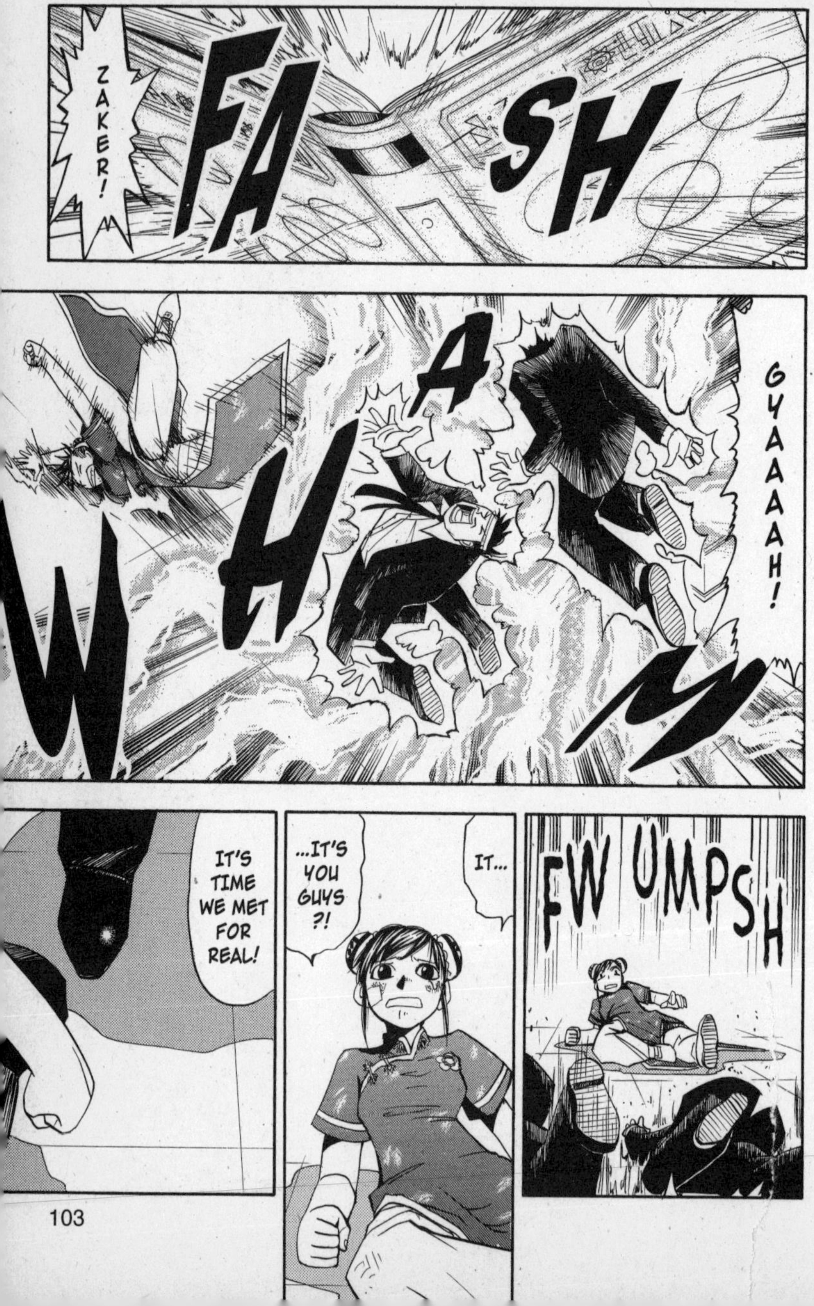
ZAKER!
FA-SH
GYAAAAAH!
WHAM
FWUMPSH
IT...
...IT'S YOU GUYS?!
IT'S TIME WE MET FOR REAL!

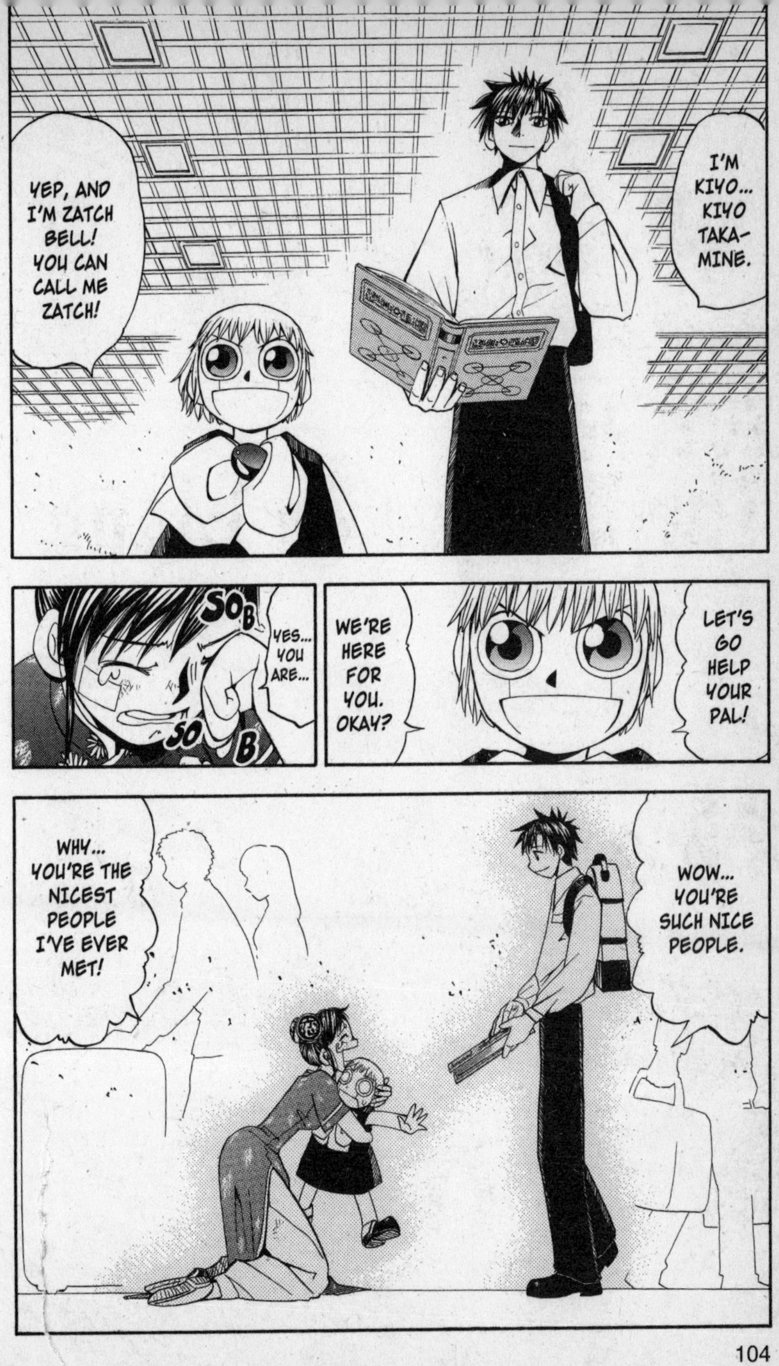
I'M KIYO... KIYO TAKA-MINE.
YEP, AND I'M ZATCH BELL! YOU CAN CALL ME ZATCH!
LET'S GO HELP YOUR PAL!
WE'RE HERE FOR YOU. OKAY?
SOB
YES... YOU ARE...
SOB
WOW... YOU'RE SUCH NICE PEOPLE.
WHY... YOU'RE THE NICEST PEOPLE I'VE EVER MET!

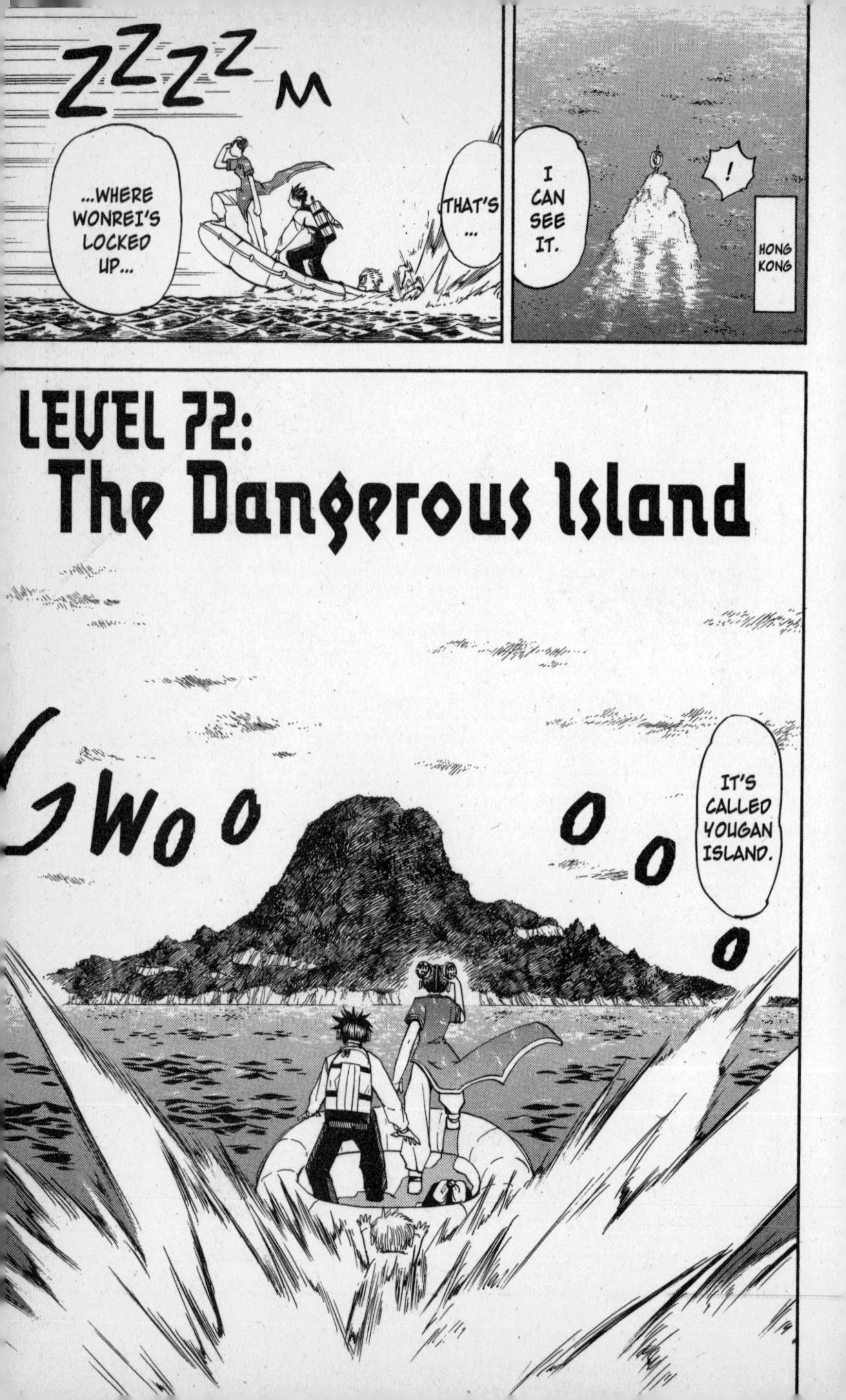
HONG KONG
!
I CAN SEE IT.
THAT'S ...
...WHERE WONREI'S LOCKED UP...
ZZZZZM
LEVEL 72: The Dangerous Island
IT'S CALLED YOUGAN ISLAND.
GWOOOOO

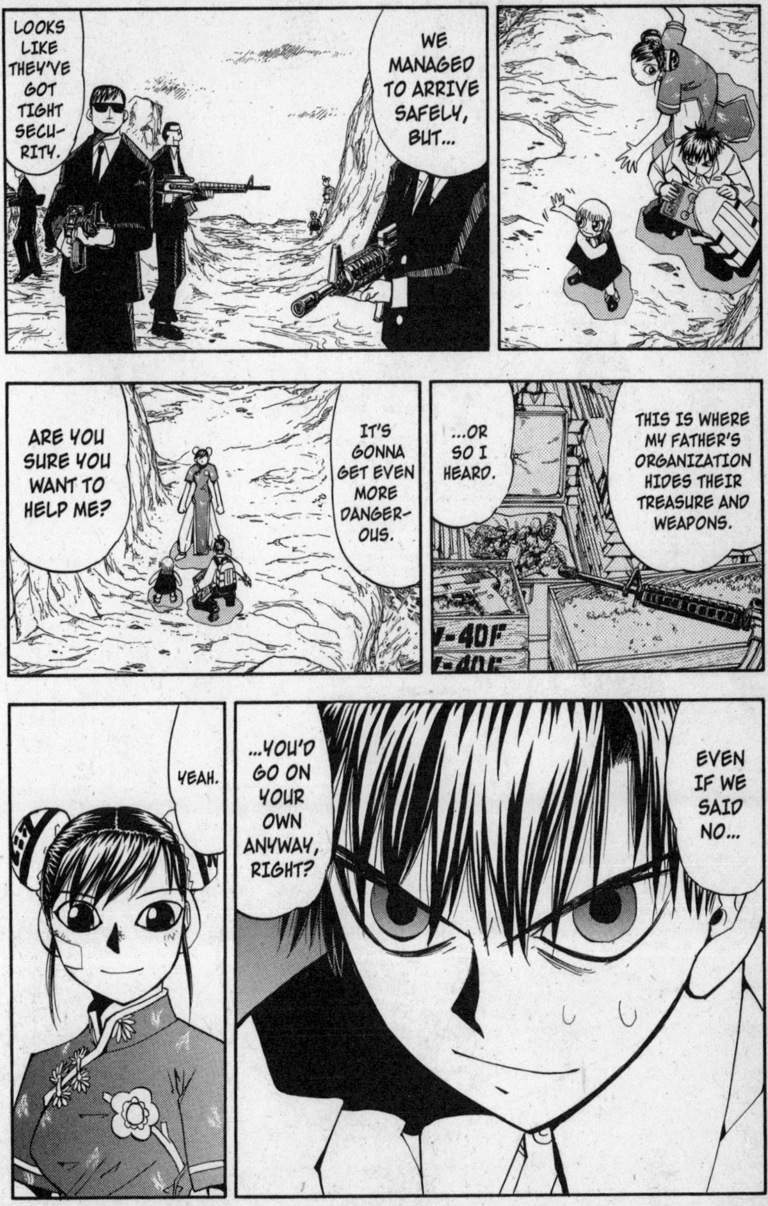
WE MANAGED TO ARRIVE SAFELY, BUT...
LOOKS LIKE THEY'VE GOT TIGHT SECU-RITY.
THIS IS WHERE MY FATHER'S ORGANIZATION HIDES THEIR TREASURE AND WEAPONS.
...OR SO I HEARD.
IT'S GONNA GET EVEN MORE DANGER-OUS.
ARE YOU SURE YOU WANT TO HELP ME?
EVEN IF WE SAID NO...
...YOU'D GO ON YOUR OWN ANYWAY, RIGHT?
YEAH.

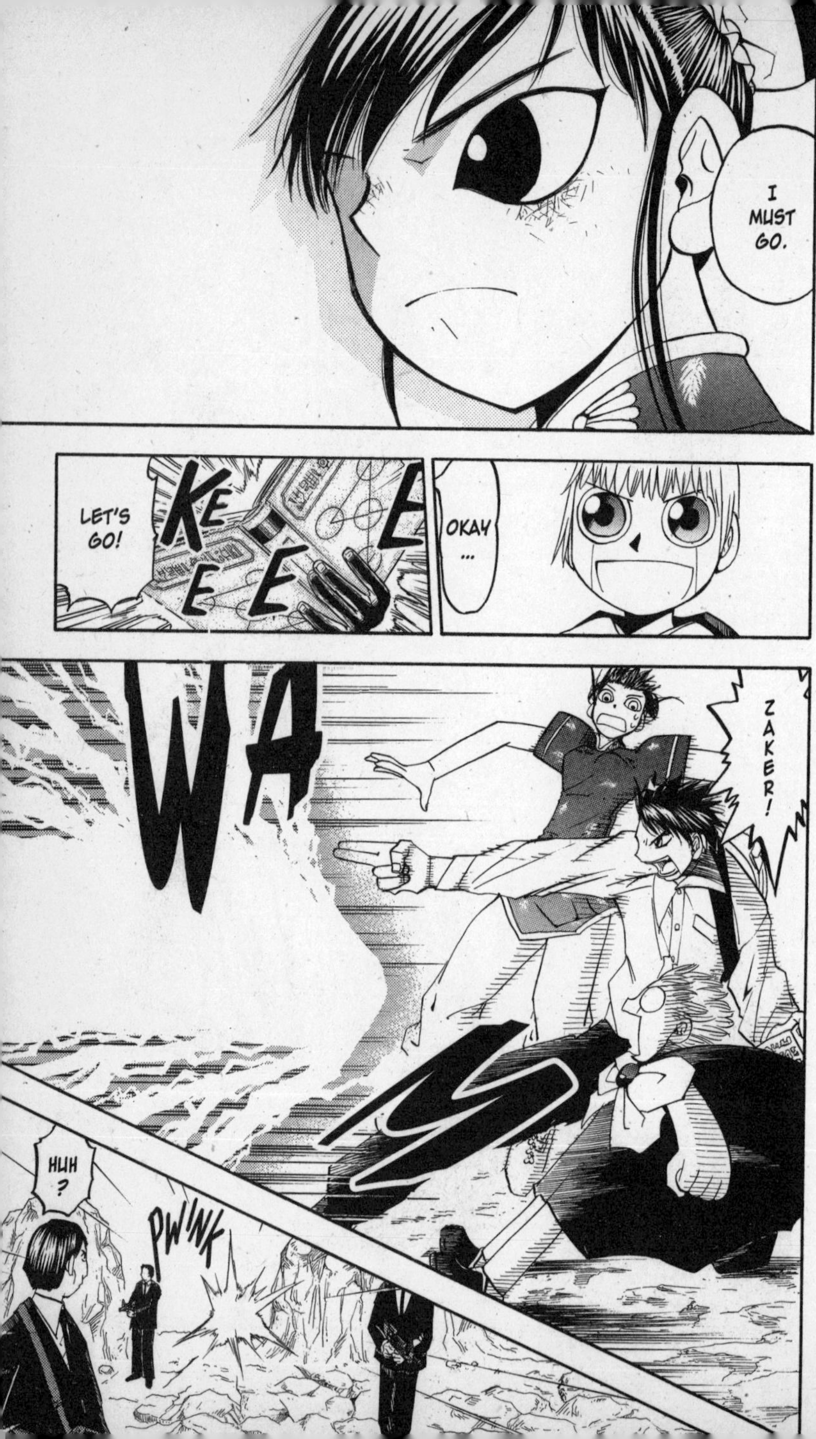
I MUST GO.
OKAY ...
LET'S GO!
KEEEEW
ZAKER!
WA
HUH ?
PWINK

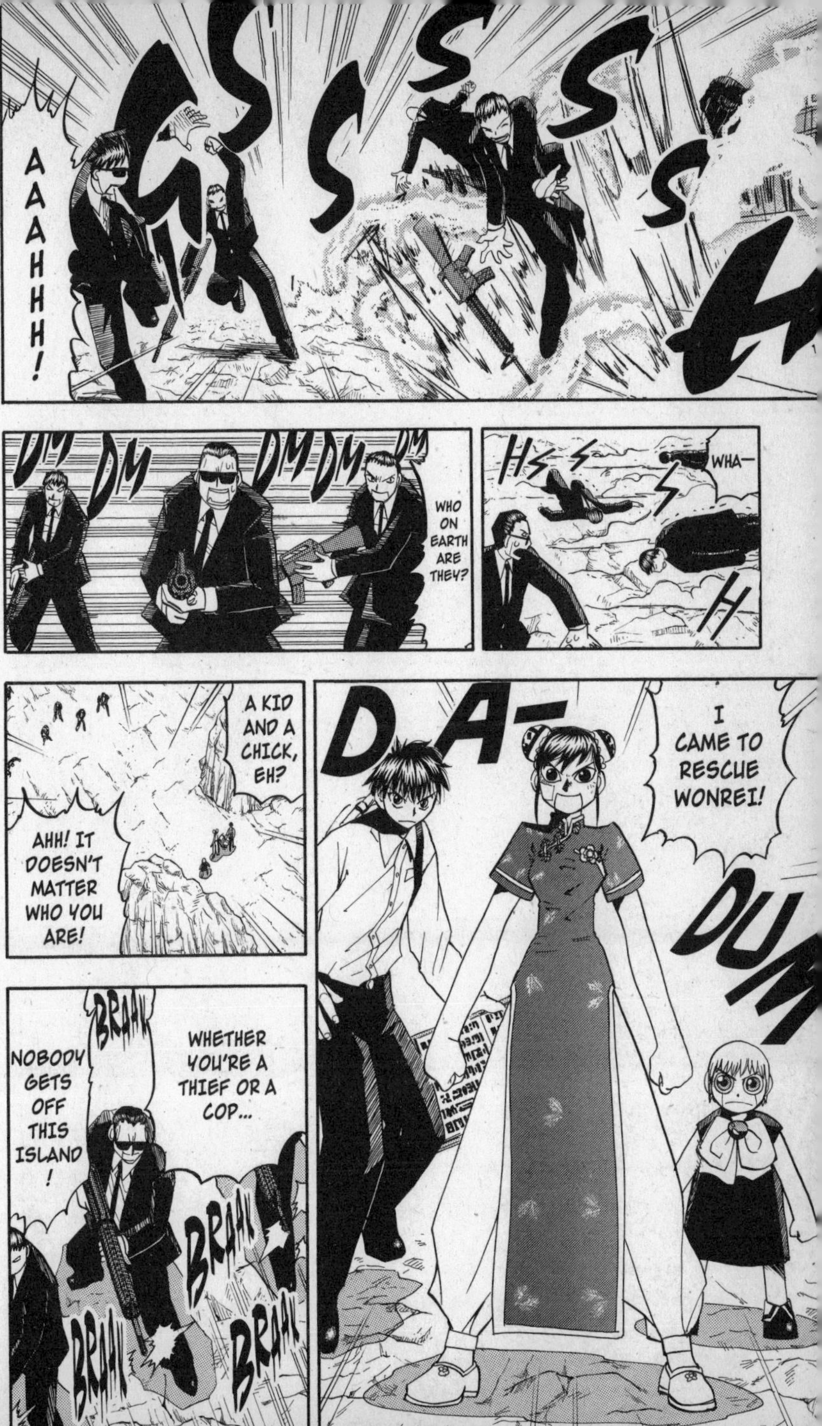
AAAAHHH!
WHA—
WHO ON EARTH ARE THEY?
DM DM DM DM DM
D A- DUM
I CAME TO RESCUE WONREI!
A KID AND A CHICK, EH?
AHH! IT DOESN'T MATTER WHO YOU ARE!
WHETHER YOU'RE A THIEF OR A COP...
NOBODY GETS OFF THIS ISLAND!

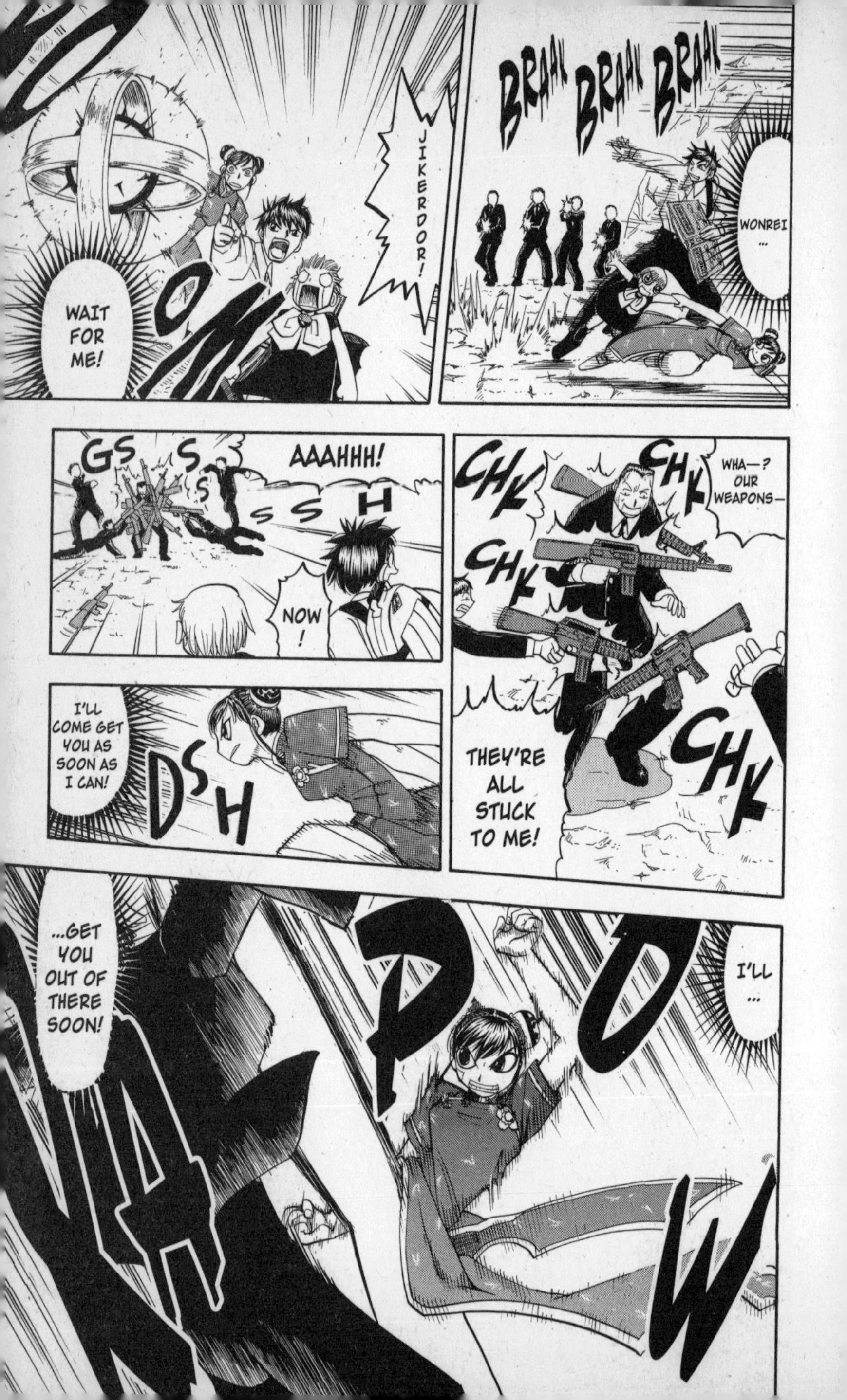
BRAAK BRAAK BRAAK
WONREI...
JIKERDOR!
WAIT FOR ME!
CHK CHK CHK CHK
WHA—? OUR WEAPONS—
THEY'RE ALL STUCK TO ME!
GSSSSH
AAAHHH!
NOW!
I'LL COME GET YOU AS SOON AS I CAN!
DSH
I'LL...
...GET YOU OUT OF THERE SOON!

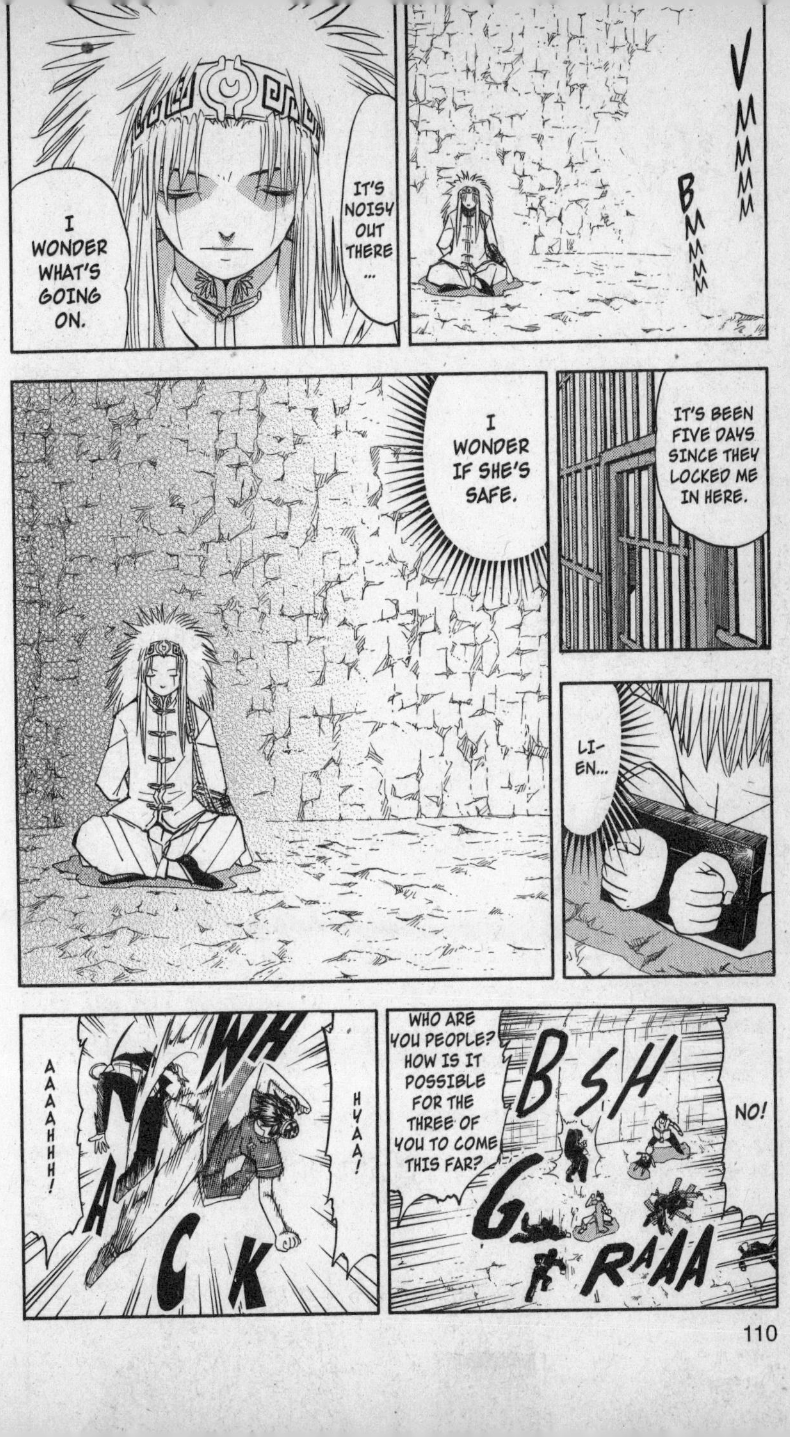
VMMMM
BMMMM
IT'S NOISY OUT THERE ...
I WONDER WHAT'S GOING ON.
IT'S BEEN FIVE DAYS SINCE THEY LOCKED ME IN HERE.
LI-EN...
I WONDER IF SHE'S SAFE.
NO!
BSH
G
RAAA
WHO ARE YOU PEOPLE? HOW IS IT POSSIBLE FOR THE THREE OF YOU TO COME THIS FAR?
HYAA!
WHACK
AAAAHHH!

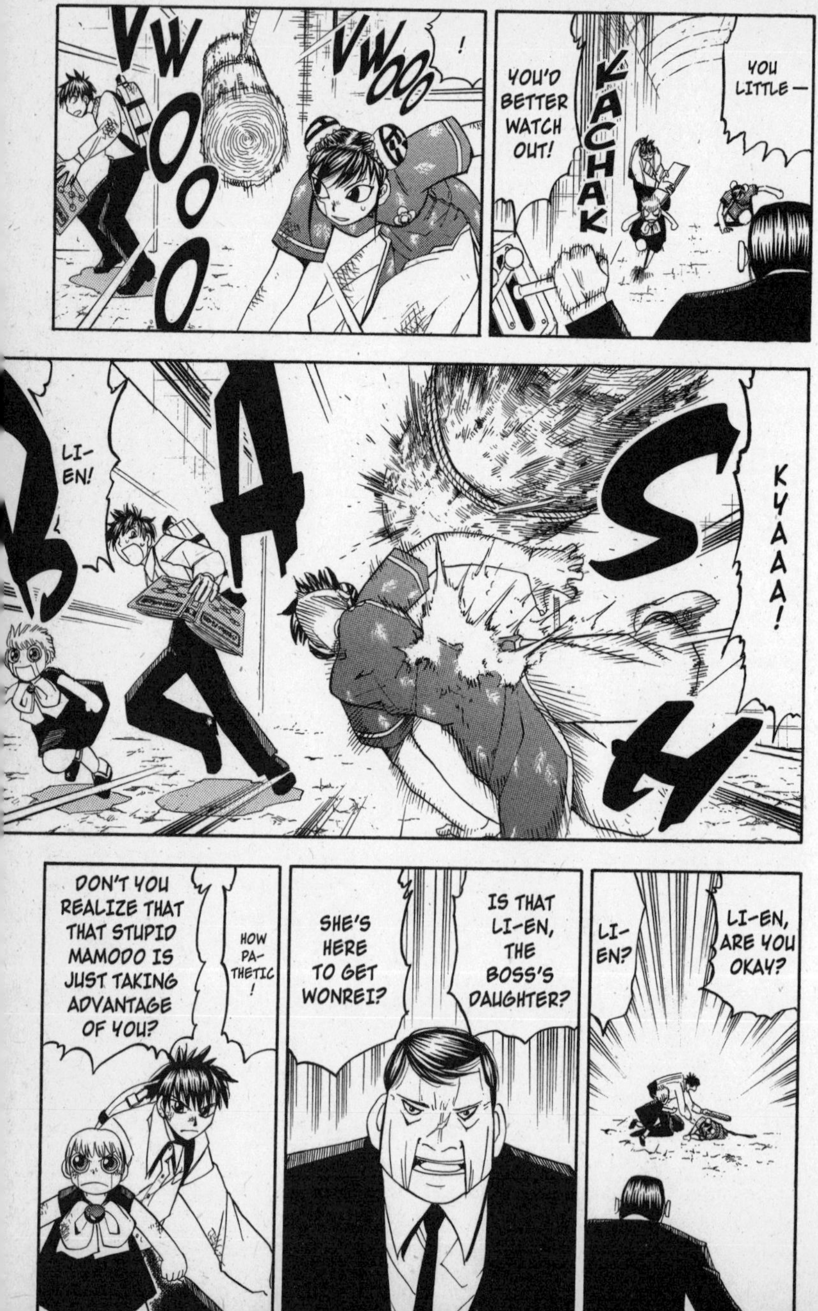
YOU LITTLE—
YOU'D BETTER WATCH OUT!
KACHAK
VWOOO
VWOOOO
!
KYAAAA!
BASH
LI-EN!
LI-EN, ARE YOU OKAY?
LI-EN?
IS THAT LI-EN, THE BOSS'S DAUGHTER?
SHE'S HERE TO GET WONREI?
HOW PATHETIC!
DON'T YOU REALIZE THAT THAT STUPID MAMODO IS JUST TAKING ADVANTAGE OF YOU?

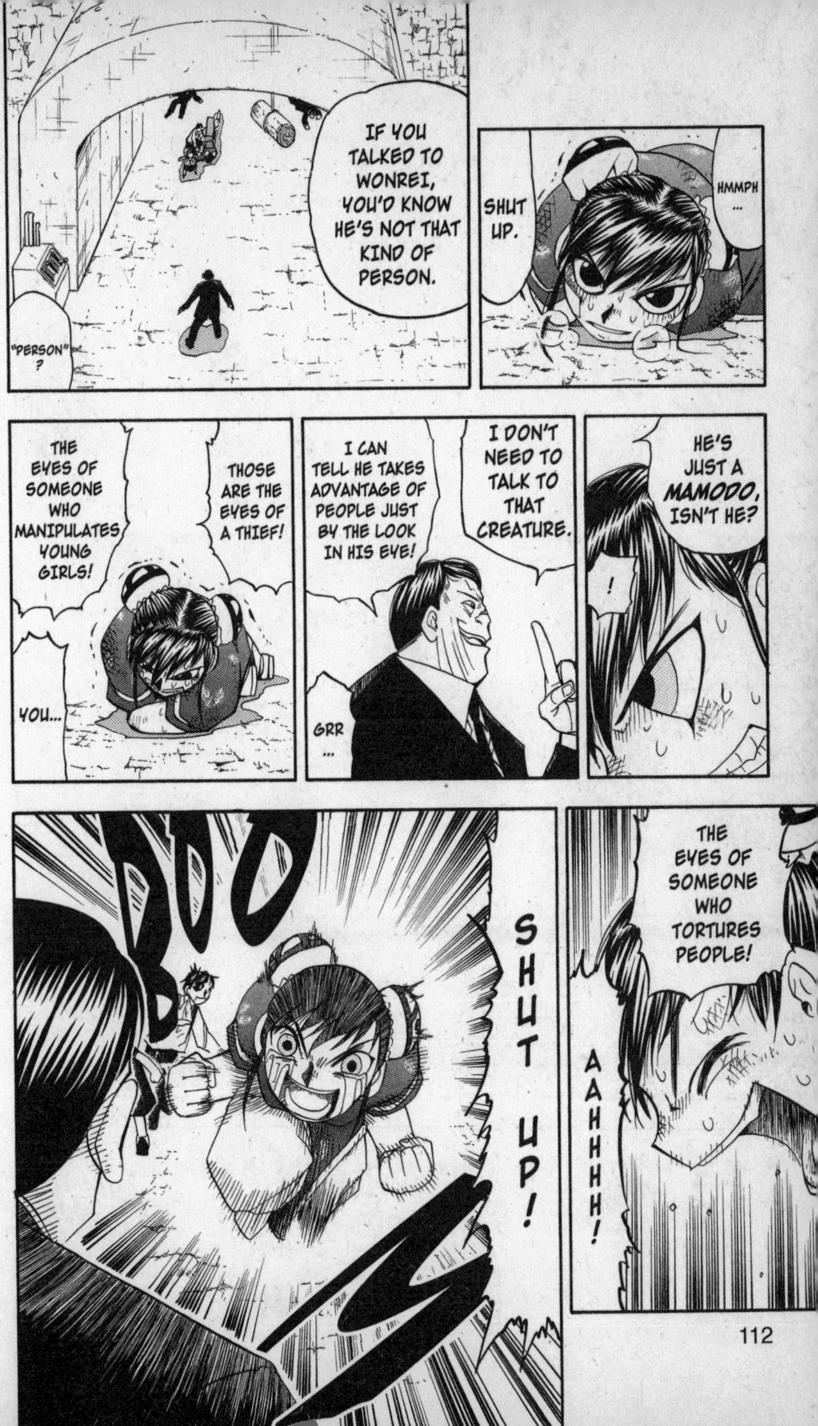
HMMPH ...
SHUT UP.
IF YOU TALKED TO WONREI, YOU'D KNOW HE'S NOT THAT KIND OF PERSON.
"PERSON"?
HE'S JUST A *MAMODO*, ISN'T HE?
!
I DON'T NEED TO TALK TO THAT CREATURE.
I CAN TELL HE TAKES ADVANTAGE OF PEOPLE JUST BY THE LOOK IN HIS EYE!
GRR ...
THOSE ARE THE EYES OF A THIEF!
THE EYES OF SOMEONE WHO MANIPULATES YOUNG GIRLS!
YOU...
THE EYES OF SOMEONE WHO TORTURES PEOPLE!
AAHHHH!
SHUT UP!

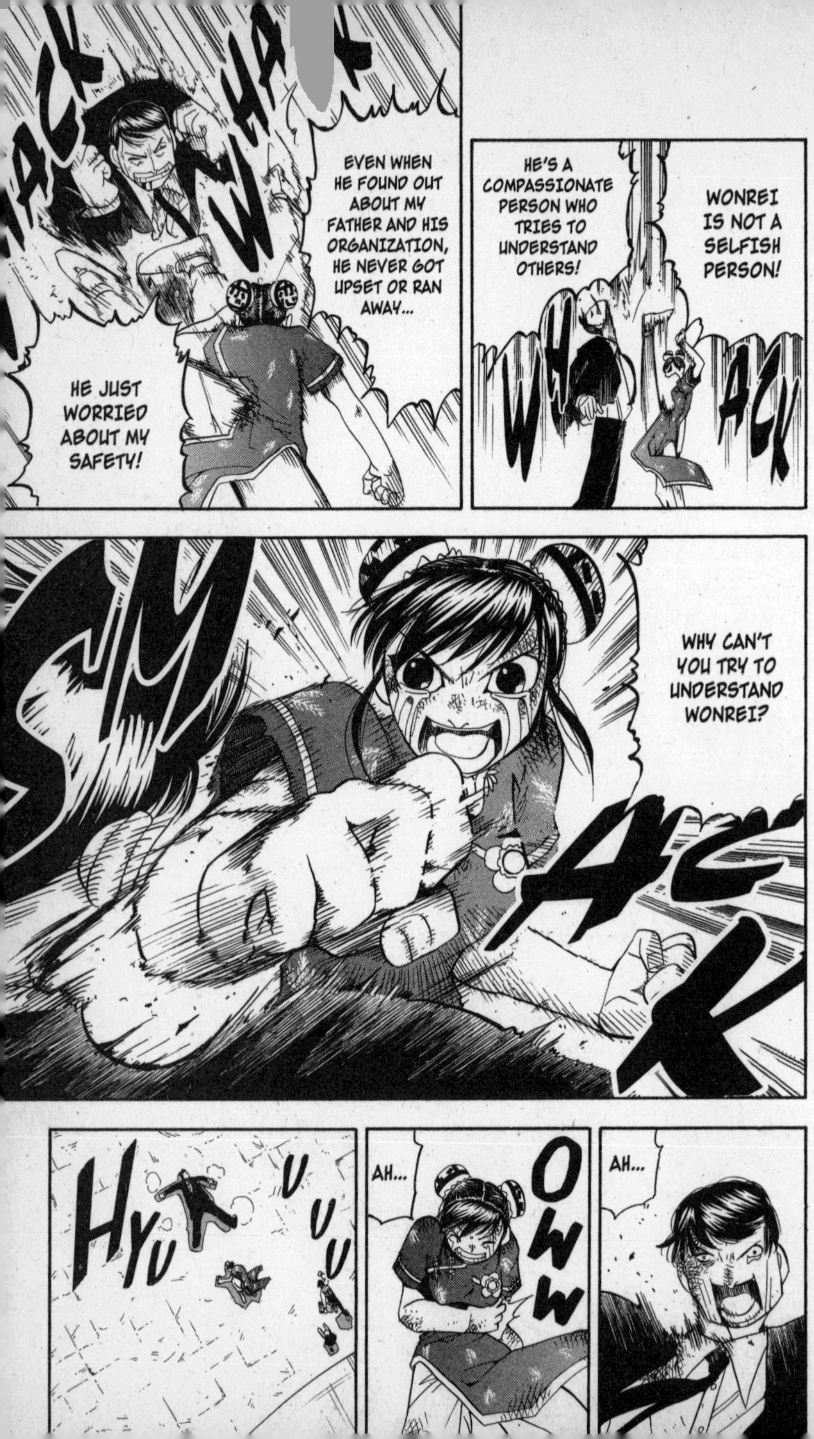
WONREI IS NOT A SELFISH PERSON!
HE'S A COMPASSIONATE PERSON WHO TRIES TO UNDERSTAND OTHERS!
EVEN WHEN HE FOUND OUT ABOUT MY FATHER AND HIS ORGANIZATION, HE NEVER GOT UPSET OR RAN AWAY...
HE JUST WORRIED ABOUT MY SAFETY!
WHY CAN'T YOU TRY TO UNDERSTAND WONREI?
AH...
AH...
OWW

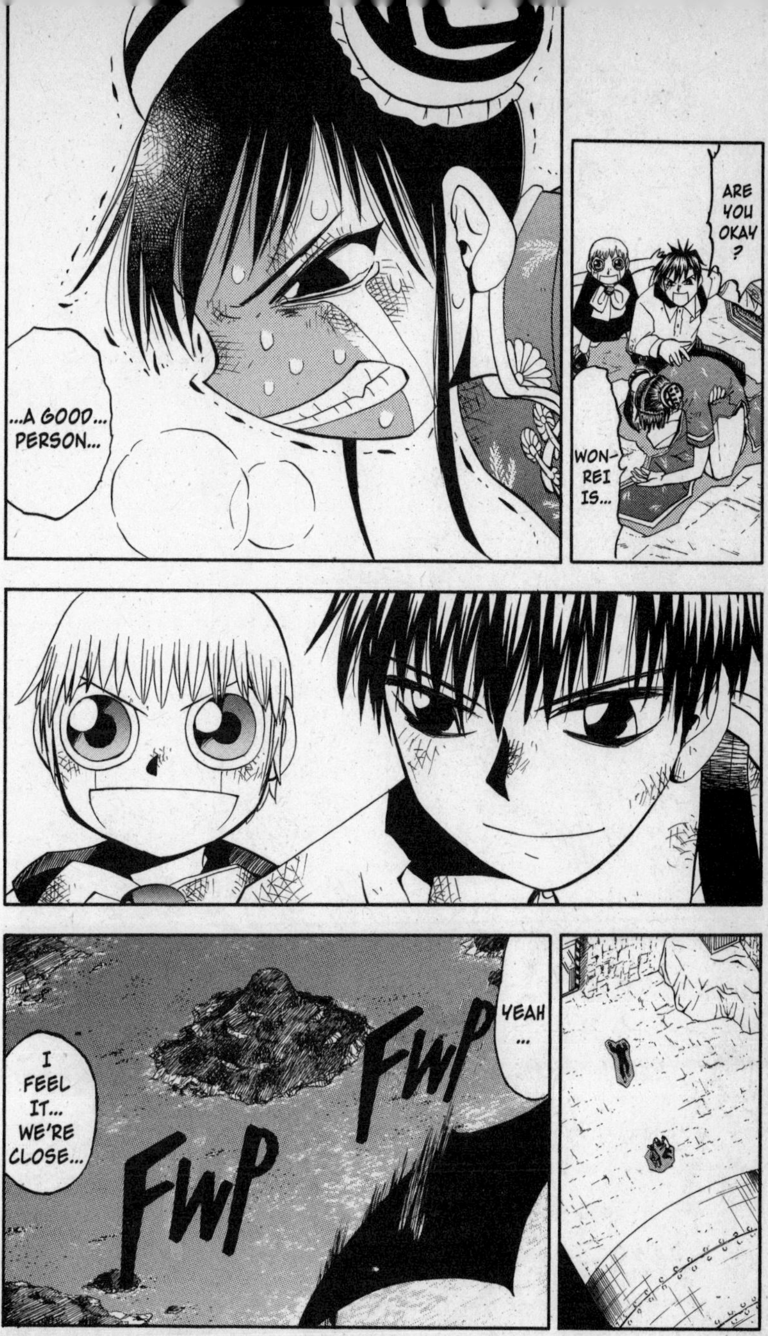
ARE YOU OKAY?
WON-REI IS...
...A GOOD... PERSON...
YEAH...
I FEEL IT... WE'RE CLOSE...
FWP
FWP

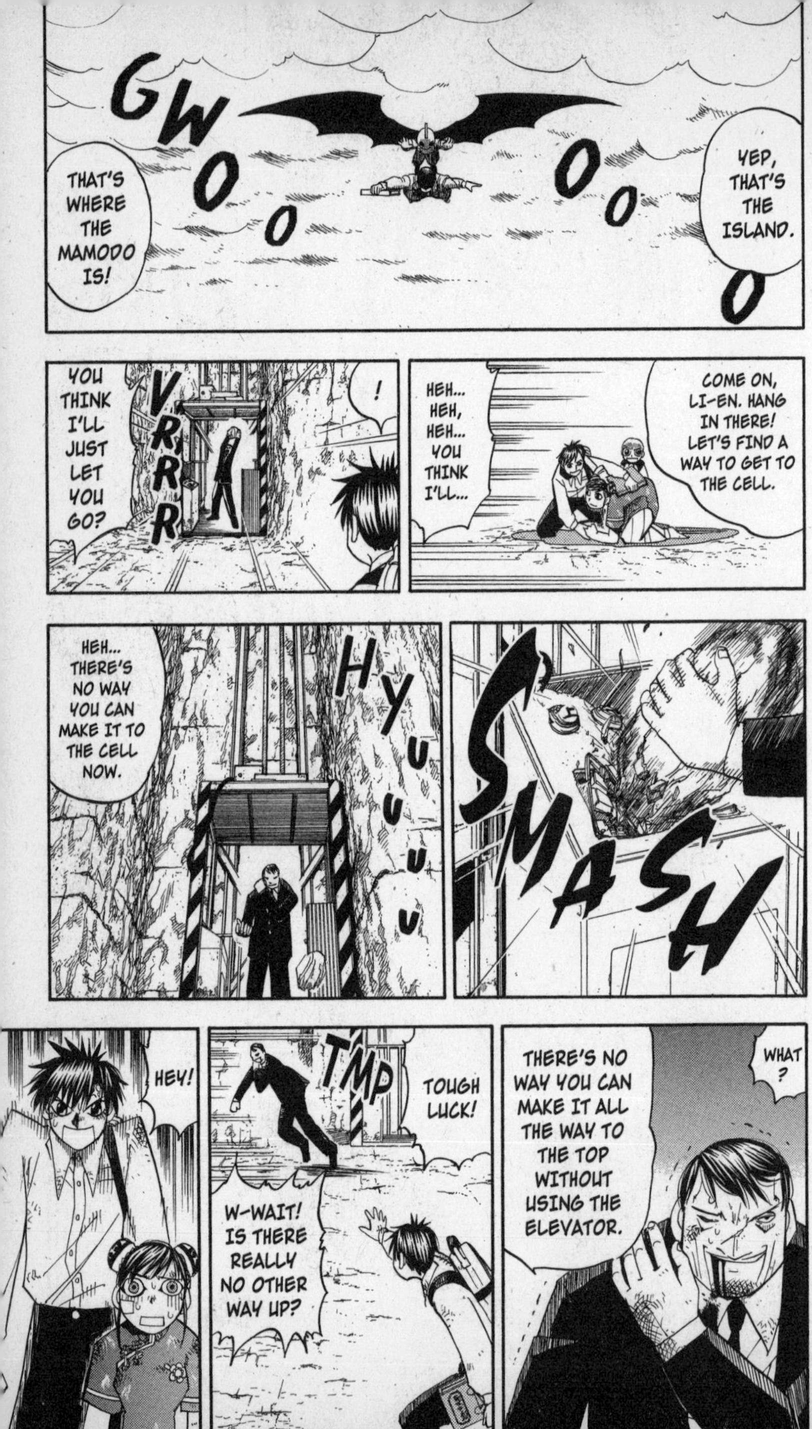
GWOOOOOOO
THAT'S WHERE THE MAMODO IS!
YEP, THAT'S THE ISLAND.
YOU THINK I'LL JUST LET YOU GO?
VRRRR
!
HEH... HEH, HEH... YOU THINK I'LL...
COME ON, LI-EN. HANG IN THERE! LET'S FIND A WAY TO GET TO THE CELL.
HEH... THERE'S NO WAY YOU CAN MAKE IT TO THE CELL NOW.
HYUUUUU
SMASH
HEY!
TMP
TOUGH LUCK!
W-WAIT! IS THERE REALLY NO OTHER WAY UP?
THERE'S NO WAY YOU CAN MAKE IT ALL THE WAY TO THE TOP WITHOUT USING THE ELEVATOR.
WHAT?

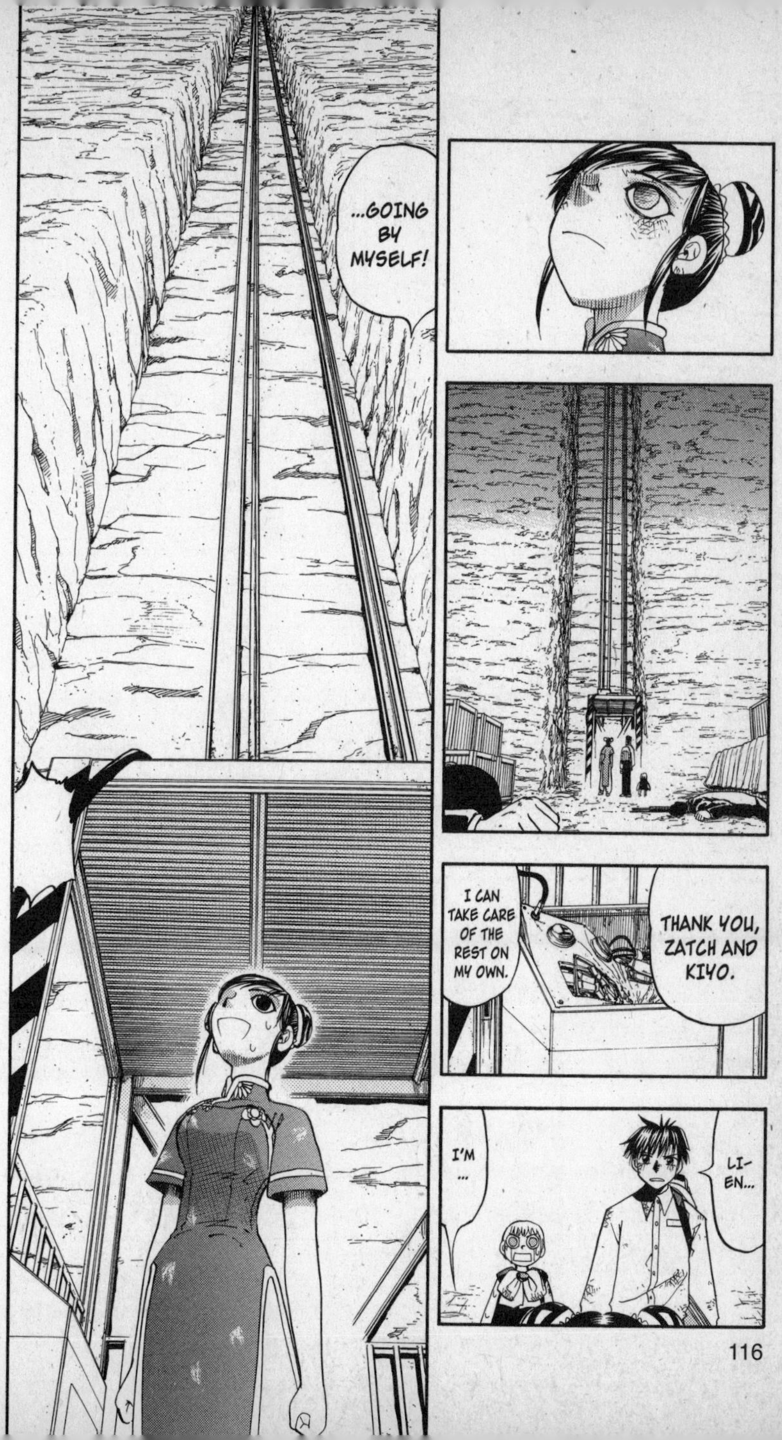
...GOING BY MYSELF!
THANK YOU, ZATCH AND KIYO.
I CAN TAKE CARE OF THE REST ON MY OWN.
LI-EN...
I'M ...

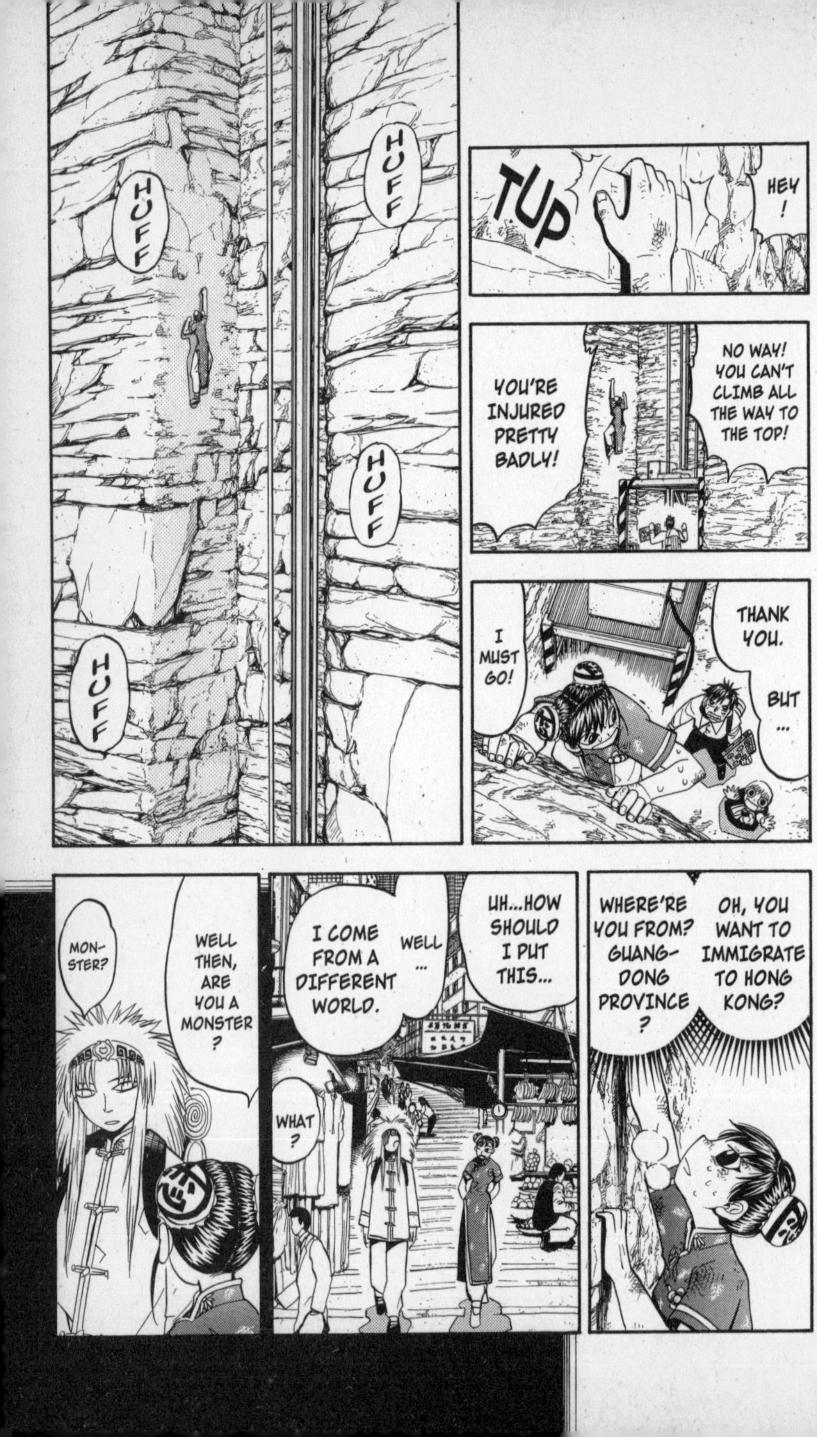
TUP
HEY!
NO WAY! YOU CAN'T CLIMB ALL THE WAY TO THE TOP!
YOU'RE INJURED PRETTY BADLY!
THANK YOU.
BUT ...
I MUST GO!
HUFF
HUFF
HUFF
HUFF
OH, YOU WANT TO IMMIGRATE TO HONG KONG?
WHERE'RE YOU FROM? GUANG-DONG PROVINCE?
UH...HOW SHOULD I PUT THIS...
WELL ...
I COME FROM A DIFFERENT WORLD.
WHAT?
WELL THEN, ARE YOU A MONSTER?
MON-STER?

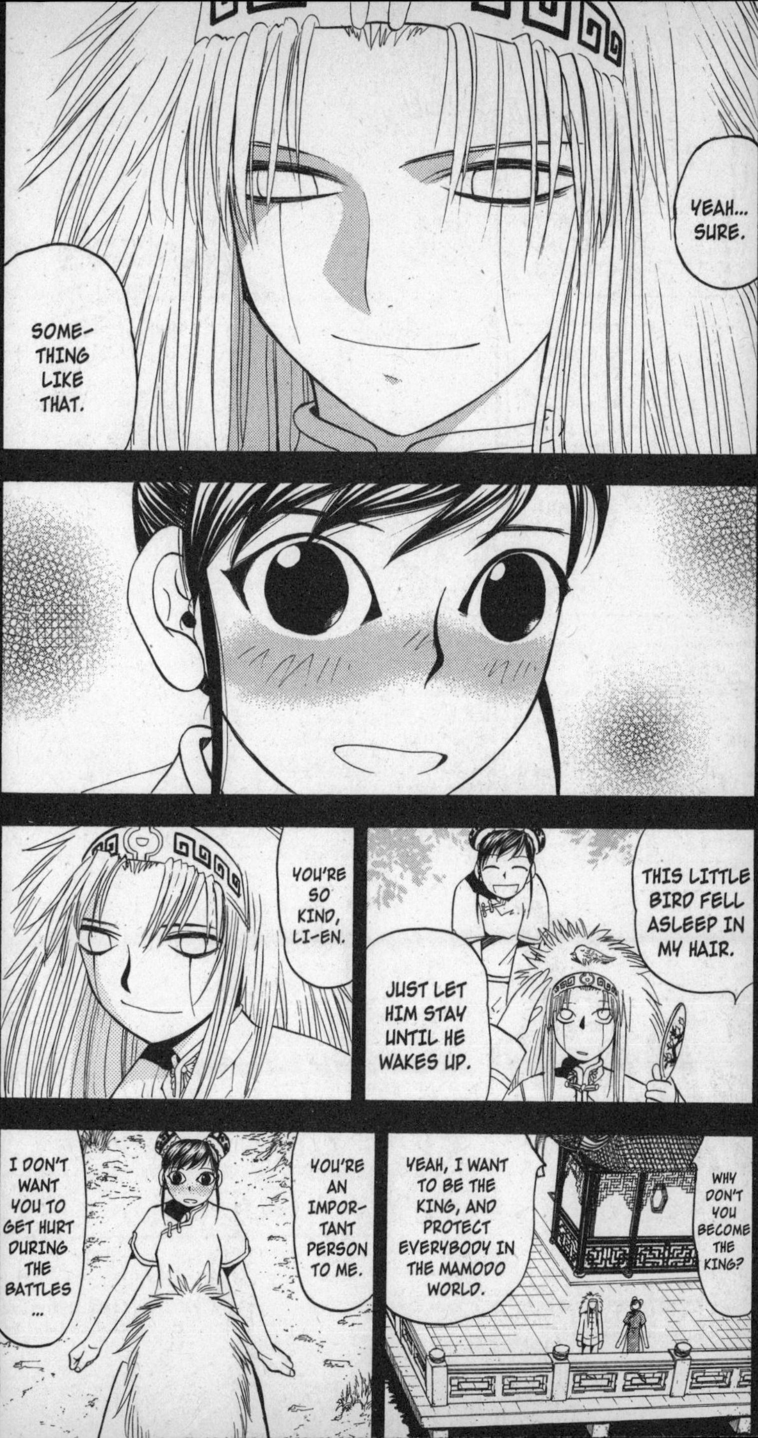
YEAH... SURE.
SOME-THING LIKE THAT.
THIS LITTLE BIRD FELL ASLEEP IN MY HAIR.
JUST LET HIM STAY UNTIL HE WAKES UP.
YOU'RE SO KIND, LI-EN.
WHY DON'T YOU BECOME THE KING?
YEAH, I WANT TO BE THE KING, AND PROTECT EVERYBODY IN THE MAMODO WORLD.
YOU'RE AN IMPOR-TANT PERSON TO ME.
I DON'T WANT YOU TO GET HURT DURING THE BATTLES ...

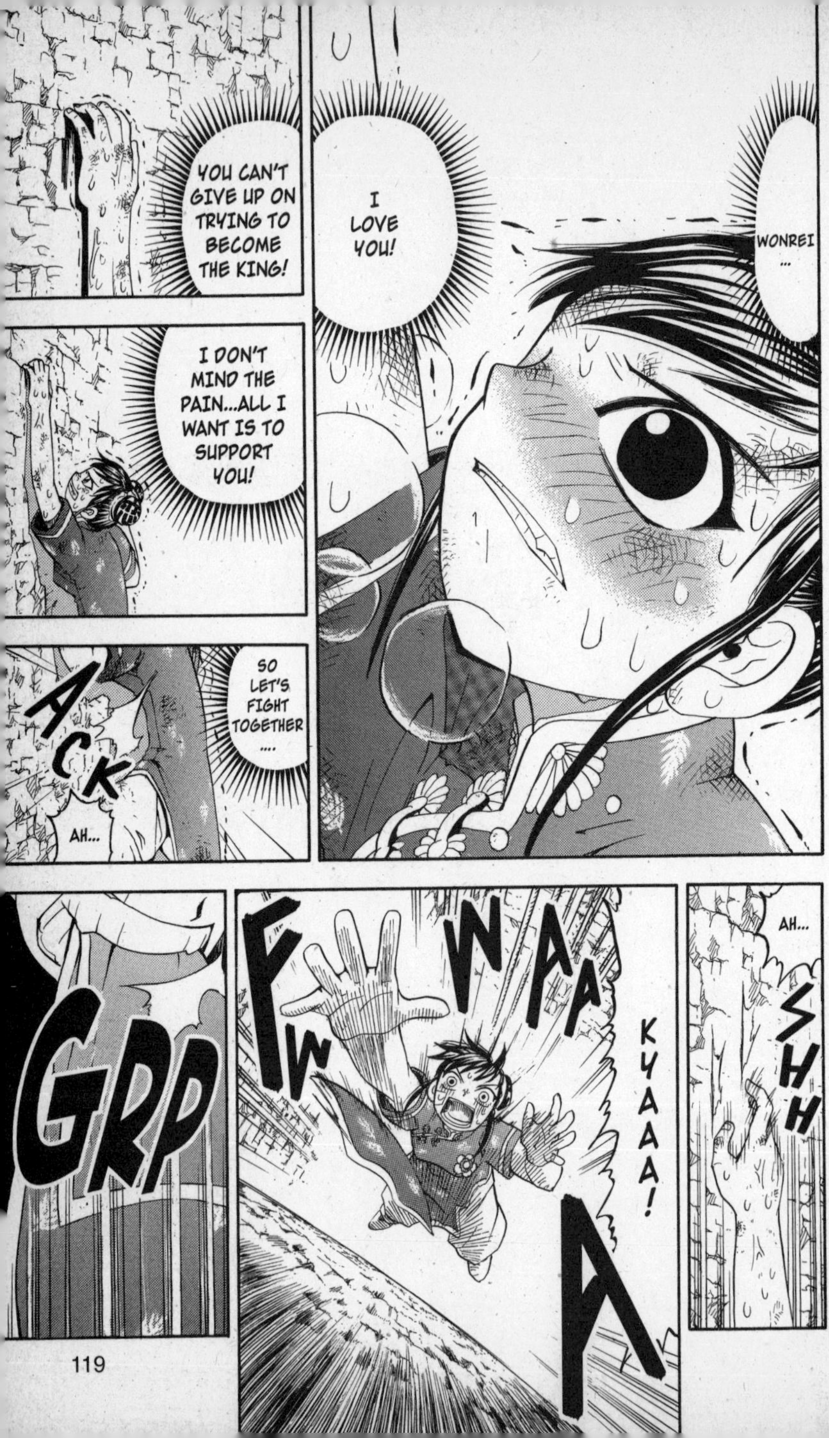
WONREI
...
I LOVE YOU!
YOU CAN'T GIVE UP ON TRYING TO BECOME THE KING!
I DON'T MIND THE PAIN...ALL I WANT IS TO SUPPORT YOU!
SO LET'S FIGHT TOGETHER....
ACK
AH...
AH...
SHH
KYAAAA!
FWWAAA
GRP

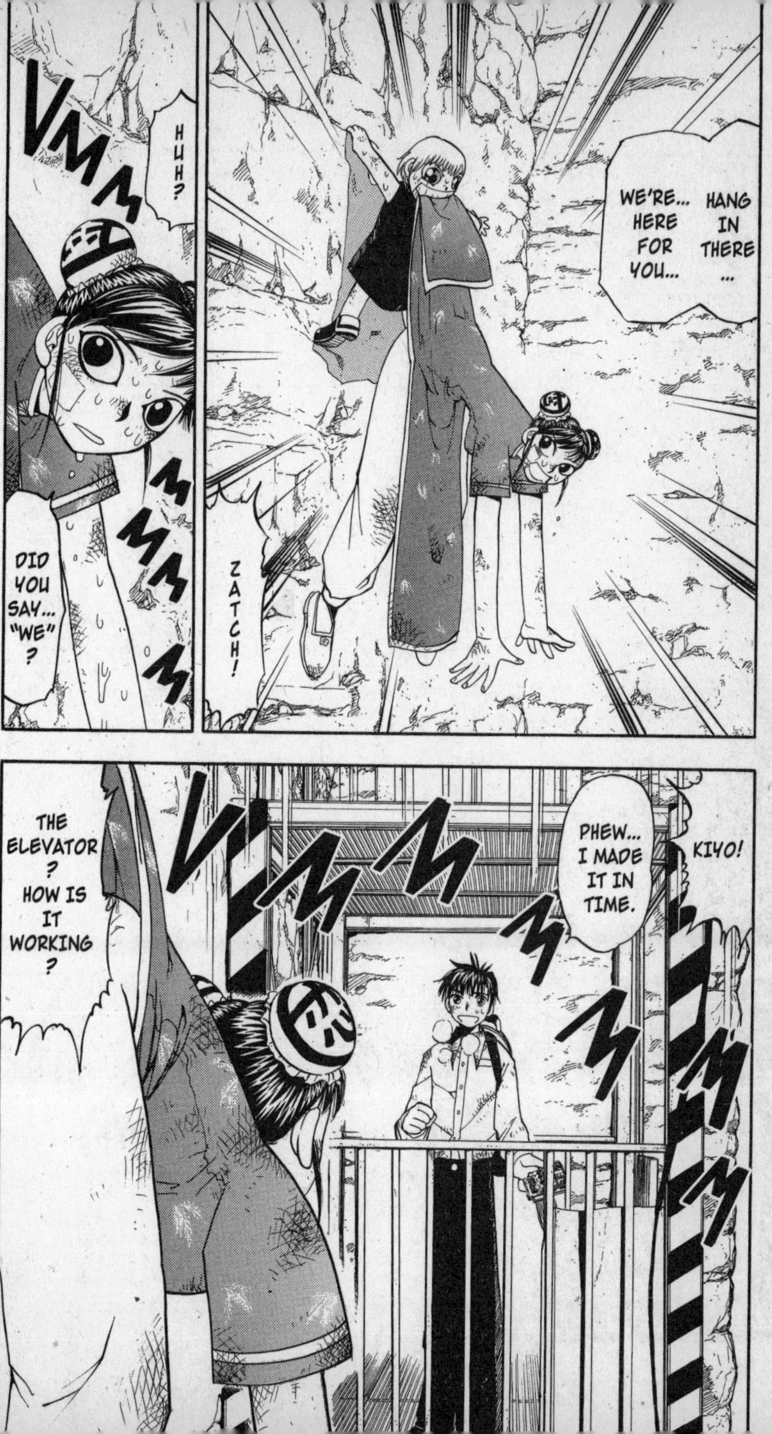
HANG IN THERE...
WE'RE... HERE FOR YOU...
ZATCH!
HUH?
VMMMMMMMM
DID YOU SAY... "WE"?
KIYO!
PHEW... I MADE IT IN TIME.
VMMMMMMMM
THE ELEVATOR? HOW IS IT WORKING?

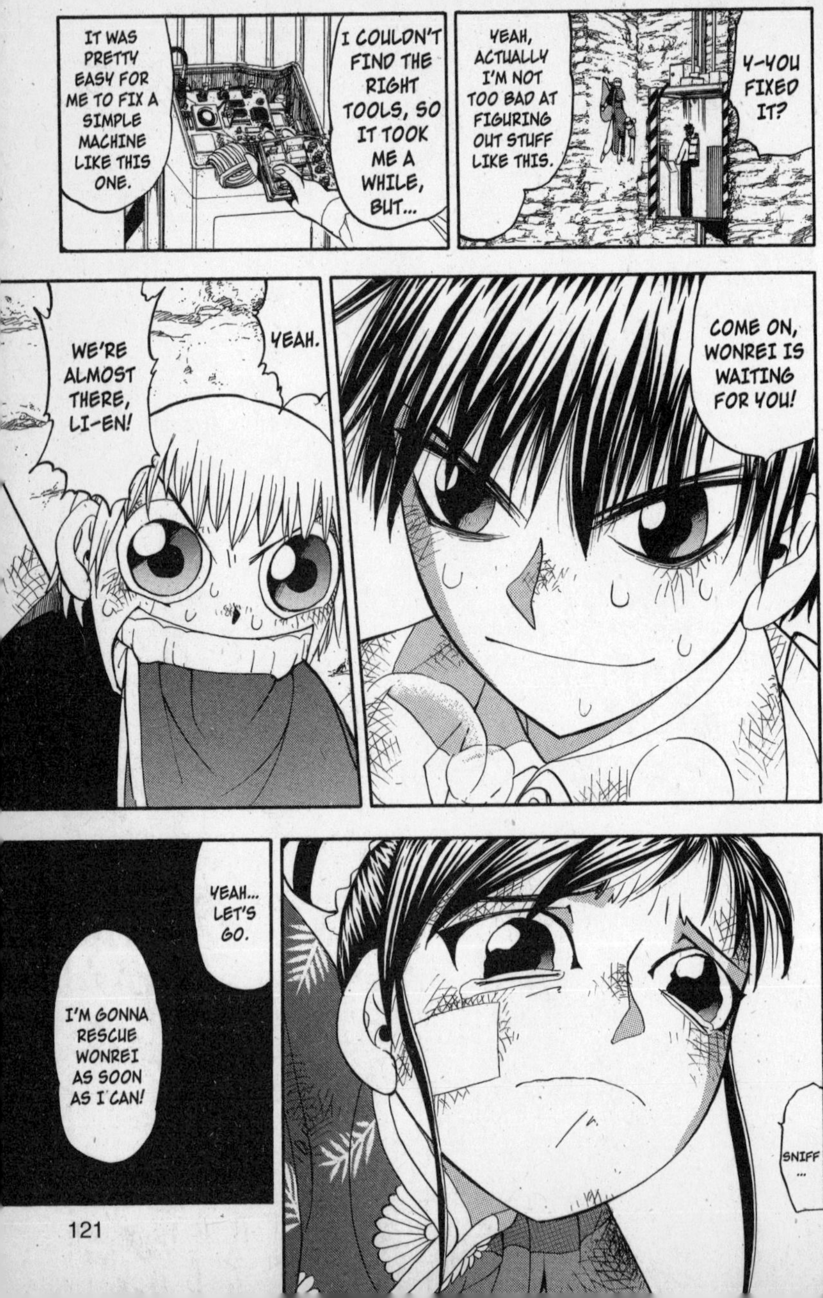
Y-YOU FIXED IT?
YEAH, ACTUALLY I'M NOT TOO BAD AT FIGURING OUT STUFF LIKE THIS.
I COULDN'T FIND THE RIGHT TOOLS, SO IT TOOK ME A WHILE, BUT...
IT WAS PRETTY EASY FOR ME TO FIX A SIMPLE MACHINE LIKE THIS ONE.
COME ON, WONREI IS WAITING FOR YOU!
YEAH.
WE'RE ALMOST THERE, LI-EN!
SNIFF...
YEAH... LET'S GO.
I'M GONNA RESCUE WONREI AS SOON AS I CAN!

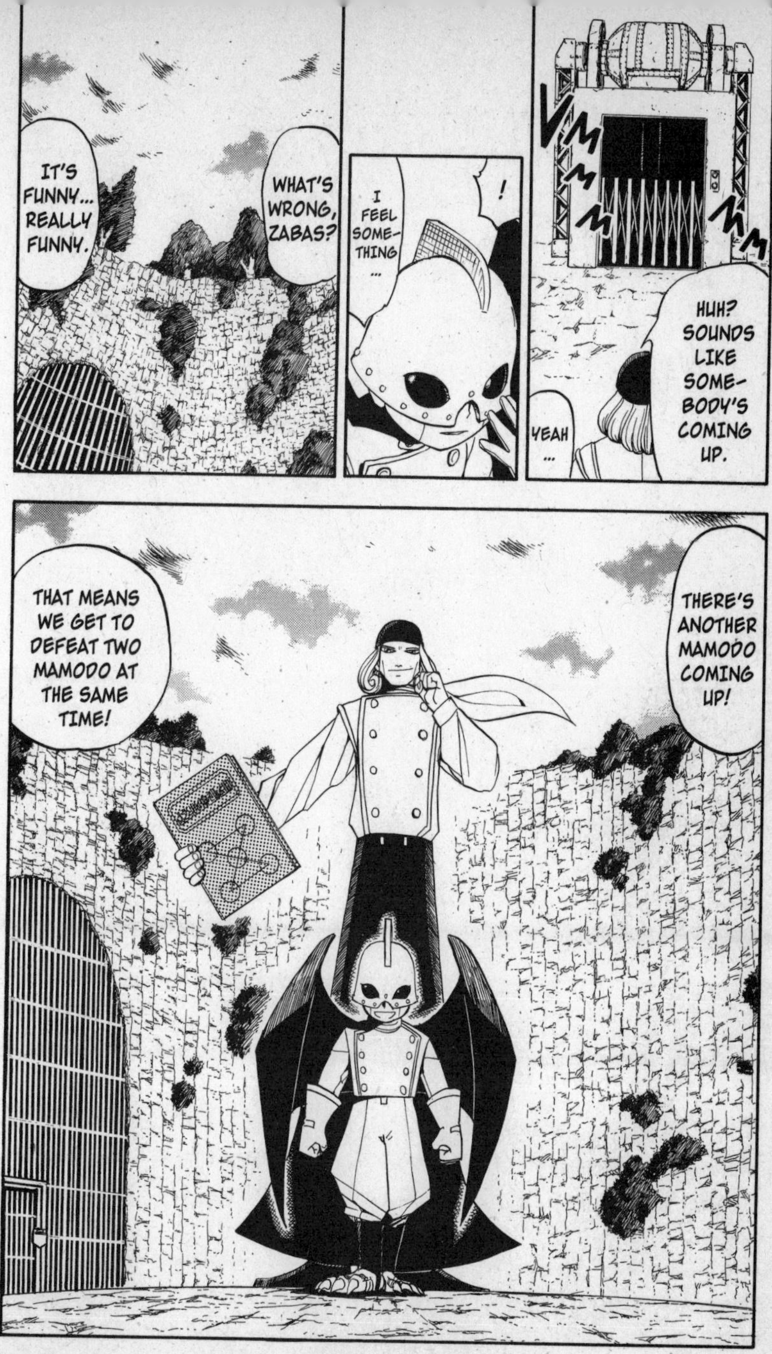
IT'S FUNNY... REALLY FUNNY.
WHAT'S WRONG, ZABAS?
I FEEL SOME-THING ...
!
VMMM MMM
HUH? SOUNDS LIKE SOME-BODY'S COMING UP.
YEAH ...
THERE'S ANOTHER MAMODO COMING UP!
THAT MEANS WE GET TO DEFEAT TWO MAMODO AT THE SAME TIME!

LEVEL 73: The Courage to Fight

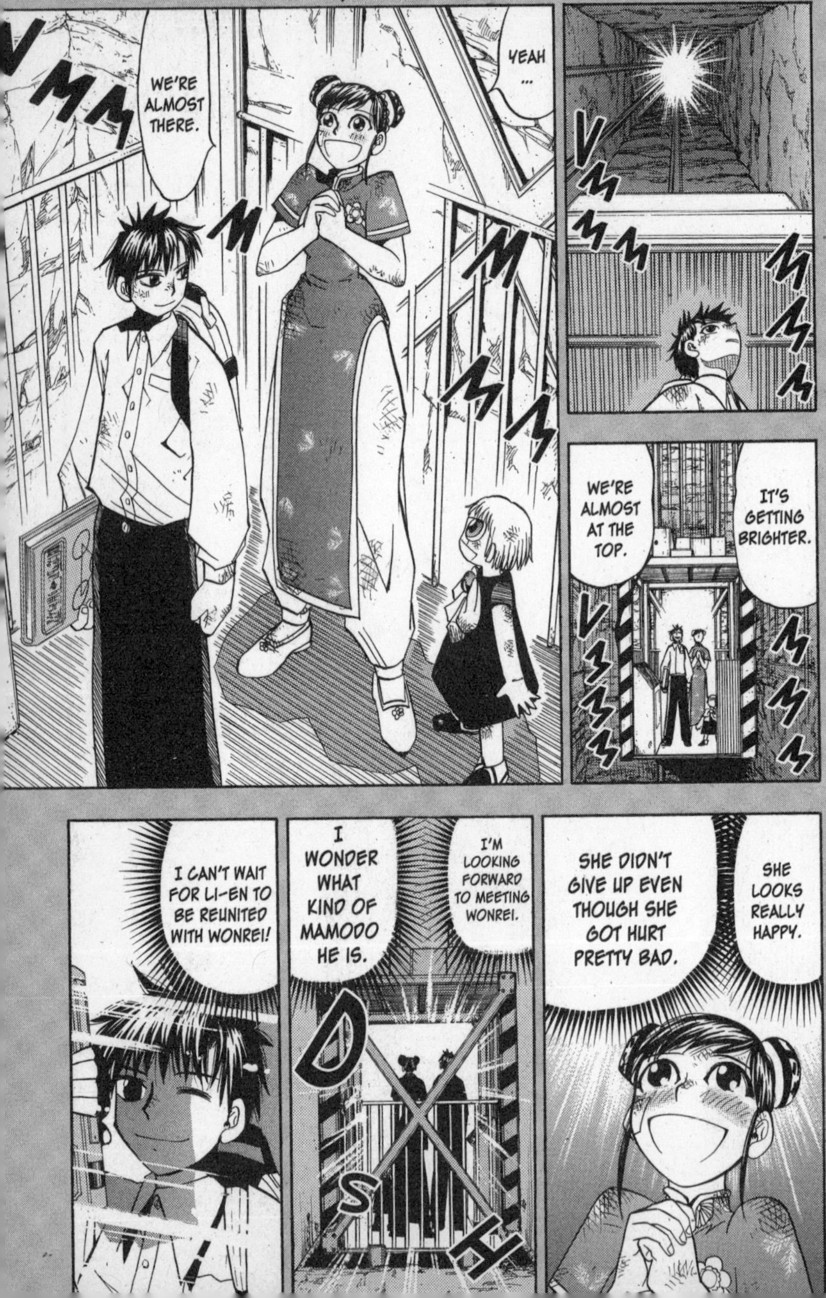
VMMM
VMMM
MMMM
IT'S GETTING BRIGHTER.
WE'RE ALMOST AT THE TOP.
VMMM
MMM
YEAH ...
WE'RE ALMOST THERE.
VMMM
MMMMM
SHE LOOKS REALLY HAPPY.
SHE DIDN'T GIVE UP EVEN THOUGH SHE GOT HURT PRETTY BAD.
I'M LOOKING FORWARD TO MEETING WONREI.
I WONDER WHAT KIND OF MAMODO HE IS.
DSH
I CAN'T WAIT FOR LI-EN TO BE REUNITED WITH WONREI!

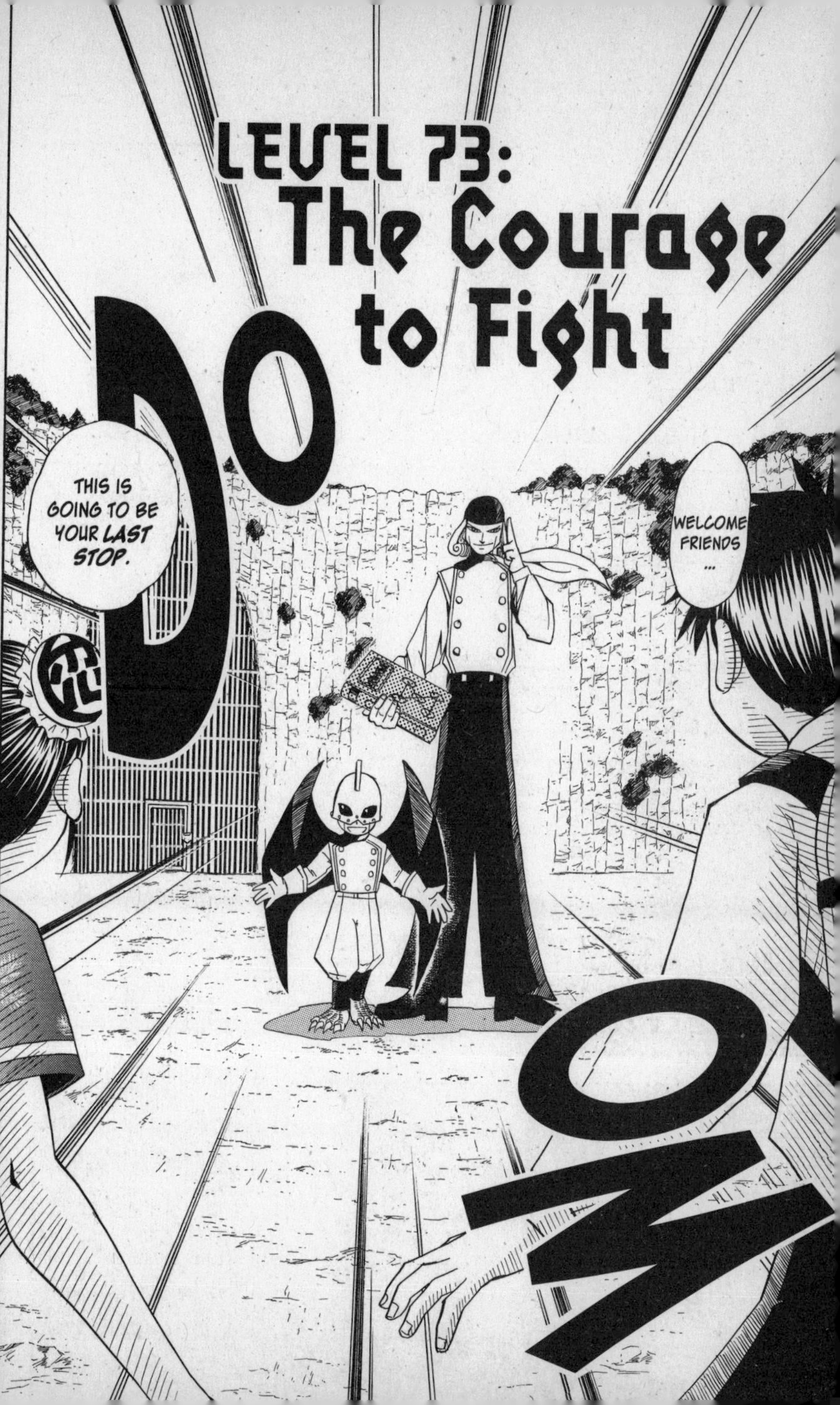
LEVEL 73:
The Courage to Fight
WELCOME FRIENDS ...
THIS IS GOING TO BE YOUR LAST STOP.

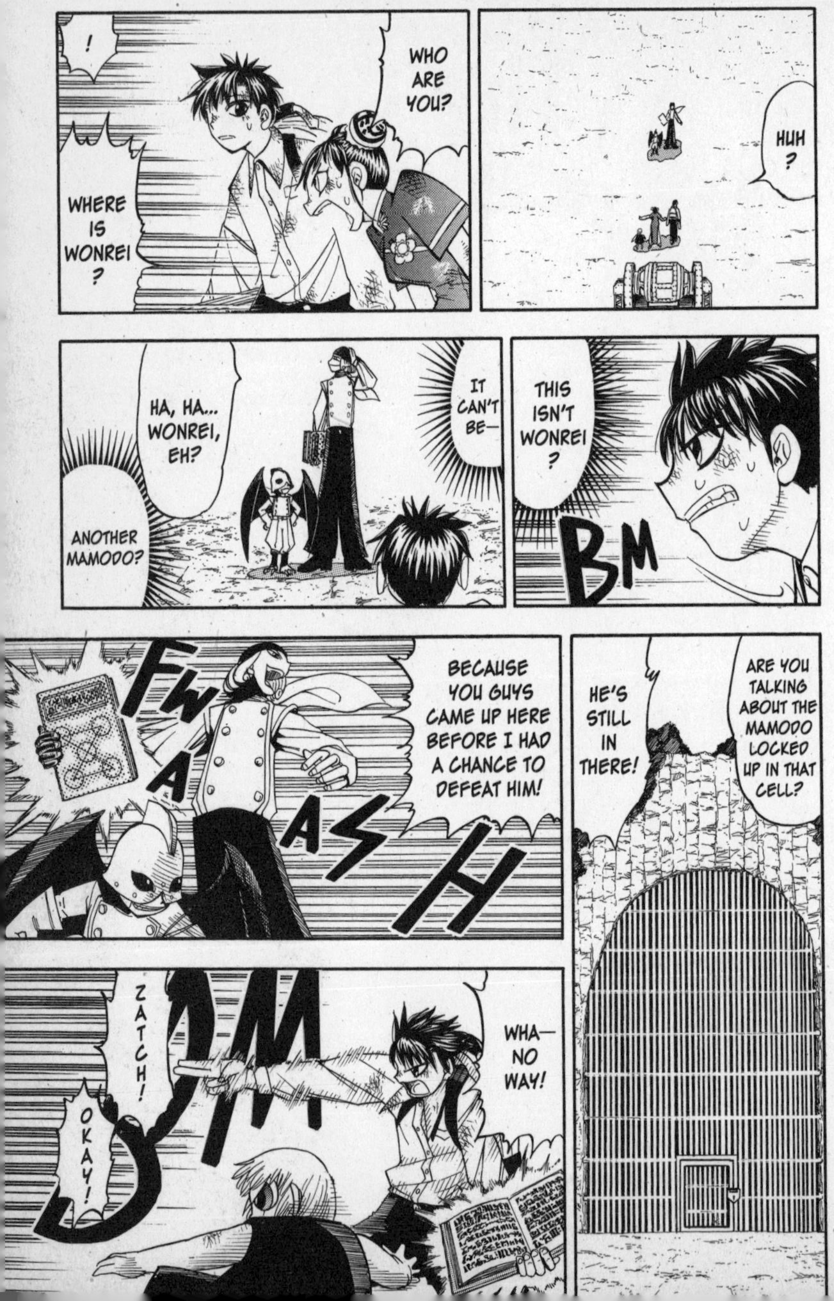
HUH?
WHO ARE YOU?
!
WHERE IS WONREI?
THIS ISN'T WONREI?
BM
IT CAN'T BE—
HA, HA... WONREI, EH?
ANOTHER MAMODO?
ARE YOU TALKING ABOUT THE MAMODO LOCKED UP IN THAT CELL?
HE'S STILL IN THERE!
BECAUSE YOU GUYS CAME UP HERE BEFORE I HAD A CHANCE TO DEFEAT HIM!
FWASH
WHA— NO WAY!
ZATCH!
OKAY!
DM

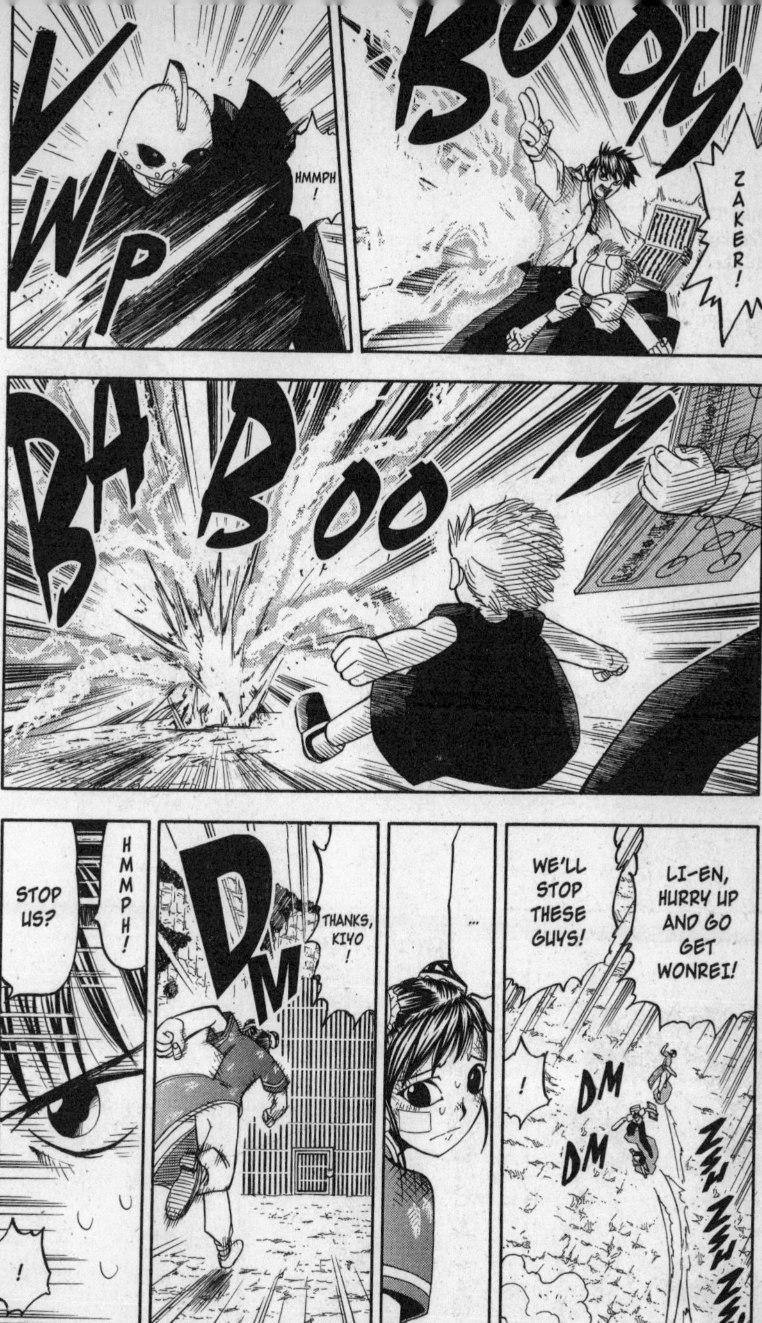
ZAKER!
BOOM
WHP
HMMPH!
BA BOOM
LI-EN, HURRY UP AND GO GET WONREI!
WE'LL STOP THESE GUYS!
!
DM
DM
ZWWWW
...
THANKS, KIYO!
DM
STOP US?
HMMPH!
!

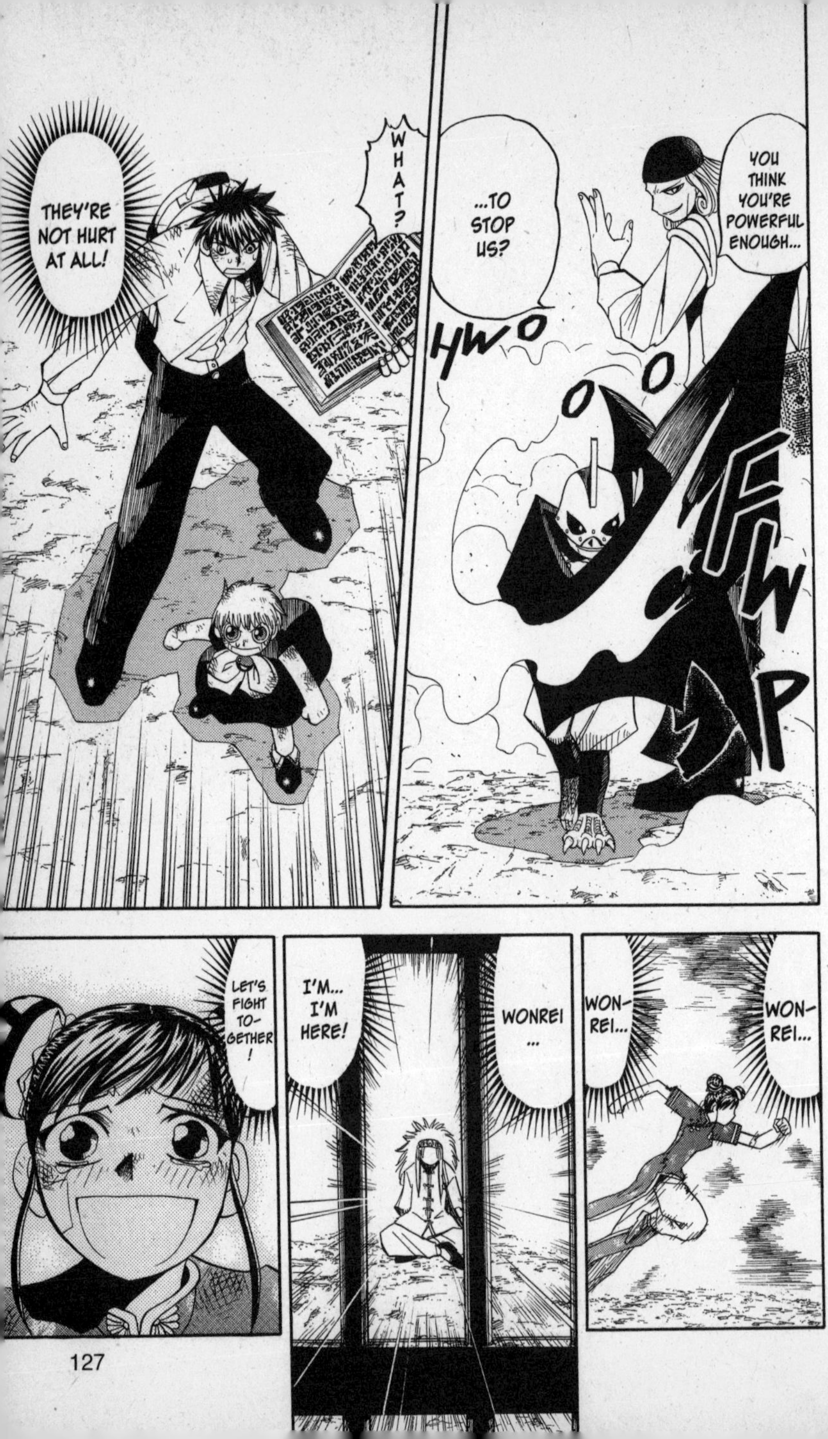

YOU THINK YOU'RE POWERFUL ENOUGH...
...TO STOP US?
HWOOO
FWP
WHAT?
THEY'RE NOT HURT AT ALL!
WON-REI...
WON-REI...
WONREI...
I'M... I'M HERE!
LET'S FIGHT TO-GETHER!

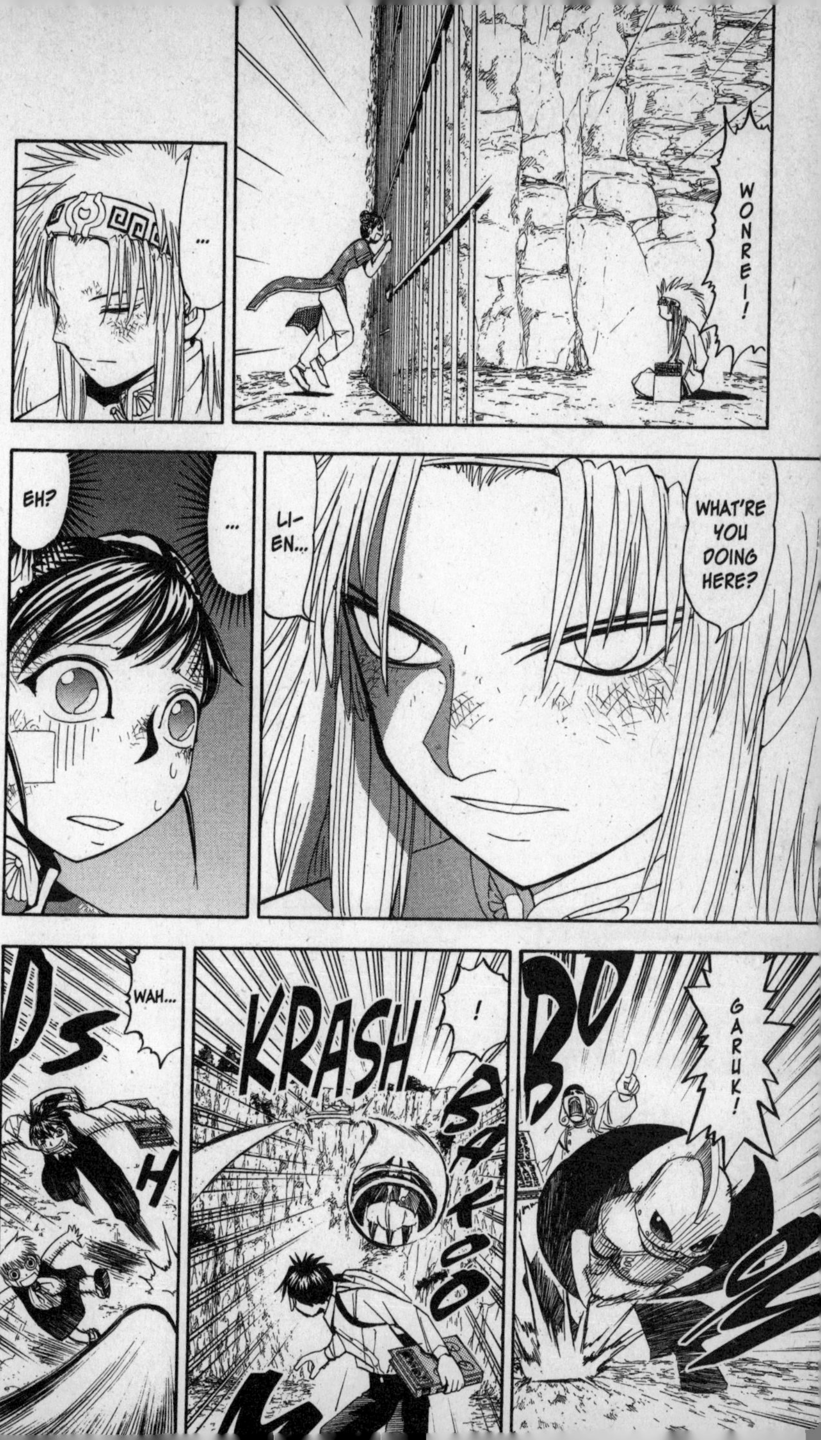
WONREI!
...
WHAT'RE YOU DOING HERE?
LI-EN...
...
EH?
GARUK!
!
BAKOOM
KRASH
WAH...
DSH

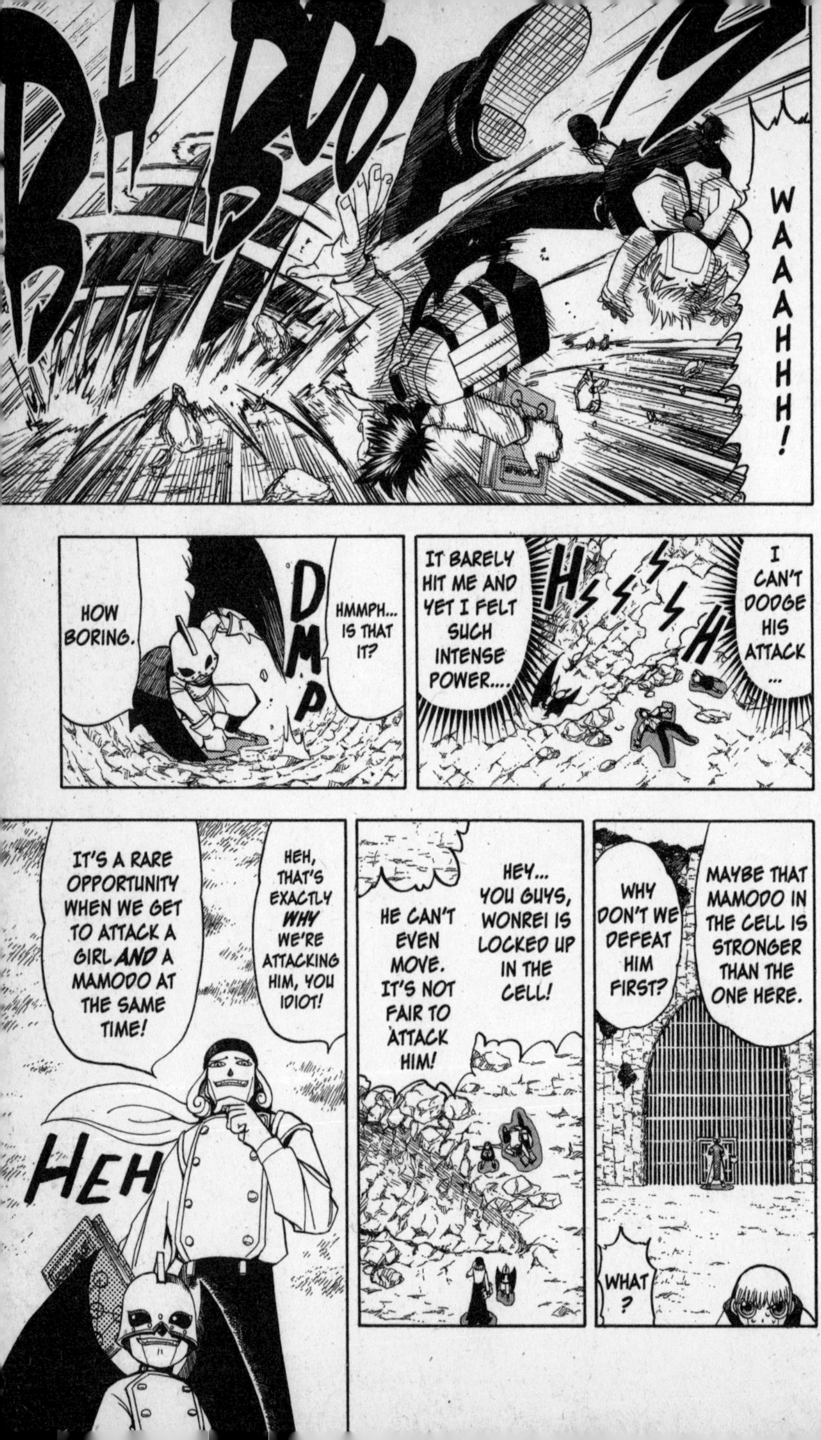
WAAAAHHH!
I CAN'T DODGE HIS ATTACK...
HSSSSH
IT BARELY HIT ME AND YET I FELT SUCH INTENSE POWER....
HMMPH... IS THAT IT?
DMP
HOW BORING.
MAYBE THAT MAMODO IN THE CELL IS STRONGER THAN THE ONE HERE.
WHY DON'T WE DEFEAT HIM FIRST?
WHAT?
HEY... YOU GUYS, WONREI IS LOCKED UP IN THE CELL!
HE CAN'T EVEN MOVE. IT'S NOT FAIR TO ATTACK HIM!
HEH, THAT'S EXACTLY WHY WE'RE ATTACKING HIM, YOU IDIOT!
IT'S A RARE OPPORTUNITY WHEN WE GET TO ATTACK A GIRL AND A MAMODO AT THE SAME TIME!
HEH

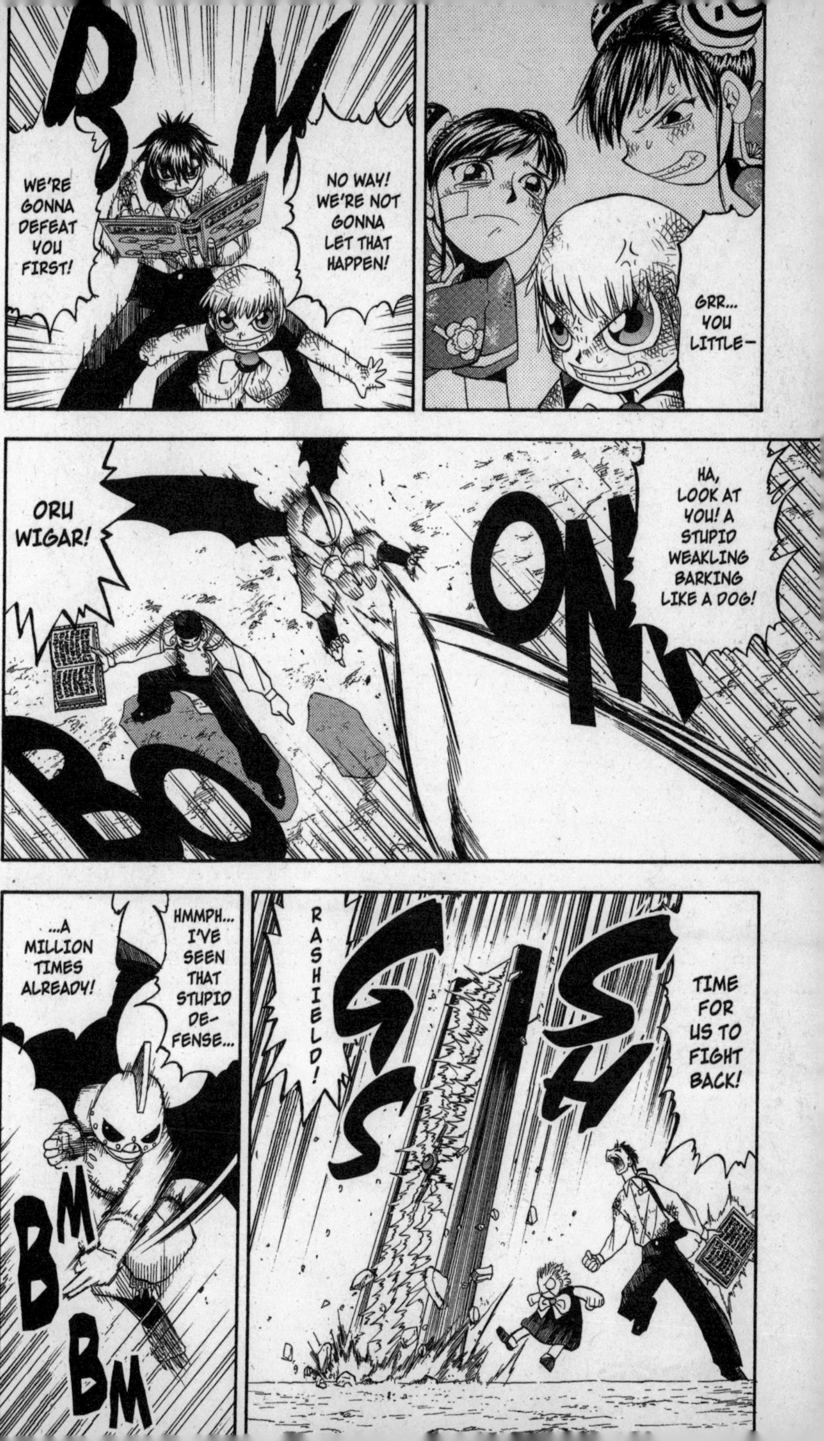
GRR... YOU LITTLE—
NO WAY! WE'RE NOT GONNA LET THAT HAPPEN!
WE'RE GONNA DEFEAT YOU FIRST!
HA, LOOK AT YOU! A STUPID WEAKLING BARKING LIKE A DOG!
ORU WIGAR!
TIME FOR US TO FIGHT BACK!
RASHIELD!
HMMPH... I'VE SEEN THAT STUPID DE-FENSE...
...A MILLION TIMES ALREADY!

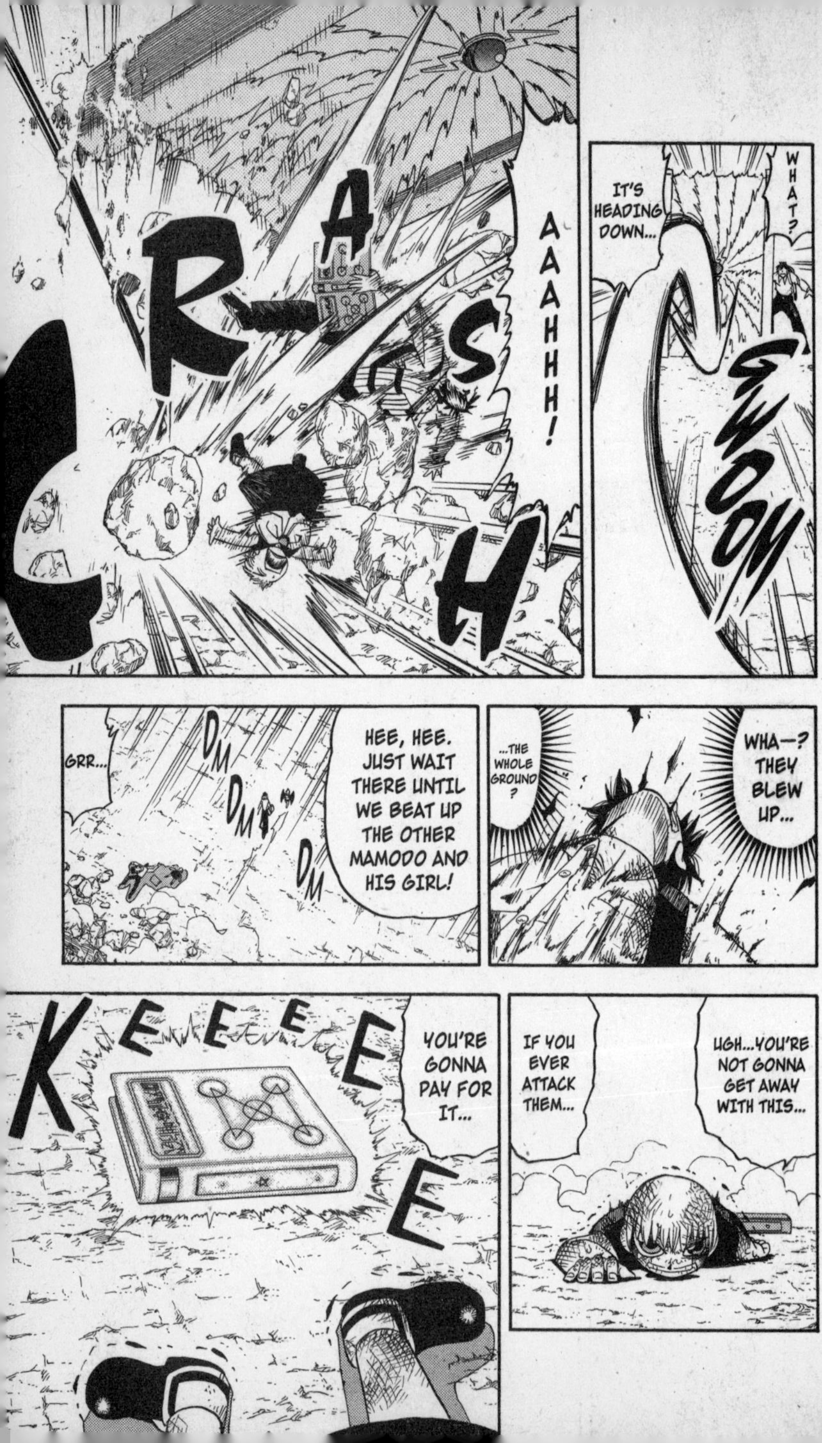

WHAT?
IT'S HEADING DOWN...
GWOOOM
AAAHHH!
CRASH
WHA—? THEY BLEW UP...
...THE WHOLE GROUND?
HEE, HEE. JUST WAIT THERE UNTIL WE BEAT UP THE OTHER MAMODO AND HIS GIRL!
DM DM DM DM
GRR...
UGH...YOU'RE NOT GONNA GET AWAY WITH THIS...
IF YOU EVER ATTACK THEM...
YOU'RE GONNA PAY FOR IT...
KEEEEEE

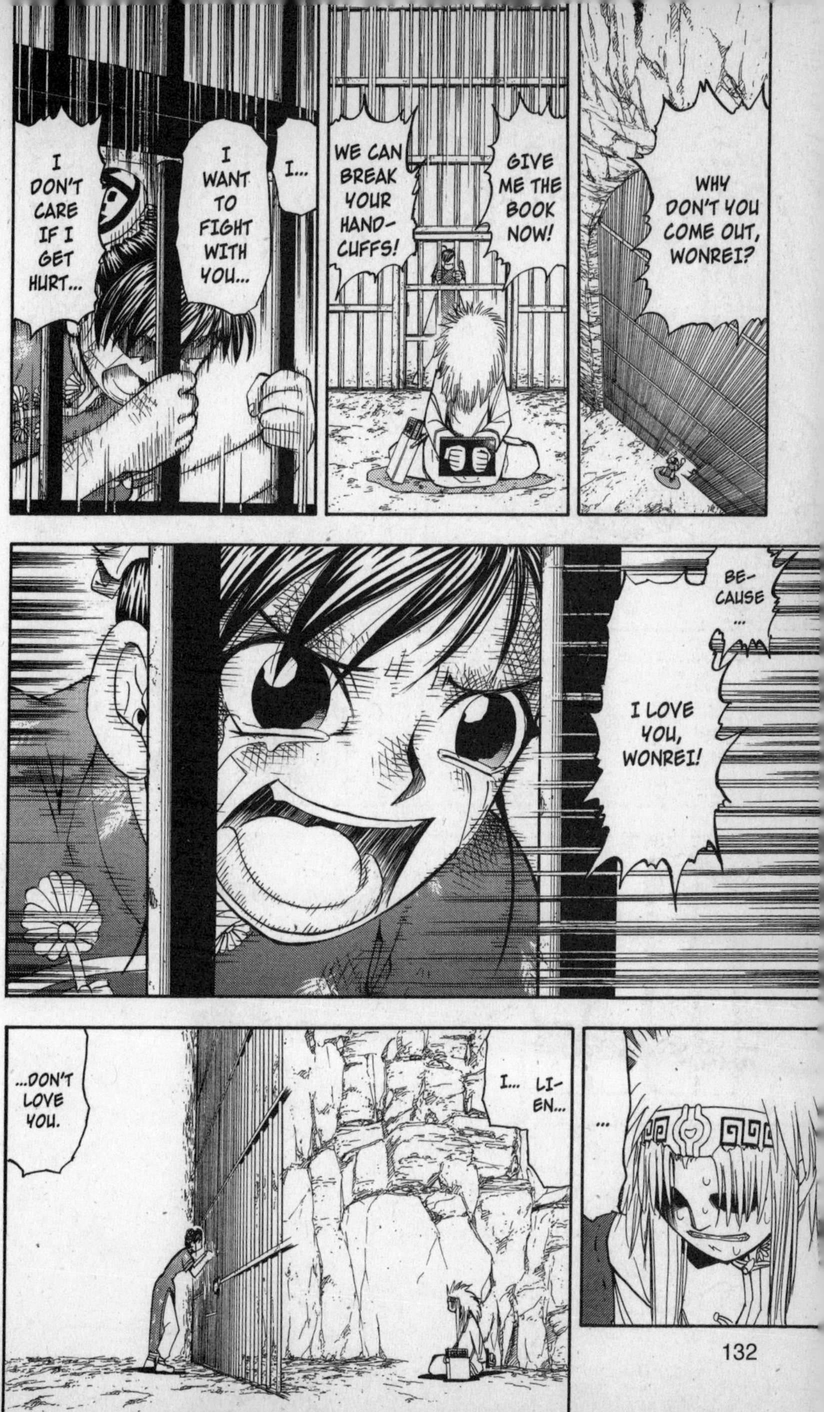

WHY DON'T YOU COME OUT, WONREI?
GIVE ME THE BOOK NOW!
WE CAN BREAK YOUR HAND-CUFFS!
I...
I WANT TO FIGHT WITH YOU...
I DON'T CARE IF I GET HURT...
BE-CAUSE ...
I LOVE YOU, WONREI!
...
LI-EN...
I...
...DON'T LOVE YOU.

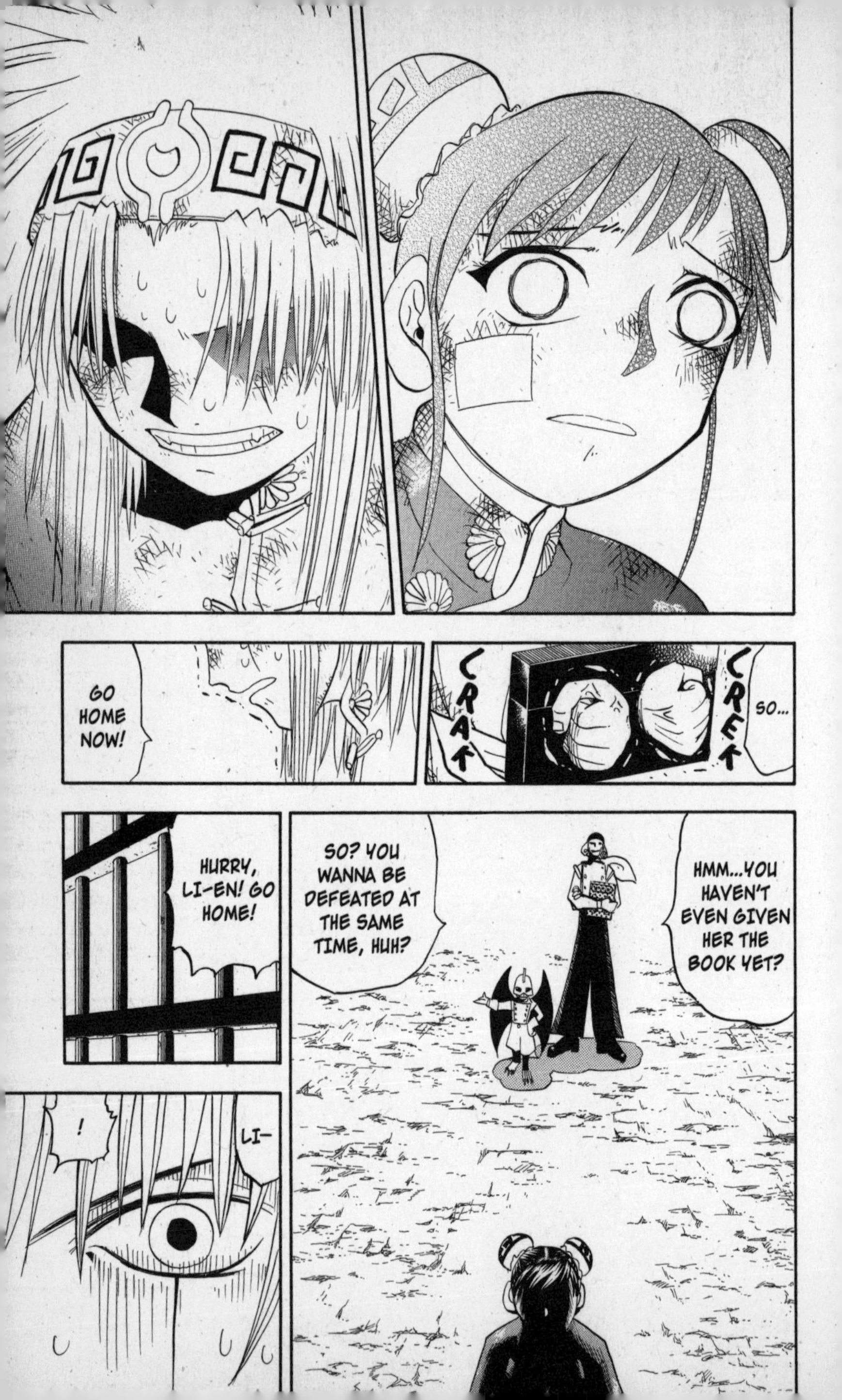
SO...
CRET
CRAT
GO HOME NOW!
HMM...YOU HAVEN'T EVEN GIVEN HER THE BOOK YET?
SO? YOU WANNA BE DEFEATED AT THE SAME TIME, HUH?
HURRY, LI-EN! GO HOME!
LI-
!

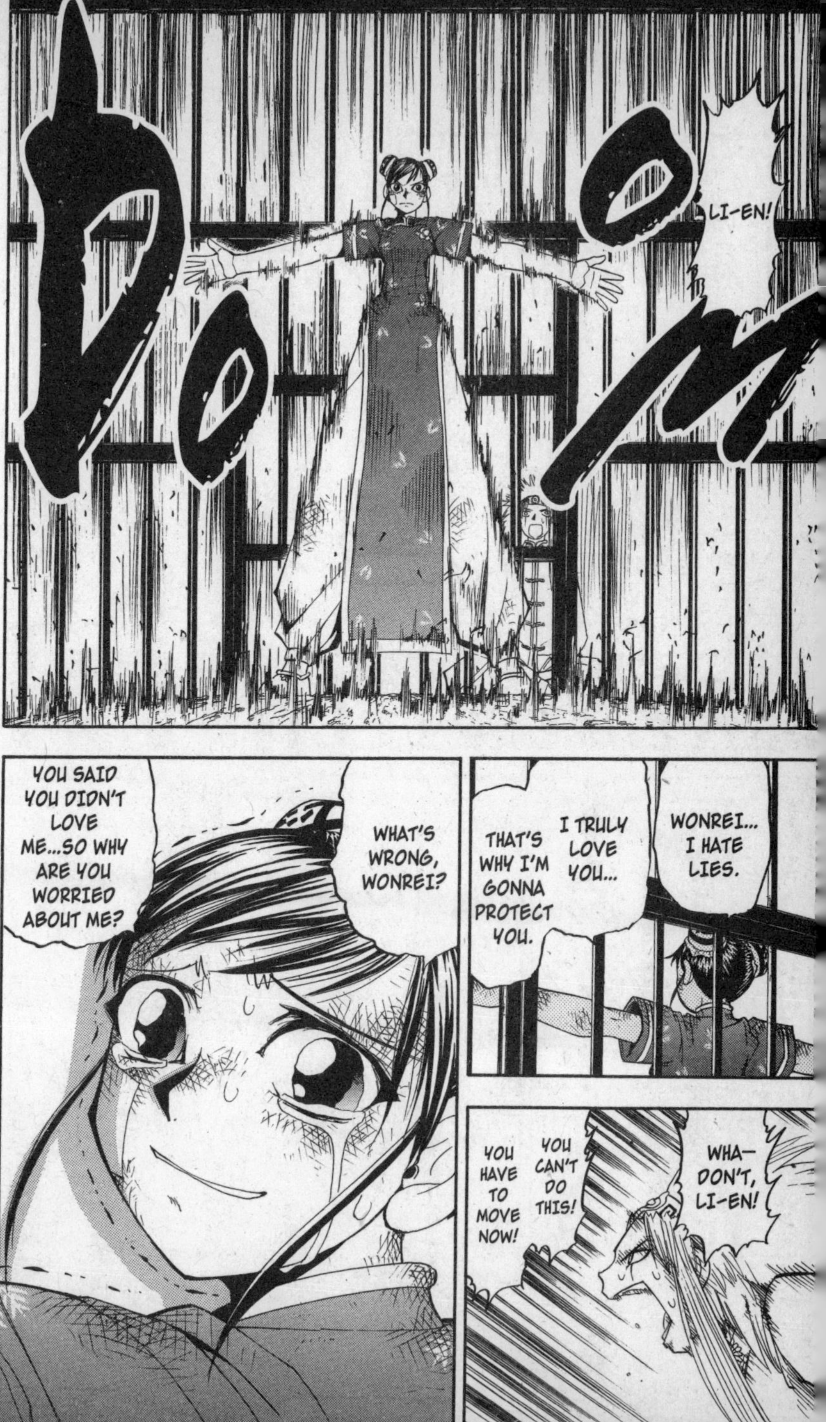
LI-EN!
DOOM
WONREI... I HATE LIES.
I TRULY LOVE YOU...
THAT'S WHY I'M GONNA PROTECT YOU.
WHAT'S WRONG, WONREI?
YOU SAID YOU DIDN'T LOVE ME...SO WHY ARE YOU WORRIED ABOUT ME?
WHA— DON'T, LI-EN!
YOU CAN'T DO THIS!
YOU HAVE TO MOVE NOW!

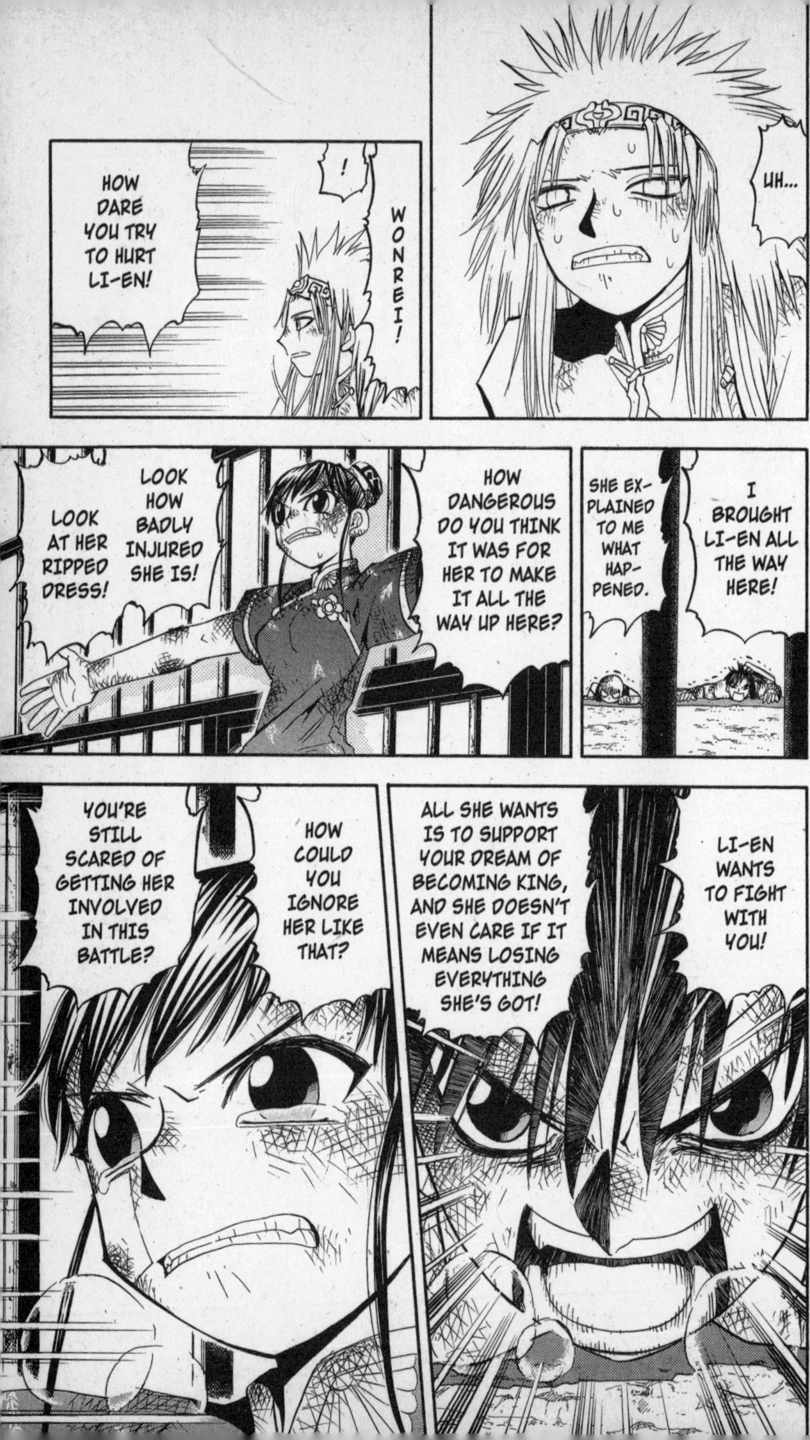
UH...
WONREI!
!
HOW DARE YOU TRY TO HURT LI-EN!
I BROUGHT LI-EN ALL THE WAY HERE!
SHE EX-PLAINED TO ME WHAT HAP-PENED.
HOW DANGEROUS DO YOU THINK IT WAS FOR HER TO MAKE IT ALL THE WAY UP HERE?
LOOK HOW BADLY INJURED SHE IS!
LOOK AT HER RIPPED DRESS!
LI-EN WANTS TO FIGHT WITH YOU!
ALL SHE WANTS IS TO SUPPORT YOUR DREAM OF BECOMING KING, AND SHE DOESN'T EVEN CARE IF IT MEANS LOSING EVERYTHING SHE'S GOT!
HOW COULD YOU IGNORE HER LIKE THAT?
YOU'RE STILL SCARED OF GETTING HER INVOLVED IN THIS BATTLE?

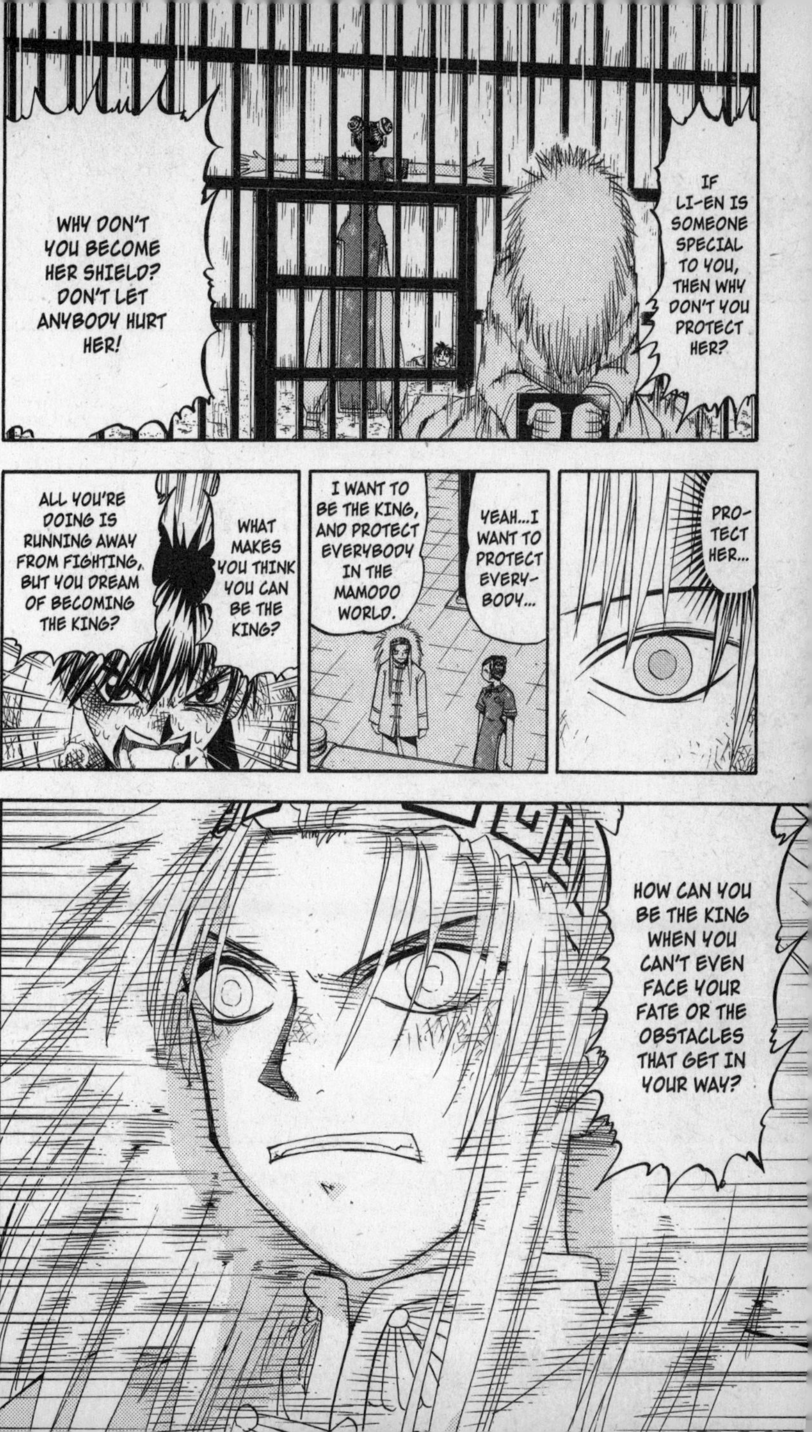
IF LI-EN IS SOMEONE SPECIAL TO YOU, THEN WHY DON'T YOU PROTECT HER?
WHY DON'T YOU BECOME HER SHIELD? DON'T LET ANYBODY HURT HER!
PROTECT HER...
YEAH...I WANT TO PROTECT EVERYBODY...
I WANT TO BE THE KING, AND PROTECT EVERYBODY IN THE MAMODO WORLD.
WHAT MAKES YOU THINK YOU CAN BE THE KING?
ALL YOU'RE DOING IS RUNNING AWAY FROM FIGHTING, BUT YOU DREAM OF BECOMING THE KING?
HOW CAN YOU BE THE KING WHEN YOU CAN'T EVEN FACE YOUR FATE OR THE OBSTACLES THAT GET IN YOUR WAY?

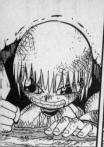

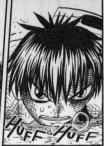

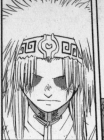

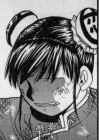

HUFF HUFF
HEE, HEE...IS THE SHOW OVER NOW? THAT WAS ENTERTAINING.
WORTHLESS FOOLS, ENOUGH BABBLING ABOUT PROTECTING THIS OR BECOMING KING OF THAT.
OH, I GET IT. WORTHLESS MAMODO TEAMED UP WITH WORTHLESS HUMANS, EH?
FINE! I'LL LET YOU WORTHLESS PAIRS GO DOWN TOGETHER!
GARUK!
LI-EN...
THE FOURTH SPELL!

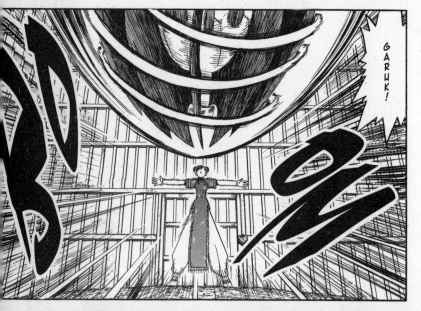

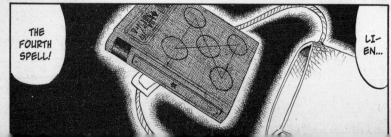

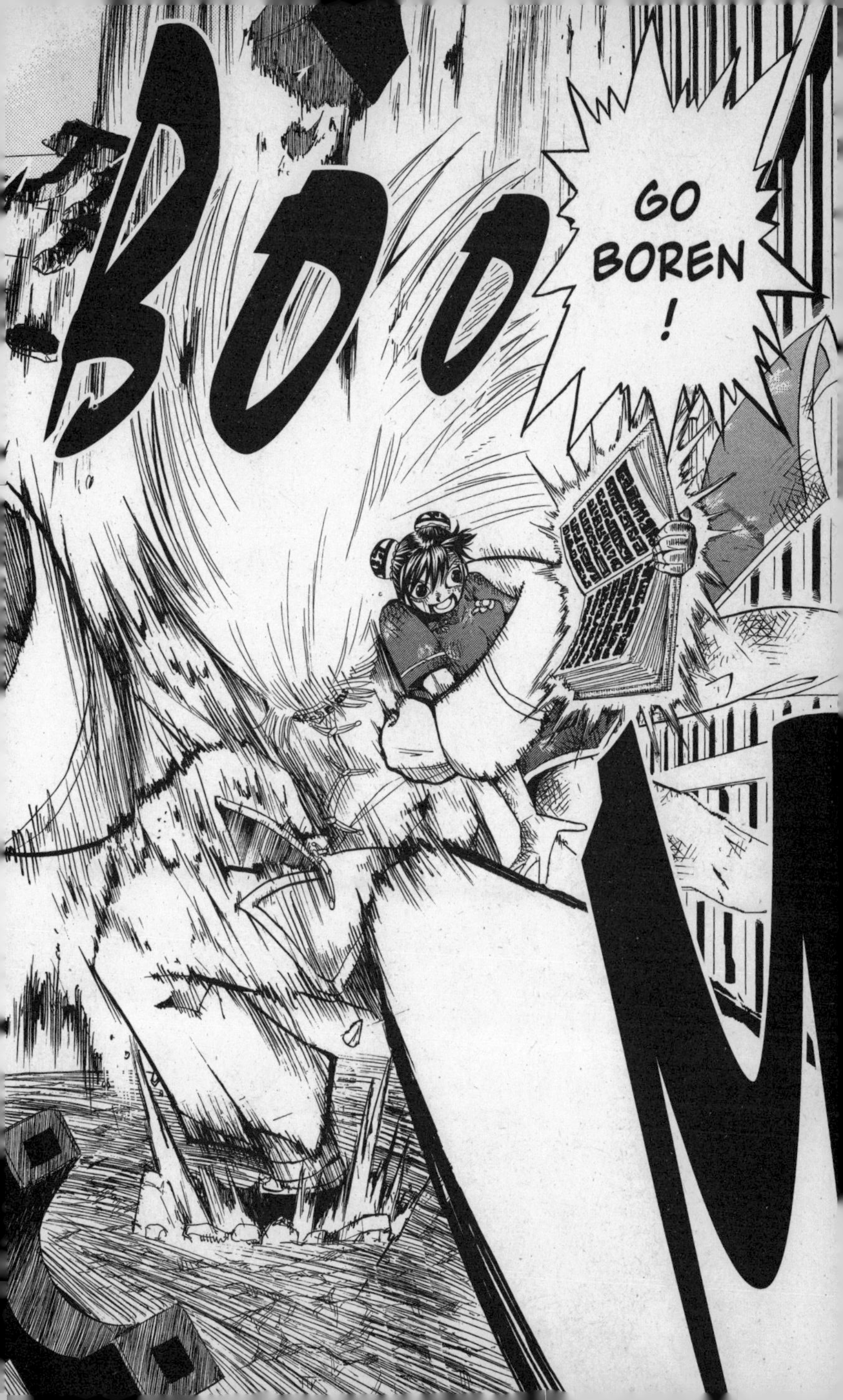
GO BOREN!
BOOM

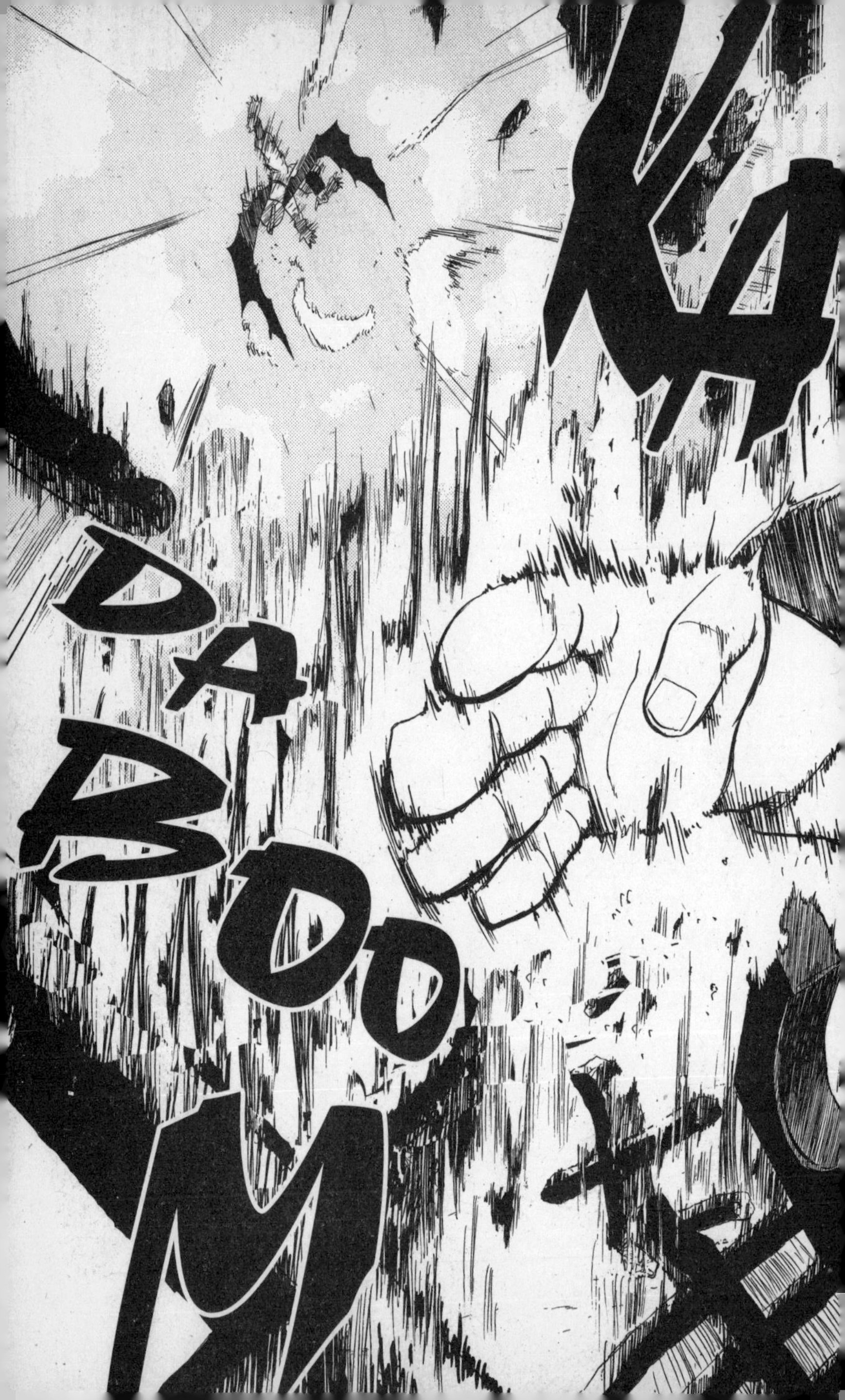
DABOOM

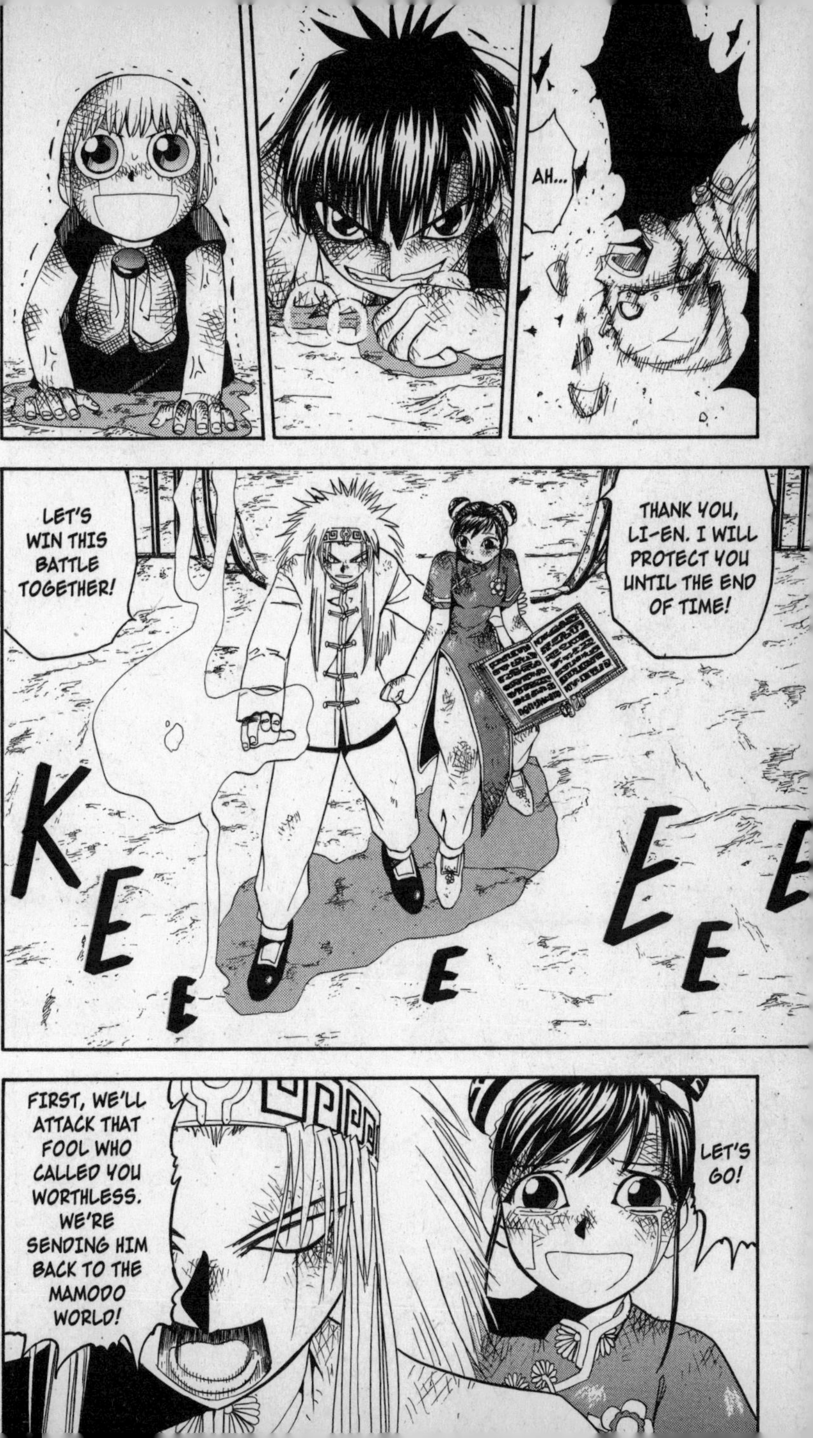
AH...
LET'S WIN THIS BATTLE TOGETHER!
THANK YOU, LI-EN. I WILL PROTECT YOU UNTIL THE END OF TIME!
KEEEEEEE
FIRST, WE'LL ATTACK THAT FOOL WHO CALLED YOU WORTHLESS. WE'RE SENDING HIM BACK TO THE MAMODO WORLD!
LET'S GO!

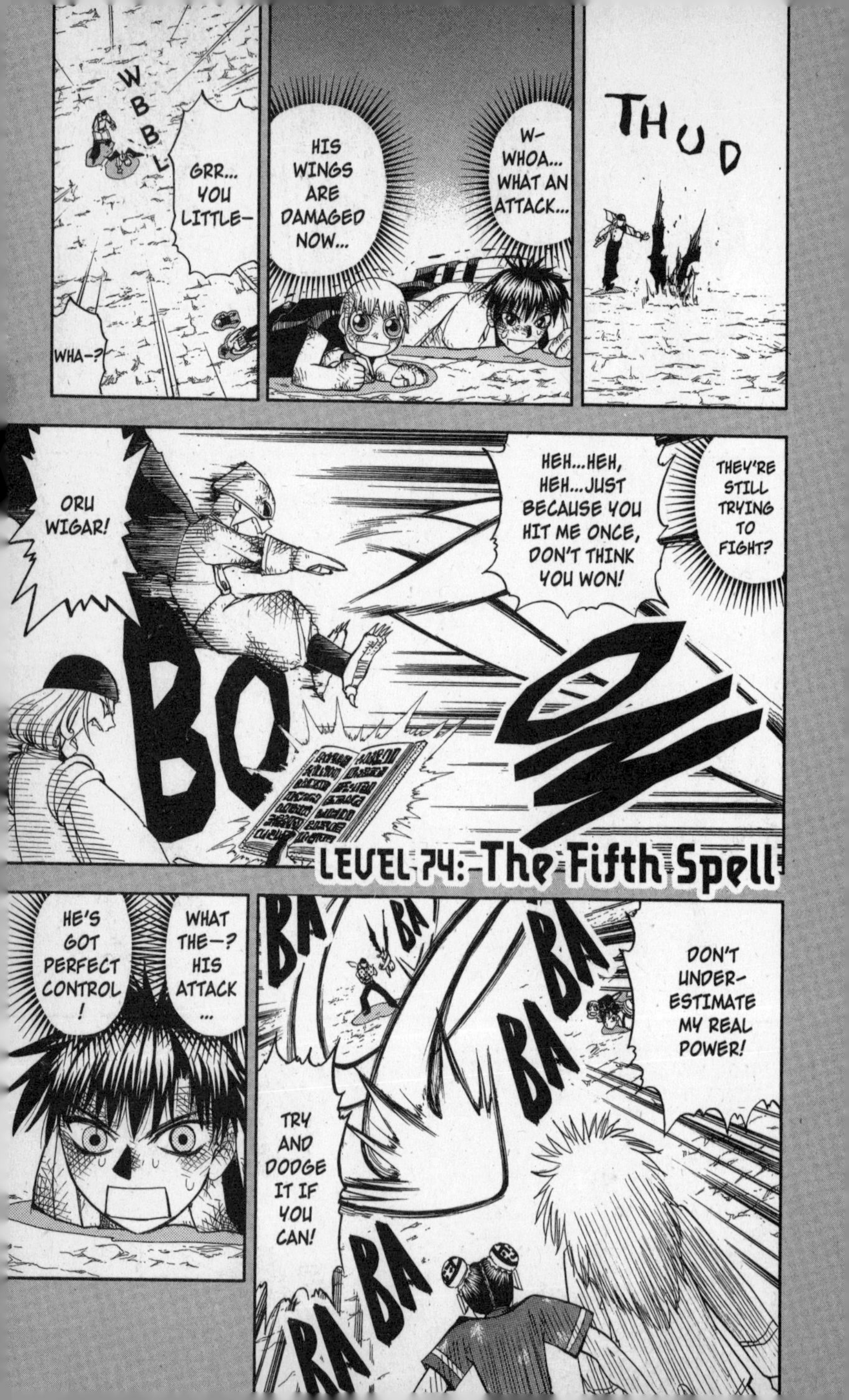
THUD
W-WHOA... WHAT AN ATTACK...
HIS WINGS ARE DAMAGED NOW...
GRR... YOU LITTLE-
WBBL
WHA-?
THEY'RE STILL TRYING TO FIGHT?
HEH...HEH, HEH...JUST BECAUSE YOU HIT ME ONCE, DON'T THINK YOU WON!
ORU WIGAR!
BOOM
LEVEL 74: The Fifth Spell
DON'T UNDER-ESTIMATE MY REAL POWER!
BA BA BA BA BA
TRY AND DODGE IT IF YOU CAN!
RA BA BA
WHAT THE—? HIS ATTACK ...
HE'S GOT PERFECT CONTROL !

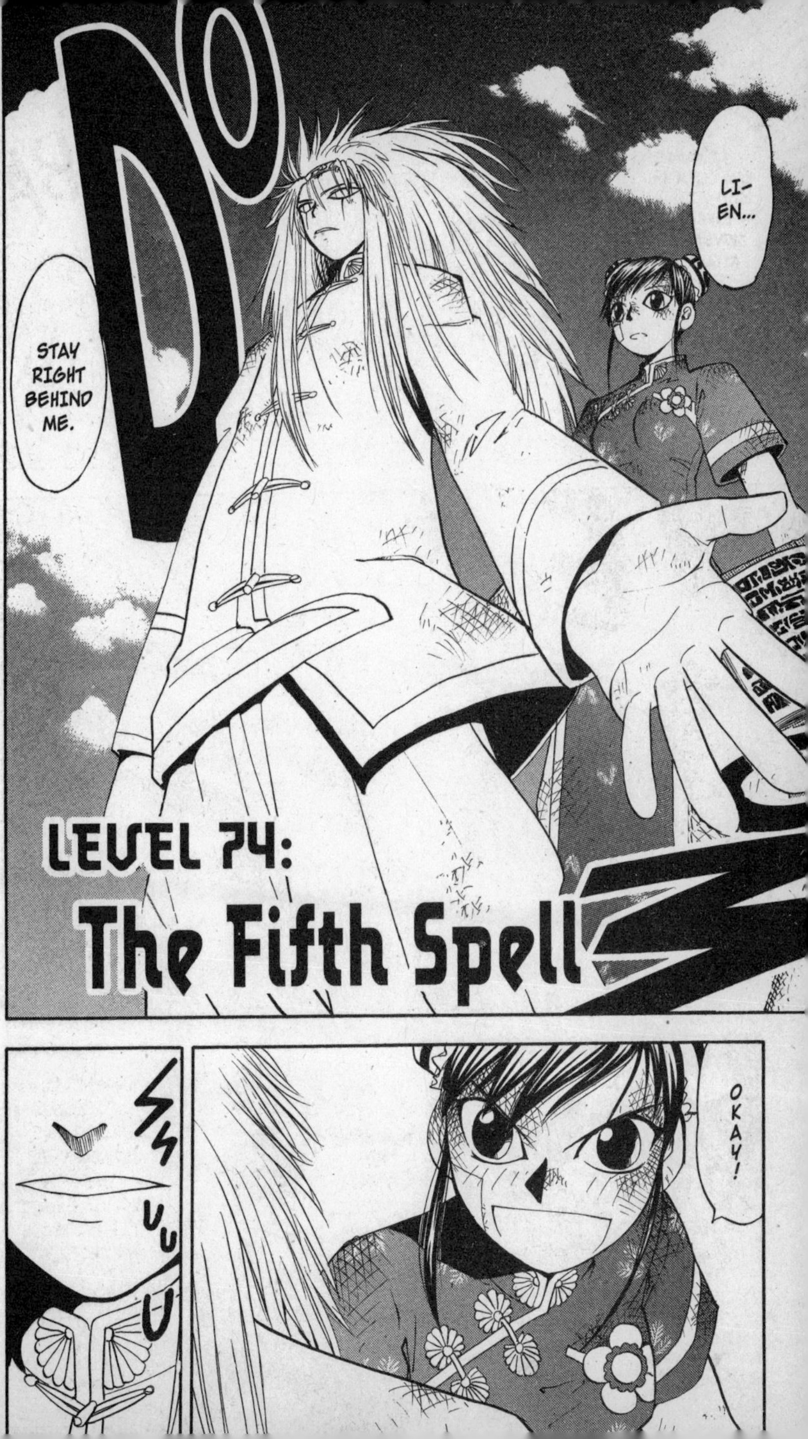
LI-EN...
DO
STAY RIGHT BEHIND ME.
LEVEL 74:
The Fifth Spell
OKAY!

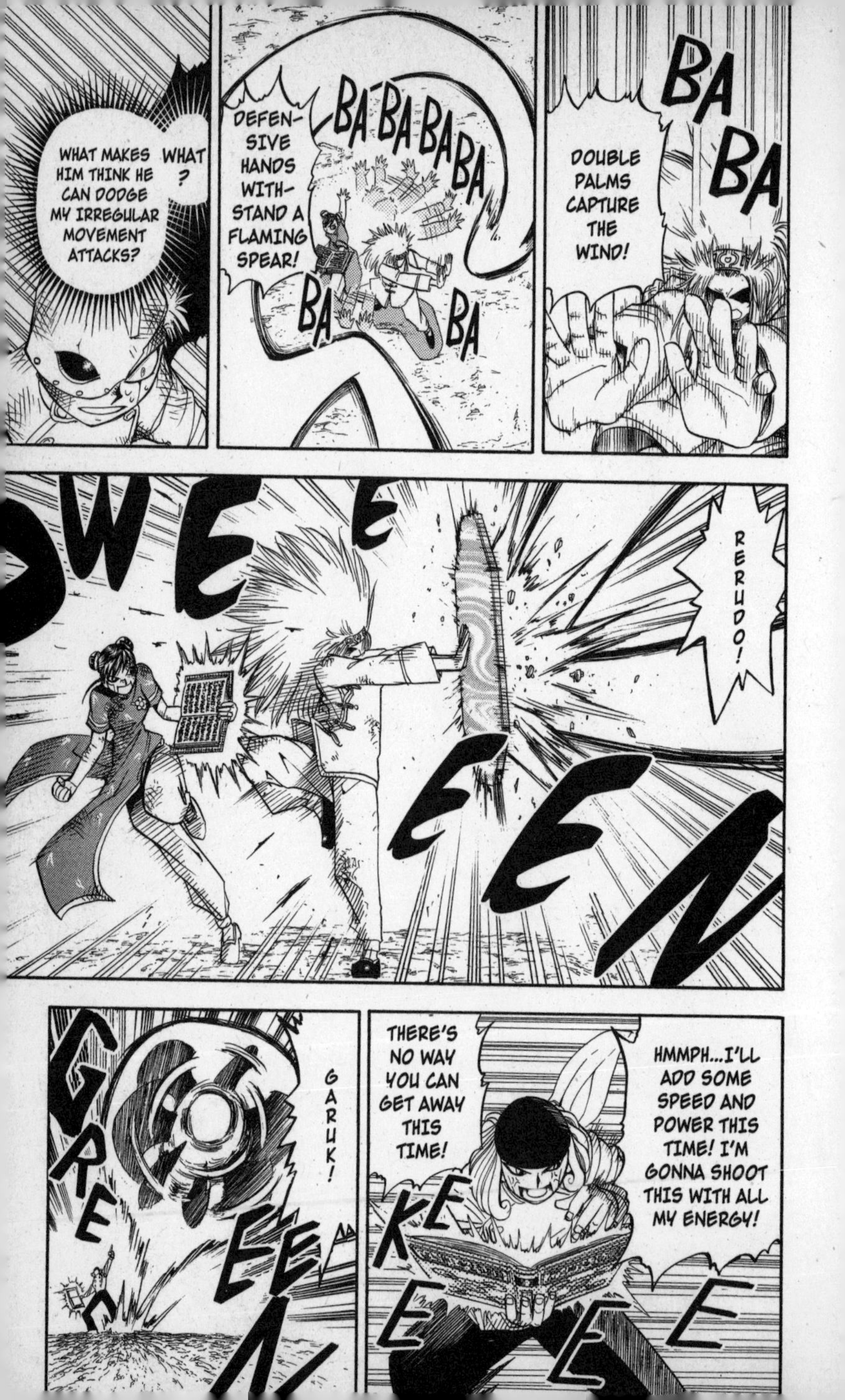
BA BA BA
DOUBLE PALMS CAPTURE THE WIND!
DEFEN-SIVE HANDS WITH-STAND A FLAMING SPEAR!
BA-BA-BA-BA-BA
BA BA
WHAT ?
WHAT MAKES HIM THINK HE CAN DODGE MY IRREGULAR MOVEMENT ATTACKS?
RERUDO!
HMMPH...I'LL ADD SOME SPEED AND POWER THIS TIME! I'M GONNA SHOOT THIS WITH ALL MY ENERGY!
THERE'S NO WAY YOU CAN GET AWAY THIS TIME!
GARUK!

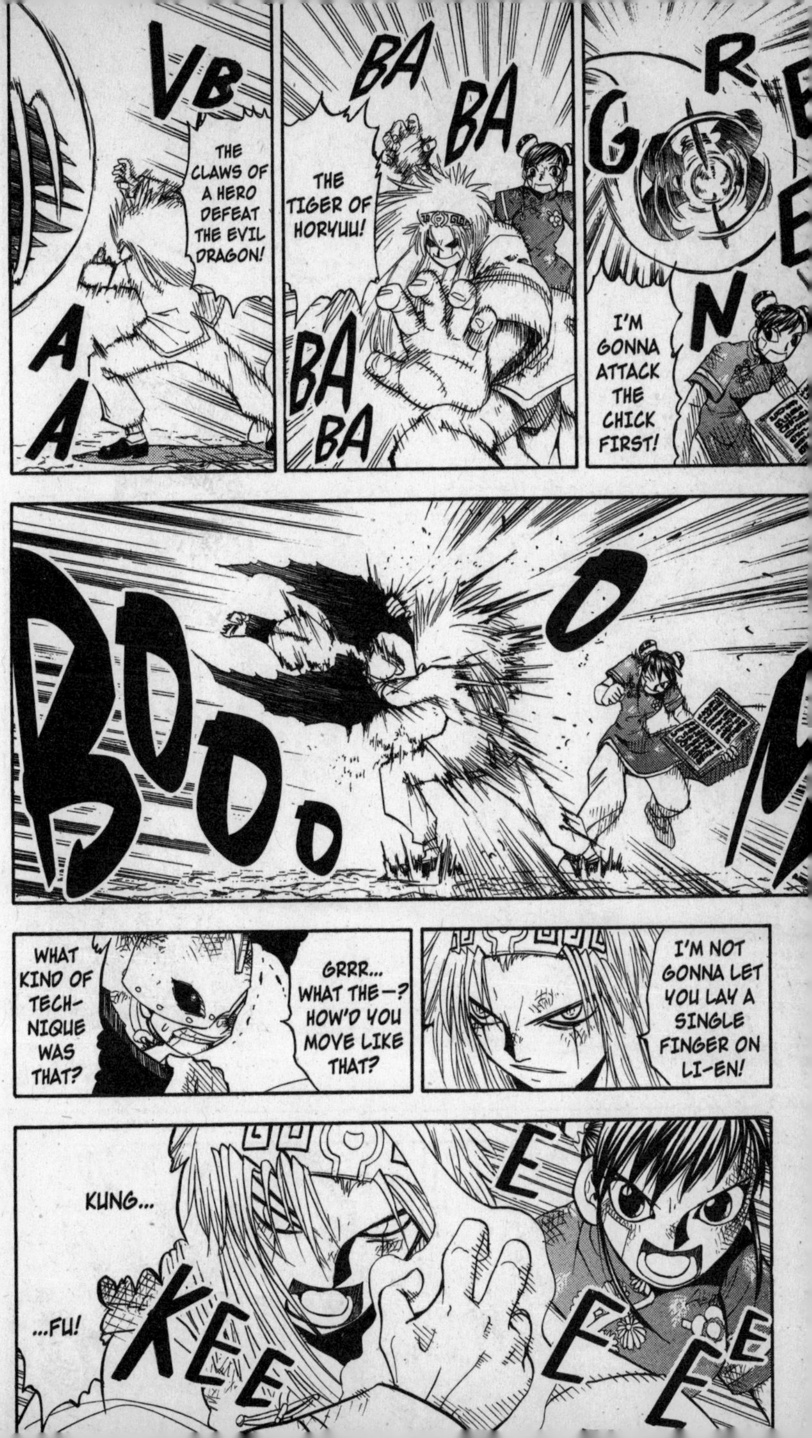
GREEN
I'M GONNA ATTACK THE CHICK FIRST!
BA BA
THE TIGER OF HORYUU!
BA BA BA
VB
THE CLAWS OF A HERO DEFEAT THE EVIL DRAGON!
AA
BDOOOM
I'M NOT GONNA LET YOU LAY A SINGLE FINGER ON LI-EN!
GRRR... WHAT THE—? HOW'D YOU MOVE LIKE THAT?
WHAT KIND OF TECH-NIQUE WAS THAT?
EEEEE
KUNG...
...FU!
KEE

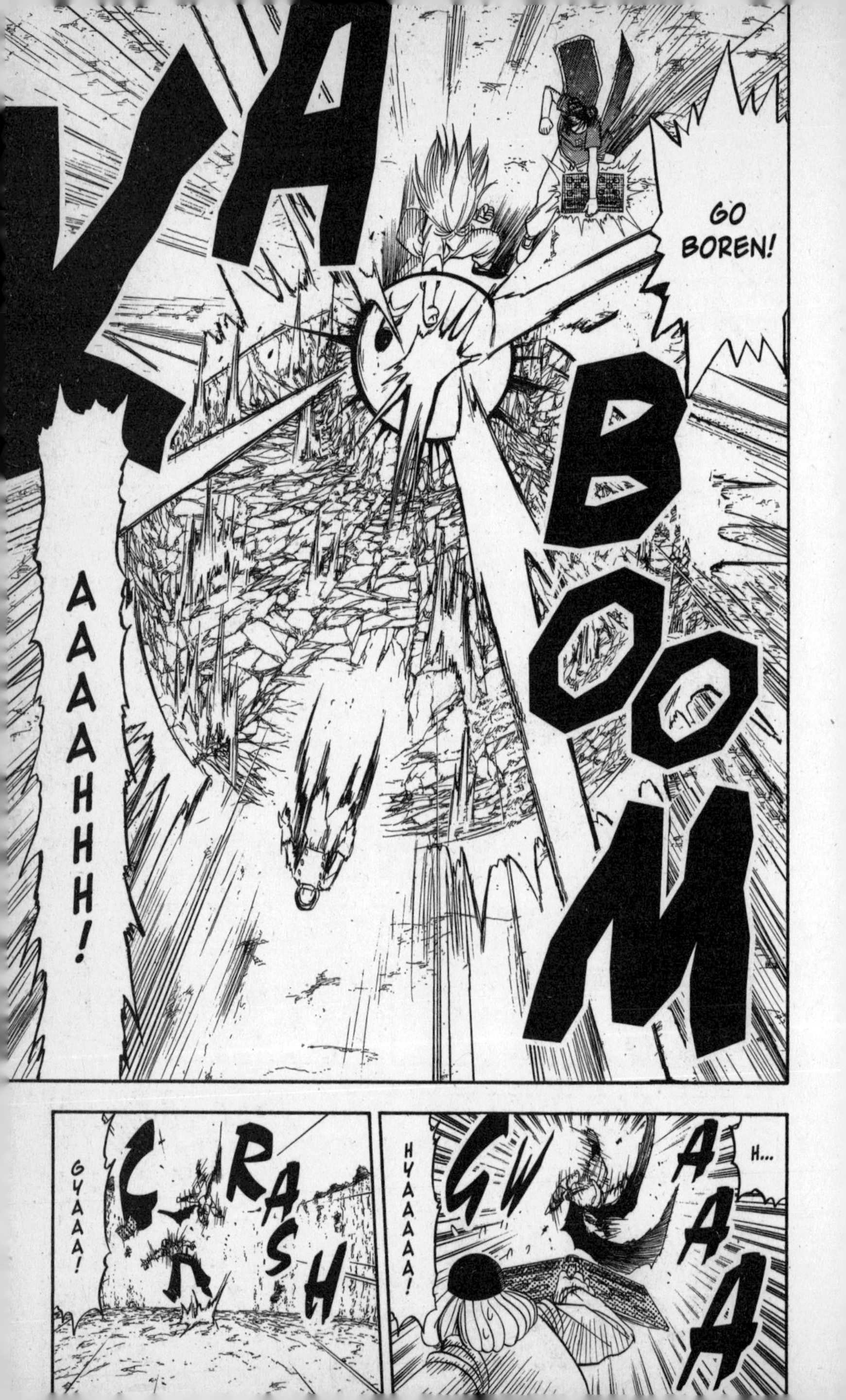
GO BOREN!
YA
BOOM
AAAAHHH!
H...
GWAAAA
HYAAAAAA!
CRASH
GYAAAA!

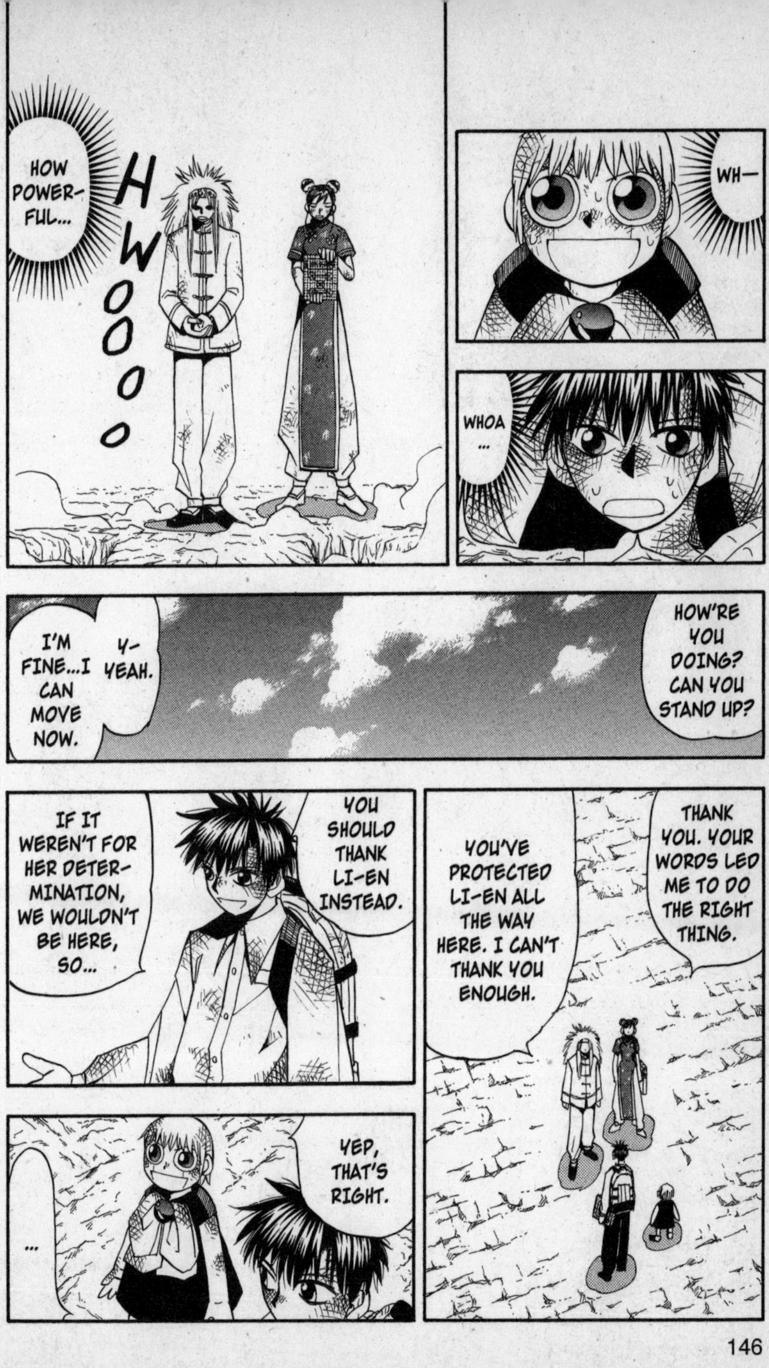
WH—
WHOA...
HWOOOO
HOW POWERFUL...
HOW'RE YOU DOING? CAN YOU STAND UP?
Y-YEAH.
I'M FINE...I CAN MOVE NOW.
THANK YOU. YOUR WORDS LED ME TO DO THE RIGHT THING.
YOU'VE PROTECTED LI-EN ALL THE WAY HERE. I CAN'T THANK YOU ENOUGH.
YOU SHOULD THANK LI-EN INSTEAD.
IF IT WEREN'T FOR HER DETERMINATION, WE WOULDN'T BE HERE, SO...
YEP, THAT'S RIGHT.
...

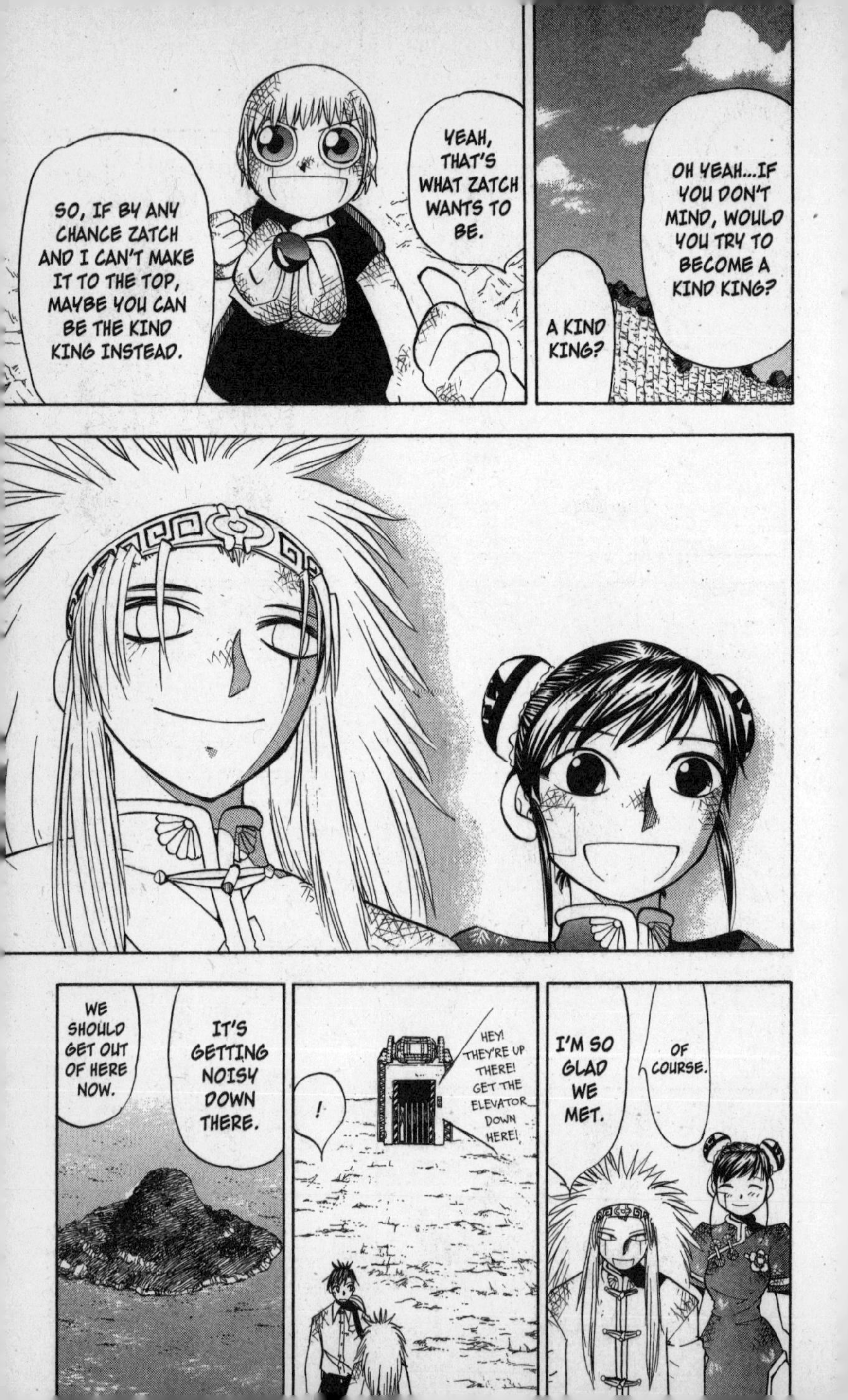
OH YEAH...IF YOU DON'T MIND, WOULD YOU TRY TO BECOME A KIND KING?
A KIND KING?
YEAH, THAT'S WHAT ZATCH WANTS TO BE.
SO, IF BY ANY CHANCE ZATCH AND I CAN'T MAKE IT TO THE TOP, MAYBE YOU CAN BE THE KIND KING INSTEAD.
OF COURSE.
I'M SO GLAD WE MET.
HEY! THEY'RE UP THERE! GET THE ELEVATOR DOWN HERE!
!
IT'S GETTING NOISY DOWN THERE.
WE SHOULD GET OUT OF HERE NOW.

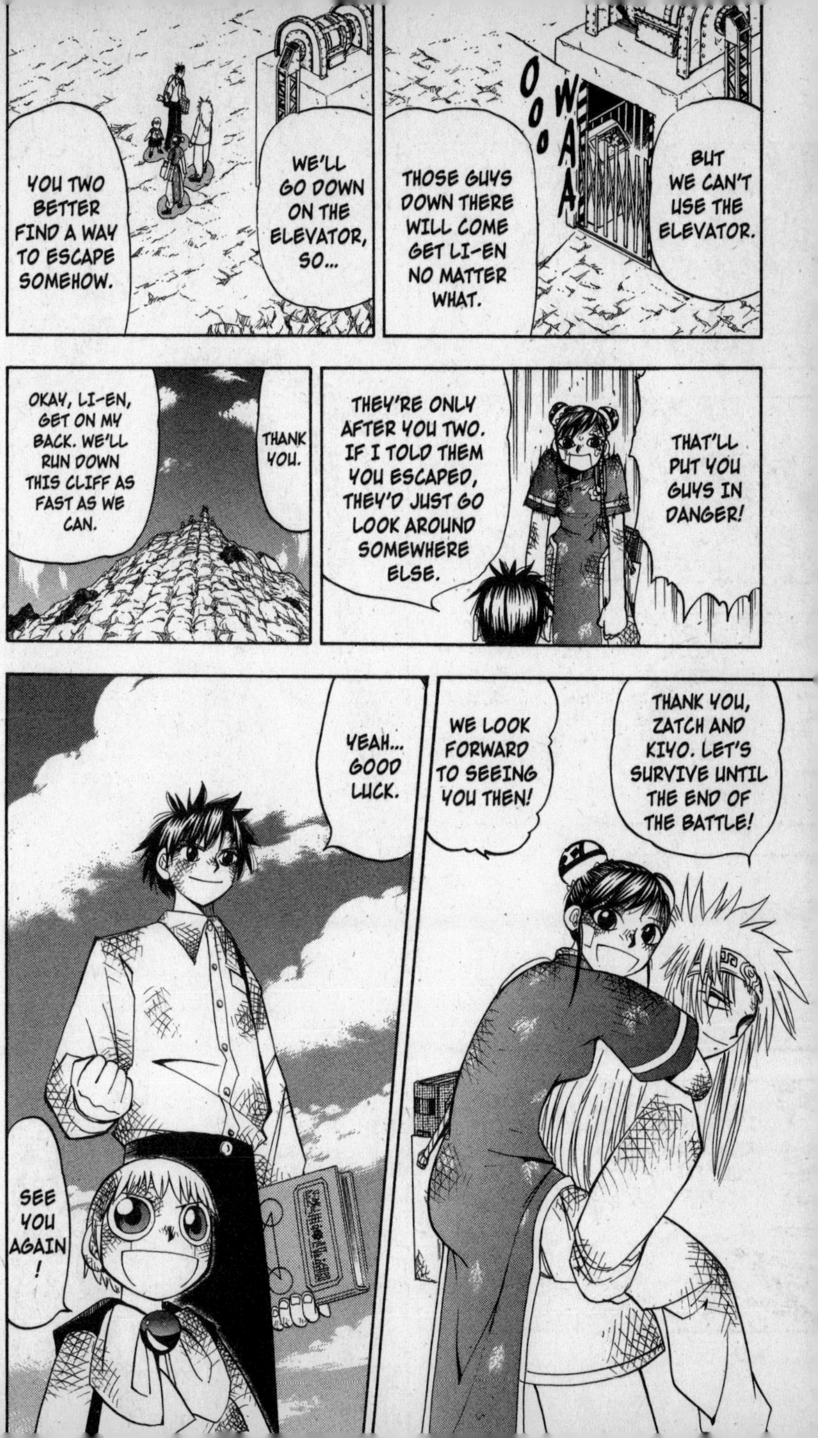
BUT WE CAN'T USE THE ELEVATOR.
THOSE GUYS DOWN THERE WILL COME GET LI-EN NO MATTER WHAT.
WE'LL GO DOWN ON THE ELEVATOR, SO...
YOU TWO BETTER FIND A WAY TO ESCAPE SOMEHOW.
THAT'LL PUT YOU GUYS IN DANGER!
THEY'RE ONLY AFTER YOU TWO. IF I TOLD THEM YOU ESCAPED, THEY'D JUST GO LOOK AROUND SOMEWHERE ELSE.
THANK YOU.
OKAY, LI-EN, GET ON MY BACK. WE'LL RUN DOWN THIS CLIFF AS FAST AS WE CAN.
THANK YOU, ZATCH AND KIYO. LET'S SURVIVE UNTIL THE END OF THE BATTLE!
WE LOOK FORWARD TO SEEING YOU THEN!
YEAH... GOOD LUCK.
SEE YOU AGAIN!

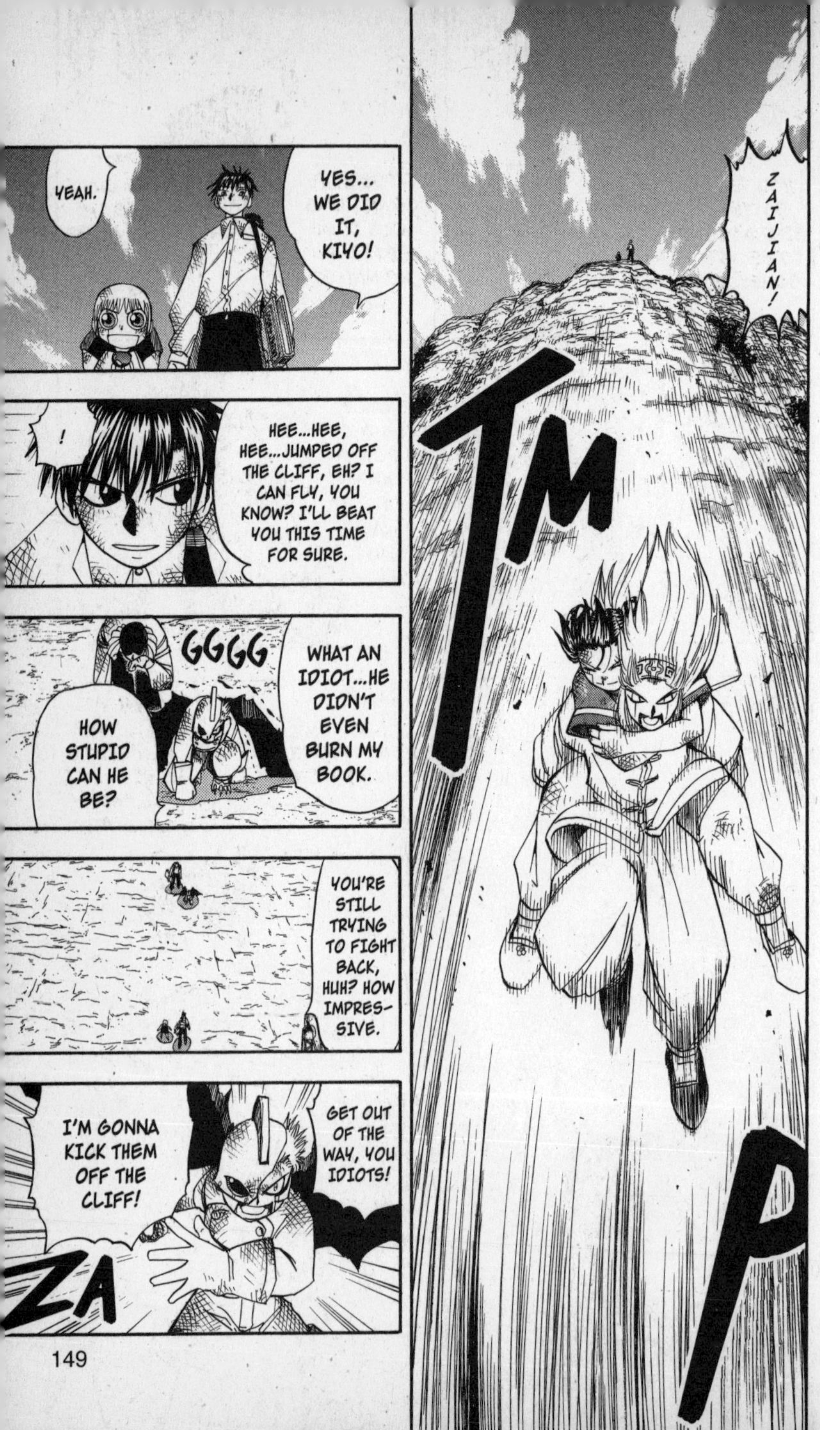
YES... WE DID IT, KIYO!
YEAH.
!
HEE...HEE, HEE...JUMPED OFF THE CLIFF, EH? I CAN FLY, YOU KNOW? I'LL BEAT YOU THIS TIME FOR SURE.
WHAT AN IDIOT...HE DIDN'T EVEN BURN MY BOOK.
GGGG
HOW STUPID CAN HE BE?
YOU'RE STILL TRYING TO FIGHT BACK, HUH? HOW IMPRES-SIVE.
GET OUT OF THE WAY, YOU IDIOTS!
I'M GONNA KICK THEM OFF THE CLIFF!
ZA
ZAIJIAN!
TM
P

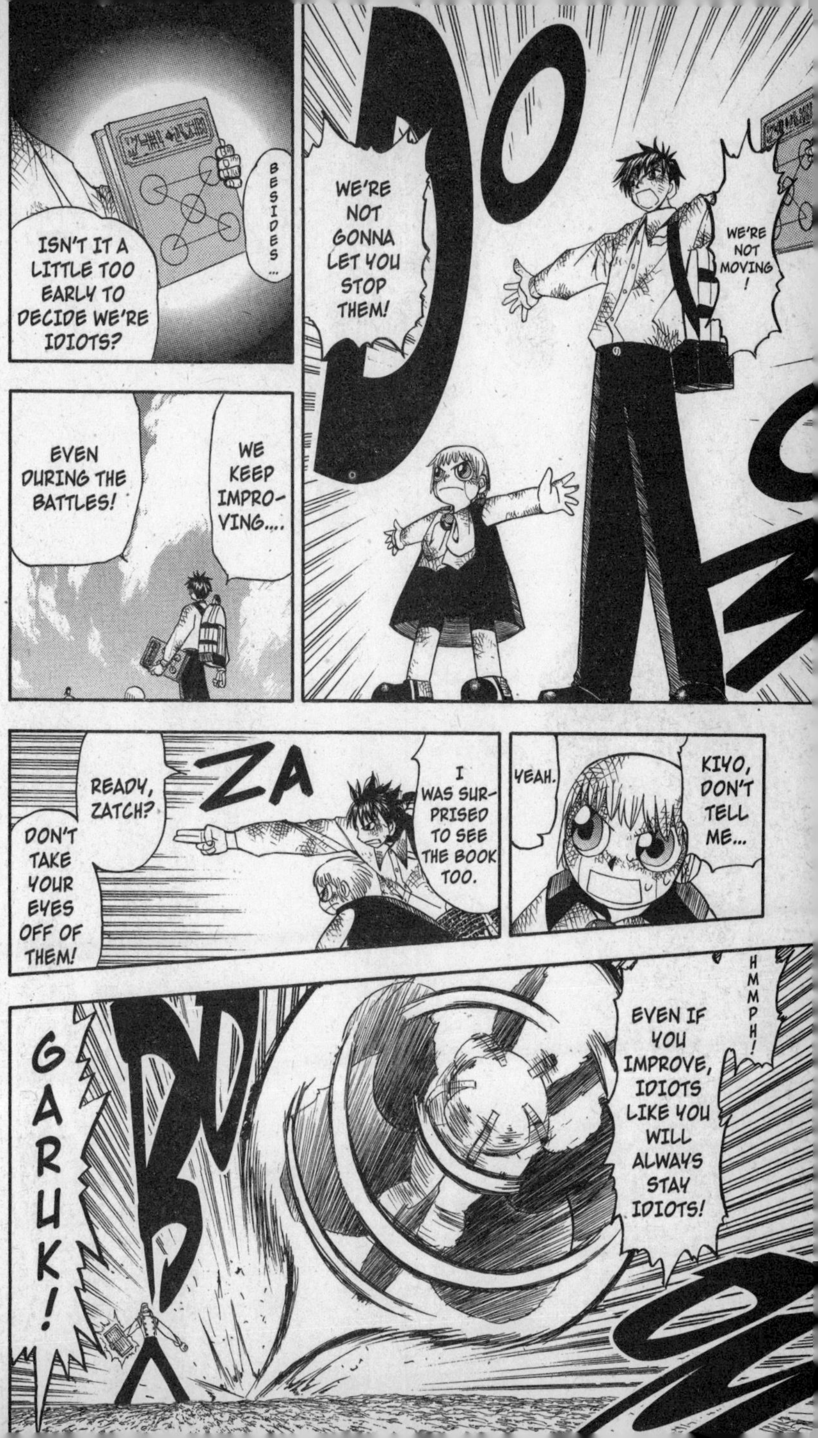
WE'RE NOT MOVING!
WE'RE NOT GONNA LET YOU STOP THEM!
DO
BESIDES...
ISN'T IT A LITTLE TOO EARLY TO DECIDE WE'RE IDIOTS?
WE KEEP IMPROVING....
EVEN DURING THE BATTLES!
KIYO, DON'T TELL ME...
YEAH.
I WAS SURPRISED TO SEE THE BOOK TOO.
ZA
READY, ZATCH?
DON'T TAKE YOUR EYES OFF OF THEM!
HMMPH!
EVEN IF YOU IMPROVE, IDIOTS LIKE YOU WILL ALWAYS STAY IDIOTS!
GARUK!

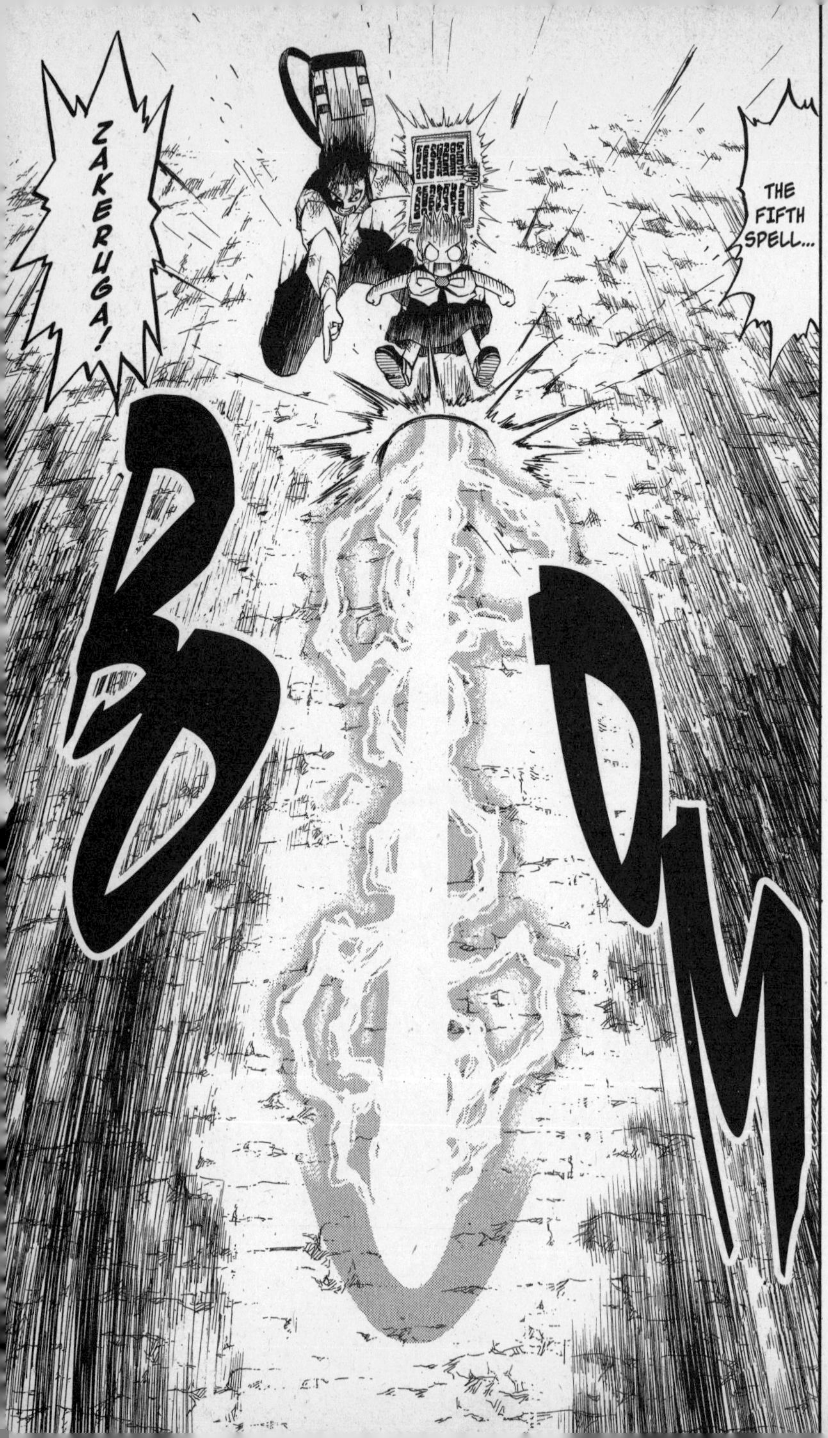
THE FIFTH SPELL...
ZAKERUGA!
BDM

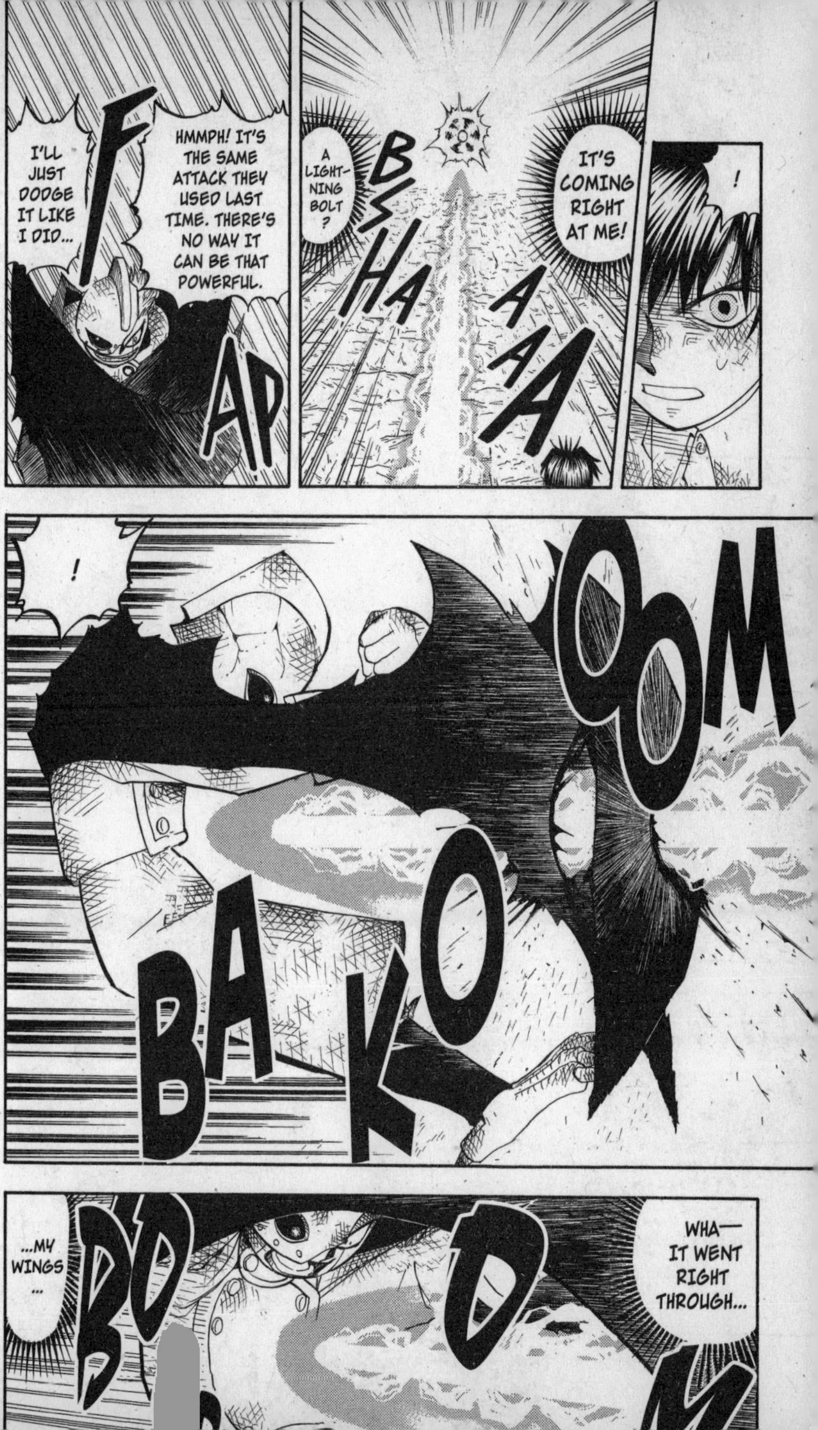
HMMPH! IT'S THE SAME ATTACK THEY USED LAST TIME. THERE'S NO WAY IT CAN BE THAT POWERFUL.
I'LL JUST DODGE IT LIKE I DID...
FAP
A LIGHTNING BOLT?
BSHAAAA
IT'S COMING RIGHT AT ME!
!
!
BAKOOOM
WHA— IT WENT RIGHT THROUGH...
...MY WINGS...
BDOOM

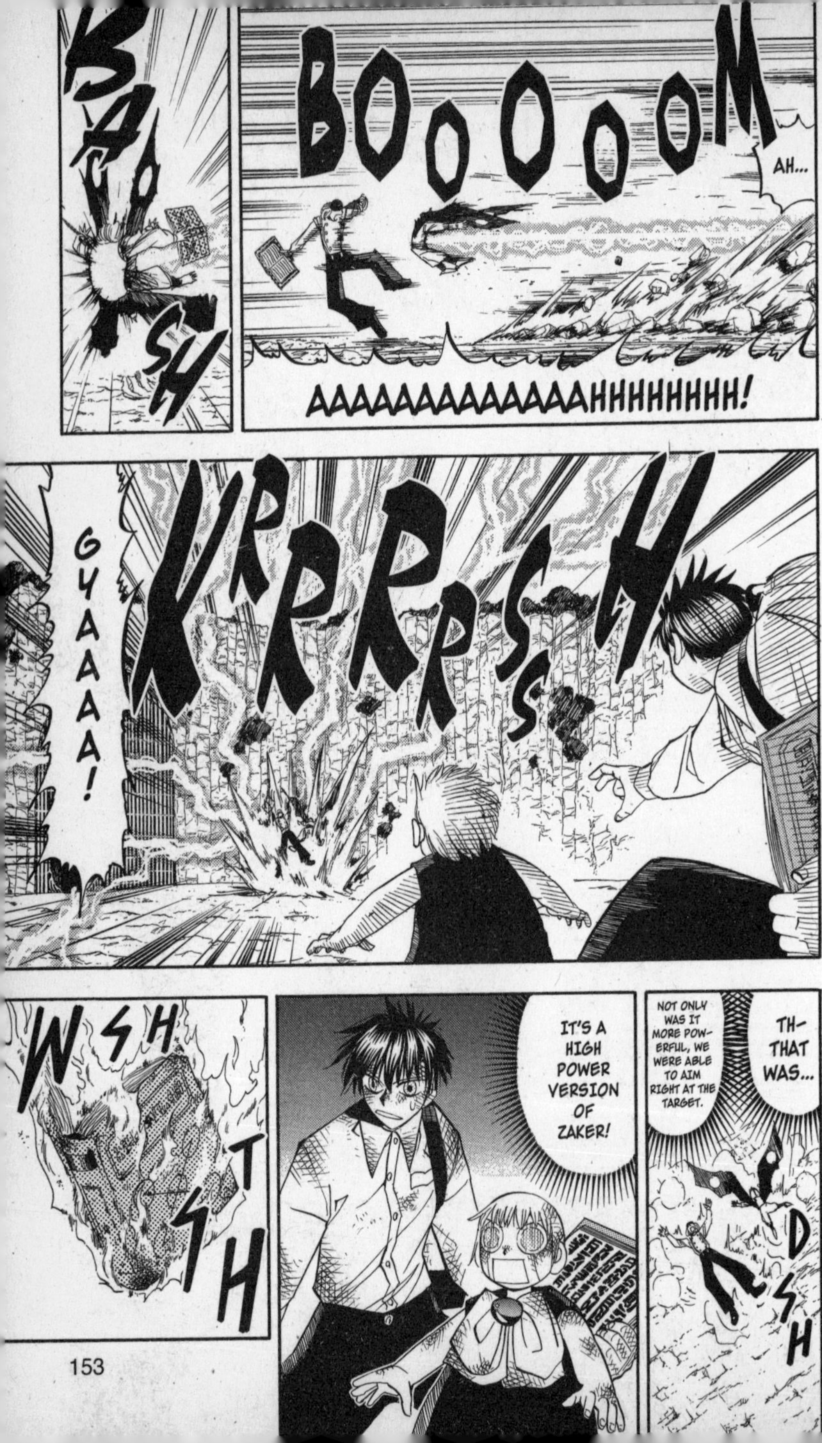
BOOOOOM
AH...
BASH
AAAAAAAAAAAAAAHHHHHHHH!
KRRRSH
GYAAAAA!
TH-THAT WAS...
NOT ONLY WAS IT MORE POW-ERFUL, WE WERE ABLE TO AIM RIGHT AT THE TARGET.
IT'S A HIGH POWER VERSION OF ZAKER!
DSH
WSH
TSH

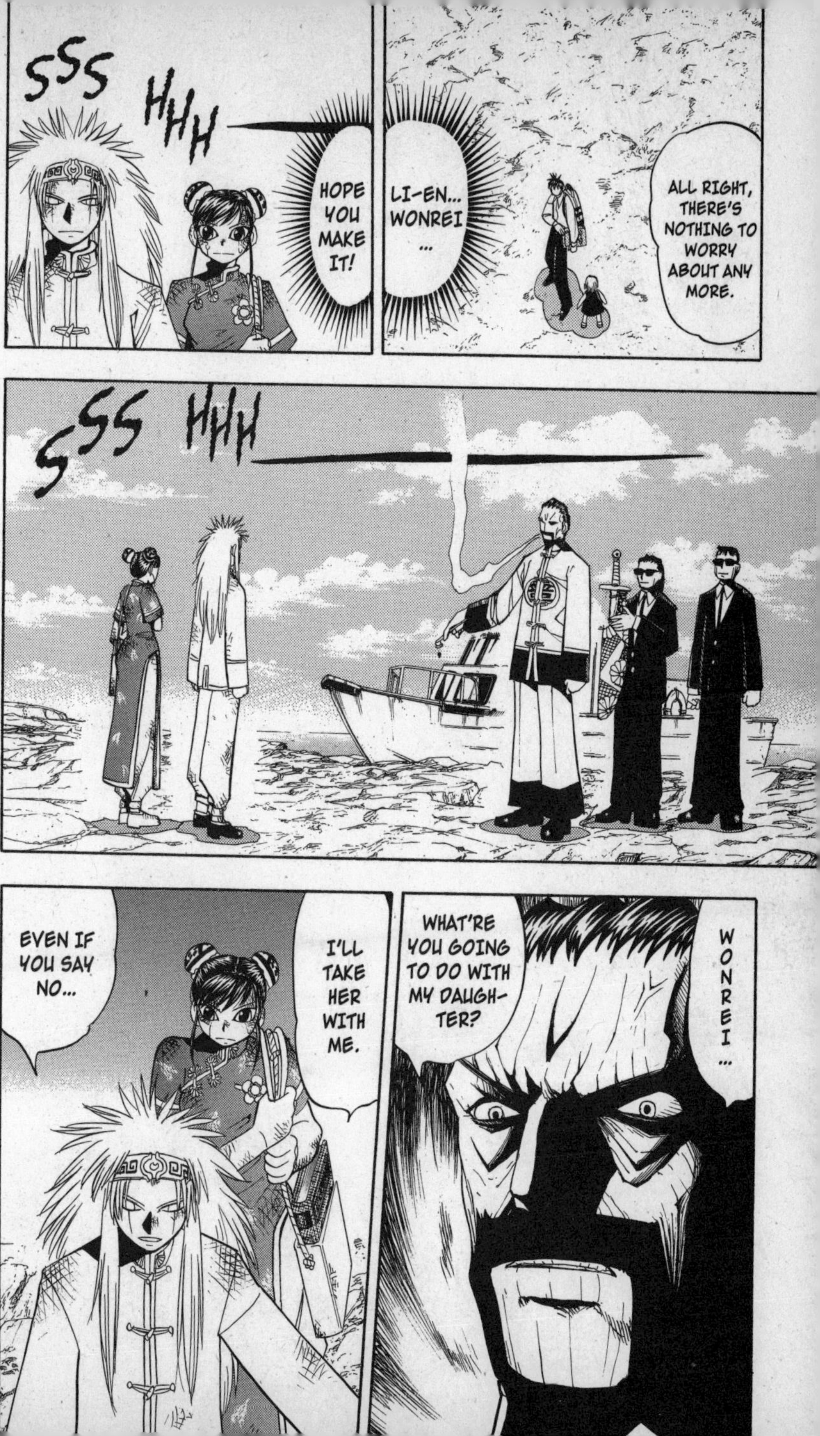
ALL RIGHT, THERE'S NOTHING TO WORRY ABOUT ANY MORE.
LI-EN... WONREI ...
HOPE YOU MAKE IT!
SSS HHH
SSS HHH
WONREI ...
WHAT'RE YOU GOING TO DO WITH MY DAUGH-TER?
I'LL TAKE HER WITH ME.
EVEN IF YOU SAY NO...

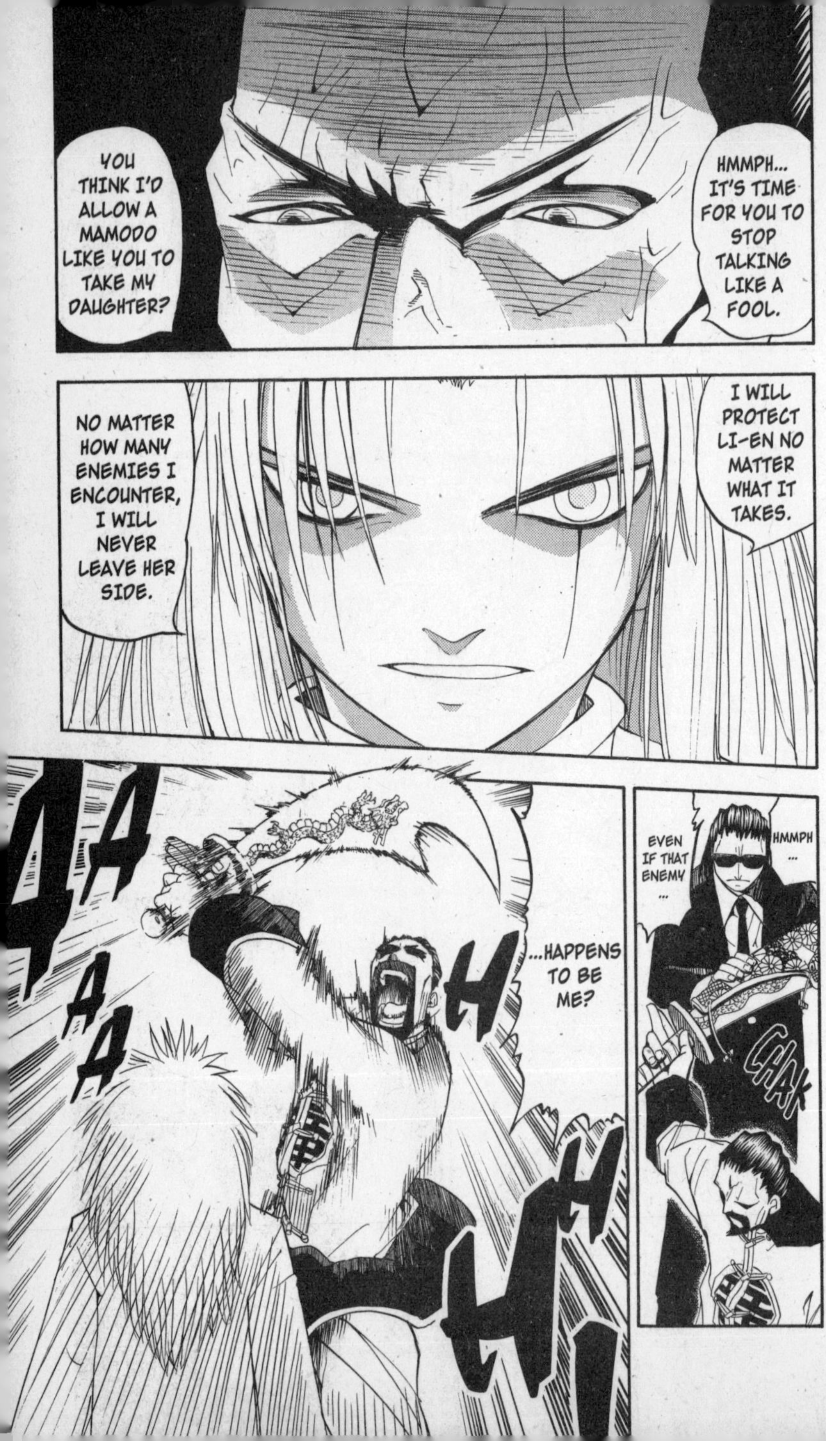
HMMPH... IT'S TIME FOR YOU TO STOP TALKING LIKE A FOOL.
YOU THINK I'D ALLOW A MAMODO LIKE YOU TO TAKE MY DAUGHTER?
I WILL PROTECT LI-EN NO MATTER WHAT IT TAKES.
NO MATTER HOW MANY ENEMIES I ENCOUNTER, I WILL NEVER LEAVE HER SIDE.
HMMPH ...
EVEN IF THAT ENEMY ...
CHAK
...HAPPENS TO BE ME?
AAAAHHH

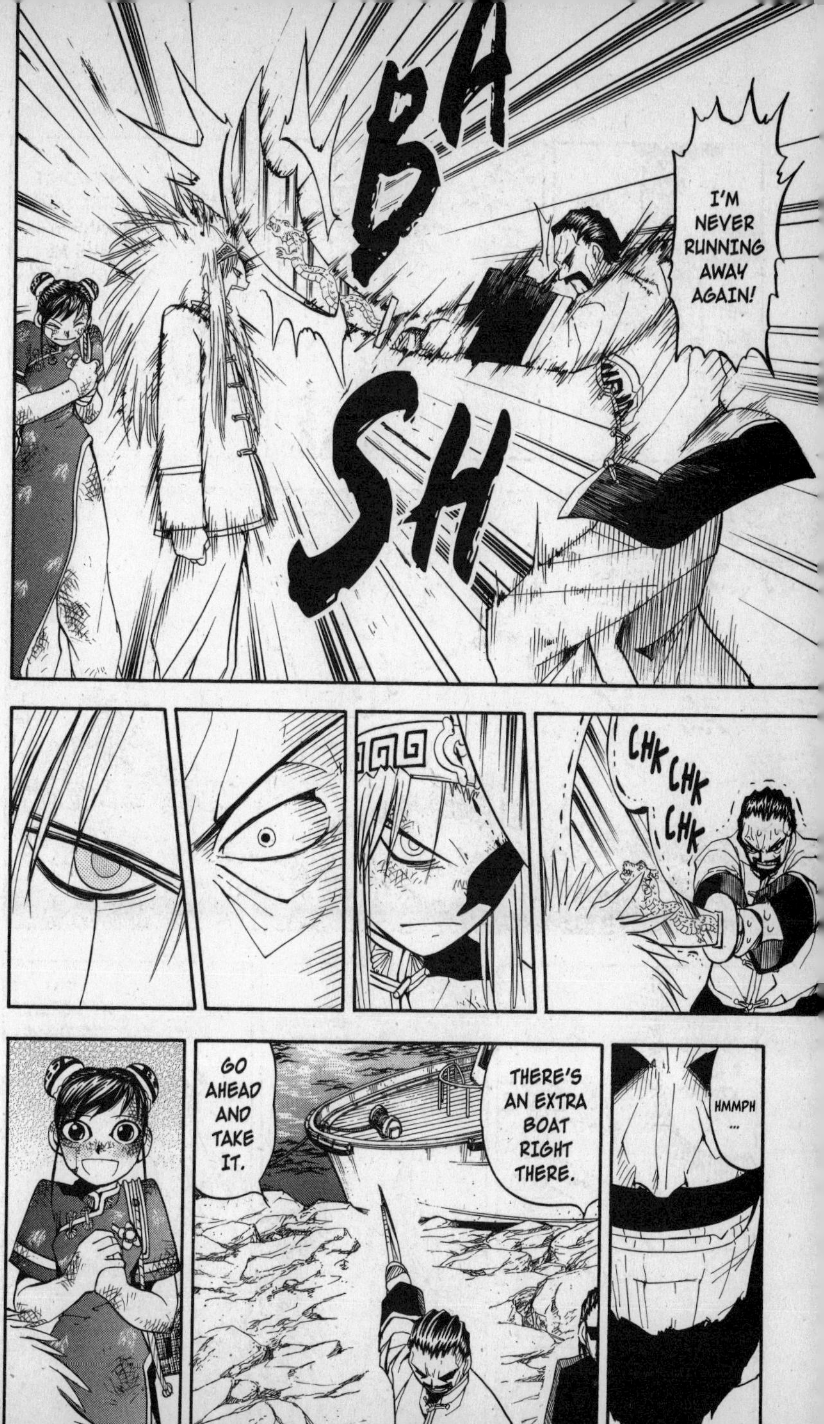
BA
SH
I'M NEVER RUNNING AWAY AGAIN!
CHK CHK CHK
HMMPH ...
THERE'S AN EXTRA BOAT RIGHT THERE.
GO AHEAD AND TAKE IT.

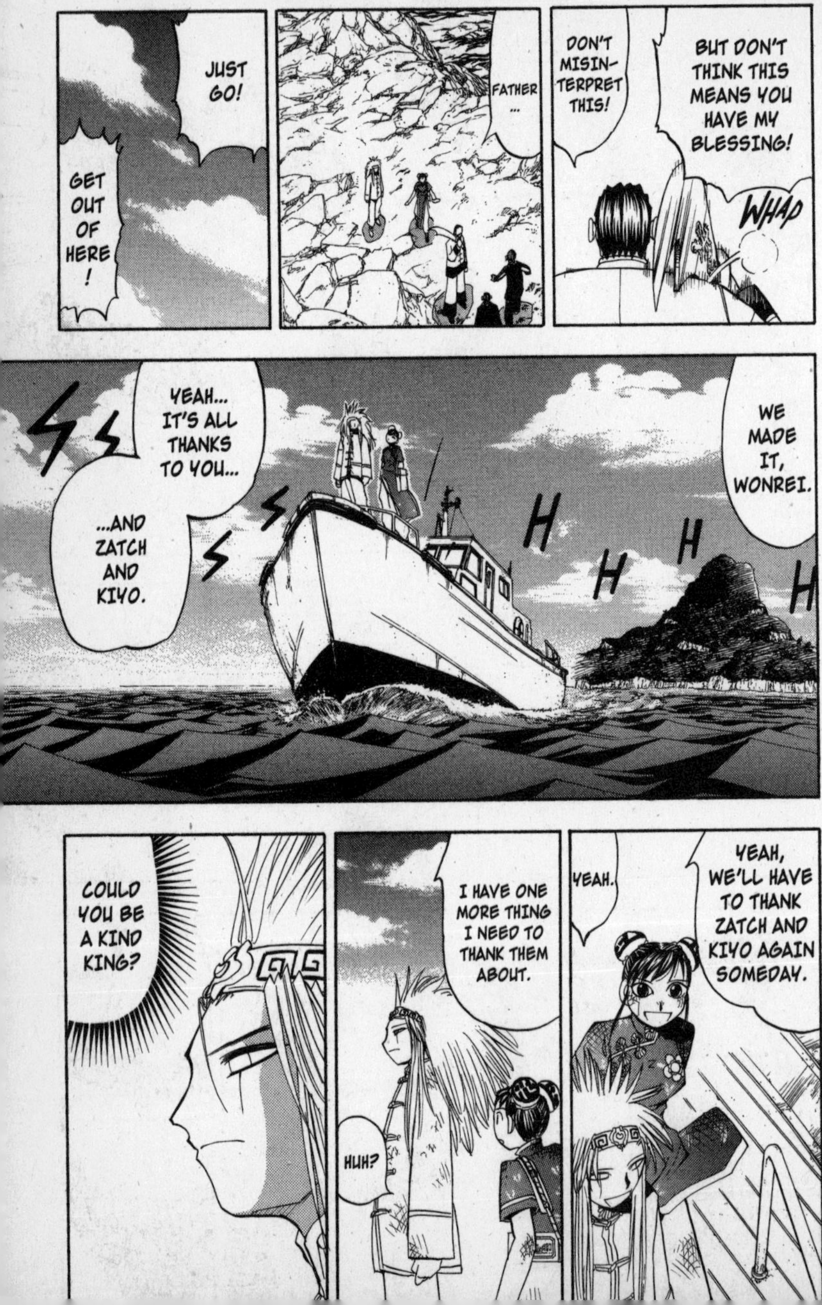
BUT DON'T THINK THIS MEANS YOU HAVE MY BLESSING!
DON'T MISINTERPRET THIS!
WHAP
FATHER ...
JUST GO!
GET OUT OF HERE!
WE MADE IT, WONREI.
YEAH... IT'S ALL THANKS TO YOU...
...AND ZATCH AND KIYO.
YEAH, WE'LL HAVE TO THANK ZATCH AND KIYO AGAIN SOMEDAY.
YEAH.
I HAVE ONE MORE THING I NEED TO THANK THEM ABOUT.
HUH?
COULD YOU BE A KIND KING?

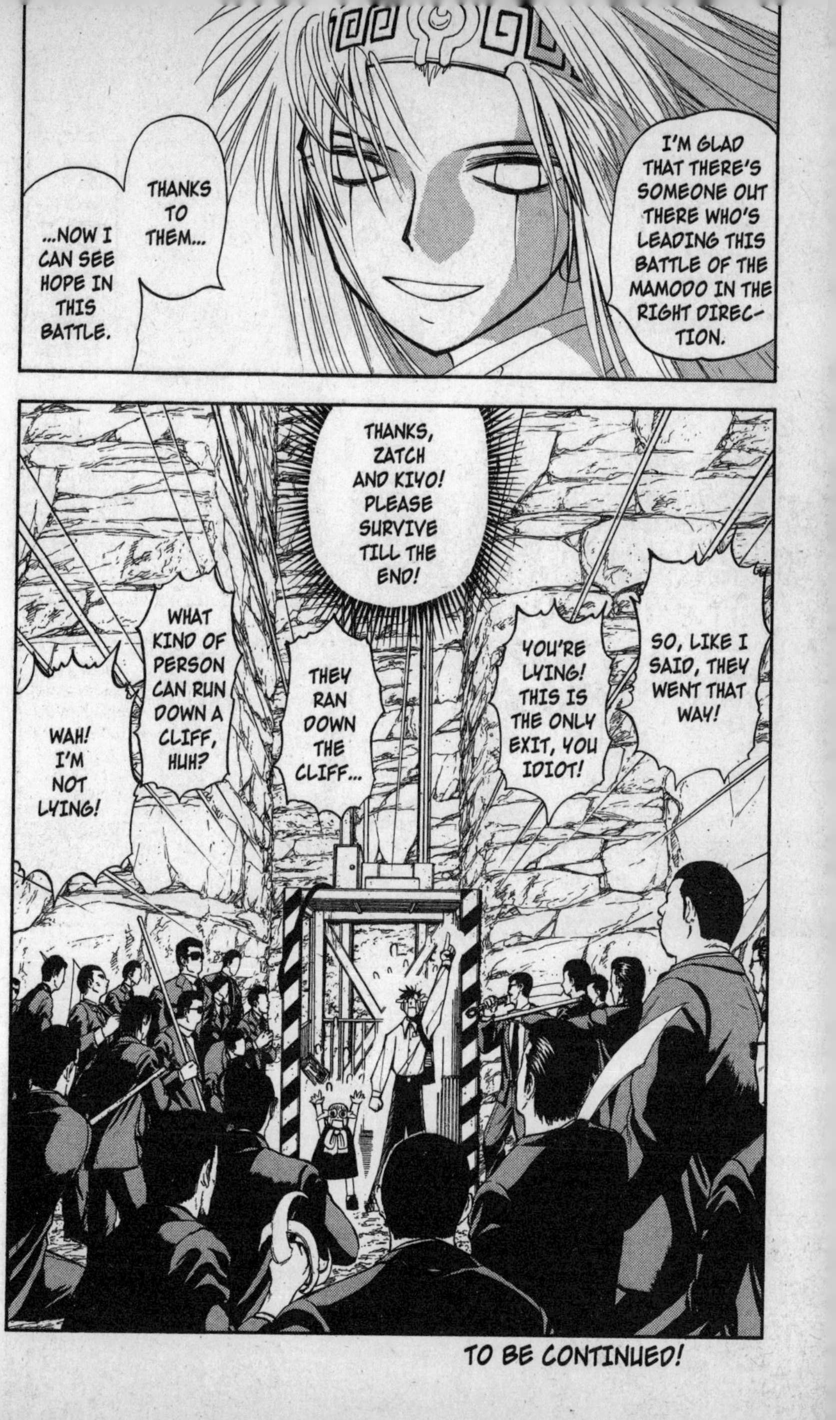
I'M GLAD THAT THERE'S SOMEONE OUT THERE WHO'S LEADING THIS BATTLE OF THE MAMODO IN THE RIGHT DIRECTION.
THANKS TO THEM...
...NOW I CAN SEE HOPE IN THIS BATTLE.
THANKS, ZATCH AND KIYO! PLEASE SURVIVE TILL THE END!
SO, LIKE I SAID, THEY WENT THAT WAY!
YOU'RE LYING! THIS IS THE ONLY EXIT, YOU IDIOT!
THEY RAN DOWN THE CLIFF...
WHAT KIND OF PERSON CAN RUN DOWN A CLIFF, HUH?
WAH! I'M NOT LYING!

TO BE CONTINUED!

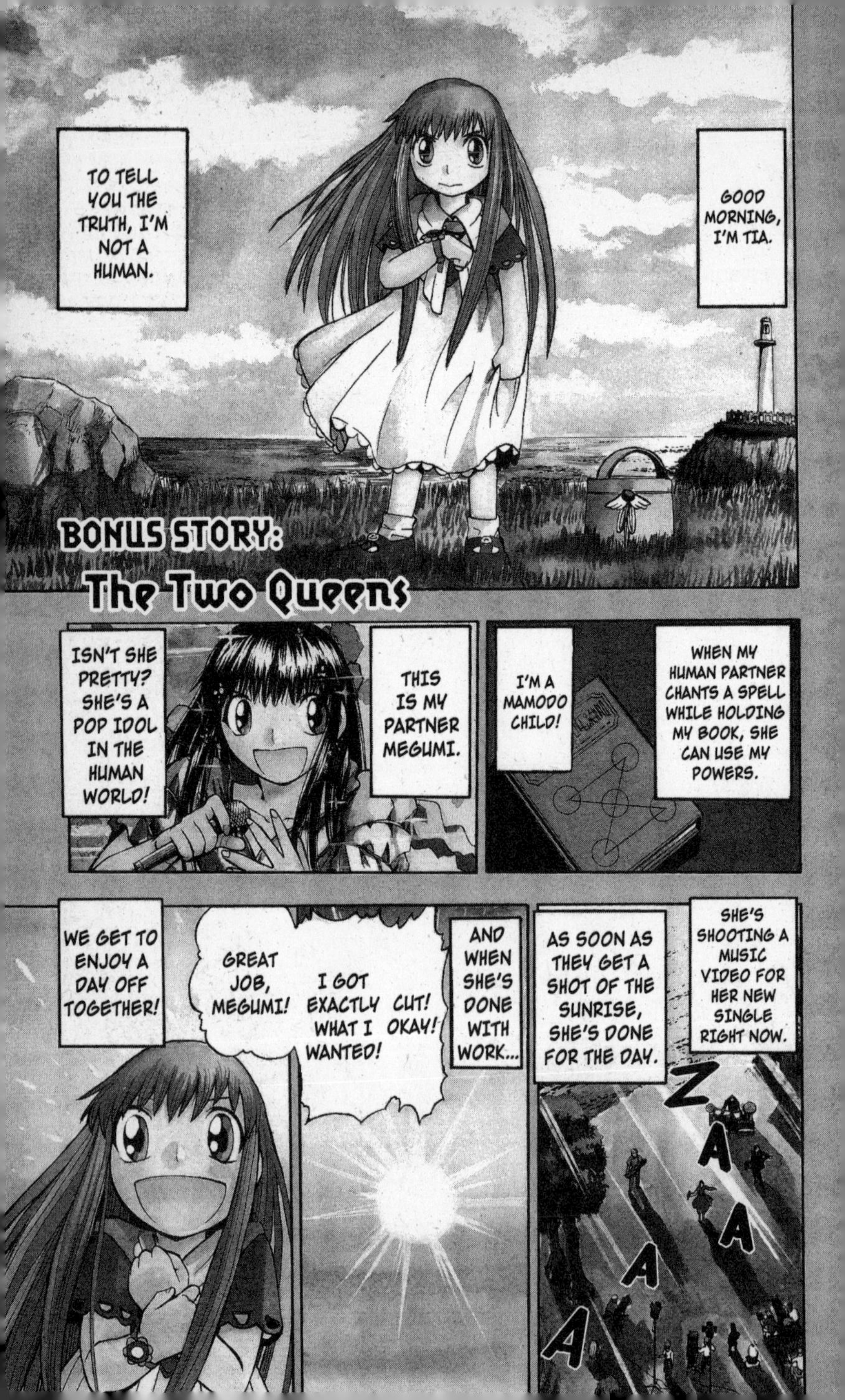
GOOD MORNING, I'M TIA.
TO TELL YOU THE TRUTH, I'M NOT A HUMAN.
BONUS STORY:
The Two Queens
I'M A MAMODO CHILD!
WHEN MY HUMAN PARTNER CHANTS A SPELL WHILE HOLDING MY BOOK, SHE CAN USE MY POWERS.
THIS IS MY PARTNER MEGUMI.
ISN'T SHE PRETTY? SHE'S A POP IDOL IN THE HUMAN WORLD!
SHE'S SHOOTING A MUSIC VIDEO FOR HER NEW SINGLE RIGHT NOW.
ZAAAA
AS SOON AS THEY GET A SHOT OF THE SUNRISE, SHE'S DONE FOR THE DAY.
AND WHEN SHE'S DONE WITH WORK...
CUT! OKAY!
I GOT EXACTLY WHAT I WANTED!
GREAT JOB, MEGUMI!
WE GET TO ENJOY A DAY OFF TOGETHER!

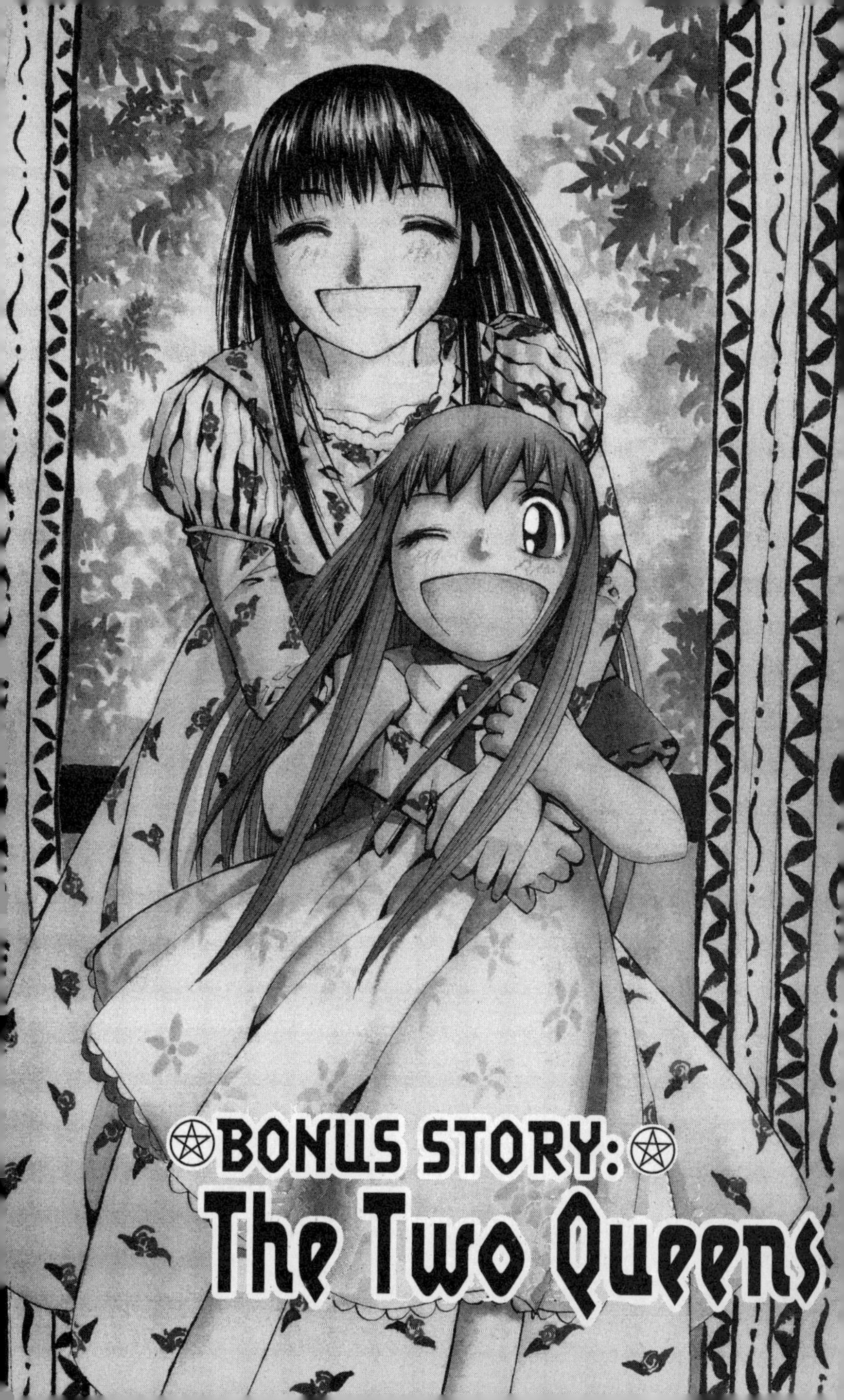
BONUS STORY:
The Two Queens

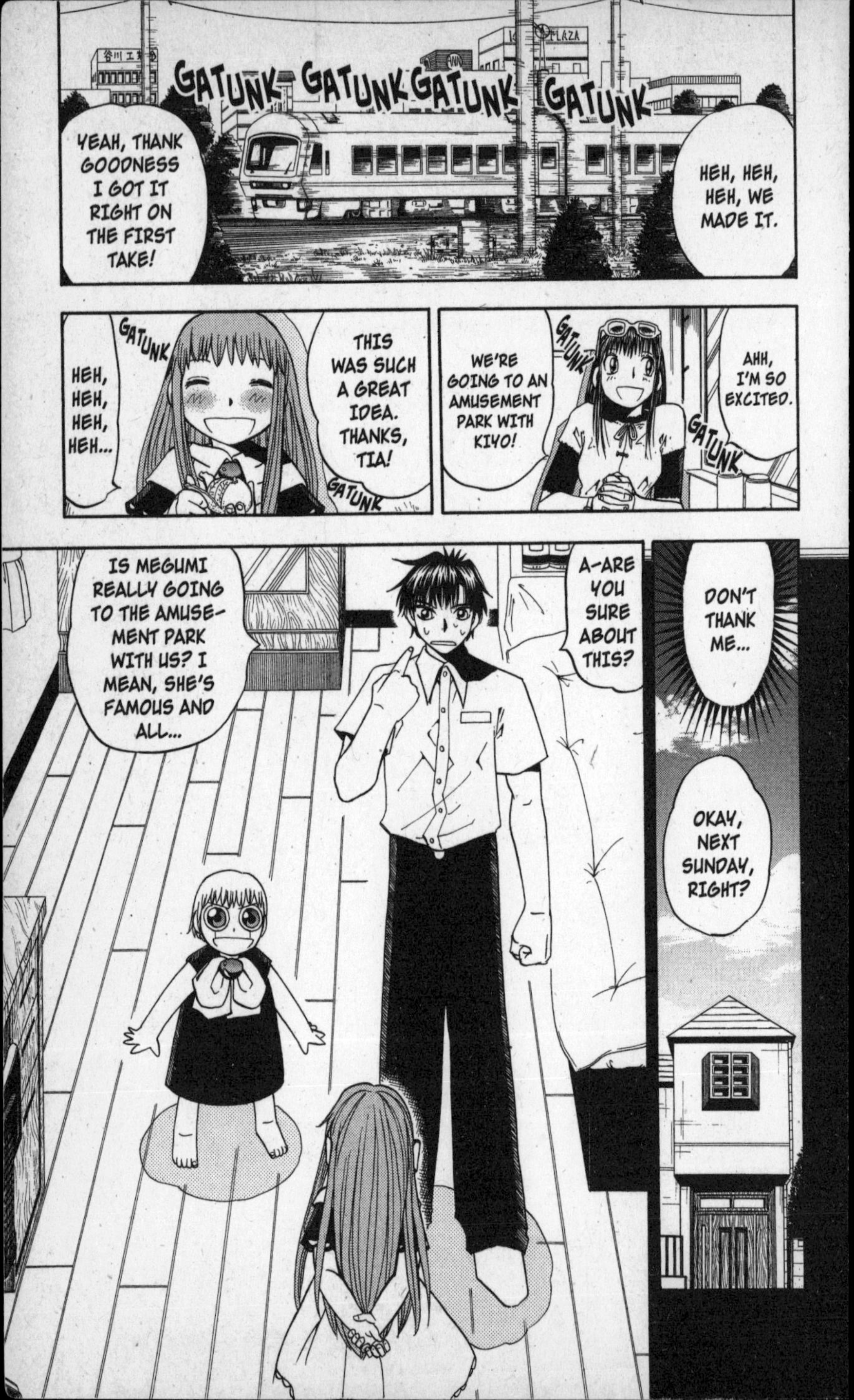
GATUNK GATUNK GATUNK GATUNK
HEH, HEH, HEH, WE MADE IT.
YEAH, THANK GOODNESS I GOT IT RIGHT ON THE FIRST TAKE!
GATUNK
GATUNK
AHH, I'M SO EXCITED.
WE'RE GOING TO AN AMUSEMENT PARK WITH KIYO!
GATUNK
GATUNK
THIS WAS SUCH A GREAT IDEA. THANKS, TIA!
HEH, HEH, HEH, HEH...
DON'T THANK ME...
OKAY, NEXT SUNDAY, RIGHT?
A-ARE YOU SURE ABOUT THIS?
IS MEGUMI REALLY GOING TO THE AMUSEMENT PARK WITH US? I MEAN, SHE'S FAMOUS AND ALL...

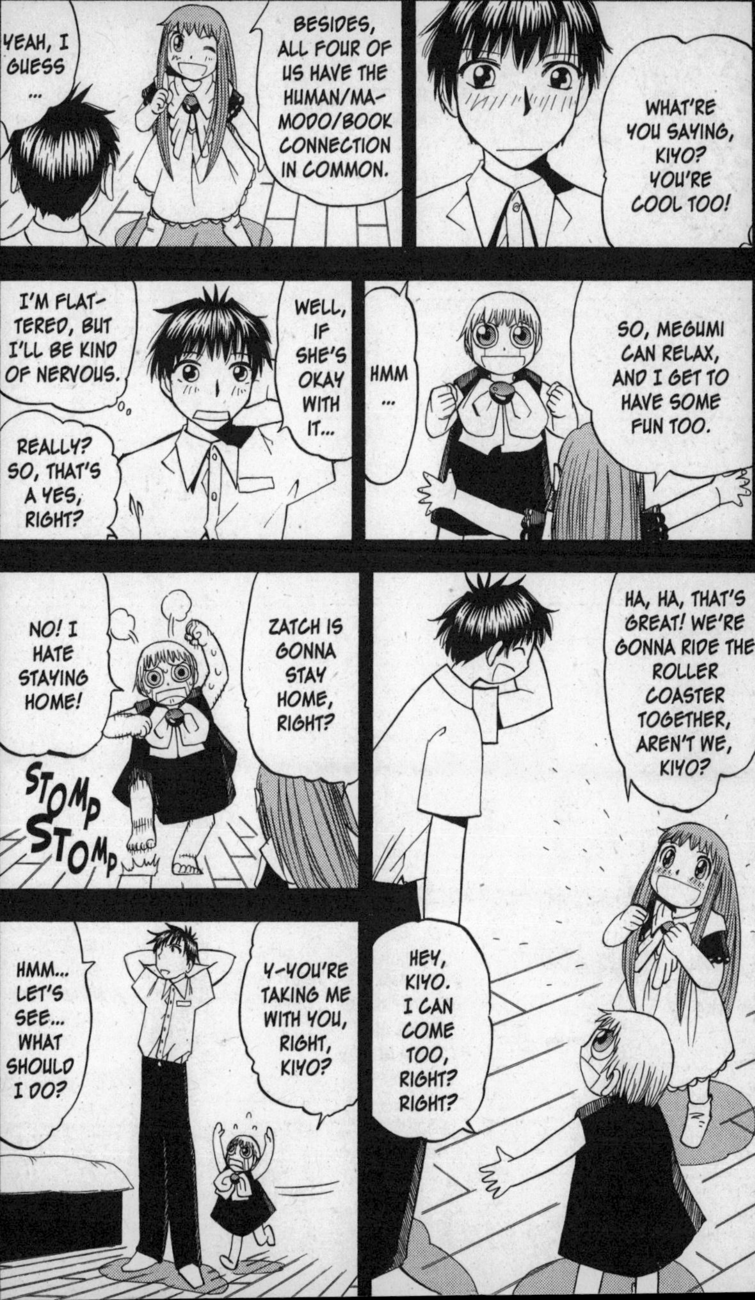
WHAT'RE YOU SAYING, KIYO? YOU'RE COOL TOO!
BESIDES, ALL FOUR OF US HAVE THE HUMAN/MA-MODO/BOOK CONNECTION IN COMMON.
YEAH, I GUESS ...
SO, MEGUMI CAN RELAX, AND I GET TO HAVE SOME FUN TOO.
HMM ...
WELL, IF SHE'S OKAY WITH IT...
I'M FLAT-TERED, BUT I'LL BE KIND OF NERVOUS.
REALLY? SO, THAT'S A YES, RIGHT?
HA, HA, THAT'S GREAT! WE'RE GONNA RIDE THE ROLLER COASTER TOGETHER, AREN'T WE, KIYO?
ZATCH IS GONNA STAY HOME, RIGHT?
NO! I HATE STAYING HOME!
STOMP STOMP
HEY, KIYO. I CAN COME TOO, RIGHT? RIGHT?
Y-YOU'RE TAKING ME WITH YOU, RIGHT, KIYO?
HMM... LET'S SEE... WHAT SHOULD I DO?

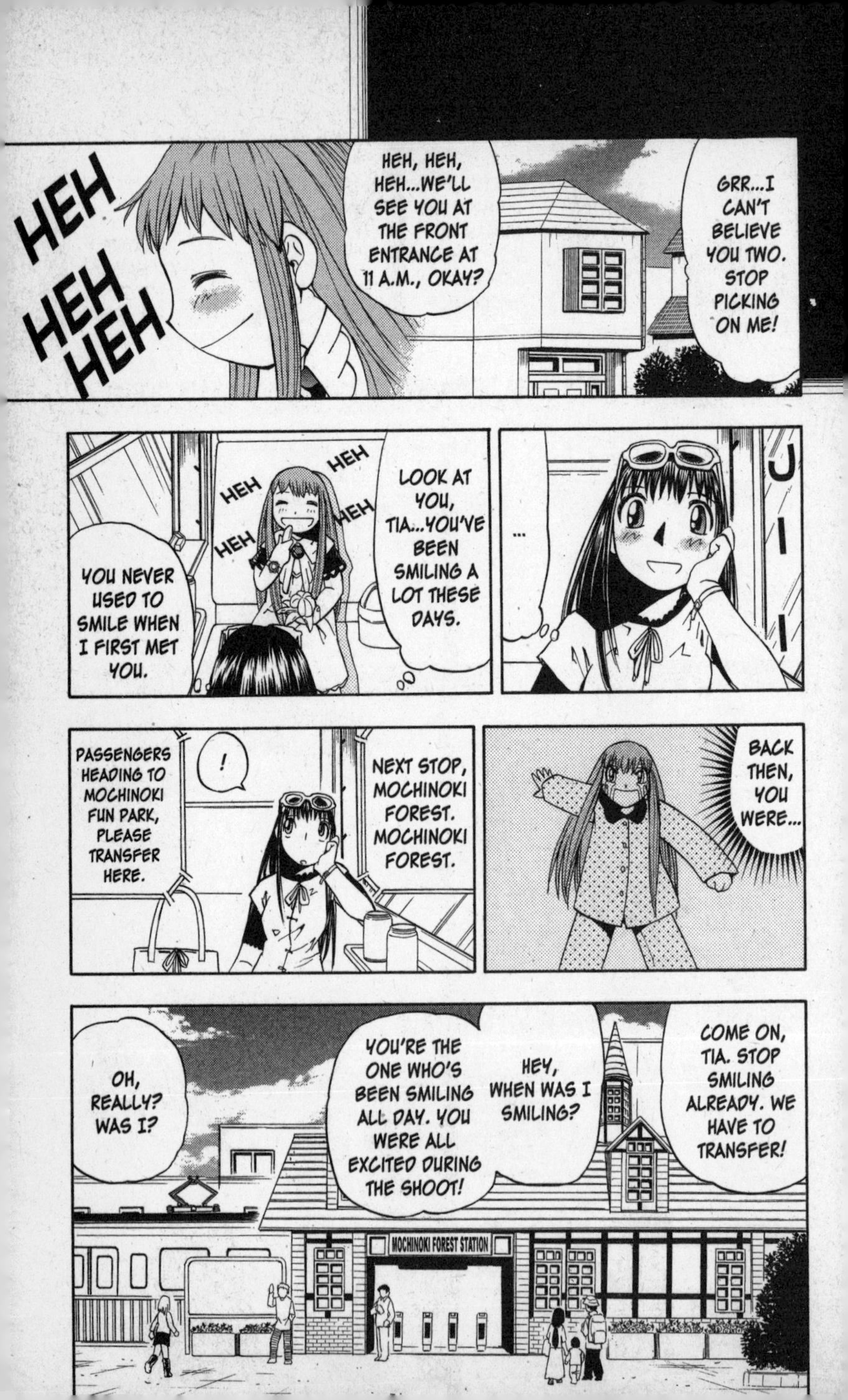
GRR...I CAN'T BELIEVE YOU TWO. STOP PICKING ON ME!
HEH, HEH, HEH...WE'LL SEE YOU AT THE FRONT ENTRANCE AT 11 A.M., OKAY?
HEH HEH HEH
JIII
...
LOOK AT YOU, TIA...YOU'VE BEEN SMILING A LOT THESE DAYS.
HEH HEH HEH HEH
YOU NEVER USED TO SMILE WHEN I FIRST MET YOU.
BACK THEN, YOU WERE...
NEXT STOP, MOCHINOKI FOREST. MOCHINOKI FOREST.
!
PASSENGERS HEADING TO MOCHINOKI FUN PARK, PLEASE TRANSFER HERE.
COME ON, TIA. STOP SMILING ALREADY. WE HAVE TO TRANSFER!
HEY, WHEN WAS I SMILING?
YOU'RE THE ONE WHO'S BEEN SMILING ALL DAY. YOU WERE ALL EXCITED DURING THE SHOOT!
OH, REALLY? WAS I?
MOCHINOKI FOREST STATION

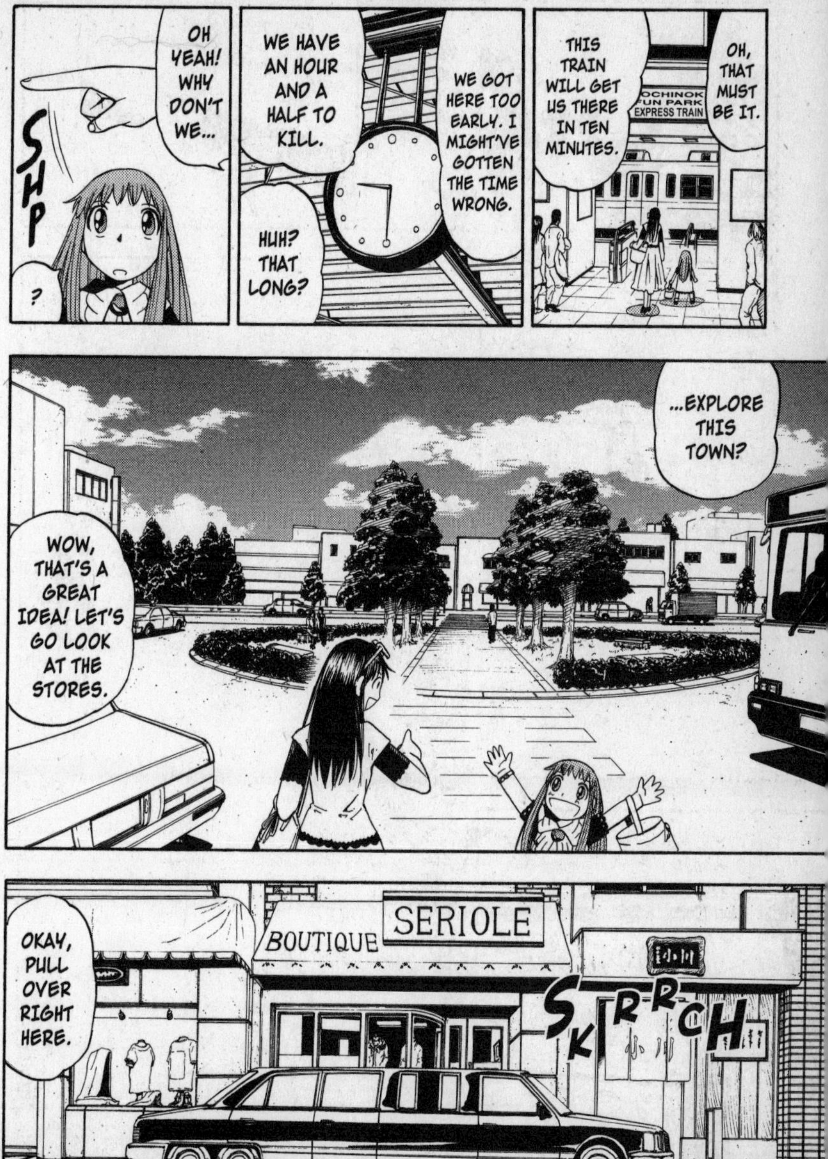
OH, THAT MUST BE IT.
OCHINOK FUN PARK EXPRESS TRAIN
THIS TRAIN WILL GET US THERE IN TEN MINUTES.
WE GOT HERE TOO EARLY. I MIGHT'VE GOTTEN THE TIME WRONG.
HUH? THAT LONG?
WE HAVE AN HOUR AND A HALF TO KILL.
OH YEAH! WHY DON'T WE...
SHP
?
...EXPLORE THIS TOWN?
WOW, THAT'S A GREAT IDEA! LET'S GO LOOK AT THE STORES.
BOUTIQUE SERIOLE
SKRRRCH
OKAY, PULL OVER RIGHT HERE.

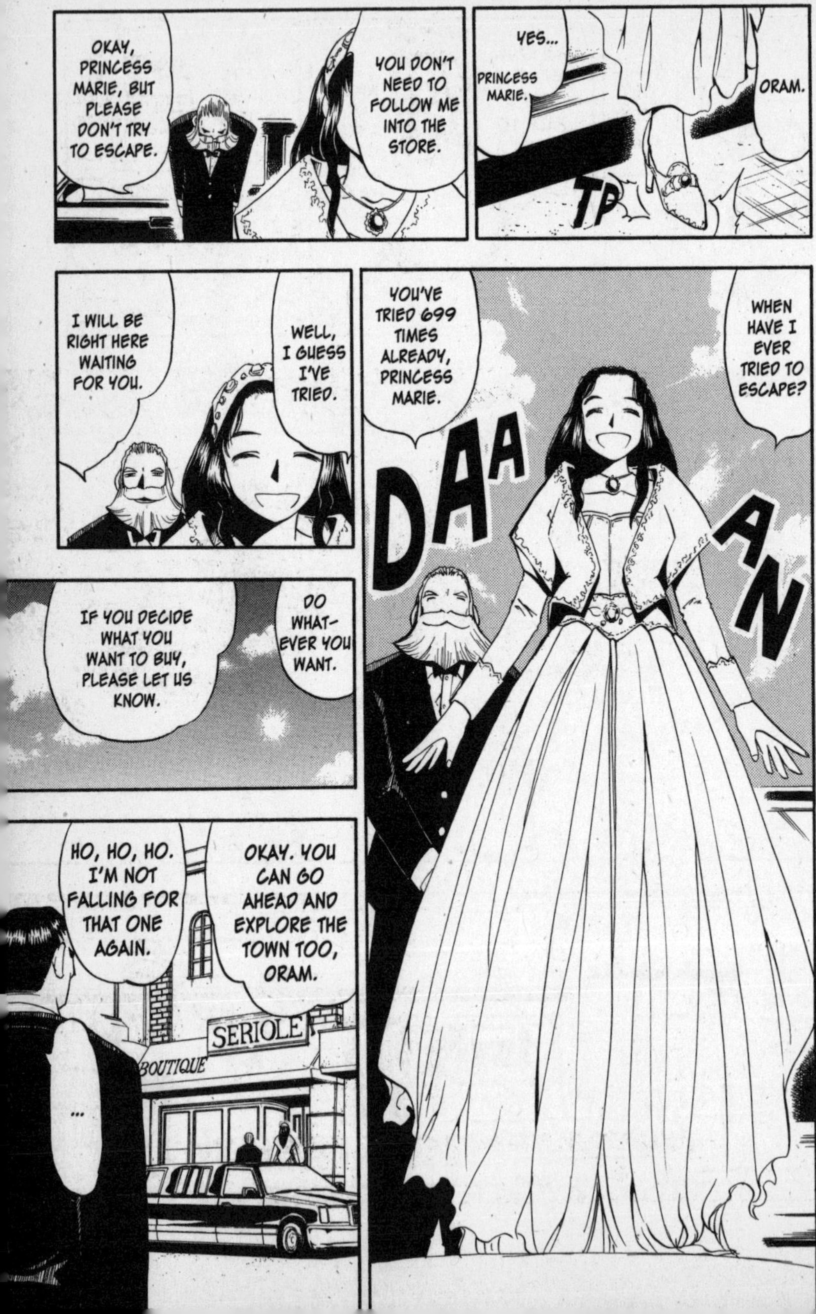
ORAM.
YES...
PRINCESS MARIE.
TP
YOU DON'T NEED TO FOLLOW ME INTO THE STORE.
OKAY, PRINCESS MARIE, BUT PLEASE DON'T TRY TO ESCAPE.
WHEN HAVE I EVER TRIED TO ESCAPE?
YOU'VE TRIED 699 TIMES ALREADY, PRINCESS MARIE.
DAAAN
WELL, I GUESS I'VE TRIED.
I WILL BE RIGHT HERE WAITING FOR YOU.
DO WHATEVER YOU WANT.
IF YOU DECIDE WHAT YOU WANT TO BUY, PLEASE LET US KNOW.
OKAY. YOU CAN GO AHEAD AND EXPLORE THE TOWN TOO, ORAM.
HO, HO, HO. I'M NOT FALLING FOR THAT ONE AGAIN.
SERIOLE
BOUTIQUE
...

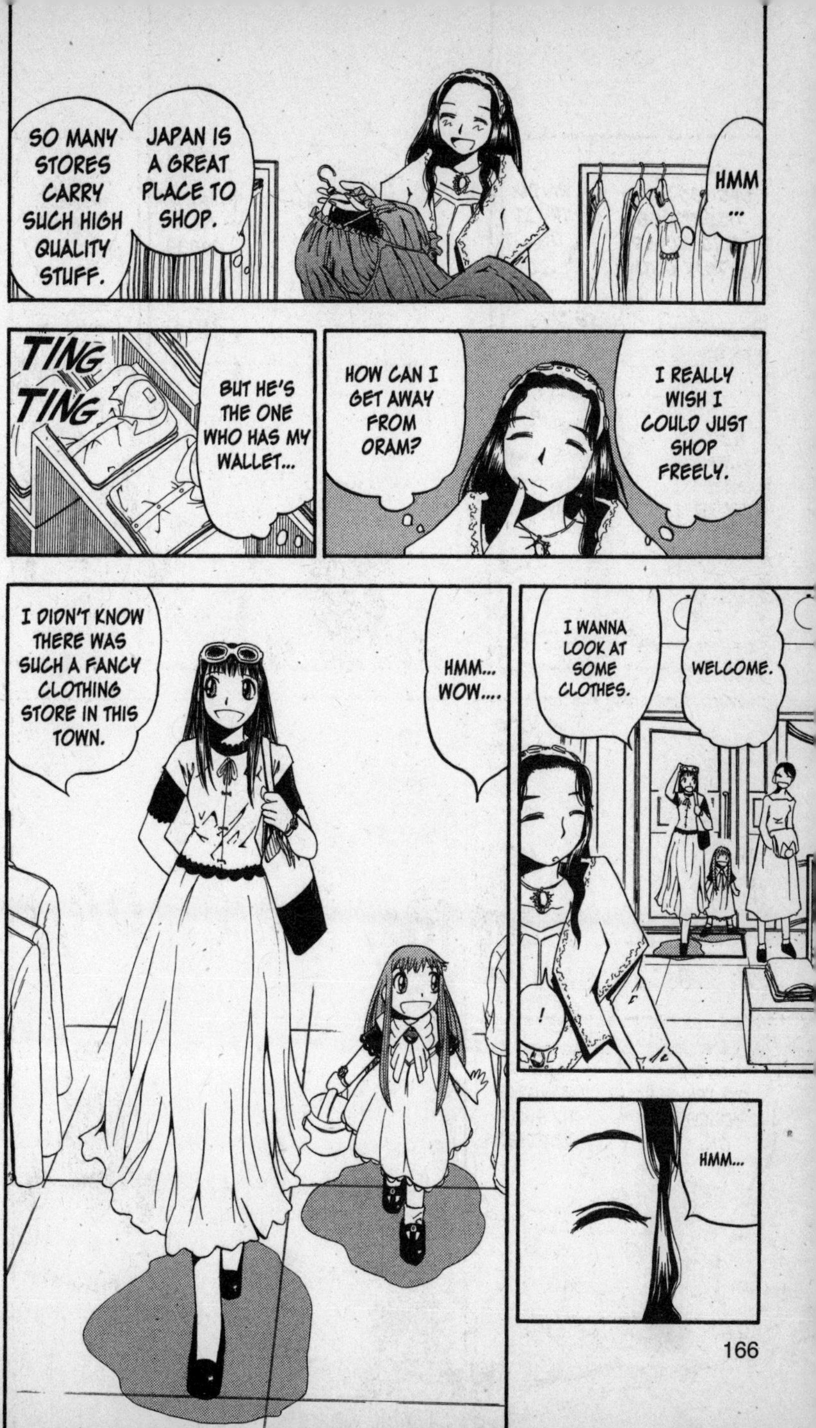
HMM ...
JAPAN IS A GREAT PLACE TO SHOP.
SO MANY STORES CARRY SUCH HIGH QUALITY STUFF.
I REALLY WISH I COULD JUST SHOP FREELY.
HOW CAN I GET AWAY FROM ORAM?
BUT HE'S THE ONE WHO HAS MY WALLET...
TING TING
WELCOME.
I WANNA LOOK AT SOME CLOTHES.
!
HMM...
HMM... WOW....
I DIDN'T KNOW THERE WAS SUCH A FANCY CLOTHING STORE IN THIS TOWN.

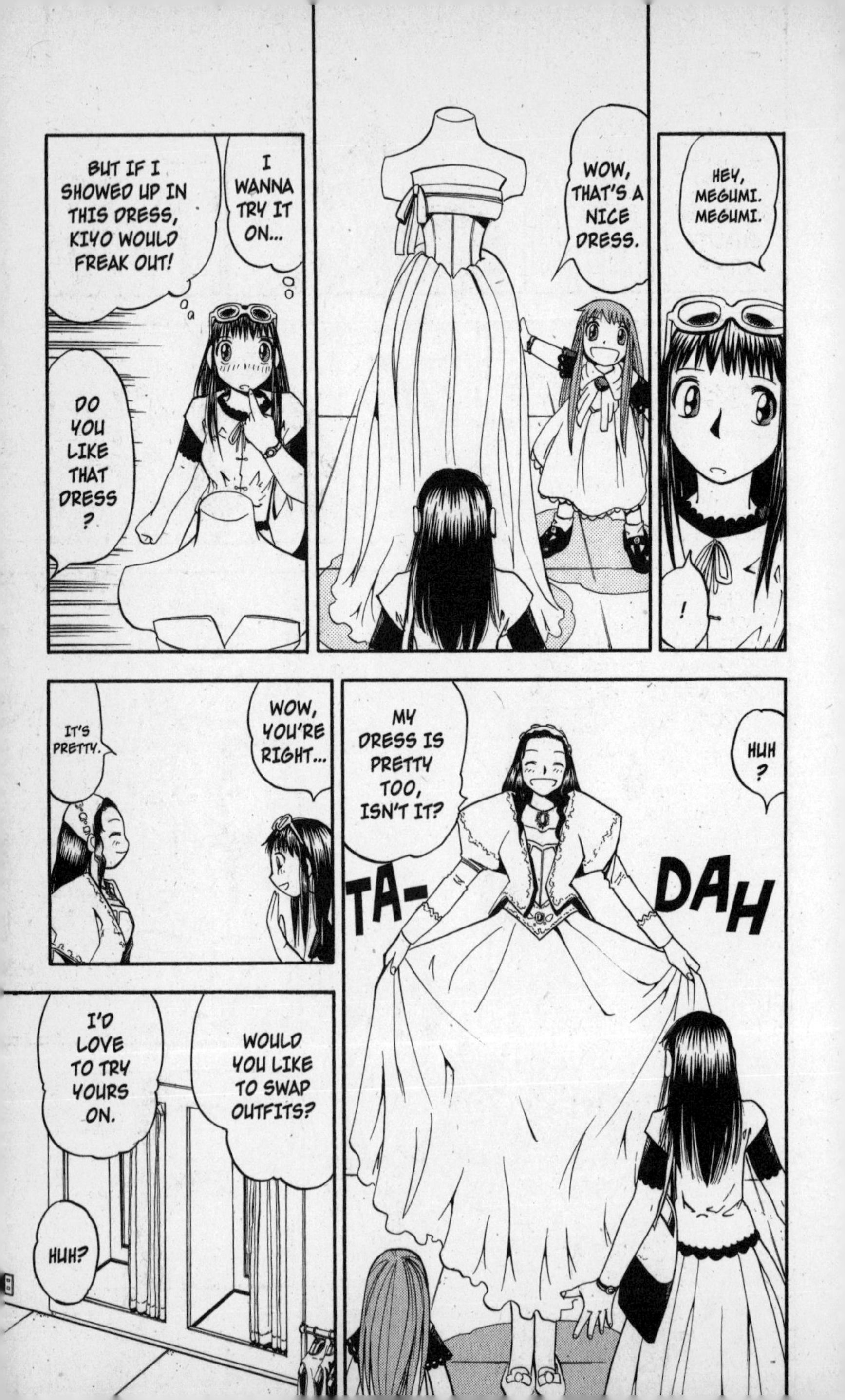
HEY, MEGUMI. MEGUMI.
!
WOW, THAT'S A NICE DRESS.
I WANNA TRY IT ON...
BUT IF I SHOWED UP IN THIS DRESS, KIYO WOULD FREAK OUT!
DO YOU LIKE THAT DRESS ?
HUH ?
MY DRESS IS PRETTY TOO, ISN'T IT?
TA-DAH
WOW, YOU'RE RIGHT...
IT'S PRETTY.
WOULD YOU LIKE TO SWAP OUTFITS?
I'D LOVE TO TRY YOURS ON.
HUH?

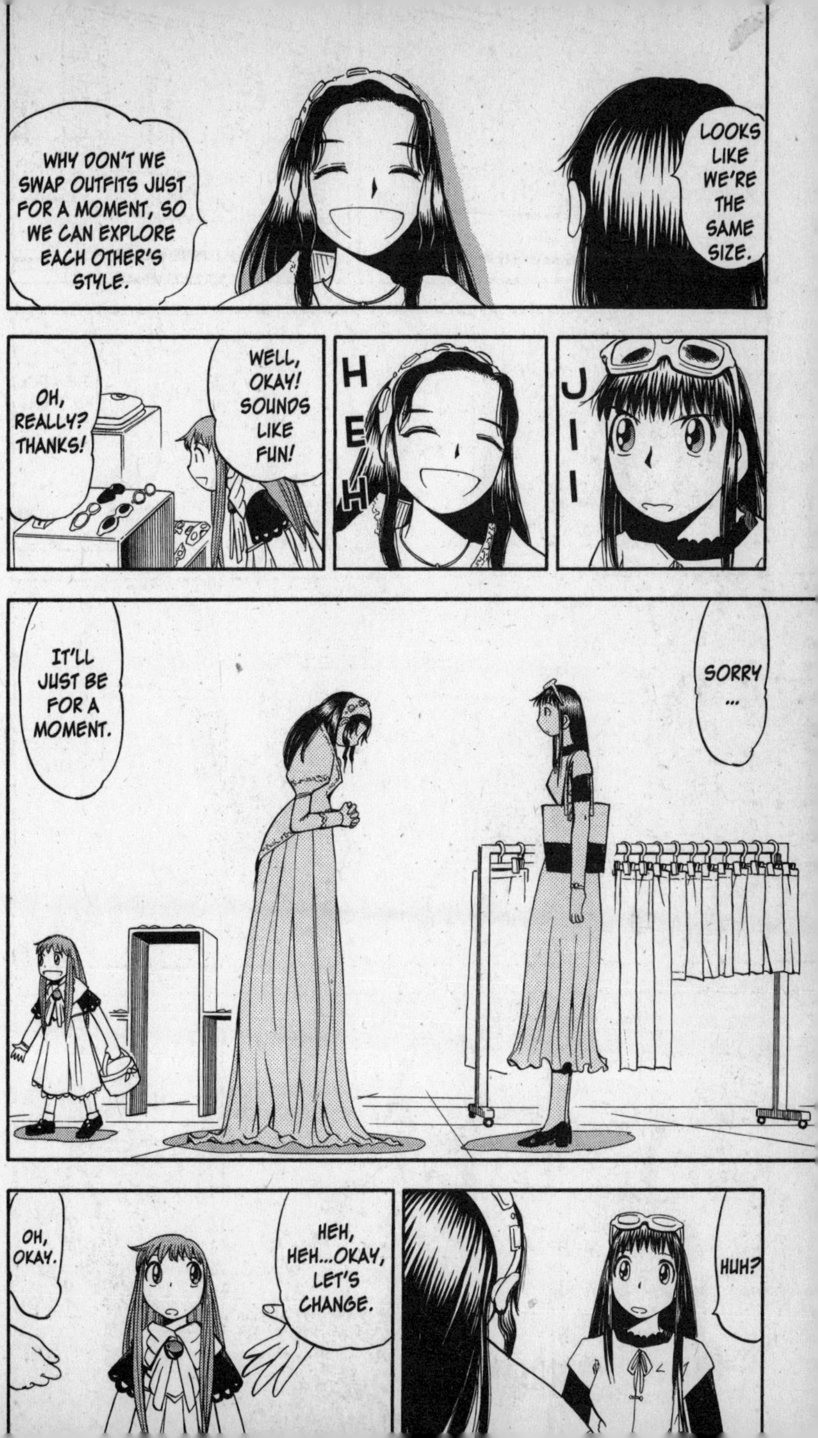
LOOKS LIKE WE'RE THE SAME SIZE.
WHY DON'T WE SWAP OUTFITS JUST FOR A MOMENT, SO WE CAN EXPLORE EACH OTHER'S STYLE.
JIII
HEHEH
WELL, OKAY! SOUNDS LIKE FUN!
OH, REALLY? THANKS!
SORRY ...
IT'LL JUST BE FOR A MOMENT.
HUH?
HEH, HEH...OKAY, LET'S CHANGE.
OH, OKAY.

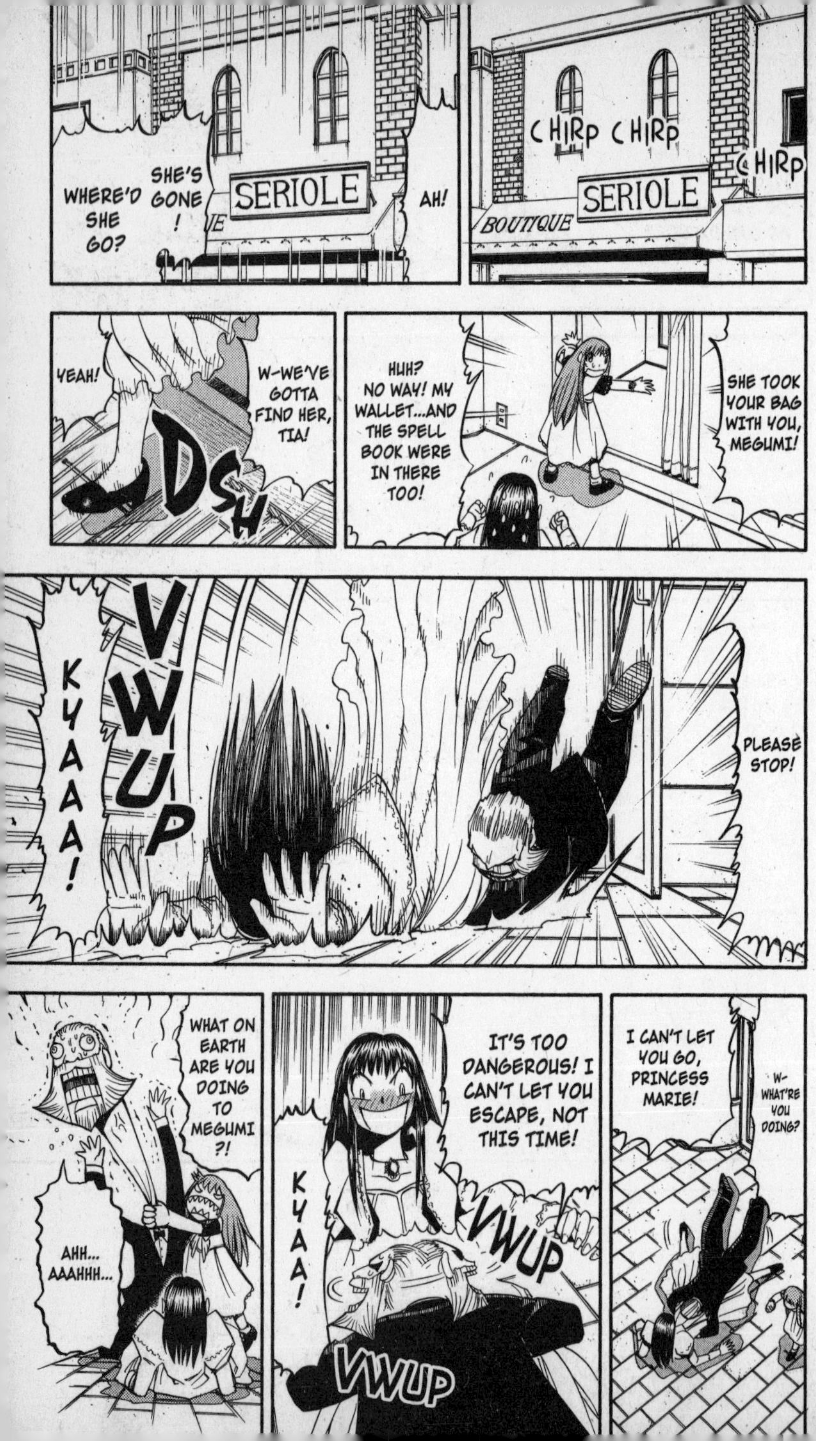
CHIRP CHIRP
CHIRP
SERIOLE
BOUTIQUE
AH!
SHE'S GONE!
WHERE'D SHE GO?
SERIOLE
SHE TOOK YOUR BAG WITH YOU, MEGUMI!
HUH? NO WAY! MY WALLET...AND THE SPELL BOOK WERE IN THERE TOO!
W-WE'VE GOTTA FIND HER, TIA!
YEAH!
DSH
PLEASE STOP!
VWUP
KYAAAA!
W-WHAT'RE YOU DOING?
I CAN'T LET YOU GO, PRINCESS MARIE!
IT'S TOO DANGEROUS! I CAN'T LET YOU ESCAPE, NOT THIS TIME!
VWUP
KYAA!
VWUP
WHAT ON EARTH ARE YOU DOING TO MEGUMI?!
AHH... AAAHHH...

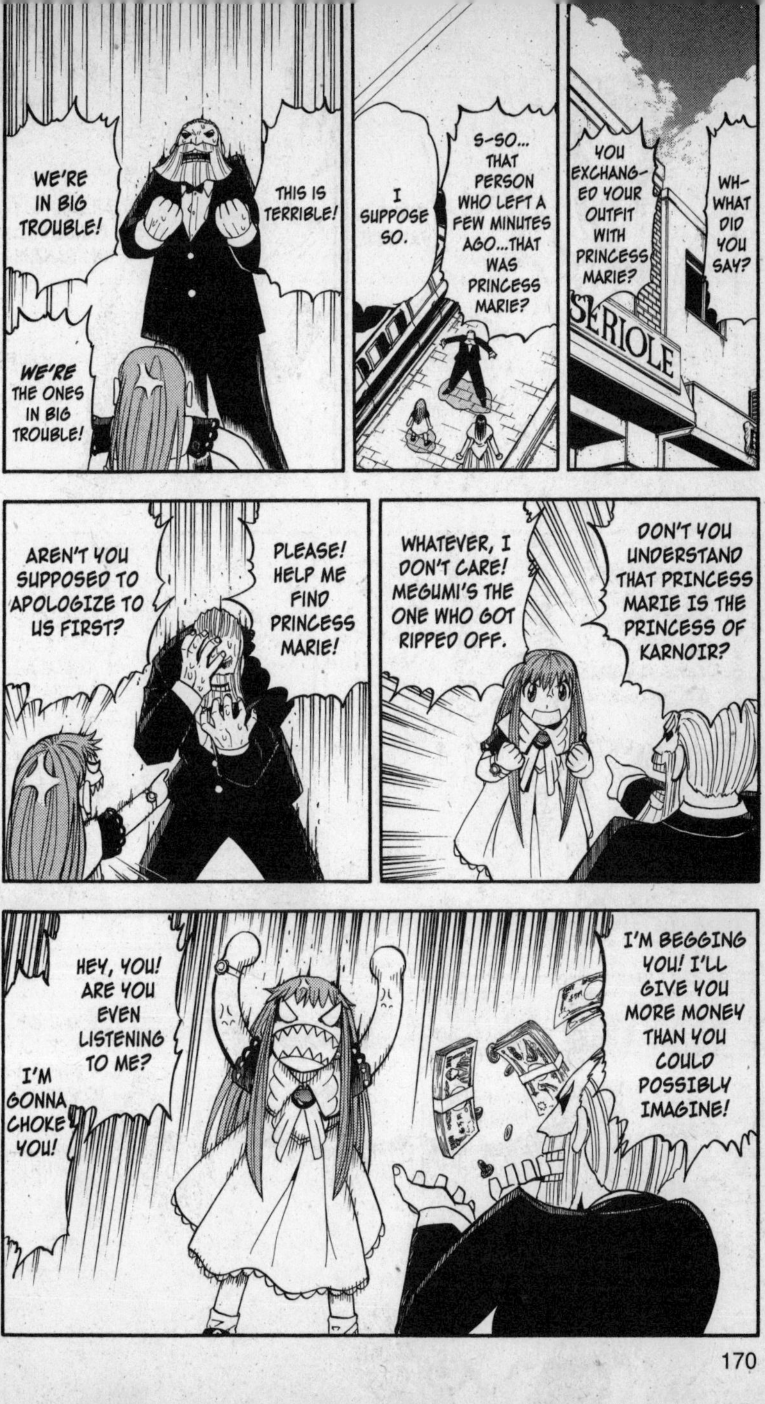
WH-WHAT DID YOU SAY?
YOU EXCHANGED YOUR OUTFIT WITH PRINCESS MARIE?
SERIOLE
S-SO... THAT PERSON WHO LEFT A FEW MINUTES AGO...THAT WAS PRINCESS MARIE?
I SUPPOSE SO.
THIS IS TERRIBLE!
WE'RE IN BIG TROUBLE!
WE'RE THE ONES IN BIG TROUBLE!
DON'T YOU UNDERSTAND THAT PRINCESS MARIE IS THE PRINCESS OF KARNOIR?
WHATEVER, I DON'T CARE! MEGUMI'S THE ONE WHO GOT RIPPED OFF.
PLEASE! HELP ME FIND PRINCESS MARIE!
AREN'T YOU SUPPOSED TO APOLOGIZE TO US FIRST?
I'M BEGGING YOU! I'LL GIVE YOU MORE MONEY THAN YOU COULD POSSIBLY IMAGINE!
HEY, YOU! ARE YOU EVEN LISTENING TO ME?
I'M GONNA CHOKE YOU!

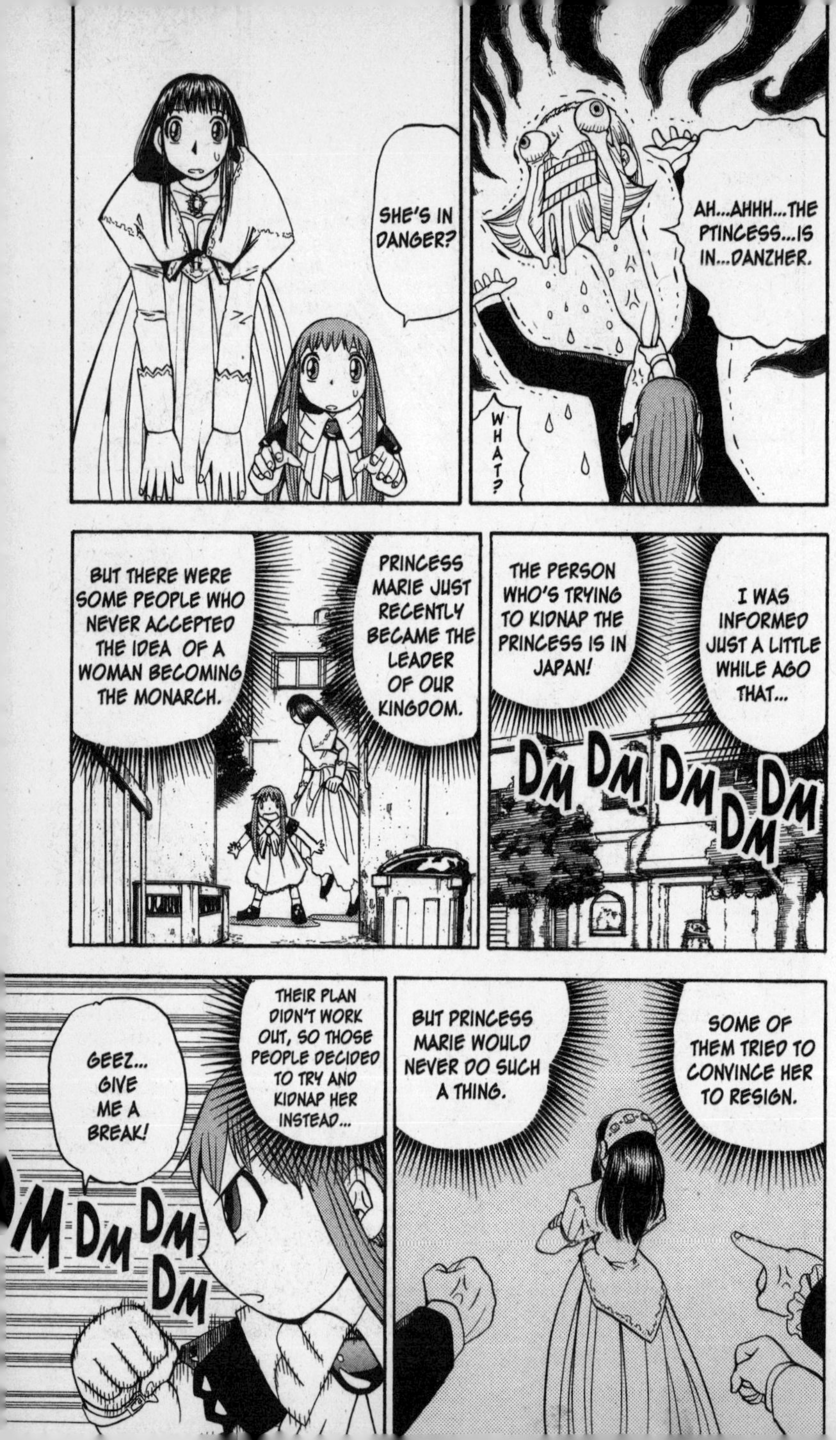
AH...AHHH...THE PTINCESS...IS IN...DANZHER.
WHAT?
SHE'S IN DANGER?
I WAS INFORMED JUST A LITTLE WHILE AGO THAT...
THE PERSON WHO'S TRYING TO KIDNAP THE PRINCESS IS IN JAPAN!
DM DM DM DM DM
PRINCESS MARIE JUST RECENTLY BECAME THE LEADER OF OUR KINGDOM.
BUT THERE WERE SOME PEOPLE WHO NEVER ACCEPTED THE IDEA OF A WOMAN BECOMING THE MONARCH.
SOME OF THEM TRIED TO CONVINCE HER TO RESIGN.
BUT PRINCESS MARIE WOULD NEVER DO SUCH A THING.
THEIR PLAN DIDN'T WORK OUT, SO THOSE PEOPLE DECIDED TO TRY AND KIDNAP HER INSTEAD...
GEEZ... GIVE ME A BREAK!
DM DM DM DM

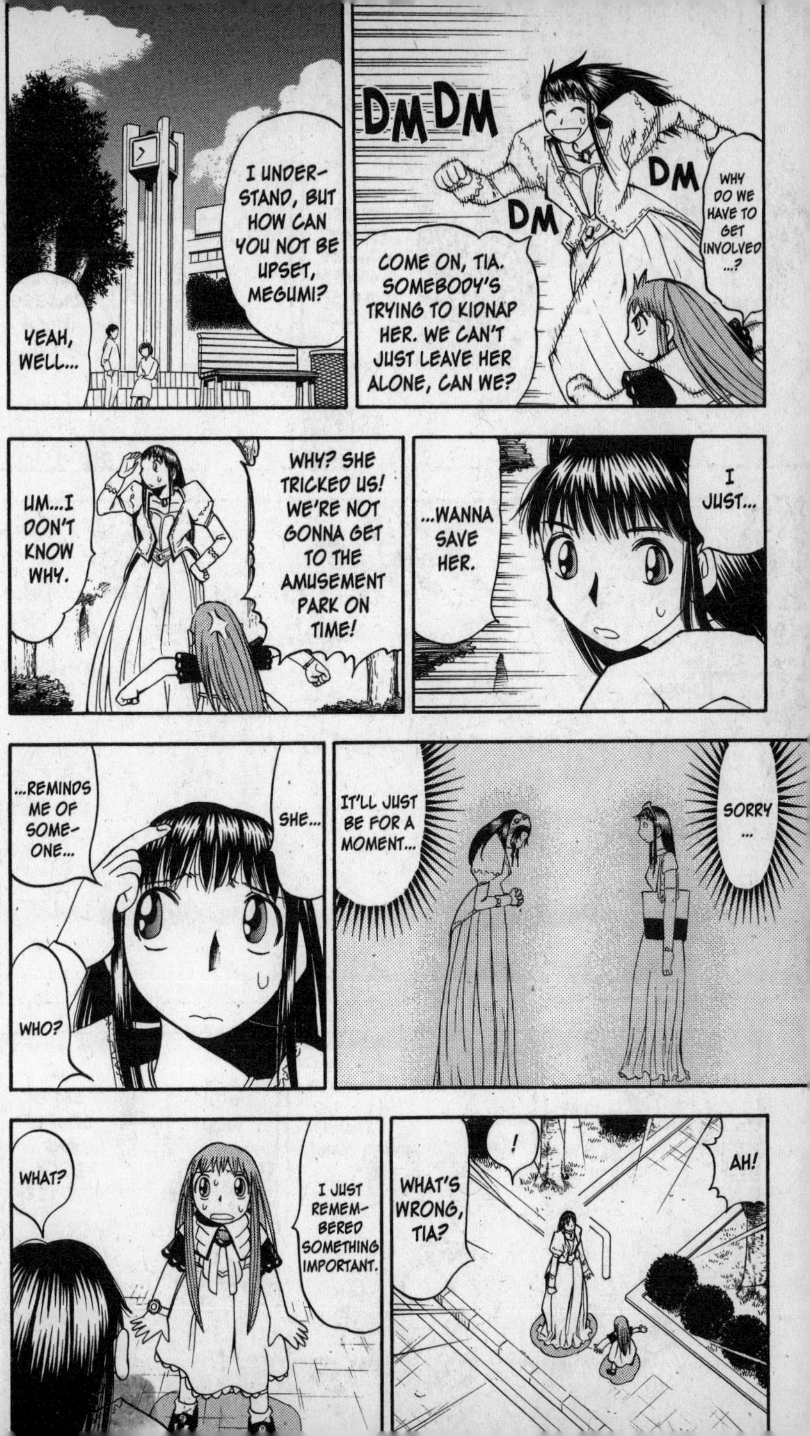
DMDM
DM
DM
WHY DO WE HAVE TO GET INVOLVED ...?
COME ON, TIA. SOMEBODY'S TRYING TO KIDNAP HER. WE CAN'T JUST LEAVE HER ALONE, CAN WE?
I UNDER-STAND, BUT HOW CAN YOU NOT BE UPSET, MEGUMI?
YEAH, WELL...
I JUST...
...WANNA SAVE HER.
WHY? SHE TRICKED US! WE'RE NOT GONNA GET TO THE AMUSEMENT PARK ON TIME!
UM...I DON'T KNOW WHY.
SORRY ...
IT'LL JUST BE FOR A MOMENT...
SHE...
...REMINDS ME OF SOME-ONE...
WHO?
AH!
!
WHAT'S WRONG, TIA?
I JUST REMEM-BERED SOMETHING IMPORTANT.
WHAT?

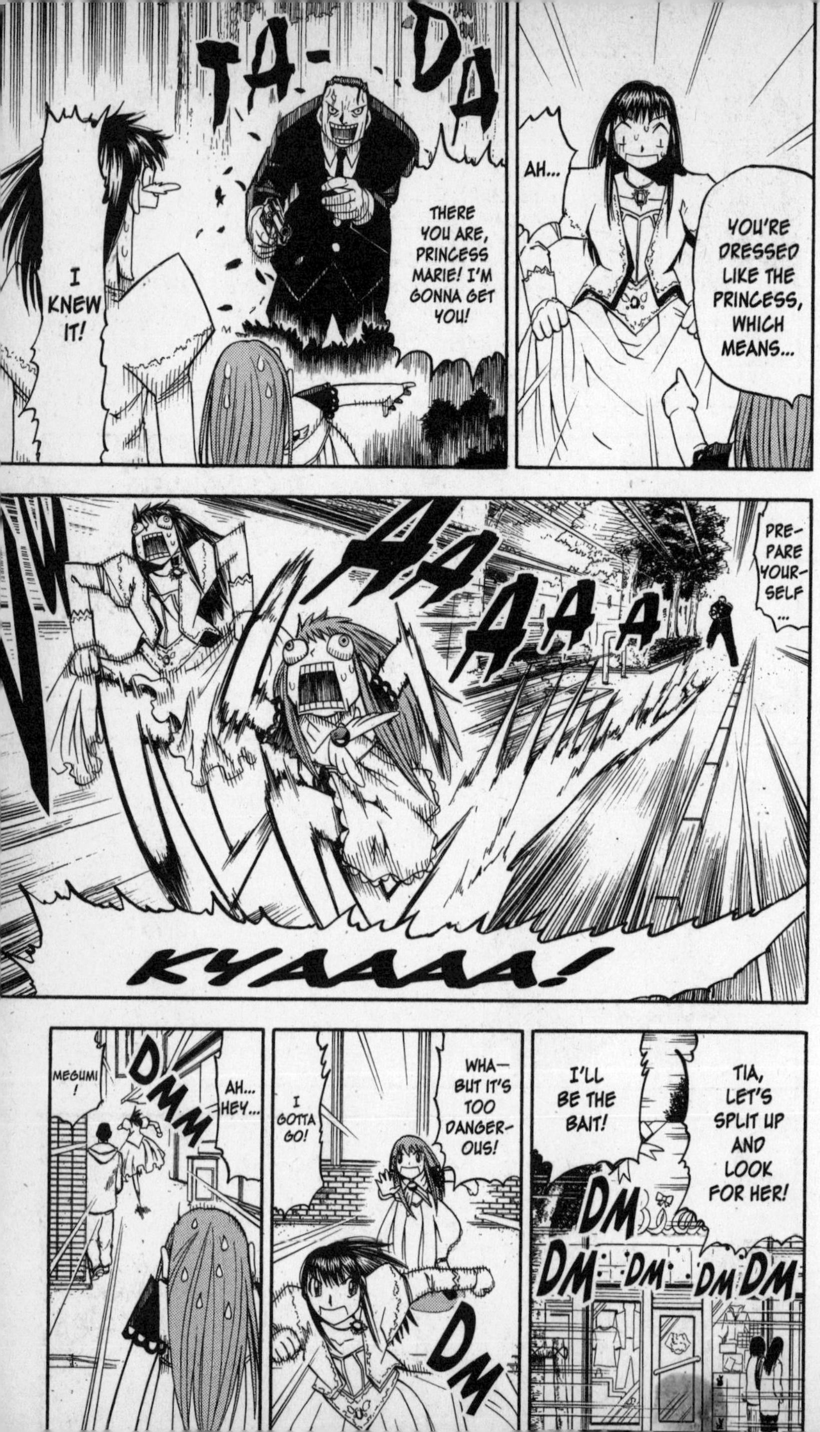
AH...
YOU'RE DRESSED LIKE THE PRINCESS, WHICH MEANS...
TA-DA
THERE YOU ARE, PRINCESS MARIE! I'M GONNA GET YOU!
I KNEW IT!
PRE-PARE YOURSELF...
AAAAAA
KYAAAA!
TIA, LET'S SPLIT UP AND LOOK FOR HER!
I'LL BE THE BAIT!
DM DM DM DM DM DM
WHA— BUT IT'S TOO DANGEROUS!
I GOTTA GO!
DM
AH... HEY...
DMM
MEGUMI!

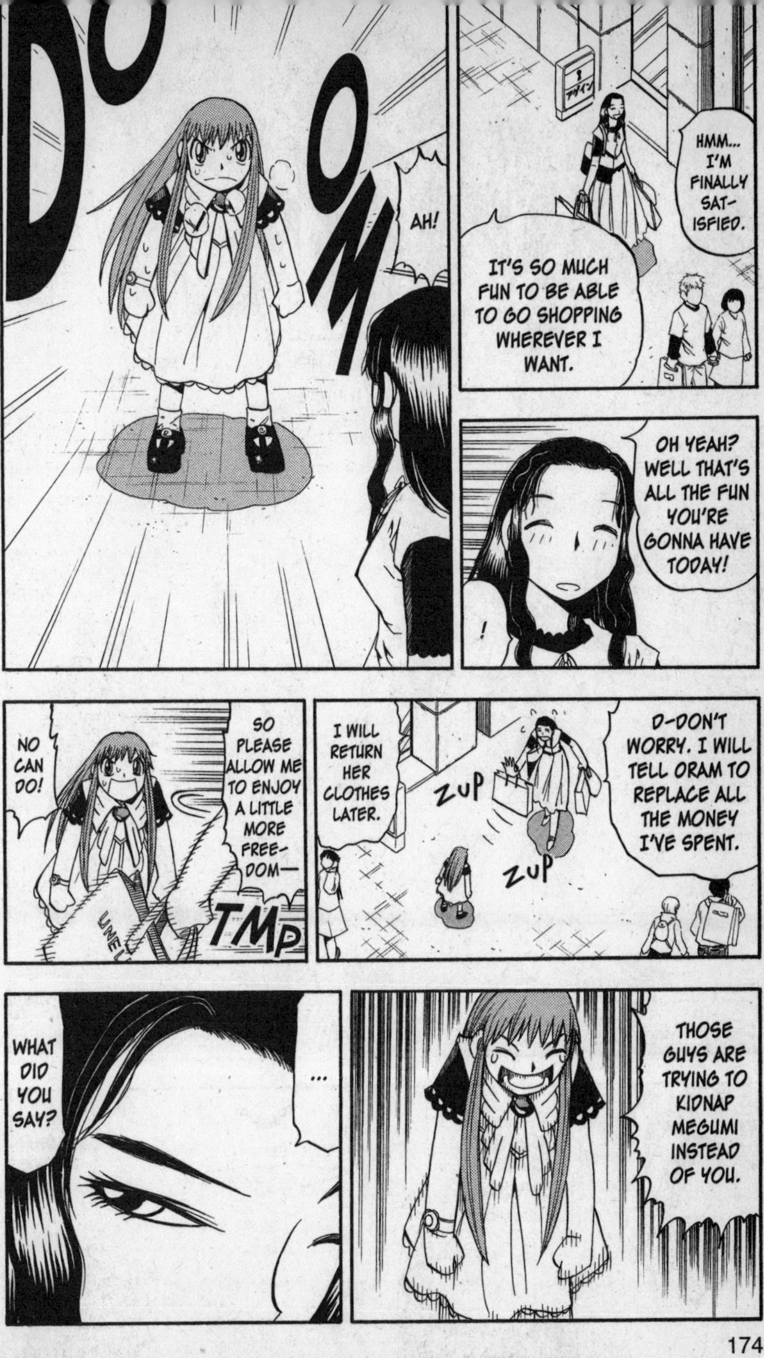
HMM... I'M FINALLY SAT-ISFIED.
IT'S SO MUCH FUN TO BE ABLE TO GO SHOPPING WHEREVER I WANT.
DOOM
AH!
OH YEAH? WELL THAT'S ALL THE FUN YOU'RE GONNA HAVE TODAY!
!
D-DON'T WORRY. I WILL TELL ORAM TO REPLACE ALL THE MONEY I'VE SPENT.
ZUP
ZUP
I WILL RETURN HER CLOTHES LATER.
SO PLEASE ALLOW ME TO ENJOY A LITTLE MORE FREE-DOM—
TMP
NO CAN DO!
THOSE GUYS ARE TRYING TO KIDNAP MEGUMI INSTEAD OF YOU.
...
WHAT DID YOU SAY?

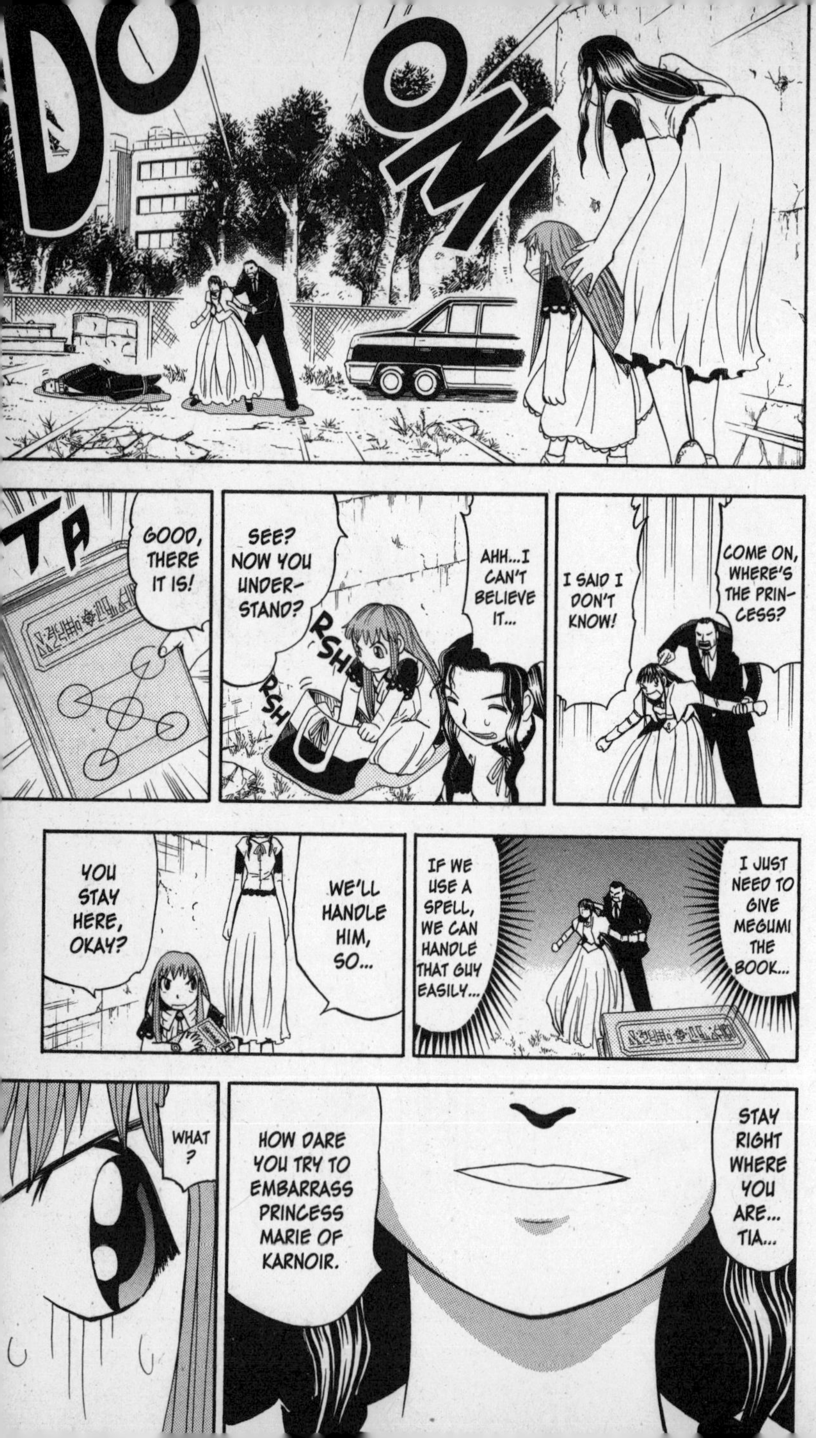
DOOM
COME ON, WHERE'S THE PRINCESS?
I SAID I DON'T KNOW!
AHH...I CAN'T BELIEVE IT...
SEE? NOW YOU UNDERSTAND?
RSH
RSH
TA
GOOD, THERE IT IS!
I JUST NEED TO GIVE MEGUMI THE BOOK...
IF WE USE A SPELL, WE CAN HANDLE THAT GUY EASILY...
WE'LL HANDLE HIM, SO...
YOU STAY HERE, OKAY?
STAY RIGHT WHERE YOU ARE... TIA...
HOW DARE YOU TRY TO EMBARRASS PRINCESS MARIE OF KARNOIR.
WHAT?

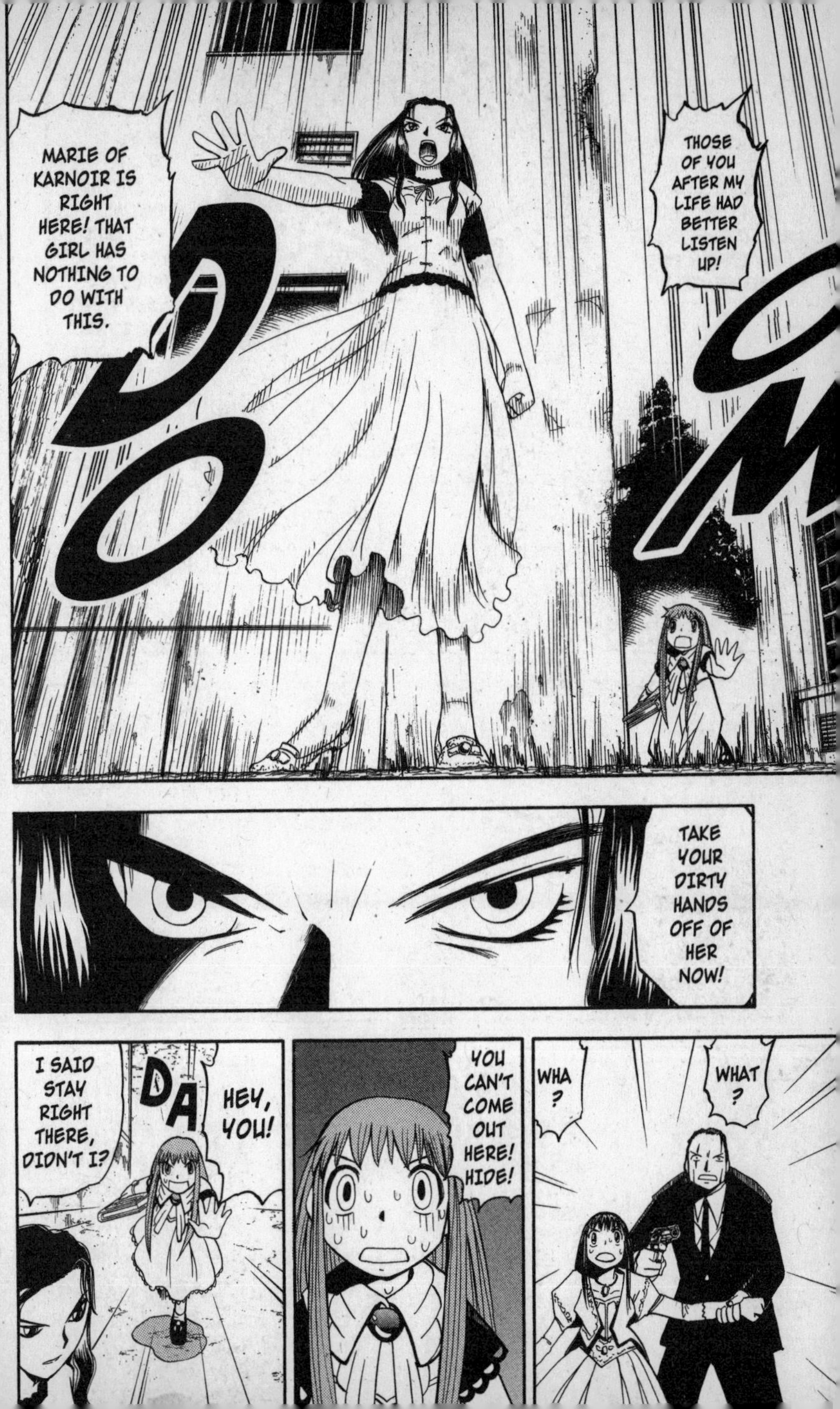
THOSE OF YOU AFTER MY LIFE HAD BETTER LISTEN UP!
MARIE OF KARNOIR IS RIGHT HERE! THAT GIRL HAS NOTHING TO DO WITH THIS.
DO
TAKE YOUR DIRTY HANDS OFF OF HER NOW!
WHAT?
WHA?
YOU CAN'T COME OUT HERE! HIDE!
HEY, YOU!
DA
I SAID STAY RIGHT THERE, DIDN'T I?

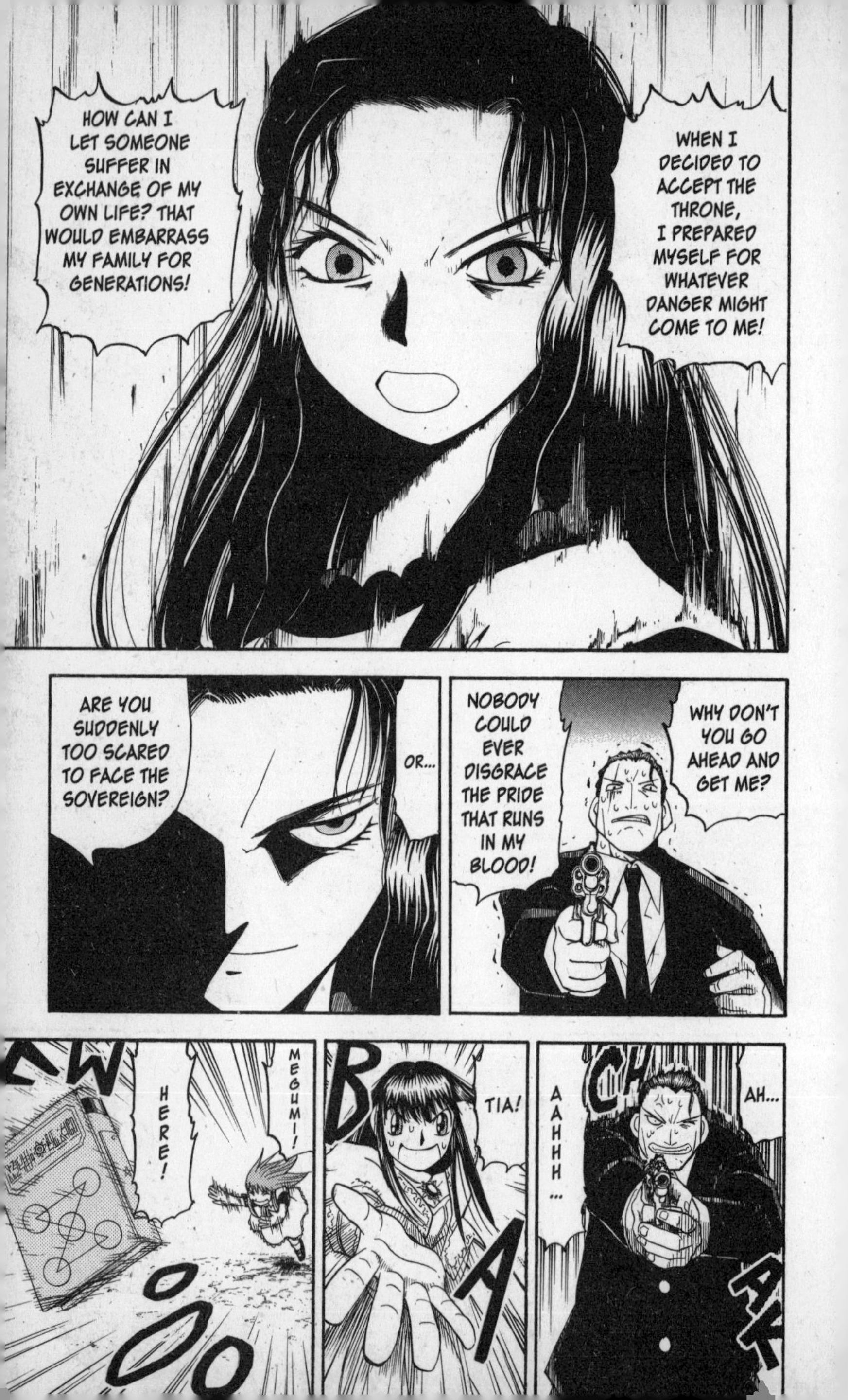
WHEN I DECIDED TO ACCEPT THE THRONE, I PREPARED MYSELF FOR WHATEVER DANGER MIGHT COME TO ME!
HOW CAN I LET SOMEONE SUFFER IN EXCHANGE OF MY OWN LIFE? THAT WOULD EMBARRASS MY FAMILY FOR GENERATIONS!
WHY DON'T YOU GO AHEAD AND GET ME?
NOBODY COULD EVER DISGRACE THE PRIDE THAT RUNS IN MY BLOOD!
OR...
ARE YOU SUDDENLY TOO SCARED TO FACE THE SOVEREIGN?
AH...
AAHHH...
TIA!
MEGUMI!
HERE!

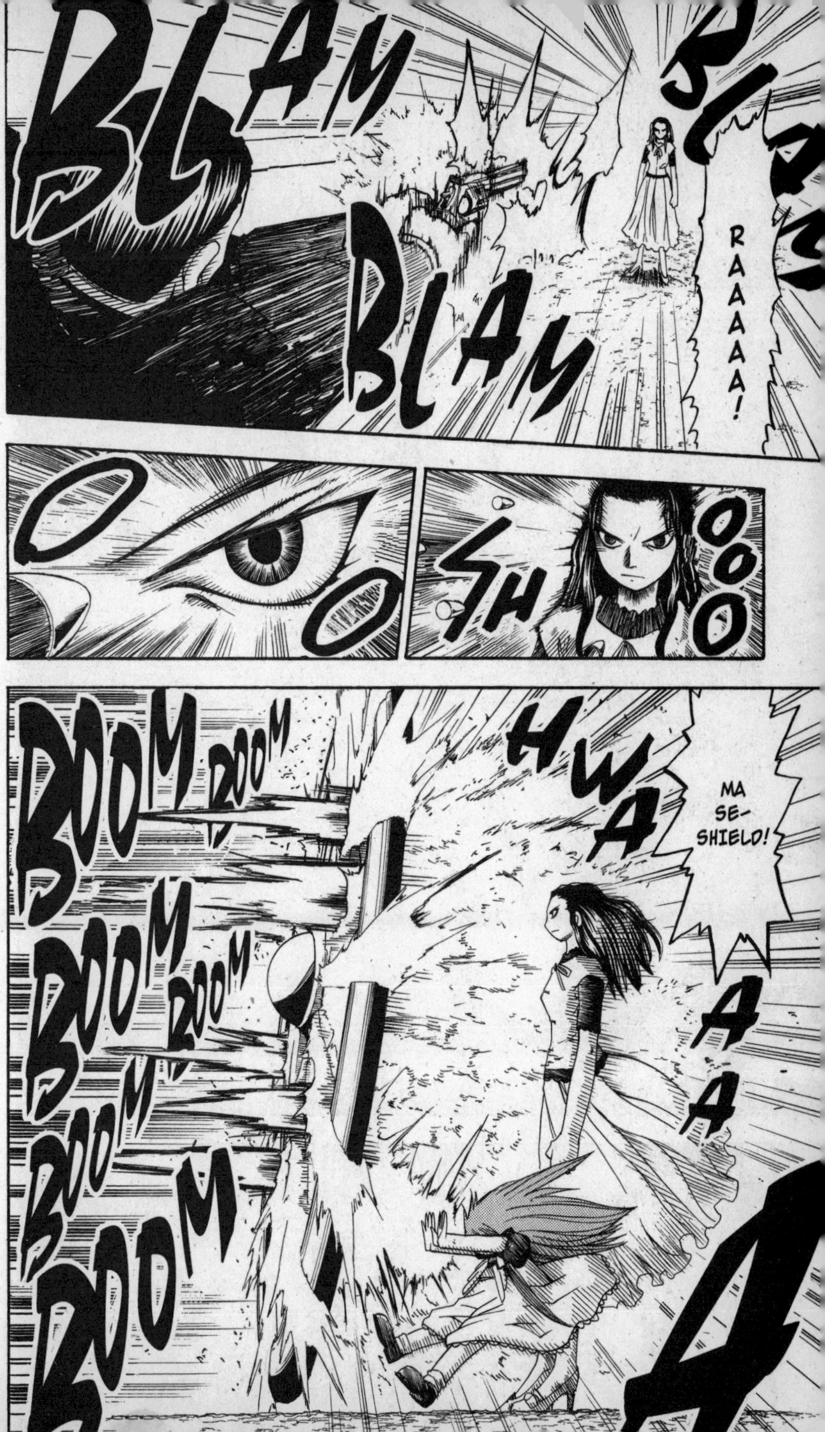

BLAM
RAAAAAA!
BLAM
BLAM
SHOOO
OO
MA SE-SHIELD!
HWAAAA
BOOM BOOM BOOM BOOM BOOM
BOOM BOOM BOOM

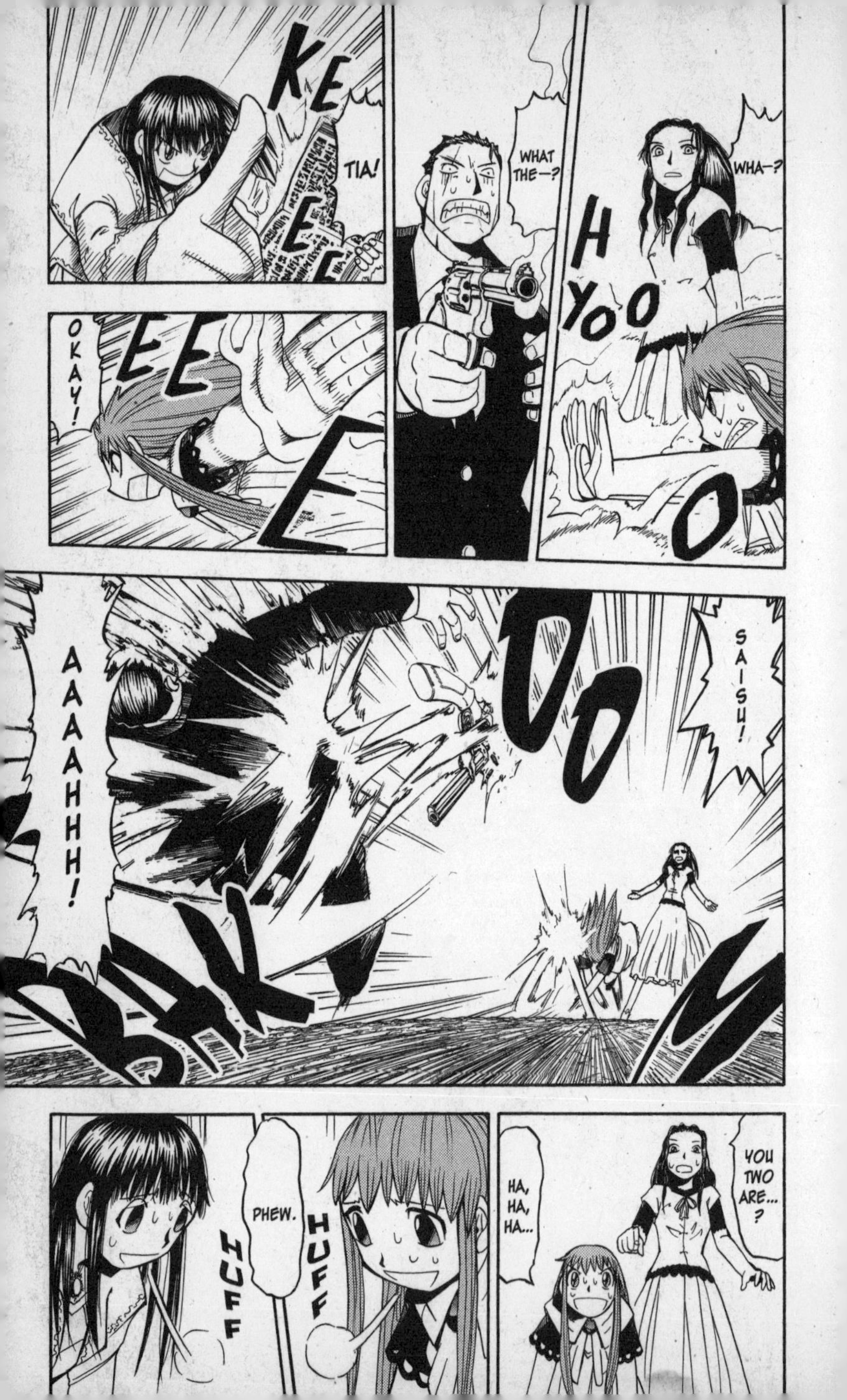
WHA–?
H
YOO
O
WHAT THE–?
KE
TIA!
OKAY!
EE
E
SAISU!
AAAAAHHH!
YOU TWO ARE...?
HA, HA, HA...
PHEW.
HUFF
HUFF

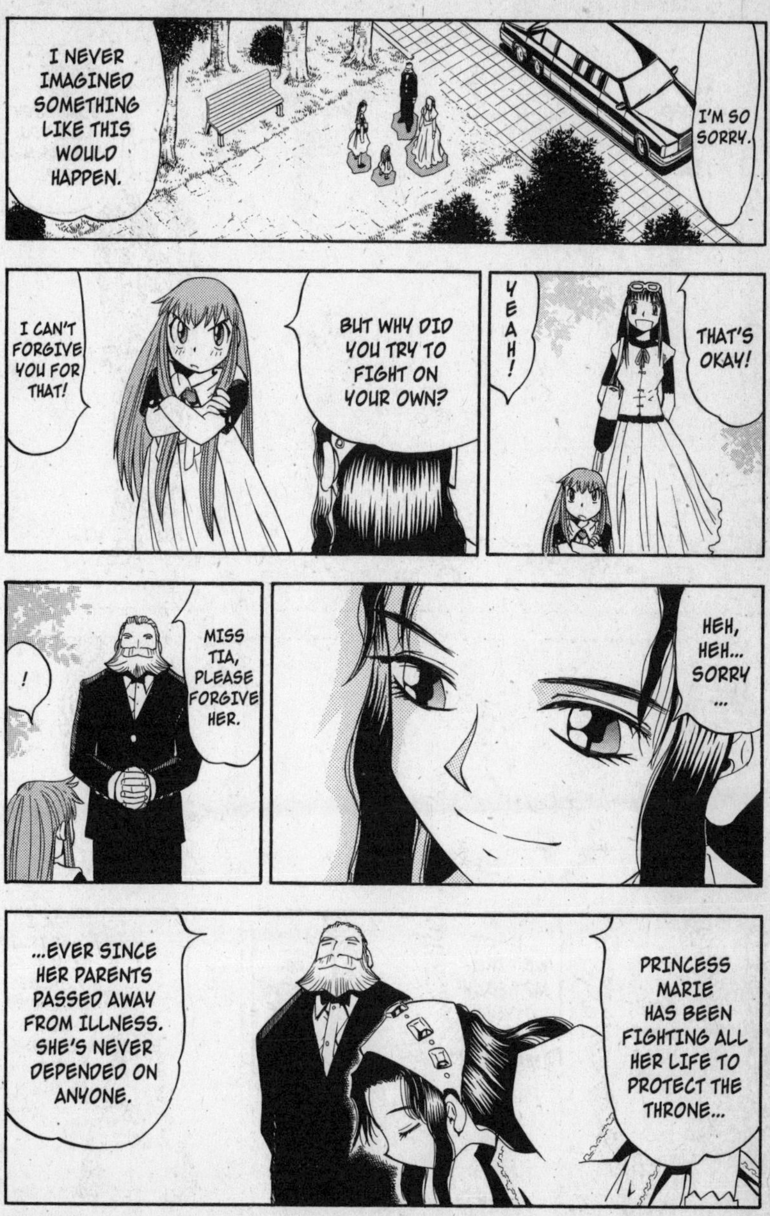
I NEVER IMAGINED SOMETHING LIKE THIS WOULD HAPPEN.
I'M SO SORRY.
THAT'S OKAY!
YEAH!
I CAN'T FORGIVE YOU FOR THAT!
BUT WHY DID YOU TRY TO FIGHT ON YOUR OWN?
!
MISS TIA, PLEASE FORGIVE HER.
HEH, HEH... SORRY...
PRINCESS MARIE HAS BEEN FIGHTING ALL HER LIFE TO PROTECT THE THRONE...
...EVER SINCE HER PARENTS PASSED AWAY FROM ILLNESS. SHE'S NEVER DEPENDED ON ANYONE.

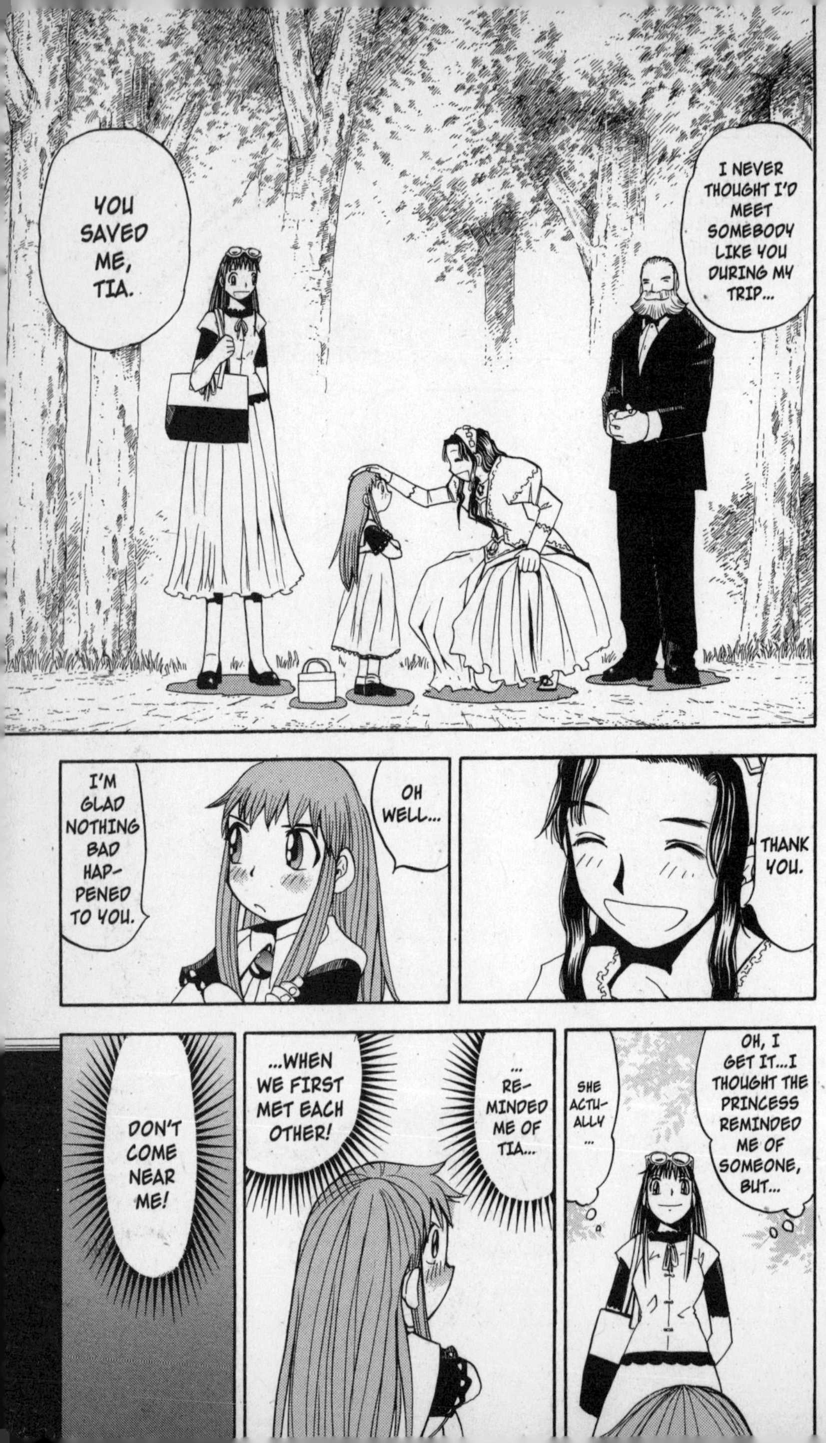
I NEVER THOUGHT I'D MEET SOMEBODY LIKE YOU DURING MY TRIP...
YOU SAVED ME, TIA.
THANK YOU.
OH WELL...
I'M GLAD NOTHING BAD HAP-PENED TO YOU.
OH, I GET IT...I THOUGHT THE PRINCESS REMINDED ME OF SOMEONE, BUT...
SHE ACTU-ALLY...
...RE-MINDED ME OF TIA...
...WHEN WE FIRST MET EACH OTHER!
DON'T COME NEAR ME!

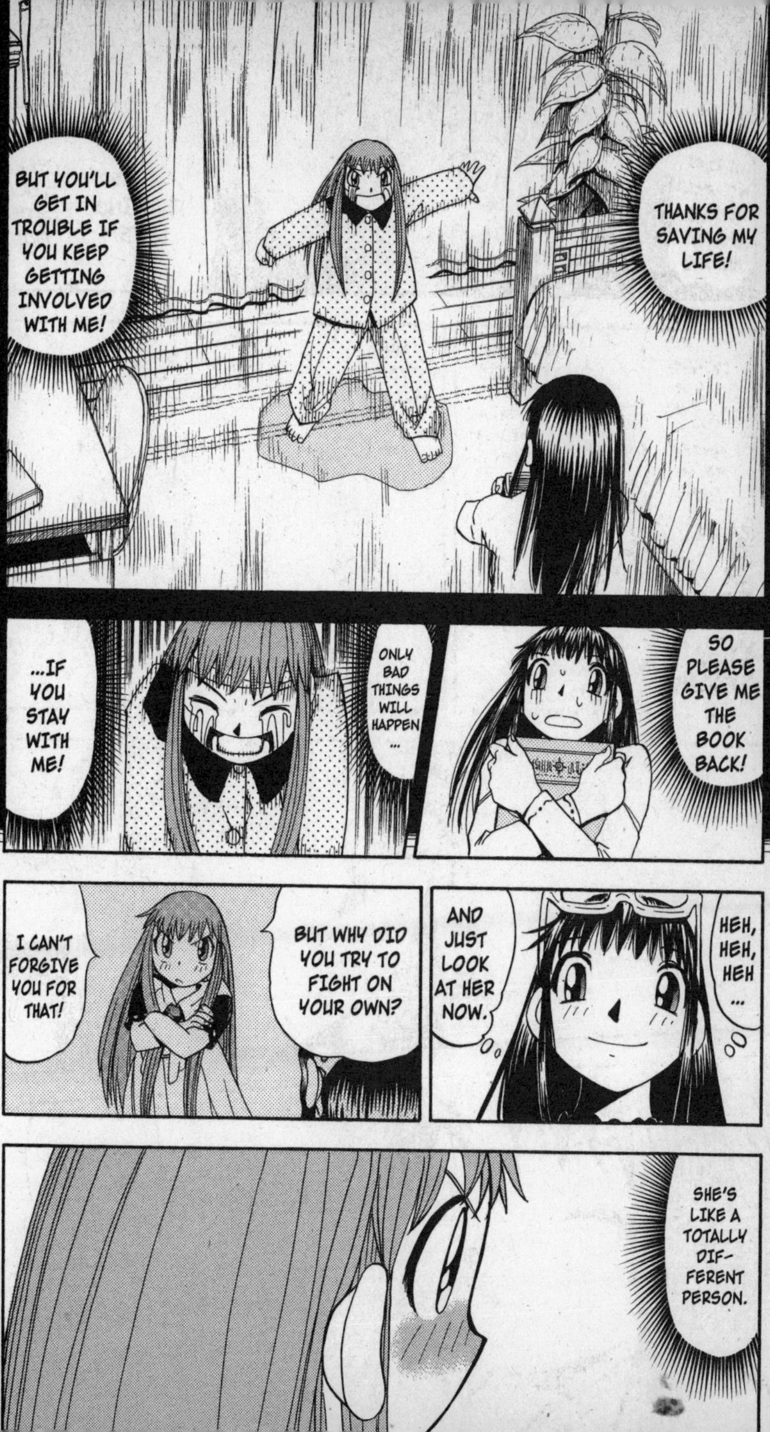
THANKS FOR SAVING MY LIFE!
BUT YOU'LL GET IN TROUBLE IF YOU KEEP GETTING INVOLVED WITH ME!
SO PLEASE GIVE ME THE BOOK BACK!
ONLY BAD THINGS WILL HAPPEN ...
...IF YOU STAY WITH ME!
HEH, HEH, HEH ...
AND JUST LOOK AT HER NOW.
BUT WHY DID YOU TRY TO FIGHT ON YOUR OWN?
I CAN'T FORGIVE YOU FOR THAT!
SHE'S LIKE A TOTALLY DIF-FERENT PERSON.

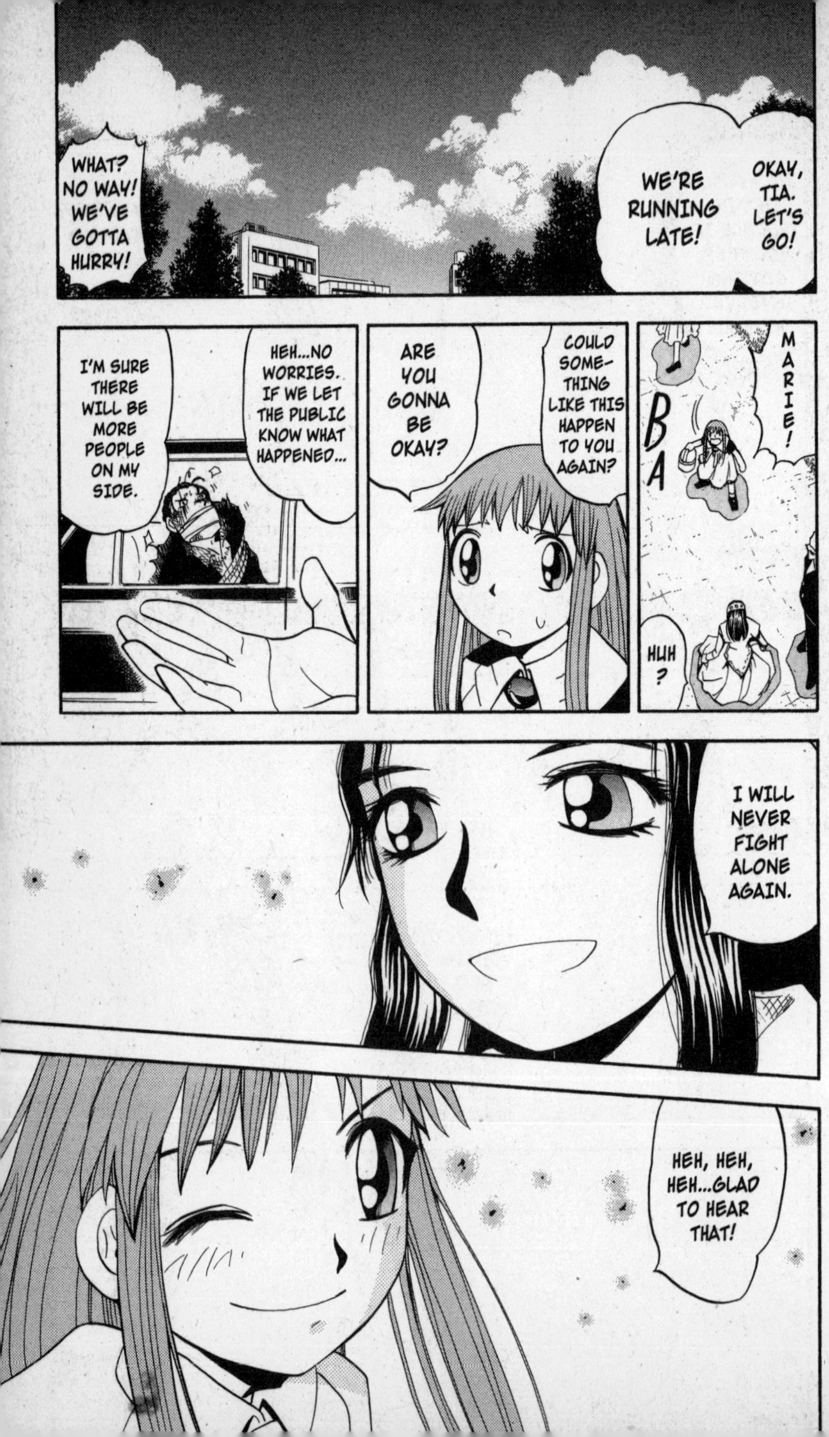
OKAY, TIA. LET'S GO!
WE'RE RUNNING LATE!
WHAT? NO WAY! WE'VE GOTTA HURRY!
MARIE!
BA
HUH?
COULD SOMETHING LIKE THIS HAPPEN TO YOU AGAIN?
ARE YOU GONNA BE OKAY?
HEH...NO WORRIES. IF WE LET THE PUBLIC KNOW WHAT HAPPENED...
I'M SURE THERE WILL BE MORE PEOPLE ON MY SIDE.
I WILL NEVER FIGHT ALONE AGAIN.
HEH, HEH, HEH...GLAD TO HEAR THAT!

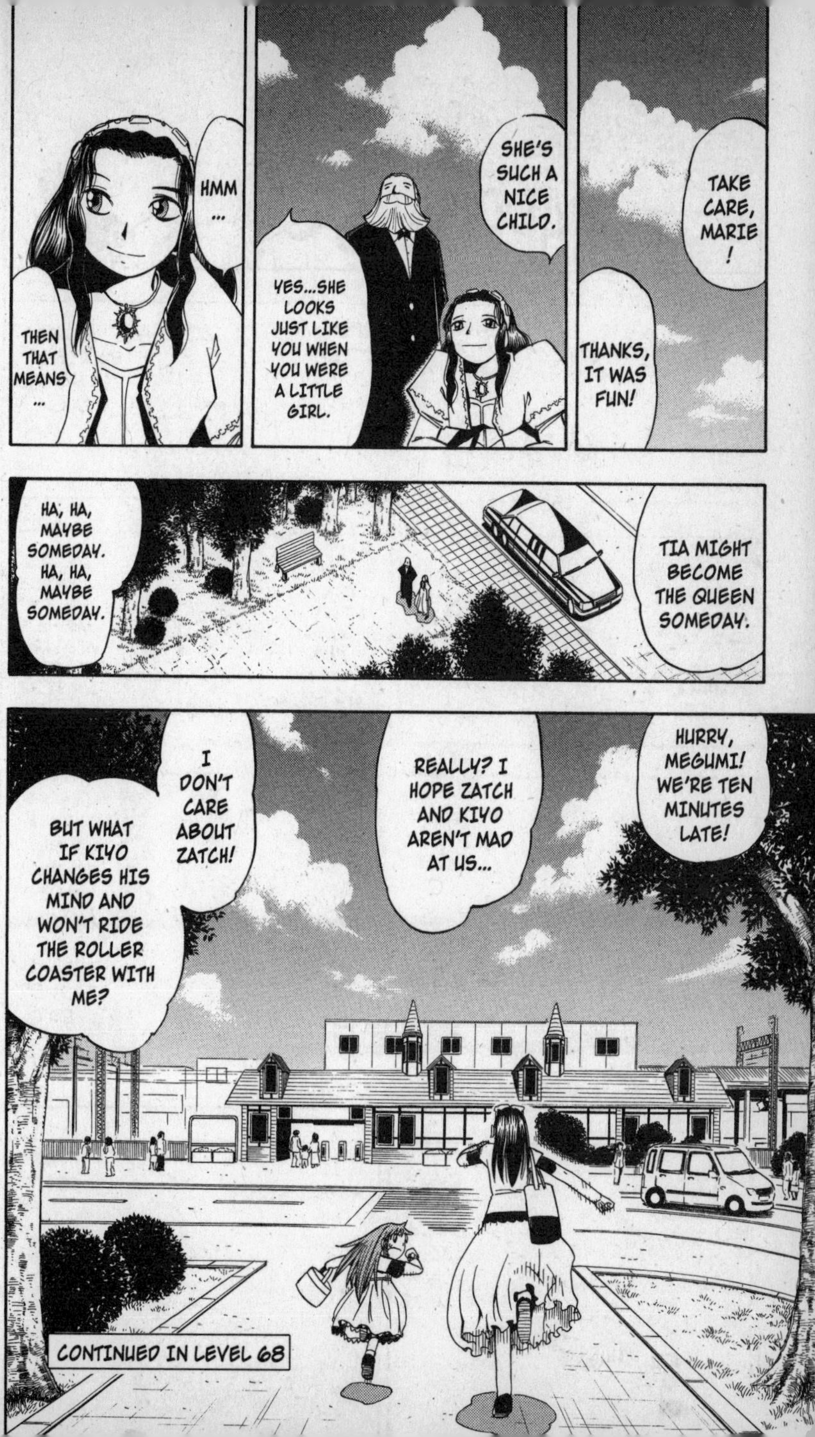
TAKE CARE, MARIE!
THANKS, IT WAS FUN!
SHE'S SUCH A NICE CHILD.
YES...SHE LOOKS JUST LIKE YOU WHEN YOU WERE A LITTLE GIRL.
HMM ...
THEN THAT MEANS ...
TIA MIGHT BECOME THE QUEEN SOMEDAY.
HA, HA, MAYBE SOMEDAY. HA, HA, MAYBE SOMEDAY.
HURRY, MEGUMI! WE'RE TEN MINUTES LATE!
REALLY? I HOPE ZATCH AND KIYO AREN'T MAD AT US...
I DON'T CARE ABOUT ZATCH!
BUT WHAT IF KIYO CHANGES HIS MIND AND WON'T RIDE THE ROLLER COASTER WITH ME?
CONTINUED IN LEVEL 68

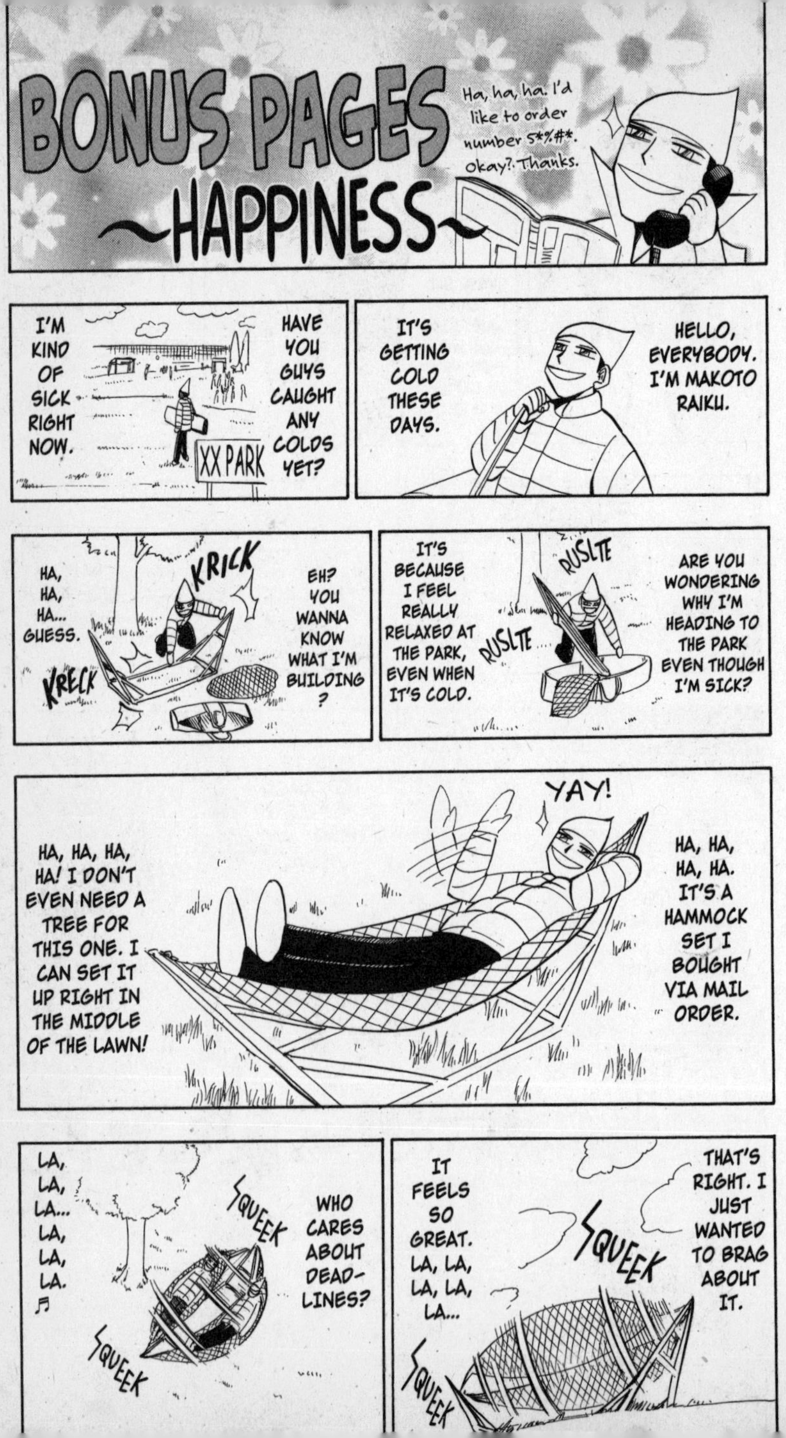
BONUS PAGES
~HAPPINESS~
Ha, ha, ha. I'd like to order number 5*%#*. Okay? Thanks.
HELLO, EVERYBODY. I'M MAKOTO RAIKU.
IT'S GETTING COLD THESE DAYS.
HAVE YOU GUYS CAUGHT ANY COLDS YET?
XX PARK
I'M KIND OF SICK RIGHT NOW.
ARE YOU WONDERING WHY I'M HEADING TO THE PARK EVEN THOUGH I'M SICK?
RUSLTE
RUSLTE
IT'S BECAUSE I FEEL REALLY RELAXED AT THE PARK, EVEN WHEN IT'S COLD.
EH? YOU WANNA KNOW WHAT I'M BUILDING?
KRICK
KRECK
HA, HA, HA... GUESS.
HA, HA, HA, HA. IT'S A HAMMOCK SET I BOUGHT VIA MAIL ORDER.
YAY!
HA, HA, HA, HA! I DON'T EVEN NEED A TREE FOR THIS ONE. I CAN SET IT UP RIGHT IN THE MIDDLE OF THE LAWN!
THAT'S RIGHT. I JUST WANTED TO BRAG ABOUT IT.
SQUEEK
IT FEELS SO GREAT. LA, LA, LA, LA, LA...
SQUEEK
WHO CARES ABOUT DEAD-LINES?
SQUEEK
LA, LA, LA... LA, LA, LA. ♬
SQUEEK

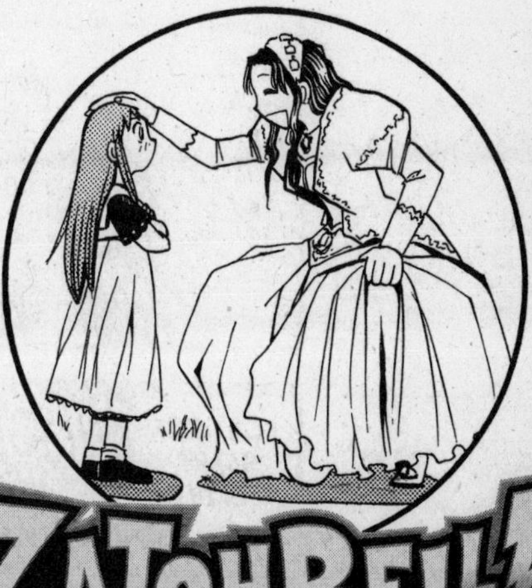

ZATCH BELL!

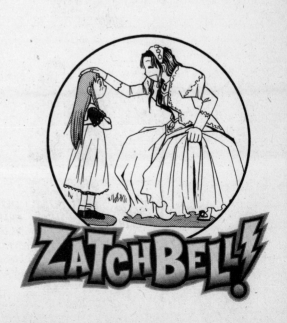

ZATCH & SUZY

BY MAKOTO RAIKU

SHAAA
SO A THEME PARK, EH? DID YOU HAVE FUN?
BOY DID I! A LOT OF FUN!
SO YOU WENT WITH TAKAMINE?
YEAH, AND MEGUMI AND TIA WENT WITH US.
MEGUMI? AND WHO IS SHE?
WELL, SHE'S JUST WHO SHE IS!
WOOM
WSSH
AND WHAT DOES MEGUMI LOOK LIKE?
YOU LOOK SCARY, SUZY.
YES YOU DO.

MAKOTO RAIKU

I heard on the radio that 90 percent of Japanese people in their twenties have cell phones these days. I'm actually one of the ten percent who doesn't have a cell phone. People tell me to get a cell phone, but I've got a phone at home, and I can send e-mails via my computer, so, uh...I don't think I need one any time soon.

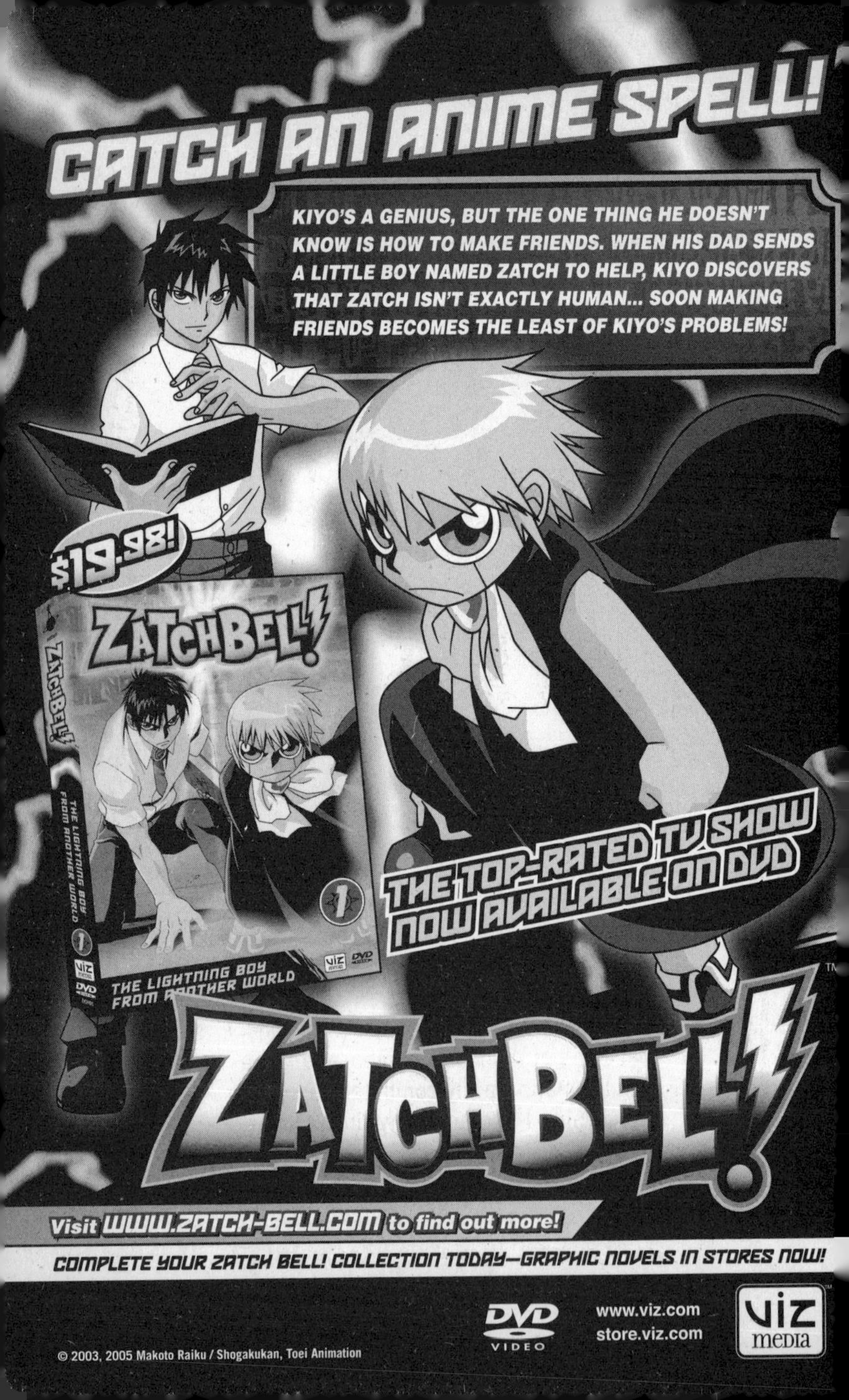
CATCH AN ANIME SPELL!
KIYO'S A GENIUS, BUT THE ONE THING HE DOESN'T KNOW IS HOW TO MAKE FRIENDS. WHEN HIS DAD SENDS A LITTLE BOY NAMED ZATCH TO HELP, KIYO DISCOVERS THAT ZATCH ISN'T EXACTLY HUMAN... SOON MAKING FRIENDS BECOMES THE LEAST OF KIYO'S PROBLEMS!
$19.98!
ZATCH BELL!
THE LIGHTNING BOY FROM ANOTHER WORLD
THE TOP-RATED TV SHOW NOW AVAILABLE ON DVD
ZATCH BELL!™
Visit WWW.ZATCH-BELL.COM to find out more!
COMPLETE YOUR ZATCH BELL! COLLECTION TODAY—GRAPHIC NOVELS IN STORES NOW!
DVD VIDEO
www.viz.com
store.viz.com
VIZ media
© 2003, 2005 Makoto Raiku / Shogakukan, Toei Animation

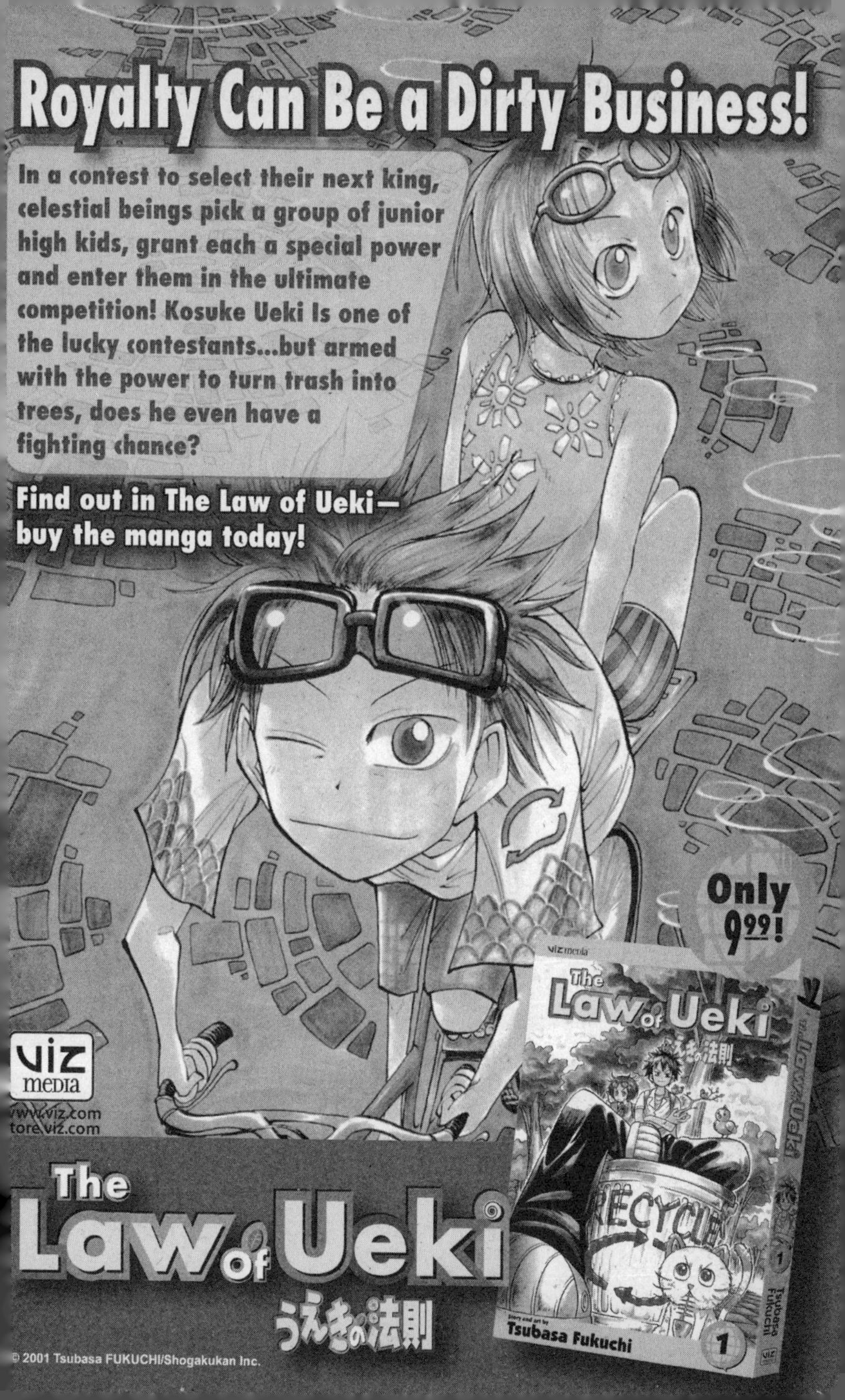
Royalty Can Be a Dirty Business!
In a contest to select their next king, celestial beings pick a group of junior high kids, grant each a special power and enter them in the ultimate competition! Kosuke Ueki Is one of the lucky contestants...but armed with the power to turn trash into trees, does he even have a fighting chance?
Find out in The Law of Ueki— buy the manga today!
Only 9.99!
viz media
www.viz.com
tore.viz.com
The Law of Ueki
うえきの法則
viz media
The Law of Ueki
Story and art by Tsubasa Fukuchi
1
RECYCLE
© 2001 Tsubasa FUKUCHI/Shogakukan Inc.

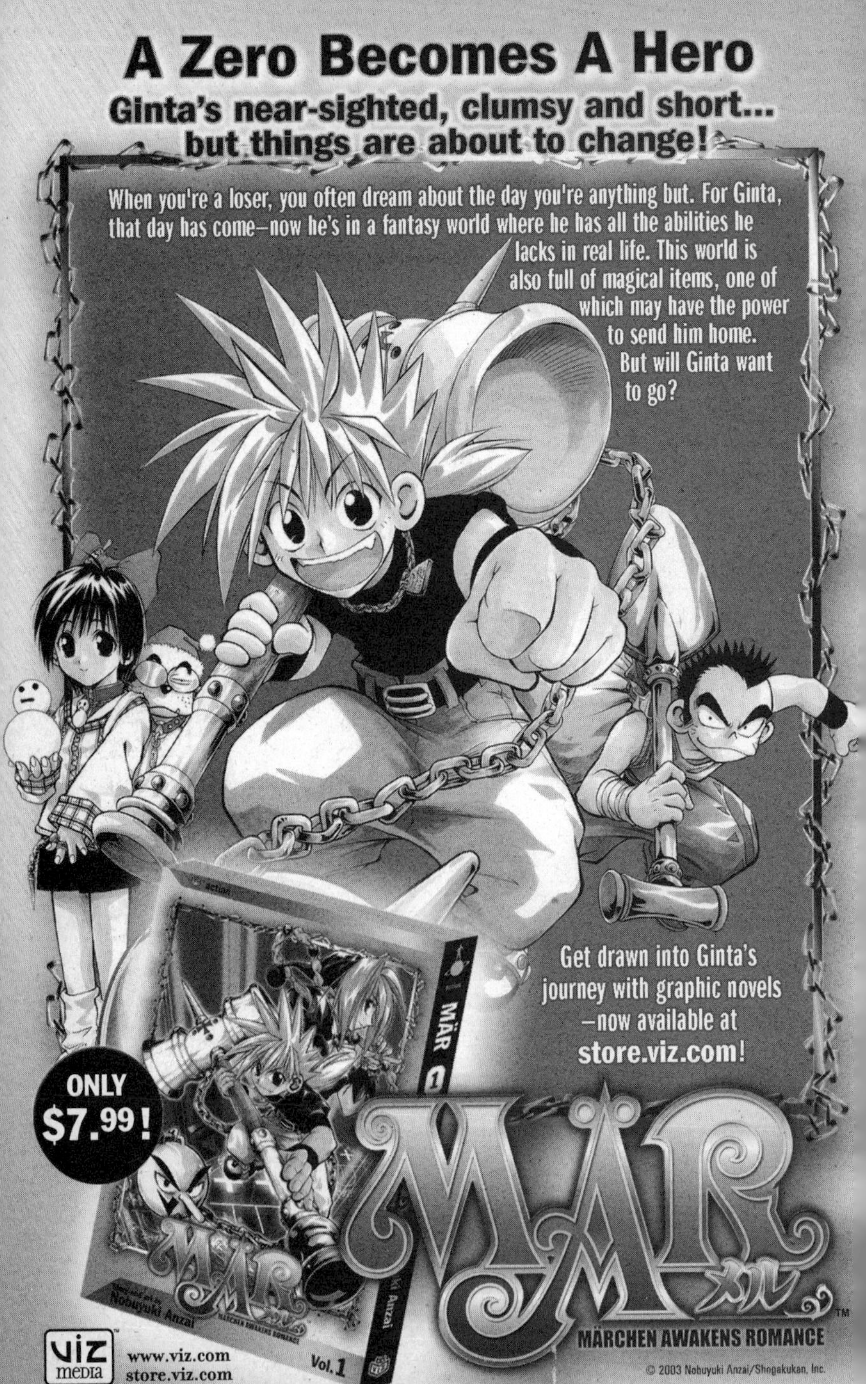
A Zero Becomes A Hero
Ginta's near-sighted, clumsy and short...
...but things are about to change!
When you're a loser, you often dream about the day you're anything but. For Ginta, that day has come—now he's in a fantasy world where he has all the abilities he lacks in real life. This world is also full of magical items, one of which may have the power to send him home. But will Ginta want to go?
Get drawn into Ginta's journey with graphic novels —now available at store.viz.com!
ONLY $7.99!
MÄR
MÄRCHEN AWAKENS ROMANCE
Nobuyuki Anzai
Vol. 1
viz media
www.viz.com
store.viz.com
© 2003 Nobuyuki Anzai/Shogakukan, Inc.

LOVE MAN

LET US KNOW WHA

OUR MANGA SURVEY IS NOW AVAILABLE ONLINE. PLEASE VISIT: VIZ.COM/MANGASURVEY

HELP US MAKE THE MANGA YOU LOVE BETTER!